Technologies and Protocols for the Future of Internet Design:

Reinventing the Web

Deo Prakash Vidyarthi
Jawaharlal Nehru University, India

Information Science
REFERENCE

Managing Director:	Lindsay Johnston
Senior Editorial Director:	Heather Probst
Book Production Manager:	Sean Woznicki
Development Manager:	Joel Gamon
Development Editor:	Myla Harty
Acquisitions Editor:	Erika Gallagher
Typesetters:	Russell Spangler
Cover Design:	Nick Newcomer, Greg Snader

Published in the United States of America by
Information Science Reference (an imprint of IGI Global)
701 E. Chocolate Avenue
Hershey PA 17033
Tel: 717-533-8845
Fax: 717-533-8661
E-mail: cust@igi-global.com
Web site: http://www.igi-global.com

Library of Congress Cataloging-in-Publication Data

Technologies and protocols for the future of Internet design : reinventing the Web / Deo Prakash Vidyarthi, editor.
     p. cm.
  Includes bibliographical references and index.
  Summary: "This book provides relevant methods and theories in the area of the Internet design, written for the research community and professionals who wish to improve their understanding of future Internet technologies and gain knowledge of new tools and techniques in future Internet design"--Provided by publisher.
  ISBN 978-1-4666-0203-8 (hardcover) -- ISBN 978-1-4666-0204-5 (ebook) -- ISBN 978-1-4666-0205-2 (print & perpetual access) 1. Internet--Technological innovations. I. Vidyarthi, Deo Prakash.
  TK5105.875.I57T454 2012
  621.39'81--dc23
                              2011049480

British Cataloguing in Publication Data
A Cataloguing in Publication record for this book is available from the British Library.

All work contributed to this book is new, previously-unpublished material. The views expressed in this book are those of the authors, but not necessarily of the publisher.

Editorial Advisory Board

Table of Contents

Foreword xiv

Preface xv

Acknowledgment xviii

Chapter 1
Historical Evolution in Internet: An Introduction 1
    Deo Prakash Vidyarthi, Jawaharlal Nehru University, India

Chapter 2
Optical Networking: Current Issues and Review 4
    Sanjeev Kumar Raghuwanshi, Indian School of Mines, India

Chapter 3
The User as a Service 37
    José C. Delgado, Instituto Superior Técnico, Technical University of Lisbon, Portugal

Chapter 4
Web Services for Healthcare Management 60
    Lucio Grandinetti, Università della Calabria, Italy
    Ornella Pisacane, Università della Calabria, Italy

Chapter 5
The Physical Layer Aspects of Wireless Networks 95
    Neetesh Purohit, Indian Institute of Information Technology, India

Chapter 6
Internet Security Using Biometrics 114
    Shrikant Tiwari, Institute of Technology, Banaras Hindu University, India
    Aruni Singh, Institute of Technology, Banaras Hindu University, India
    Ravi Shankar Singh, Institute of Technology, Banaras Hindu University, India
    Sanjay K. Singh, Institute of Technology, Banaras Hindu University, India

Chapter 7

Quality of Service (QoS) in WiMAX 143

Kashinath Basu, Oxford Brookes University, UK

Sherali Zeadally, University of the District of Columbia, USA

Farhan Siddiqui, Walden University, USA

Chapter 8

Analysis of the High-Speed Network Performance through a Prediction Feedback Based Model 162

Manjunath Ramachandra, Philips Innovation Campus, India

Pandit Pattabhirama, Philips Innovation Campus, India

Chapter 9

Optimizing Path Reliability in IPTV Systems Using Genetic Algorithm 179

Mohammad Anbar, Tishreen University, Syria

Deo Prakash Vidyarthi, Jawaharlal Nehru University, India

Chapter 10

IP Connected Low Power Wireless Personal Area Networks in the Future Internet 191

Rune Hylsberg Jacobsen, Aarhus School of Engineering, Denmark

Thomas Skjødeberg Toftegaard, Aarhus School of Engineering, Denmark

Jens Kristian Kjærgaard, Tieto, Denmark

Chapter 11

Token Based Mutual Exclusion in Peer-to-Peer Systems 214

Mayank Singh, ABV-Indian Institute of Information Technology and Management, India

Shashikala Tapaswi, ABV-Indian Institute of Information Technology and Management, India

Chapter 12

Random Early Discard (RED) Queue Evaluation for Congestion Control 229

Md. Shohidul Islam, Dhaka University of Engineering & Technology, Bangladesh

Md. Niaz Morshed, Dhaka University of Engineering & Technology, Bangladesh

Sk. Shariful Islam, Dhaka University of Engineering & Technology, Bangladesh

Md. Mejbahul Azam, Dhaka University of Engineering & Technology, Bangladesh

Chapter 13

A Comparative Study of Evolutionary Algorithms for Maximizing Reliability
of a Flow in Cellular IP Network 247

Mohammad Anbar, Tishreen University, Syria

Deo Prakash Vidyarthi, Jawaharlal Nehru University, India

Chapter 14

Blending Augmented Reality with Real World Scenarios Using Mobile Devices 258

Alexiei Dingli, University of Malta, Malta

Dylan Seychell, University of Malta, Malta

Chapter 15

Pervasive Internet via Wireless Infrastructure Based Mesh Networks 274

    Nabanita Das, Indian Statistical Institute, India

Chapter 16

Smart Rooms: A Framework for Inferencing Using Semantic Web Technology in

Ambient Intelligent Network 289

    Biplab K. Sarker, University of New Brunswick, Canada

    Julian Descottes, University of New Brunswick, Canada

    Mohsin Sohail, University of New Brunswick, Canada

    Rama Krishna Kosaraju, University of New Brunswick, Canada

Compilation of References 304

About the Contributors 323

Index 330

Detailed Table of Contents

Foreword xiv

Preface xv

Acknowledgment...xviii

Chapter 1
Historical Evolution in Internet: An Introduction... 1
    Deo Prakash Vidyarthi, Jawaharlal Nehru University, India

The spurt in the Information Technology in the recent past has been well complemented by the innovative research in communication technology. Tremendous growth in the Internet is the result of this. This chapter highlights how the Internet has evolved, over the years, since its inception. The major contributors of Internet Technology have also been pointed out in this chapter.

Chapter 2
Optical Networking: Current Issues and Review.. 4
    Sanjeev Kumar Raghuwanshi, Indian School of Mines, India

Telecommunication networks based on optical fiber technology have become a major information transmission system with high capacity optical fiber links encircling the globe in both terrestrial and undersea installation. At present there are numerous passive and active optical devices within a light wave link that perform complex networking functions in the optical domain, such as signal restoration, routing, and switching. Along with the need to understand the functions of these devices comes the necessity to measure both components and network performance and to model and simulate the complex behavior of reliable high capacity networks. This chapter presents the fundamental principles for understanding and applying these issues. This chapter is primarily about TCP/IP network protocols and Ethernet network architectures, but also briefly describes other protocol suites, network architectures, and other significant areas of networking. It explains in simple terms the way networks are put together, and how data packages are sent between networks and subnets, along with how data is routed to the Internet.

Chapter 3

The User as a Service...37

José C. Delgado, Instituto Superior Técnico, Technical University of Lisbon, Portugal

The Web has changed a lot since its inception, 20 years ago, now offering dynamic information and services. The users have also evolved and are no longer mere information consumers, but rather active producers. This calls for a paradigm shift, with the user at the center of the information, service, and collaboration networks, taking the role of active services (able to respond to requests), in equal terms with current service providers. This leads to a unified user model, in which both individual and institutional entities are users and providers, although with different emphasis. To support this approach, the authors present a new Web access device, the browserver, which includes a browser and a server working in close cooperation, with the goal of replacing the classical browser but being backwards compatible with it to ease the migration path. The authors show how it can be implemented and its advantages in the case of typical applications.

Chapter 4

Web Services for Healthcare Management...60

Lucio Grandinetti, Università della Calabria, Italy
Ornella Pisacane, Università della Calabria, Italy

Nowadays, Health Care Organizations (HCOs) are interested in defining methodologies of Information Technology (IT) for providing high quality services at minimum cost. Through modern software and hardware, they can process data and manage the three important phases: diagnosis, prognosis, and therapy. In this scenario, Web Technologies (WTs) can: provide advanced Information Systems that combine software applications; offer a heterogeneous connectivity to users; allow costs reduction; improve the delivery of the services; guarantee an interactive support of the doctors, interconnectivity between the HCOs, and effective information sharing.

Chapter 5

The Physical Layer Aspects of Wireless Networks 95

Neetesh Purohit, Indian Institute of Information Technology, India

The modern era belongs to wireless communication systems. The cellular networks, which were originally designed for voice services, have now been upgraded to accommodate Internet services. Wi-Fi and Wi-Max systems have been explicitly developed for delivering data services over wireless channels. Just like wired systems, wireless systems also follow the layered architecture for developing or accessing various Internet services; still, there exist significant differences between the technologies used at various layers for the similar purpose. Special design requirements of physical layer due to distinct properties of wireless channel have caused these differences. Low bandwidth supported by the channel, poor equipment capabilities, et cetera, features require special attention in developing various Internet services intended to be accessed by wireless devices. This chapter addresses various aspects of the physical layer of a wireless channel for developing a basic understanding of the problems, existing solutions, and proposals for future networks.

Chapter 6

Internet Security Using Biometrics... 114

Shrikant Tiwari, Institute of Technology, Banaras Hindu University, India
Aruni Singh, Institute of Technology, Banaras Hindu University, India
Ravi Shankar Singh, Institute of Technology, Banaras Hindu University, India
Sanjay K. Singh, Institute of Technology, Banaras Hindu University, India

Internet security is a big challenge for Internet users, and passwords are the primary means of authenticating users. Establishing identity is becoming difficult in this vastly interconnected society. The need for reliable Internet security techniques has increased in the wake of heightened concerns about security and rapid advancements in networking, communication, and mobility. Biometrics is the science of identifying an individual based on his physical (static) or behavioral (dynamic) characteristics, and it is beginning to gain acceptance as a legitimate method for determining an individual's identity. Biometrics has been used for many years in high security government and military applications, but the technology is now becoming affordable for use as an authentication methods and general security feature. In this chapter, the authors provide an overview of Internet security using Biometrics.

Chapter 7

Quality of Service (QoS) in WiMAX 143

Kashinath Basu, Oxford Brookes University, UK
Sherali Zeadally, University of the District of Columbia, USA
Farhan Siddiqui, Walden University, USA

The WiMAX technology provides wireless QoS-enabled broadband access for fixed and mobile users at the metropolitan level. It is end-to-end IP based and provides a rich set of QoS support for multimedia-based ubiquitous computing. The main contribution of WiMAX in terms of technology has been over its radio interface, which is based on the IEEE 802.16-2004 and 802.16e protocols. It is a two layer protocol stack, which provides a very robust QoS framework. At the physical layer, it focuses on optimising the use of radio resources. In the MAC layer, the main focus is on efficient scheduling and allocation of bandwidth to meet the QoS requirements of IP sessions. This chapter investigates the WiMAX architecture, its components, and the QoS support provided by the IEEE 802.16 protocol stack. It also examines mobility management issues, end-to-end QoS, and current and future application areas of the technology.

Chapter 8

Analysis of the High-Speed Network Performance through a Prediction Feedback Based Model......... 162

Manjunath Ramachandra, Philips Innovation Campus, India
Pandit Pattabhirama, Philips Innovation Campus, India

Performance modeling of a high speed network is challenging, especially when the size of the network is large. The high speed networks span various applications such as the transportation, wireless sensors, et cetera. The present day transportation system makes uses of Internet for efficient command and control transfers. In such a communication system, reliability and in-time data transfer is critical. In addition to the sensor information, the present day wireless networks target to support streaming of multimedia and entertainment data from mobile to infrastructure network and vice versa. In this chapter, a novel modeling method for the network and its traffic shaping is introduced, and simulation model is provided.

The performance with this model is analyzed. The case-study with wireless networks is considered. The chapter is essentially about solving the congestion control of packet loss using a differentially fed neural network controller.

Chapter 9

Optimizing Path Reliability in IPTV Systems Using Genetic Algorithm 179

Mohammad Anbar, Tishreen University, Syria
Deo Prakash Vidyarthi, Jawaharlal Nehru University, India

IPTV system is meant to provide TV services through IP networks. IPTV is a next generation technology and is growing rapidly day by day across the globe. Providing TV services through IP networks reflects the audio-video service through the IP networks in IP format. TV packets are media and real-time packets in nature, therefore delivering these packets through the IP network is a big challenge. It needs to be done with utmost care and reliably for the timely delivery of these packets to ensure reliable packet transfer is a big issue in IPTV systems. Reliability, in such systems, depends on the failure rates of various components through which the packet passes. This chapter addresses the reliability issue in IPTV systems and suggests a possible solution to maximize it using Genetic Algorithms. The proposed model explores for the most reliable path among many available paths for the packet delivery. It helps in deciding the best available route passing through which reliability is maximized. Experimental results reveal the efficacy of the model.

Chapter 10

IP Connected Low Power Wireless Personal Area Networks in the Future Internet 191

Rune Hylsberg Jacobsen, Aarhus School of Engineering, Denmark
Thomas Skjødeberg Toftegaard, Aarhus School of Engineering, Denmark
Jens Kristian Kjærgaard, Tieto, Denmark

The Internet of Things is a key concept of the Future Internet. The Internet of Things potentially interconnects billions of small devices in a large ubiquitous infrastructure based on the Internet Protocol (IP). Typically, these devices will be limited in computational capacity, memory, and available energy and will suffer a high data loss rate when integrated into a network infrastructure. This poses significant challenges in the network design. This chapter describes the assumptions, technologies, and challenges for transmitting IPv6 over low power wireless personal area networks (LoWPANs). The authors address the key mechanisms from network aspects down to device design aspects and discuss how technologies interplay to make real application deployment practical for the Internet of Things.

Chapter 11

Token Based Mutual Exclusion in Peer-to-Peer Systems 214

Mayank Singh, ABV-Indian Institute of Information Technology and Management, India
Shashikala Tapaswi, ABV-Indian Institute of Information Technology and Management, India

Mutual exclusion is one of the well-studied fundamental primitives in distributed systems, and a number of vital solutions have been proposed to achieve the same. However, the emerging Peer to Peer systems bring forward several challenges to protect consistent and concurrent access to shared resources, as classical peer-to-peer systems, like Napster, Gnutella, et cetera, have been mainly used for sharing files with read only permission. In this chapter, the authors propose a quorum based mutual exclusion algorithm that can be used over any Peer to Peer Distributed Hash Table (DHT). The proposed approach can be seen as extension to traditional Sigma protocol for mutual exclusion in Peer to Peer systems. The basic idea is to reduce message overhead with use of smart nodes present in each quorum set and message passing between the current owners of resource with next resource requester nodes.

Chapter 12
Random Early Discard (RED) Queue Evaluation for Congestion Control 229

Md. Shohidul Islam, Dhaka University of Engineering & Technology, Bangladesh
Md. Niaz Morshed, Dhaka University of Engineering & Technology, Bangladesh
Sk. Shariful Islam, Dhaka University of Engineering & Technology, Bangladesh
Md. Mejbahul Azam, Dhaka University of Engineering & Technology, Bangladesh

Congestion is an un-avoiding issue of networking, and many attempts and mechanisms have been devised to avoid and control congestion in diverse ways. Random Early Discard (RED) is one of such type of algorithm that applies the techniques of Active Queue Management (AQM) to prevent and control congestion and to provide a range of Internet performance facilities. In this chapter, performance of RED algorithm has been measured from different point of views. RED works with Transmission Control Protocol (TCP), and since TCP has several variants, the authors investigated which versions of TCP behave well with RED in terms of few network parameters. Also, performance of RED has been compared with its counterpart Drop Tail algorithm. These statistics are immensely necessary to select the best protocol for Internet performance optimization.

Chapter 13
A Comparative Study of Evolutionary Algorithms for Maximizing Reliability
of a Flow in Cellular IP Network 247

Mohammad Anbar, Tishreen University, Syria
Deo Prakash Vidyarthi, Jawaharlal Nehru University, India

The rapid development in technology, witnessed in daily communication, especially in wireless communication, is a good motivation for performance improvement in this field. Cellular IP access network is a suitable environment where a micro mobility of mobile users is implemented and managed. The reliability of Cellular IP network during the communication is an important characteristic measure and must be considered while designing a new model. Evolutionary Algorithms are powerful tools for optimization and problem solving, which require extracting the best solution from a big search space. This chapter explores the reliability issue in Cellular IP of a flow of packets passing through the route from a source to a destination. The main aim of the chapter is to maximize the reliability of the flow passing through a route having number of routers. Two Evolutionary Algorithms (EAs), Genetic Algorithm (GA) and Particle Swarm Optimization (PSO), have been used for this purpose, and a comparative study between the two is performed. Experimental studies of the proposed work have also been performed.

Chapter 14
Blending Augmented Reality with Real World Scenarios Using Mobile Devices 258

Alexiei Dingli, University of Malta, Malta
Dylan Seychell, University of Malta, Malta

In this work, the authors present methods that add value to the current Web by connecting administrators of a space such as a city with its visitors. The mobile device has nowadays become an important tool in the hands of visitors of cities and the authors present it as a gateway for the administrators to their visitors. The authors present a method that processes various environmental factors during a visit and uses these factors as a context for presenting the recommendations. In this work, the authors also propose a method that can measure queues in a city, and by knowing the overall picture of the situation, it provides individual recommendations of separate mobile devices accordingly. This chapter shows, therefore, the three main steps in the process of recommendation systems: collecting information, processing the recommendations, and presenting them in an attractive way. In this case the authors focus on presenting recommendations through augmented reality in order to provide an attractive tool for end users, which would, at the end of the day, connect them further to the city over the Internet.

Chapter 15

Pervasive Internet via Wireless Infrastructure-Based Mesh Networks..274

    Nabanita Das, Advanced Computing and Microelectronics Unit,
       Indian Statistical Institute, Calcutta, India

With the arrival of Wi-Fi, WiMax, Zigbee, and other wireless network standards, the penetration of Internet in daily life has surged significantly. While the usage of Internet access in urban areas is steadily increasing in recent years, rural people are still suffering from the effect of the digital divide, mainly due to the poor coverage by Internet service providers in remote areas. This chapter aims to provide a cost-effective reliable broadband Internet access solution for rural people in the form of Wireless Mesh Network (WMN) whose coverage can be easily extended in a multi-hop fashion. Starting from a general description of the WMN architecture and protocol developments, this chapter focuses on the primary design issues and challenges for making Internet pervasive through WMN's that demand innovations in protocols at different layers and perfect integration. The brief discussion on the research works and related experimental testbeds shows that WMN with its unique features seems to be a promising solution to provide next generation Internet access to areas that are too remote to receive it via cable or DSL, or where upgrading the landlines to broadband is highly cost-prohibitive. Finally, this chapter concludes introducing various open issues and research challenges still to be addressed and resolved in coming days to make this solution commercially viable.

Chapter 16

Smart Rooms: A Framework for Inferencing Using Semantic Web Technology in
Ambient Intelligent Network 289

    Biplab K. Sarker, University of New Brunswick, Canada
    Julian Descottes, University of New Brunswick, Canada
    Mohsin Sohail, University of New Brunswick, Canada
    Rama Krishna Kosaraju, University of New Brunswick, Canada

In this chapter, the authors present a framework to provide useful and accurate information to users based on data collected from rooms in a building comprised of wireless sensor networks. The authors call a room "smart room" when a room is considered suitable for a particular purpose. For instance, a dark room for a conference, a bright room for a party, et cetera, which can be determined according to the data available from various positions of sensors located in each room and a sensor network of a building. The authors undertook the task of designing a semantic inferencing framework for a smart room. This led to automatic extraction of information from the central repository or even when the data is in a transient state(dynamic) in the network. The chapter discusses a practical way of building a query system using semantic Web technology and tools. Similar systems are becoming more feasible nowadays, and industrial leaders are moving forward to build them from commercial view point. The chapter is concluded with some future directions of the system.

Compilation of References 304

About the Contributors 323

Index 330

Foreword

It is an honour to be asked by the editor (Dr. D.P.Vidyarthi, Jawaharlal Nehru University) to write a foreword for this book, and it is my pleasure to congratulate the editor and the authors for a job well done. The quality of the presentations and the scope of recent topics provide the reader with an up-to-the-moment resource in the area of Future Internet.

As one of the determining elements, the Internet Protocol makes today's Internet work. The Internet base protocols and systems were mainly devised in the 1970s and 1980s. In 1974, the IEEE published a paper entitled "A Protocol for Packet Network Interconnection," in which Vint Cerf and Bob Kahn described an internetworking protocol for sharing resources using packet-switching among the nodes. A central control component of this model was the "Transmission Control Program" (TCP). The model became well known as TCP/IP, the dominant internetworking protocol in the Internet Layer in use today.

Some parts of the Internet are now over 40 years old, and the Internet does need to implement a lot of functions that were not included in the original design. Future Internet is about the further development of the original Internet. This book is unique as it brings together in one place relevant theoretical frameworks and the latest empirical research findings in the area. These topics are becoming ubiquitous throughout performance, reliability, scalability, security, and many other categories including societal, economical, and business aspects. This book has been written by the research community dedicated to the public awareness. It describes how the Internet will reshape itself in the future.

Frank Zhigang Wang
IEEE Computer Society, UK and Republic of Ireland &, University of Kent, UK

Frank Wang *is Head of School, School of Computing, University of Kent, UK. In 1987 the Computing Laboratory Extension was formally opened by Her Majesty the Queen. Professor Wang was elected as the Chairman (UK & Republic of Ireland Chapter) of the IEEE Computer Society in 2005. He is Fellow of British Computer Society. He serves the High End Computing Panel for Science Foundation Ireland (SFI) and the UK Government EPSRC e-Science Panel. Professor Wang's research interest includes next generation Internet, future computing, green computing, Grid/Cloud Computing, and data storage & data communication. He and his group have been developing a novel data communication protocol that can universally accelerate office/database/Web/media applications by a factor up to ten. This work won an ACM/IEEE Super Computing Finalist Award.*

Preface

The Internet is forty years old now, and by revisiting the history of the Internet, it has evolved tremendously since its birth. It is not a simple network collection to pass the data from one computer to another, the idea with which it was conceived. It is also not only the simple information repository, but incorporates all essential tools for day-to-day information processing. Be it a small shop, mid-level organization, or big corporation, governmental organization or non-governmental, all rely on Internet in contemporary world. As it was viewed a few years back, evolution in Information Technology complemented well by the network technology has resulted in total change in the Internet design. The drastic makeover in the Internet is well complemented by the revolution in Communication Technology. Thus, Information Technology and network communication technology together have made the Internet a complete utility for all types of affair. Grid Computing and Cloud Computing are few of the innovations, the backbone of which is Internet technology. Cyberworld is the name often used to pronounce the Internet world. The Cyberworld is changing at a rapid pace and has tremendously evolved since its inception. Many organizations are now equipped with Cybercell to look after Cyberworld affairs. Now Internet has become part and parcel of each individual well supported by all IT and communication infrastructure.

This book aims to provide relevant theoretical frameworks and the latest empirical research findings in the area of the Internet design. It is written for the research community and professionals who wish to improve their understanding of the Future Internet Technologies. It is to foresee how the Internet will reshape itself in the future and will be supported by the latest technology. This will also be a reference book for the students/researchers working in the field of computer science, Information Technology, communication technology, Cyberworld, et cetera.

In the year 1969, the Internet was conceived in a lab at the University of California, Los Angles to connect two big computers with 15-foot cables to pass the data. Since then, it has grown enormously. The first chapter of this book briefs the historical evolution of the Internet design in chronological order. Optical networking is an upcoming technology for both LAN and MAN. There are many related research issues with the optical networking technology that are pointed out in the second chapter. This also lists the current state of affairs in optical networks.

Since its inception, Web has changed a lot and so have its users. The Web now offers dynamic information and services. Users are also not mere information consumers, but are active producers now. The third chapter proposes a unified user model, in terms of a new Web access device, the *browserver*, which includes a browser and a server working in close cooperation. The objective is to replace the classical browser and stay backward compatible to ease the migration path.

Healthcare is an essential service. Health Care Organizations (HCOs) are now defining methodologies of the Information Technology (IT) that can provide high quality services at minimum cost. Internet technology can add a lot in this endeavor of HCO. The fourth chapter elaborates on the uses of Web technology for healthcare services.

Cellular networks, originally designed for voice services, have been upgraded to accommodate Internet services. WiFi and WiMax systems have been explicitly developed for delivering data services over wireless channels. Special design requirements of physical layer due to distinct properties of wireless channel have caused some differences with those of wired networks. Low bandwidth supported by the channel, poor equipment capabilities, and other features require special attention in developing various Internet services intended to be accessed by wireless devices. Chapter five addresses various aspects of physical layer of wireless channel for developing basic understanding of the problems, existing solutions and proposals for the future networks.

Internet security is a big challenge and is a prime issue for all Internet based technology (e.g. Grid and Cloud computing). Identification based on biological features is emerging as a foolproof solution to all kinds of security threats. Chapter six discusses Internet security using biometrics. WiMAX technology provides wireless Quality of Service QoS-enabled broadband access for fixed and mobile users. It is end-to-end and IP based and provides a rich set of QoS support for multimedia-based ubiquitous computing. The seventh chapter investigates the WiMAX architecture and the QoS support provided by the IEEE 802.16 protocol stack. This chapter also examines mobility management issues, end-to-end QoS, and current and future application areas of the WiMAX technology.

The present day transportation system makes uses of Internet for efficient command and control transfers. In such a communication system, reliability and on-time data transfer are critical. The sensor network supports streaming of multimedia and entertainment data from mobile to infrastructure network and vice versa in addition to the sensor information. The eighth chapter proposes a novel modeling method for the network and its traffic shaping. It also looks at the congestion control of packet loss using a differentially fed neural network controller. IPTV is an upcoming technology for audio-visual communication over the IP based network. Reliable data transfer is very important, more so as it is the transfer of real time data. Chapter nine proposes a model for reliability optimization in IPTV systems using Genetic Algorithms.

The Internet interconnects billions of small devices often limited in computational capacity, memory, and available energy and may suffer a high data loss rate when integrated into a network infrastructure. The tenth chapter describes the assumptions, technologies, and challenges for transmitting IPv6 over low power wireless personal area networks (LoWPANs). It addresses the key mechanisms from network aspects down to device design aspects. Mutual exclusion is one of the well-studied fundamental primitives in distributed systems. However, the emerging Peer to Peer systems bring forward several challenges to protect consistent and concurrent access to shared resources, as classical peer-to-peer systems like Napster, Gnutella, et cetera have been mainly used for sharing files with read only permission. Chapter eleven proposes a quorum based mutual exclusion algorithm, which can be used over any Peer to Peer Distributed Hash Table (DHT). The approach is an extension to traditional Sigma protocol for mutual exclusion in Peer to Peer systems.

Chapter twelve discusses Random Early Discard (RED) algorithm. This applies the technique of Active Queue Management (AQM) to prevent and control congestion and also to provide a range of Internet performance facilities. Chapter thirteen is the comparative study of the two models based on the two evolutionary algorithms, i.e. GA and PSO. It optimizes the path reliability of a flow in Cellular IP network.

The mobile device has nowadays become an important tool that can work as a gateway for the administrators to their visitors of the city. Chapter fourteen presents a method to process various environmental factors during a visit of the visitor and uses these factors as a context for presenting the recommendations. This chapter presents three main steps in the process of recommendation systems: collecting information, processing the recommendations, and presenting them in an attractive way. Focus of the chapter is the recommendations through augmented reality in order to provide an attractive tool for end users.

Growing Internet usage has invited to make the Internet pervasive so that it can be exploited to maximum possible extent. Today, the Internet is being utilized for multiple useful purposes. Chapter fifteen talks about making Internet pervasive via wireless mesh network.

A smart room is one that can adapt to the requirement from time to time. A semantic inference framework for a smart room has been designed in the last chapter of the book. It proposes a framework to provide useful and accurate information to users based on data collected from rooms in a building comprised of wireless sensor networks.

Overall, this book is a good collection of chapters comprised of useful research output towards the future Internet design.

Deo Prakash Vidyarthi
Jawaharlal Nehru University, India

Acknowledgment

I express my deepest sense of gratitude to all the authors of different chapters of this book who not only visualized and conceived the idea for future Internet design, but also detailed their work in chapters. It is their effort and commitment that has resulted in the form of this book.

I am grateful to all the editorial board members of this book who spared their valuable time to review the chapters of this book. Their sincere efforts have resulted in quality production of this book. I wish to express my sincere thanks to Prof. Frank Zhigang Wang, University of Kent, Canterbury, UK for writing a foreword for this book

I am indebted to my research students and colleagues in Jawaharlal Nehru University for their continuous support and valuable suggestions.

The team at IGI Global truly deserves word of appreciation as their valuable advice has helped me a lot in modeling this book. I am also thankful to them for the best compilation of the book.

I would like also to convey my love, respect, and gratitude to my dear parents who are always a source of inspiration in my life. It is because of their support and blessings that I was able to conceive this idea of the book.

I am grateful to my wife Meenu who provided me with the time and support to design this book. My love and affection to my son Prashast and daughter Navya for their patience and assistance to make this work possible.

During the course of life, we encounter many people who help us, share their valuable time with us, and provide support so that we can achieve our goals of life, I would like to thank all of them.

D.P. Vidyarthi
Jawaharlal Nehru University, India

Chapter 1
Historical Evolution in Internet:
An Introduction

Deo Prakash Vidyarthi
Jawaharlal Nehru University, India

ABSTRACT

The spurt in the Information Technology in the recent past has been well complemented by the innovative research in communication technology. Tremendous growth in the Internet is the result of this. This chapter highlights how the Internet has evolved, over the years, since its inception. The major contributors of Internet Technology have also been pointed out in this chapter.

INTRODUCTION

Recently, on September 2, 2010, Internet turned to the age of 40 years. We never have imagined in the past such a boom in the Information technology attributed to the design of the Internet. Its stunning success has changed the way we work, learn and play. It has proved its worth by its support to vast number of applications. It is possible only by the evolution in the underlying network technology. As of today, Internet has become an essential component of our daily life assisting in most of our activities.

DOI: 10.4018/978-1-4666-0203-8.ch001

However, Internet's increasing ubiquity has brought a number of challenges for which the current architecture is ill suited. It warrants the changes in the Future Internet Design.

Going down the line, it is just a group of small people which conceived the idea of the network, which has resulted in such a huge global network. In the year 1969 around 20 people sat together in a lab at the University of California, Los Angles to connect two big computers with 15 fit big cables to pass the data. This event is supposed to be the inception of the Internet. Over the years, Internet has evolved drastically and may sound miracle, the way it has changed the life of human being. It is impossible to think of the modern world today without World Wide Web (WWW). The term WWW is often mistakenly used as a synonym for the Internet. In reality, Web is a service that operates over the Internet, e.g. e-mail.

The development of the Internet, over the years, may be listed in chronological order as below.

In the year 1969 on September 2, in first test of Arpanet, two computers at the University of California, exchange meaningless data. Arpanet was an experimental military network. On October 29 in the same year, the first connection between the two sites UCLA and the Stanford Research Institute in Menlo Park, California took place. This is to note that the network crashed just after the first two letters of the word "logon." Arpanet got its first East Coast node, at Bolt, Beranek and Newman in Cambridge, Mass in the year 1970. It was Ray Tomlinson, who brought e-mail to the network in the year 1972. He selected @ symbol to specify e-mail addresses belonging to other systems.

Famous communications technique called TCP protocol was developed by Vint Cerf and Bob Kahn in the year 1974. Before formal adoption of this protocol on January 1, 1983, it was divided into TCP/IP. The robust naming mechanism, Domain Name System (DNS) was also proposed in the year 1983, though the famous suffixes *.com, .edu* etc. came a year later.

America Online service for Macintosh and Apple II was introduced by Quantum Computer Services (now AOL) in the year 1989. It is supposed to connect nearly 27 million Americans online by 2002. While inventing ways to control computers remotely at European Organization for Nuclear Research CERN, Tim Berners-Lee created the World Wide Web in 1990. It is one of the biggest milestones in the development of current Internet. In fact several names were considered for WWW i.e. *The Information Mesh, The Information Mine* (both abbreviates to TIM) or *Mine of Information* (MOI) but ultimately was settled on *World Wide Web*.

Burner Lee along-with his one of the colleagues developed a Hypertext Technology in the year 1990. All the necessary tools e.g. HTML (Hyper Text Markup Language), HTTP (Hyper Text Transfer Protocol) for working with Internet was developed by them by the year 1990.

Mosaic was the first Web browser to combine graphics and text on a single page. It was created by Marc Andreessen and colleagues at University of Illinois create in the year 1993. First commercial Web browser, Netscape, was also developed by Andreessen and others on the Mosaic team in the year 1994. In the year 1995, Amazon.com Inc. opens its virtual doors for users. In 1998, Google Inc. was formed out of a project in Stanford. Internet Corporation for Assigned Names and Numbers (ICANN) was also formed by the US government in 1998. Eventually, in the year 1999, Napster popularizes the music and file-sharing. World Internet population also grows to 250 million by 1999. It was the year 2000 in which Amazon.com, eBay and other sites are crippled in one of the first widespread uses of the denial-of-service attack. This flooded the site with a huge bogus traffic and prevented legitimate users. Successive years only see the world Internet population to grow like anything. It was 500 million in 2002, which increased to 1.5 billion in 2008 and reaching to 2 billion now. Many web browsers; Firefox, MS Internet Explorer, chrome etc. have been developed during this development.

The concept of the Semantic Web came around the year 2003 by the Tim Berner Lee. His vision of the Semantic Web is as follows:

I have a dream for the Web in which computers become capable of analyzing all the data on the Web – the content, links, and transactions between people and computers. A 'Semantic Web', which should make this possible, has yet to emerge, but when it does, the day-to-day mechanisms of trade, bureaucracy and our daily lives will be handled by machines talking to machines. The 'intelligent agents' people have touted for ages will finally materialize. – Time Berner Lee

Three ex-PayPal employees formed a video viewing website called YouTube in the year 2005. Over the years as Internet connectivity becomes ubiquitous; it is possible to leverage the expanded computing power to enhance their usability and capability. Intelligent Device Management focuses on connecting devices to the Internet. Through Internet connectivity, manufacturers are now able to interact with the devices they have sold and shipped to their customers, and customers are able to interact with the manufacturer to access new content.

Two parallel bodies Internet Research Task Force (IRTF) and Internet Engineering Task Force (IETF) exist today to look into all aspects of Internet. IRTF concentrates on long term research issues related to the Internet while the IETF focuses on the short term issues of engineering and Internet standardization.

Many malicious things also happened along with the invention of Internet. Internet worms, bombs, viruses, etc. had been developed that crippled the computer world wide. Nonetheless, the positive developments are much more in comparison to the negative one and thus lead the Internet to a stage where it has become essential part of our daily activity.

From the beginning till today Internet has evolved so much and it has come a full circle. It is high time to think of reinventing the Internet. This book has been designed keeping in mind the kind of shape Internet will take in the years to come.

REFERENCES

Berners-Lee, T., & Fischetti, M. (1999). *Weaving the Web: The original design and ultimate destiny of the World Wide Web by its inventor*. San Francisco, CA: Harper.

Gillies, J., & Cailliau, R. (2000). *How the Web was born: The story of the World Wide Web*. Oxford, UK: Oxford University Press.

Herman, A. (2000). *The World Wide Web and contemporary cultural theory: Magic, metaphor, power* (1st ed.). Routledge.

ADDITIONAL READING

http://en.wikipedia.org

http://www.ietf.org

http://www.irtf.org

Chapter 2
Optical Networking:
Current Issues and Review

Sanjeev Kumar Raghuwanshi
Indian School of Mines, India

ABSTRACT

Telecommunication networks based on optical fiber technology have become a major information transmission system with high capacity optical fiber links encircling the globe in both terrestrial and undersea installation. At present there are numerous passive and active optical devices within a light wave link that perform complex networking functions in the optical domain, such as signal restoration, routing, and switching. Along with the need to understand the functions of these devices comes the necessity to measure both components and network performance and to model and simulate the complex behavior of reliable high capacity networks. This chapter presents the fundamental principles for understanding and applying these issues. This chapter is primarily about TCP/IP network protocols and Ethernet network architectures, but also briefly describes other protocol suites, network architectures, and other significant areas of networking. It explains in simple terms the way networks are put together, and how data packages are sent between networks and subnets, along with how data is routed to the Internet.

OPTICAL NETWORKING

Key features of this chapter for accomplishing these issues are as follows: history, types, principle and operation of optical networking; wavelength division multiplexing (WDM) routed optical net-

works; main characteristics of optical switching; IP over WDM issues: routing problem and routing protocols used in IP network; current typical protocol stacks and classification of routing schemes; topology of optical network: star network, ring network and tree network, et cetera; types of optical networks, and network categories. Hence this chapter treats more complex optical networks that

DOI: 10.4018/978-1-4666-0203-8.ch002

can be utilized in local, metropolitan or wide area networks to connect hundreds or thousands of users with a wide range of transmission capacities and speeds (Modiano, 1999).

As the name suggests, optical networks form a class of networks where optical, rather than electronic, components are the building blocks of the network. Compared to metallic cable, fiber optic systems offer greater bandwidths, lower attenuation, and no crosstalk or electrical interference. Those advantages have led to the dramatic growth of fiber optic systems worldwide. This chapter is primarily about TCP/IP network protocols and Ethernet network architectures, but also briefly describes other protocol suites, network architectures, and other significant areas of networking. This chapter is written for all audiences, even those with little or no networking experience. It explains in simple terms the way networks are put together, and how data packages are sent between networks and subnets along with how data is routed to the internet (Gerstel & Ramaswami, 2000; Modiano & Narula Tam, 2002; Manchester et al., 1998).

Today, nearly all long-haul telecommunications depend on the use of optical networks for their large capacity and robust performance.

- The purpose of the management and control systems for optical networks is to provide for the efficient delivery of highly available, highly reliable communication services.
- These services consist of a variety of different types of connections between end users of the optical network.

Standards

Standards for fiber optic cable and other optical components have been developed over the last 20 years primarily by the American National Standards Institute (ANSI) and the International Telecommunications Union (ITU). Standards for fiber optic transmission have been developed initially

in North America under the name Synchronous Optical Network (SONET) and later by the ITU using the name Synchronous Digital Hierarchy

Historical Milestones

- **1958:** Discovery of laser
- **Mid-60s:** Demonstration of guided wave optics
- **1970:** Production of low-loss fibers, which made long-distance optical transmission possible
- **1970:** Invention of semiconductor laser diode, which made highly refined optical transceivers possible
- **70s-80s:** Use of fiber in telephony: SONET/SDH standards from ITU
- **Mid-80s:** LANs/MANs: broadcast-and-select architectures
- **1988:** First trans-Atlantic optical fiber laid
- **Late-80s:** Development of EDFA (optical amplifier), which greatly alleviated distance limitations
- **Mid/late-90s:** DWDM systems explode
- **Late-90s:** Intelligent Optical networks
- **20??:** Soliton transmission with optical TDM

Optical Networking: Why

The "traditional" networks consist, for the most part, of a collection of electronic switches interconnected by point-to-point optical fiber links, which can span local, metropolitan, or wide area networks. To accommodate continually increasing demand for bandwidth and flexibility, such networks are being enhanced by adding more fibers and switches, increasing the bit rate per fiber, and upgrading the switches' size, throughput and functionality. Such enhancements eventually lead to very large and complex networks that are difficult and expensive to construct, operate and maintain. Recent and emerging advances in optical technology promise revolutionary all-optical networks capable of providing improved economy, flexibility and robustness while still capable of making use of the large existing fiber base Baransel, Dobosiz, & Gewicburzynski, 1995).

PRINCIPLES AND OPERATION

An optical fiber is a cylindrical waveguide made of two transparent materials each with a different index of refraction. The two materials, usually high-quality glass, are arranged concentrically to form an inner core and an outer cladding. Different entry angles of the light source result in multiple modes of wave propagation. Propagation can be restricted to a single mode by using a small-diameter core. The choice between single-mode and multimode fiber depends on the desired repeater spacing or transmission rate; single mode is the preferred choice for long-haul or high data-rate systems. The earliest form of multimode fiber was the step-index, where the core has a uniform index of refraction and the concentric cladding also has a uniform but lower index. In this case the propagation velocity within the core is constant, so that rays traveling a longer path arrive behind rays traveling a shorter path, thus producing pulse spreading, or dispersion. These dispersive effects may be remedied by constructing a fiber whose refractive index increases toward the axis, with a resulting refractive index profile that is parabolic. With a graded-index fiber, rays that travel longer paths have greater velocity than rays traveling the shorter paths due to decreasing refractive index with radial distance. The various modes then tend to have the same arrival time, such that dispersion is minimized and greater bandwidths become possible for multimode fibers.

Within the spectrum available in a fiber optic system, there are three low-loss windows, at wavelengths of approximately 850, 1300, and 1550 nm. Early applications of fiber optics for communications applications were based on the short-wavelength band of roughly 800 to 860

nm. Operation in the longer-wavelength bands, particularly at 1300 and 1550 -nm, is attractive because of improved attenuation and dispersion characteristics at these wavelengths. Typically today the shorter-wavelength band is used for short-haul, low data rate systems, and the longer-wavelength bands are applied to long-haul, high data rate systems. Special fibers have been developed that shift the minimum dispersion to about 1550 nm to take advantage of lower attenuation as well as minimum dispersion. These fibers are called dispersion-shifted fibers, and are important to single-mode fiber applications. Low-data rate, short-haul fiber optic systems tend toward multimode cable, LED transmitters, and PIN diode receivers. High-data rate, long-haul systems tend toward single-mode cable, laser diode transmitters, and avalanche photodiode receivers. Latest generation fiber optic systems have introduced innovations that have significantly improved the bandwidth and repeater spacing possible. Coherent detection via either homodyne or heterodyne techniques allows much greater bandwidths to be realized. Several wavelengths can be transmitted simultaneously in wavelength-division multiplexing, analogous to frequency-division multiplexing used in telephony. Optical amplifiers are now available that eliminate electronics and instead use specially doped fiber or semiconductor laser devices. The use of optical amplifiers will allow a fiber optic system to be upgraded in bit rate without replacement of the repeaters. Optical amplifiers have also been used to achieve ultra-long distances via soliton transmission, which is the transmission of an idealized pulse without loss of pulse shape (Mukherjee et al., 1996).

WAVELENGTH DIVISION MULTIPLEXING (WDM) IN OPTICAL NETWORKS

In fiber-optic communications, wavelength-division multiplexing (WDM) is a technology which multiplexes a number of optical carrier signals onto a single optical fiber by using different wavelengths (colours) of laser light. This technique enables bidirectional communications over one strand of fiber, as well as multiplication of capacity. The term wavelength-division multiplexing is commonly applied to an optical carrier (which is typically described by its wavelength), whereas frequency-division multiplexing typically applies to a radio carrier (which is more often described by frequency). Since wavelength and frequency are tied together through a simple relationship, the two terms actually describe the same concept. A WDM system uses a multiplexer at the transmitter to join the signals together and a de-multiplexer at the receiver to split them apart. With the right type of fiber it is possible to have a device that does both simultaneously, and can function as an optical add-drop multiplexer. The optical filtering devices used have traditionally been etalons, stable solid-state single frequency Fabry Perot interferometers in the form of thin-film-coated optical glass. The concept was first published in 1970, and by 1978 WDM systems were being realized in the laboratory. The first WDM systems only combined two signals. Modern systems can handle up to 160 signals and can thus expand a basic 10 G-bit/s system over a single fiber pair to over 1.6 T-bit/s. WDM systems are popular with telecommunications companies because they allow them to expand the capacity of the network without laying more fiber. By using WDM and optical amplifiers, they can accommodate several generations of technology development in their optical infrastructure without having to overhaul the backbone network. Capacity of a given link can be expanded by simply upgrading the multiplexers and de-multiplexers at each end. This is often done by using optical-to-electrical-to-optical (O/E/O) translation at the very edge of the transport network, thus permitting interoperation with existing equipment with optical interfaces. Most WDM systems operate on single mode fiber optical cables, which have a core diameter of 9 µm.

Also certain forms of WDM can also be used in multi-mode fiber cables (also known as premises cables) which have core diameters of 50 or 62.5 µm. Early WDM systems were expensive and complicated to run. However, recent standardization and better understanding of the dynamics of WDM systems have made WDM less expensive to deploy (Neely & Modiano, 2007). Optical receivers, in contrast to laser sources, tend to be wideband devices. Therefore the de-multiplexer must provide the wavelength selectivity of the receiver in the WDM system. WDM systems are divided in different wavelength patterns, conventional or coarse and dense WDM. Conventional WDM systems provide up to 8 channels in the 3rd transmission window (C-Band) of silica fibers around 1550 nm. Dense wavelength division multiplexing (DWDM) uses the same transmission window but with denser channel spacing. Channel plans vary, but a typical system would use 40 channels at 100 GHz spacing or 80 channels with 50 GHz spacing. Some technologies are capable of 25 GHz spacing (sometimes called ultra dense WDM). New amplification options (Raman amplification) enable the extension of the usable wavelengths to the L-band, more or less doubling these numbers. Coarse wavelength division multiplexing (CWDM) in contrast to conventional WDM and DWDM uses increased channel spacing to allow less sophisticated and thus cheaper transceiver designs. To again provide 8 channels on a single fiber CWDM uses the entire frequency band between second and third transmission window (1310/1550 nm respectively) including both windows (minimum dispersion window and minimum attenuation window) but also the critical area where OH scattering may occur, recommending the use of OH-free silica fibers in case the wavelengths between second and third transmission window shall also be used. Avoiding this region, the channels 31, 49, 51, 53, 55, 57, 59, 61 remain and these are the most commonly used. WDM, DWDM and CWDM are based on the same concept of using multiple wavelengths of light on a single fiber, but differ in the spacing of the wavelengths, number of channels, and the ability to amplify the multiplexed signals in the optical space. EDFA provide efficient wideband amplification for the C-band, Raman amplification adds a mechanism for amplification in the L-band. For CWDM wideband optical amplification is not available, limiting the optical spans to several tens of kilometers. Some key point is given below:

History of WDM Networks

- In the late 70s
  - First fiber based optical transmission system
- Before 1995
  - Mostly a single high-speed optical channel
  - All multiplexing done in electrical domain(TDM)
  - 50Mb/s to 10Gb/s data services
- After 1995
  - WDM allows simultaneously transmitting multiple high-speed channels on different frequencies (Up to 160 wavelengths today)
  - 40G per l (OC768)
  - Total link capacity = 160[INSERT FIGURE 002]40G =6.4 T-bps

Background

- Three transmission pass bands in the near-IR region of the light spectrum
- Each of band has 25,000 GHz (10^6 s^{-1}) of capacity (equivalent to peak hour of phone calls in the U.S)
- Capacity is also equivalent to 1000 times the entire RF spectrum (radio waves) in free space
- WDM as a transmission technology
- Use WDM multiplexers/de-multiplexers
- Increased bandwidth - immediate value

Optical Networks - Current Usage

- Video Network Conferencing
- Real –Time Medical Imaging
- Scientific Visualization
- High-Speed Supercomputing

Use of Fiber Optics in Networks

- **First generation:** All copper networks. Contained a lot of noise (electron-electron interactions) (Figure 1).
- **Second generation:** Partially fiber/copper. Better signal to noise ratio. A lot of optical – electrical / electrical – optical conversion.
- **Third generation:** All optical networks. The only conversions occur at the transmitters / receivers. Higher bandwidth and little noise.

Coarse-WDM

Originally, the term "coarse wavelength division multiplexing (CWDM)" was fairly generic, and meant a number of different things. In general, these things shared the fact that the choice of channel spacing's and frequency stability was such that erbium doped fiber amplifiers (EDFAs) could not be utilized. Prior to the relatively recent ITU standardization of the term, one common meaning for coarse WDM meant two (or possibly more) signals multiplexed onto a single fiber, where one signal was in the 1550 nm band, and the other in

Figure 1. Generation of fiber optics in network

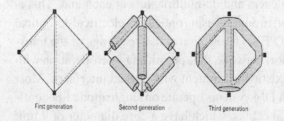

First generation   Second generation   Third generation

the 1310 nm band. In 2002 the ITU standardized a channel spacing grid for use with CWDM (ITU-T G.694.2), using the wavelengths from 1270 nm through 1610 nm with a channel spacing of 20 nm (Chen, Modiano, & Saengudomlert, 2006; Brzezinski & Modiano, 2005).

Dense-WDM

Dense wavelength division multiplexing, or DWDM for short, refers originally to optical signals multiplexed within the 1550 nm band so as to leverage the capabilities (and cost) of erbium doped fiber amplifiers (EDFAs), which are effective for wavelengths between approximately 1525-1565 nm (C band), or 1570-1610 nm (L band). EDFAs were originally developed to replace SONET/SDH optical-electrical-optical (OEO) regenerators, which they have made practically obsolete. EDFAs can amplify any optical signal in their operating range, regardless of the modulated bit rate. In terms of multi-wavelength signals, so long as the EDFA has enough pump energy available to it, it can amplify as many optical signals as can be multiplexed into its amplification band (though signal densities are limited by choice of modulation format). EDFAs therefore allow a single-channel optical link to be upgraded in bit rate by replacing only equipment at the ends of the link, while retaining the existing EDFA or series of EDFAs through a long haul route. Furthermore, single-wavelength links using EDFAs can similarly be upgraded to WDM links at reasonable cost. The EDFAs cost is thus leveraged across as many channels as can be multiplexed into the 1550 nm band.

DWDM Systems

At this stage, a basic DWDM system contains several main components:

1. A DWDM terminal multiplexer actually contains one wavelength converting transponder for each wavelength signal it will carry. The wavelength converting transponders receive the input optical signal (i.e., from a client-layer SONET/SDH or other signal), convert that signal into the electrical domain, and retransmit the signal using a 1550 nm band laser. Early DWDM systems contained 4 or 8 wavelength converting transponders in the mid 1990s. By 2000 or so, commercial systems capable of carrying 128 signals were available. The terminal mux also contains an optical multiplexer, which takes the various 1550 nm band signals and places them onto a single fiber (e.g. SMF-28 fiber). The terminal multiplexer may or may not also support a local EDFA for power amplification of the multi-wavelength optical signal.

2. An intermediate line repeater is placed approx. every 80 – 100 km for compensating the loss in optical power, while the signal travels along the fiber. The signal is amplified by an EDFA, which usually consists of several amplifier stages.

3. An intermediate optical terminal or Optical Add-drop multiplexer. This is a remote amplification site that amplifies the multi-wavelength signal that may have traversed up to 140 km or more before reaching the remote site. Optical diagnostics and telemetry are often extracted or inserted at such a site, to allow for localization of any fiber breaks or signal impairments. In more sophisticated systems (which are no longer point-to-point), several signals out of the multi-wavelength signal may be removed and dropped locally.

4. A DWDM terminal demultiplexer breaks the multi-wavelength signal back into individual signals and outputs them on separate fibers for client-layer systems (such as SONET/SDH) to detect. Originally, this de-multiplexing was performed entirely passively, except for some telemetry, as most SONET systems can receive 1550-nm signals. However, in order to allow for transmission to remote

client-layer systems (and to allow for digital domain signal integrity determination) such de-multiplexed signals are usually sent to O/E/O output transponders prior to being relayed to their client-layer systems. Often, the functionality of output transponder has been integrated into that of input transponder, so that most commercial systems have transponders that support bi-directional interfaces on both their 1550-nm (i.e., internal) side, and external (i.e., client-facing) side. Transponders in some systems supporting 40 GHz nominal operation may also perform forward error correction (FEC) via 'digital wrapper' technology, as described in the ITU-TG.709 standard.

5. Optical Supervisory Channel (OSC) is an additional wavelength usually outside the EDFA amplification band (at 1510 nm, 1620 nm, 1310 nm or another proprietary wavelength). The OSC carries information about the multi-wavelength optical signal as well as remote conditions at the optical terminal or EDFA site. It is also normally used for remote software upgrades and user (i.e., network operator) Network Management information. It is the multi-wavelength analogue to SONET's DCC (or supervisory channel). ITU standards suggest that the OSC should utilize an OC-3 signal structure, though some vendors have opted to use 100 megabit Ethernet or another signal format. Unlike the 1550 nm band client signal-carrying wavelengths, the OSC is always terminated at intermediate amplifier sites, where it receives local information before retransmission.

The introduction of the ITU-T G. 694.1 frequency grid in 2002 has made it easier to integrate WDM with older but more standard SONET/SDH systems. WDM wavelengths are positioned in a grid having exactly 100 GHz (about 0.8 nm) spacing in optical frequency, with a reference frequency fixed at 193.10 THz (1552.52 nm). The main grid is placed inside the optical fiber amplifier bandwidth, but can be extended to wider bandwidths. Today's DWDM systems use 50 GHz or even 25 GHz channel spacing for up to 160 channel operation. DWDM systems have to maintain more stable wavelength or frequency than those needed for CWDM because of the closer spacing of the wavelengths. Precision temperature control of laser transmitter is required in DWDM systems to prevent "drift" off a very narrow frequency window of the order of a few GHz. In addition, since DWDM provides greater maximum capacity it tends to be used at a higher level in the communications hierarchy than CWDM, for example on the Internet backbone and is therefore associated with higher modulation rates, thus creating a smaller market for DWDM devices with very high performance levels. These factors of smaller volume and higher performance result in DWDM systems typically being more expensive than CWDM.

Recent innovations in DWDM transport systems include pluggable and software-tunable transceiver modules capable of operating on 40 or 80 channels. This dramatically reduces the need for discrete spare pluggable modules, when a handful of pluggable devices can handle the full range of wavelengths (Berry & Modiano, 2005).

Wavelength Converting Transponders

At this stage, some details concerning Wavelength Converting Transponders should be discussed, as this will clarify the role played by current DWDM technology as an additional optical transport layer. It will also serve to outline the evolution of such systems over the last 10 or so years. As stated above, wavelength converting transponders served originally to translate the transmit wavelength of a client-layer signal into one of the DWDM system's internal wavelengths in the 1550 nm band (note that even external wavelengths in the

1550 nm will most likely need to be translated, as they will almost certainly not have the required frequency stability tolerances nor will it have the optical power necessary for the system's EDFA). In the mid-1990s, however, wavelength converting transponders rapidly took on the additional function of signal regeneration. Signal regeneration in transponders quickly evolved through 1R to 2R to 3R and into overhead-monitoring multi-bit-rate 3R regenerators. These differences are outlined below:

- **1R (Re-transmit):** Basically, early transponders were "garbage in garbage out" in that their output was nearly an analogue 'copy' of the received optical signal, with little signal cleanup occurring. This limited the reach of early DWDM systems because the signal had to be handed off to a client-layer receiver (likely from a different vendor) before the signal deteriorated too far. Signal monitoring was basically confined to optical domain parameters such as received power (Chen & Modiano, 2004).

- **2R (Re-time and re-transmit):** Transponders of this type were not very common and utilized a quasi-digital Schmitt-triggering method for signal cleanup. Some rudimentary signal quality monitoring was done by such transmitters that basically looked at analogue parameters.

- **3R (Re-time, re-transmit, re-shape):** 3R Transponders were fully digital and normally able to view SONET/SDH section layer overhead bytes such as A1 and A2 to determine signal quality health. Many systems will offer 2.5 Gbit/s transponders, which will normally mean the transponder is able to perform 3R regeneration on OC-3/12/48 signals, and possibly gigabit Ethernet, and reporting on signal health by monitoring SONET/SDH section layer

overhead bytes. Many transponders will be able to perform full multi-rate 3R in both directions. Some vendors offer 10 Gbit/s transponders, which will perform Section layer overhead monitoring to all rates up to and including OC-192.

Muxponder

The muxponder (from multiplexed transponder) has different names depending on vendor. It essentially performs some relatively simple time division multiplexing of lower rate signals into a higher rate carrier within the system (a common example is the ability to accept 4 OC-48s and then output a single OC-192 in the 1550 nm band). More recent muxponder designs have absorbed more and more TDM functionality, in some cases obviating the need for traditional SONET/SDH transport equipment.

Reconfigurable Optical Add-Drop Multiplexer (ROADM)

As mentioned above, intermediate optical amplification sites in DWDM systems may allow for the dropping and adding of certain wavelength channels. In most systems deployed as of August 2006 this is done infrequently, because adding or dropping wavelengths requires manually inserting or replacing wavelength-selective cards. This is costly, and in some systems requires that all active traffic be removed from the DWDM system, because inserting or removing the wavelength-specific cards interrupts the multi-wavelength optical signal. With a ROADM, network operators can remotely reconfigure the multiplexer by sending soft commands. The architecture of the ROADM is such that dropping or adding wavelengths does not interrupt the 'pass-through' channels (Berry & Modiano, 2004).

Transceivers vs. Transponders

Transceivers

Since communication over a single wavelength is one-way (simplex communication), and most practical communication systems require two-way (duplex communication) communication, two wavelengths will be required (which might or might not be on the same fiber, but typically they will be each on a separate fiber in a so-called fiber pair). As a result, at each end both a transmitter (to send a signal over a first wavelength) and a receiver (to receive a signal over a second wavelength) will be required. A combination of a transmitter and a receiver is called a transceiver; it converts an electrical signal to and from an optical signal.

Transponder

In practice, the signal inputs and outputs will not be electrical but optical instead (typically at 1550 nm). This means that in effect we need wavelength converters instead, which is exactly what a transponder is. A transponder can be made up of two transceivers placed after each other: the first transceiver converting the 1550 nm optical signal to/from an electrical signal, and the second transceiver converting the electrical signal to/from an optical signal at the required wavelength. Transponders that don't use an intermediate electrical signal (all-optical transponders) are in development.

WDM NETWORK COMPONENTS

It is possible to pack many channels into a SONET/SDH network, using the principle of time division multiplexing (TDM). However, available technology puts an upper limit to the realizable band width. OC-48/STM-16 with a speed of 2.488 M-bit/sec is most popular today. More expensive OC-192/ STM-64 with a 10 Gigabit/sec is available. A practical upper limit using developing technology is 40 G-bps. An alternative is to assign different frequencies to different channels, multiplex them for carrying information over fibers and finally de-multiplex at the receiver end. The wavelength division multiplexing (WDM) is the same as frequency division, excepting that the terminology is used for optical frequencies. The essential components of a WDM system are primarily those of any network, viz., transmitters, link and receivers. In addition, the system would require other components such as switches, modulators, amplifiers etc. In case of WDM technology, the transmitters are laser sources with stable tunable wavelengths (Narula, Modiano, & Brzezinksi, 2004). Before sending the signal through the link, multiplexers mix the wavelengths. Link is low loss optical fiber while at the receiver end there are photo detectors and wavelength de-multiplexers.

- **Optical Amplifiers:** Inline signal amplification is done by placing optical amplifiers along the fiber span. Erbium doped fiber amplifiers (EDFA) are generally used in WDM applications. Key performance parameters of amplifiers are gain, gain-flatness, noise level and power output. Gains greater than 30 dB over a wide spectral width (~80 nm) with low noise are characteristics of EDFAs which are available in both L-band and C-band. Signal gain provided by EDFAs has reasonably flat wavelength response. However, the flatness can be improved by gain flattening optical filters. Signal can travel over 100 km between amplifiers. If longer haul is required, it will be necessary to regenerate signal.
- **Regenerators:** In addition to amplifying signals, perform what is known as 3R-operations, viz., reshaping, retiming and retransmitting. As the total gain in EDFA is shared between different wavelength channels the gain per channel decreases.

As there are OADMs in the network, this would result in different channels being received with different power at the receiver end. The problem is addressed by equalizing filters which attenuate wavelengths that are strongly amplified.

Multiplexers (MUX)

At first sight it would seem that multiplexing different wavelengths would be a relatively simple job of simply allowing different wavelength signals to fall on an optical fiber within the latter's angle of acceptance. However, one has to take care to see that the noise associated with each channel is kept to a minimum. Channels must be isolated to ensure that noise at a different wavelength does not interfere with the signal that is being carried. A wavelength multiplexer (MUX) combines incident wavelengths and launches the output to the fiber. At the receiving end a de-multiplexer (DEMUX) reverses the above and separates the signal into the components. Multiplexers are generally based on one of two principles, viz., angular dispersion and optical filtering. Prism and reflection gratings are used for separating wavelengths. The same elements can combine wavelengths on reversing the direction of the beams. Reflection gratings can also be used to separate wavelengths. By choosing a suitable periodic structure for the grating, it is possible to coincide the directions of constructive interference and specular reflection from the grating for a given order and wavelength. The technique is known as **blazing**. In blazing light consisting of a mixture of different wavelengths enters a GRIN lens which collimates the beam to fall on the grating. After reflection, the components are spatially separated and focused by the lens as outputs to fibers carrying different wavelengths. Multiplexers may also be made using interference filters. Optical filters can be designed using various techniques, the cheapest being deposition of thin films of varying refractive indices on a substrate. When incident light falls on such a material, it encounters stacks of boundaries which produce constructive interference for some wavelengths and destructive interference for some others. As the number of stacks increases, the resolution becomes better and the band of selected wavelengths becomes narrower. The essential difference between filters based on reflection gratings and interference filters is that gratings selectively reflect a narrow range of wavelengths while the interference filters transmit a narrow range of wavelengths (Modiano, 1999).

OADM

In its passage from the MUX to DEMUX, the signal passes through one or more Optical Add-Drop Multiplexer (OADM). The function of an OADM is to selectively drop one or more wavelengths by rerouting its data content to another fiber. The OADM may just allow the remaining traffic to pass or add a different data set at a wavelength equal to that of a dropped data. This helps to create a virtual point-to-point circuit. An OADM is generally a device such as a Bragg grating which could be used to selectively reflect a wavelength that is to be dropped while allowing the others to be transmitted. OADMs are passive components of the network. They are manufactured to operate either at fixed wavelengths or at dynamically selectable wavelengths. In case of fixed wavelengths, the wavelengths to be dropped or added are pre-selected. Figure 2 shows the typical Optical Add-Drop Multiplexers.

The following Figure 3 illustrates the design of an OADM. Several wavelengths from a multiplexer are fed into port 1 of the first optical circulator. The signal passes to port 2 and then on to a fiber grating which selectively reflects λ_1, which, in turn, becomes input to port 2.

The signal of wavelength λ_1 then outputs to port 3, where it is dropped. A second signal with wavelength λ_1 arrives at the port 4 of the second circulator (whose ports are numbered 4, 5, and 6

Figure 2. Optical Add-Drop Multiplexers

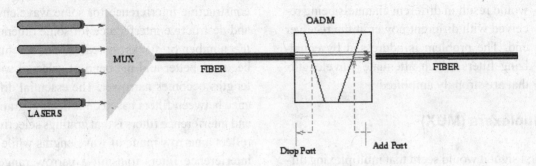

to avoid confusion). This added signal proceeds to port 5, reflected by Bragg grating and re-enters port 5 as an input. The signal, along with λ_2, λ_3 is output at port 6.

Bidirectional OADM Using Optical Circulators and FBG

Bidirectional OADM can be designed using two four port circulators and wavelength selective fiber gratings. In the Figure 4, the circulator OC-1 whose ports are numbered from 1 to 4 is used to transform the wavelengths $\lambda_1, \lambda_3, \lambda_5, \lambda_7$ from west to east and the circulator OC-2 to transform $\lambda_2, \lambda_4, \lambda_6, \lambda_8$ from east to west. The second circulator OC-2 is used to drop λ_1 and λ_2 at port 8 and add λ_1' and λ_2' at port 5. Signals $\lambda_1, \lambda_3, \lambda_5, \lambda_7$ enter port 1 of OC-1 and leave from port 2. All wavelengths other than λ_1, are reflected by FBG, re-enter port 2 and leave OC-1 through port 3

travelling east. Now λ_1, enters port 6 of OC-2, travels to port-7, reflected by FBG to re-enter port 7, and travels to port 8 and is dropped there. In a similar way λ_2, is dropped at port 8 while $\lambda_4, \lambda_6, \lambda_8$ travelling towards west leave OC-1 through port 1. Wavelengths λ_1' and λ_2', added at port 5, respectively leave OC-1 through ports 3 and 1.

Optical Cross Connects (OXC)

Cross connects are essential components of any communication system. Optical cross connects (OXC) are essentially switches which connect any of the input ports to any of the output ports. In the hybrid version of optical switches, switching was done by first converting optical signal to electrical signals, do switching electronically and then reconvert the electrical signals to optical signals. An OXC is all optical switches which work entirely at photonic level. Because of the high cost of OXCs, hybrid switches are still used

Figure 3. Function of an optical add-drop multiplexers with circulators.

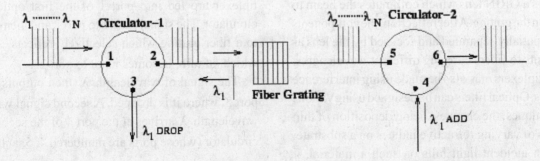

Figure 4. Bidirectional OADM using optical circulators and FBG

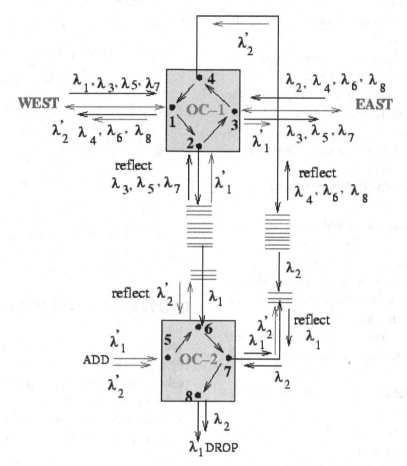

today. However, in large bandwidth applications, OXCs are more effective. Various types of OXCs are made depending on the type of function. Fiber Cross Connects (FXC) is those which connect one fiber channel to another. For wavelength switching Wavelength Switching Cross Connects (WSXC) switch wavelength from one port to a port which might be carrying a different wavelength without having to resort to wavelength conversion (Modiano & Barry, 1999). Wavelength Interchanging Cross Connects (WIXCs) is switches which provide for wavelength conversion in switching from one fiber to another. Summary of WDM concepts outlines below:

- Partitions the optical bandwidth into a large number of channels
- Allows multiple data streams to be transferred along the same piece of fiber at the same time
- Consists of nodes interconnected by fiber optic links.
- It seems like we can model this with a graph theoretic approach.
- Circuit switches
  ○ Optical add/drop multiplexers (OADM)
  ○ Optical cross-connects (OXC)
  ○ Commercially available
  ○ We assume that WDM switches are of this variety for this talk

- Packet switches
  - In research laboratories; optical buffering issues
- Retrospect the goal of IP over WDM
  - Avoid electronic bottlenecks
  - Decrease the cost by simplifying the multiple layer architecture
- Optical burst switching (OBS) is one proposal of how to realize such a network

Optical Burst Packet Switching

- Resources are allocated using one way reservation
  - Sender sends a request
  - Sender sends burst without waiting for an acknowledgement of its reservation request
  - Switch does preparation for the burst when getting the request
- Bursts can have variable lengths
- Burst switching does not necessarily require buffering
- The schemes differ in the way bandwidth release is triggered.
- In-band-terminator (IBT) – header carries the routing information, and then the payload followed by silence (needs to be done optically).
- Tell-and-go (TAG) – a control packet is sent out to reserve resources and then the burst is sent without waiting for acknowledgement. Refresh packets are sent to keep the path alive.

Main Characteristics of Optical Burst Switching

- There is a time separation (offset time) between header and data
- Header and data are usually carried on different channels

Figure 5. IP over WDM

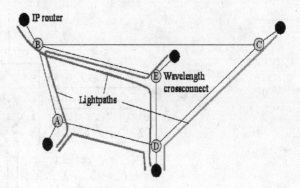

  - Header goes through sophisticated electronic processing
  - Data is kept in optical domain

IP OVER WDM: MOTIVATIONS

Establish high-speed optical layer connections (light paths). IP routers connected through light paths rather than fiber as shown in Figure 5. It is the matter of the fact that traffic volumes on the internet double every six months. Aggregate bandwidth required by the Internet in the US by the year 2005 was expected to be in excess of 35 Terabytes/sec. To meet this anticipated need, carriers in the US are in the process of deploying high capacity networks (OC-48~2.5 G-bps, and soon OC-192 ~10Gbps) for the sole purpose of delivering Internet data. Some new carriers are building networks customized for IP traffic (most

Figure 6. Wavelength conversions between nodes

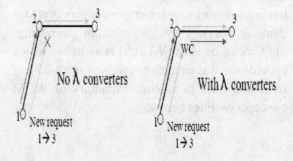

Figure 7. Virtual topology re-configuration

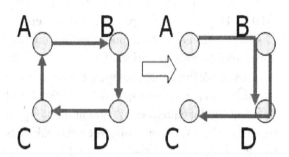

Figure 8. WDM protocol

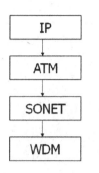
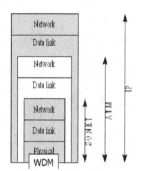

existing "transport" networks were built primarily for voice traffic). IP-centric and IP multi-service networks: Voice over IP, Video over IP.

- In an increasingly competitive world, Service Providers have to differentiate themselves.
  - Optical data networking solutions should be able to accommodate each Service Provider's unique data networking vision.
- WDM reduces costly Mux /De-mux function, reuses existing optical fibers.
  - Alternative to new fiber installation
  - Consolidation of legacy systems
  - Maximizes capacity of leased fibers
  - Future-proofing of new fiber routes

WDM allows high flexibility in expanding bandwidth. Cost reduction due to an integrating optics and eliminating Mux stages. Operation efficiency can increased by eliminate of redundant protocol layers. Transport efficiency can also increased by eliminate transport protocol overhead. Emergent technology is evolving WDM from optical transport (point-to-point line systems) to true optical networking (add-drop multiplexers and cross-connects)

Challenge for IP Over WDM Network

- WDM-aware Electronic layer (Figure 6 and Figure 7)
  - Reconfiguration and load balancing
  - Protection and restoration
  - Optical flow switching
  - Network management/control
  - Cross-layer optimization
- Reconfigurable (within milliseconds) OXC
- Wavelength Converters

Current Typical Protocol Stacks

A WDM protocol and Internet Protocol (IP) over WDM protocol stacks are shown in Figure 8 and Figure 9 respectively. The meaning of the various terminologies given below:

- AAL5: ATM Adaptation Layer 5
- ATM: Asynchronous Transfer Mode
- SONET: Synchronous Optical Network
- PPP: Point-to-Point Protocol
- HDLC: High-level Data Link Control
- WDM: Wavelength Division Multiplexing
- SDL: Simplified Data Link

Figure 10 show the Network architectures. There are two standard optical architectures, linear and ring, both of which can provide network protection and restoration of services. SONET

Figure 9. IP over WDM protocol stacks

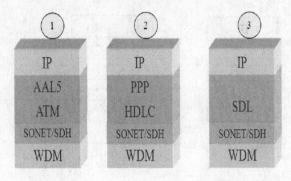

rings are the most widely deployed architecture. They can be thought of linear networks folded back to create a loop or ring. But unlike linear architectures, rings are designed to guarantee automatic restoration of services when cable or nodes fails, by use of loops around the failed component. Because of this automatic protection against failures, these rings are called self-healing. There are several SONET ring architectures that depend on the number of fibers, transmission direction, and level of switching protection. Originally developed in the United States, the

SONET standard was adopted by the ITU-T but renamed as the Synchronous Digital Hierarchy (SDH). These standards provide a complete set of specifications to allow national and international connections at various levels. Optical interfaces are defined that provide a universal fiber interface and permit mid span interconnection of different vendor equipment. A standardized signal structure allows any existing hierarchical rates (for example, DS-1, DS-3, E-1, and E-3) to be accommodated. Overhead within the SONET signals facilitate synchronization, add and drop multiplexing, electronic switching, performance monitoring and network management of the composite and tributary signals. The SONET hierarchy is built on synchronous multiplexing of a basic SONET rate of 51.84 Mb/s, so that higher SONET rates are simply N x 51.84 Mb/s. The basic signal structure provides sufficient flexibility to carry a variety of lower-level rates within the 51.84 Mb/s signal. All three protocol stacks can be used in conjunction with SONET/SDH multiplexing (Chan et al., 1998). Even without SONET/SDH multiplexing (for example

Figure 10. Network architectures

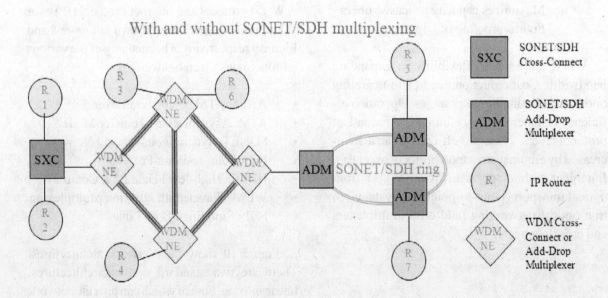

Figure 11. Optical fiber network with electronic bottleneck

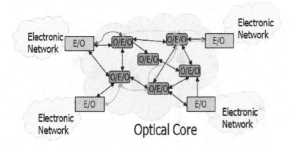

R3 to R6 communication), since IP routers have SONET/SDH interfaces, IP over WDM could involve a SONET/SDH layer

Disadvantage of Current Multi-Layer Protocol Stack

- Inefficient
  - In IP over ATM over SONET over WDM network, 22% bandwidth used for protocol overhead
- Layers often do not work in concert

- Every layer now runs at its own speed. So, low speed devices cannot fill the wavelength bandwidth.
  - When detecting of failure, different layers compete for protection
  - Optical layer detects failure almost immediately, restores error in 2 μs to 60 ms
  - SONET layer detects failure in 2.3 - 100 μs, restores error in 60 ms
- Functional overlap: So many layers are doing the same thing
  - Routing
  - Protections
- Slow speed
  - Electronic devices can not catch the transmission speed available at optical layer
- Latencies of connection

Historical Reason for Multi-Layer

- SONET over WDM
  - Conventional WDM deployment is using SONET as standard interface to higher layers
- IP over ATM

Figure 12. Current typical protocol stack and simplified protocol stack

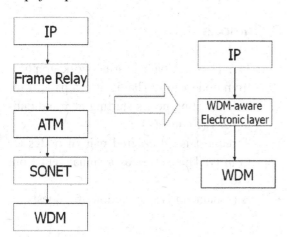

Figure 13. Wavelength routing assignment in an optical fiber networks

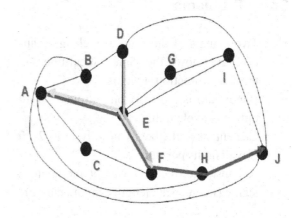

Figure 14. Optical network dipath

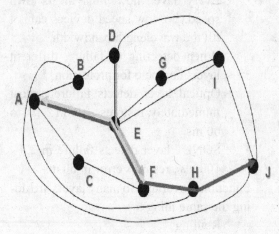

Figure 15. Optical network G with a routing R containing all colored paths in this particular instance I

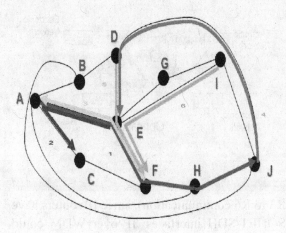

- ◦ IP packets need to be mapped into ATM cells before transporting over WDM using SONET frame
- OEO conversions at every node is easier to build than all optical switch (Figure 11)

Simplified Protocol Stacks

The protocol stacks are shown in Figure 12.

- IP layer routing is the bottleneck of present Internet
- Solution: Routing long duration flows at lower layers

Some Problems

- Two signals of the same wavelength cannot travel down the same optical fiber (in the same direction) (Figure 13)
- Bandwidth is typically only around 30-40 optical wavelengths
- Current optical fibers can only hold 2-20 wavelengths per fiber
- A transmitter/receiver cannot modulate a signal (i.e. its wavelength cannot change)

Why not Model This as a Graph Problem

- Each vertex (node) is a receiver/transmitter
- Each edge/arc is a piece of optical fiber connecting two nodes
  - ◦ In Figure 13 Colored arrows starting at one node and ending at another are directed paths representing signals of a certain wavelength being transmitted from one node to another
- The graph is considered to be a digraph since edge {a, b} is different from edge {b, a}. Thus edges will be considered as directed arcs.

Definitions

- $P(x, y)$ is a dipath in a network graph G from node x to y. That is, it is a path of interconnecting nodes starting at x and ending at y (Figure 14).
- A request is an ordered pair of nodes (x, y) in G. This serves as a signal sent from x to y.
- An instance I is a collection of requests.

Figure 16. The conflict graph of G associated with the routing R in G at a particular instance I

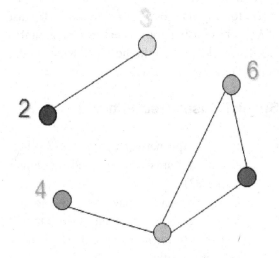

Figure 17. C (G) = 3 due to K_3 in the conflict graph

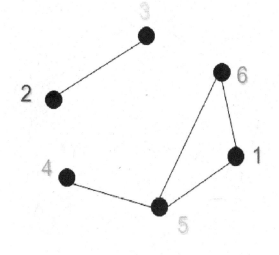

- A routing R for an instance I is a set of dipaths:

$$R = \{P(x,y) / (x,y)\} \in I$$

- $P(A, J)$ is a dipath from A to J which also represents a request from A to J
- $P(A, J)$, $P(D, F)$, and $P(F, A)$ are an instance I of requests
- The routing R consists of all dipaths $\{P(A, J), P(D, F),$ and $P(F, A)\}$ in the instance I (Figure 15 & Figure 16)

Solving Network Problems

- We know that two signals of the same wavelength cannot travel down the same optical fiber in the same direction (Figure 17).
- Let the chromatic number of the conflict graph be $c(G)$.
- Finding $c(G)$ means we have properly colored the conflict graph and so no vertex is adjacent to another vertex of the same color. Thus, $c(G)$ optical wavelengths are needed in this instance.

Another Definition: The Load of G

The load $\pi(G)$ of G is the maximum number of paths which share the same directed arc. So $c(G) = 3$ and $\pi(G) = 2$.

Lemma: c $(G) \geq \pi(G)$ for any instance I in any network G. These are described in Figure 18 and Figure 19.

So...
$$c(G) = 3$$
$$\pi(G) = 2$$

Figure 18. The graph network G

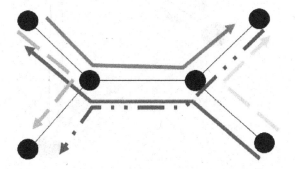

Figure 19. The conflict graph of G

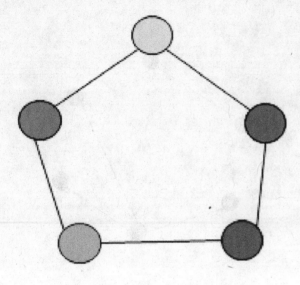

SPECIAL INSTANCES

- The all-to-all instance I_A (called gossiping) is when each vertex makes a request with every other vertex in a network G (Figure 20).
- A one-to-all instance I_0 is when one vertex makes a request with every other vertex.

Special Instance: One-to-All Instance

Theorem 1: Let G be any digraph. Then $c(G) = \pi(G)$ for any one-to-all instance in G. Because of K_3 in the conflict graph, the chromatic number is 3. The middle arc has highest load which is also three. Thus, $c(G) = \pi(G) = 3$ (Figure 21).

Special Case: Tree Network

- Let the graph network be a tree T where vertices and arcs were defined previously (Figure 22).
- Remember: Every path in T is unique. Thus there is only one path from x to y in T. Therefore for n vertices, there are $n(n-1)$ different paths.

Theorem 2: Let T be a tree and symmetric digraph. Then $c(T) = \pi(T)$, for the all-to-all gossiping instance I_A. That is the minimum number of wavelengths needed is equal to the maximum load on an arc (often called the "forwarding index" in the all-to-all instance) (Smith, 2004).

Example: All-to-all Gossiping in a Tree

Figure 20. a) All-to-all gossiping instance I_A. b) One-to-all gossiping instance I_0

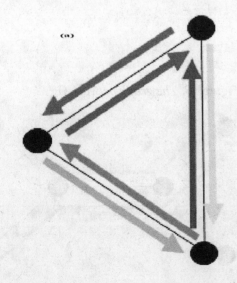
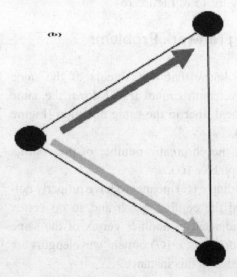

Figure 21. a) The network G and b) the conflict graph of G

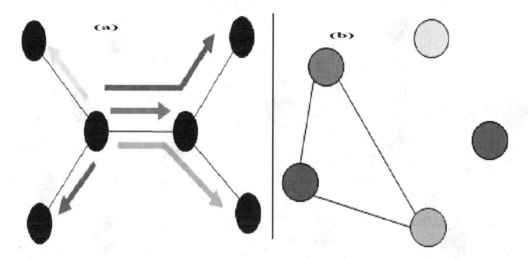

Looking in T, we see that the load on every arc is 3. Thus, by coloring the conflict graph of T, we find the chromatic number is also equal to 3. Thus $\pi(T) = c(T) = 3$.

Special Case: Star Network

Theorem 3: Let T be a symmetric tree. Then for all instances, $\pi(T) = c(T)$ if and only if T is a subdivided star. Example: Star Network (Figure 23).

Given some instance in the left network T, we find that $\pi(T) = c(T) = 2$ (Figure 24).

Special Case: Ring Network

Theorem 4: For the all-to-all instance in the ring network G with nodes N (Figure 25),

$$c(G) = \pi(G) = \frac{\left\lceil \dfrac{N^2}{4} \right\rceil}{2}$$

Figure 22. The network T

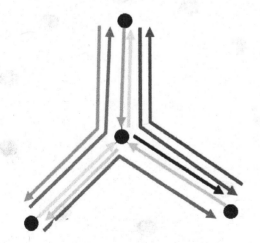

Figure 23. Star networks

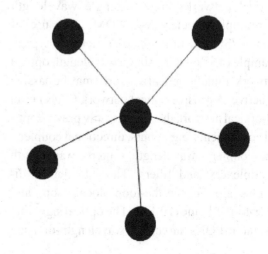

Figure 24. a) The star network T and b) the conflict graph of T

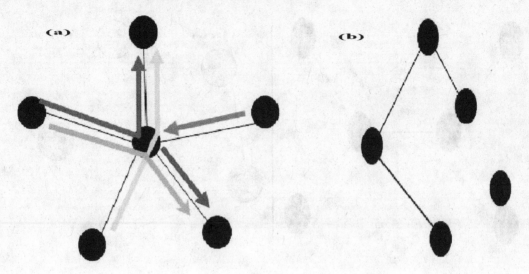

TYPES OF OPTICAL NETWORKS

Example: Ring Network

We note that the load on each arc is 1 and the chromatic number of the conflict graph is also 1. Substituting $N = 3$ into the equation in theorem 4 leads 1 (Figure 26).

TYPES OF OPTICAL NETWORKS

Optical networks may be classified in several ways. *Opaque* optical networks include optical-electronic-optical (OEO) conversion, while in all-optical *network*s each connection is totally optical (or transparent) except at the end nodes. Optical networks may be single wavelength or multiple-wavelengths (WDM). The use of SONET/SDH with a single carrier is a typical example of an opaque, single wavelength optical network. Finally, optical networks may be passive *or* active. A passive optical network (PON) is an all-optical network that utilizes only passive optical components, e.g., fibers, directional couplers, star couplers, wavelength routers, wavelength multiplexers, and filters. The intended applications are fiber-in-the-loop (local loop) and fiber-to-the-home (FTTH). The optical signaling formats in PONs can employ wavelength-division multiplexing (WDM), subcarrier multiplexing, time-division multiplexing (TDM) or any combination of these. An active all-optical network (AON) enables each of a large number of optical WDM channels (wavelengths) to propagate from source to destination over long distances and high bit rates without optical-to-electronic format conversion within the network. A network consists of multiple computers connected using some type

Figure 25. A ring network G where the number of vertices N = 10

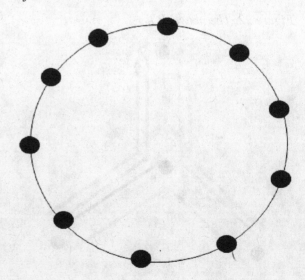

Figure 26. a) Ring network G where N = 3 b) The conflict graph of G

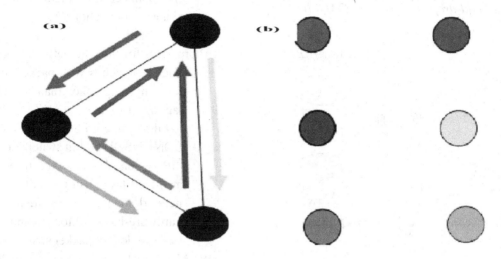

of interface, each having one or more interface devices such as a Network Interface Card (NIC) and/or a serial device for PPP networking. Each computer is supported by network software that provides the server or client functionality. The hardware used to transmit data across the network is called the media. It may include copper cable, fiber optic, or wireless transmission. The standard cabling used for the purposes of this document is 10 Base-T category 5 Ethernet cable (Ramaswami & Sivarajan, 2002). This is twisted copper cabling which appears at the surface to look similar to TV coaxial cable. It is terminated on each end by a connector that looks much like a phone connector. Its maximum segment length is 100 meters. Various optical switching technologies and their progress are shown in Figure 27.

- A network is defined by its "switching mode" and its "networking mode"
- Circuit switching vs. packet switching
  - Circuit-switching: switching based on position (space, time, λ) of arriving bits
  - Packet-switching: switching based on information in packet headers
- Connectionless vs. Connection-oriented networking:

  - CL: Packets routed based on address information in headers
  - CO: Connection set up (resources reserved) prior to data transfer

Network Categories

There are two main types of network categories which are:

1. Server based
2. Peer-to-peer

Figure 27. Various optical switching technologies and progress in optical switching technologies

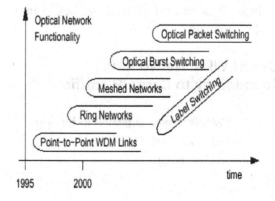

Figure 28. WDM optical cross-connects (OXC) and optical add-drop multiplexers (OADM)

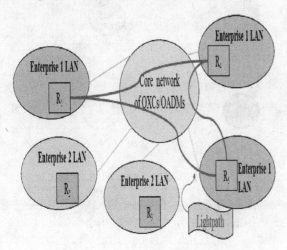

In a server based network, there are computers set up to be primary providers of services such as file service or mail service. The computers providing the service are called servers and the computers that request and use the service are called client computers. In a peer-to-peer network, various computers on the network can act both as clients and servers. For instance, many Microsoft Windows based computers will allow file and print sharing. These computers can act both as a client and a server and are also referred to as peers. Many networks are combination peer-to-peer and server based networks. The network operating system uses a network data protocol to communicate on the network to other computers. The network operating system supports the applications on that computer. A Network Operating System (NOS) includes Windows NT, Novell Netware, Linux, UNIX and others.

Use of WDM Networking Technology to Carry IP Traffic

- For WANs, usage expected to be in provisioned mode - need "CO" service for guaranteed bandwidth

    - Interconnect IP routers with provisioned (connections set up a priori) light-paths
- Alternatives for the core network nodes:
    - Packet switches with packets of format anything other than the IP datagram format, e.g. ATM, MPLS (Multi-Protocol Label Switching)
    - SONET/SDH circuit switches (TDM)
    - "IP switches" - resource reservation at the IP layer using RSVP or some network management system
    - hardware-based IP forwarding
    - variable-length packet switching
- WDM Optical cross-connects and WDM Optical add/drop multiplexers (Figure 28)
- Issues/assumptions:
    - IP traffic even in core measured to be bursty
    - Protocol layer overhead resulting from protocol encapsulation
- IP traffic even in core measured to be bursty
    - Implication: need traffic shaping at edge routers or gateways if circuit-switched alternatives are used
    - Is it possible to shape IP (self-similar) traffic to a constant rate
    - Is there a problem if the IP traffic delivered at the far-end router does not replicate burstiness
- Protocol layer overhead resulting from protocol encapsulation
    - 20% in case of ATM (TCP ACKs don't fit in one ATM cell with LLC/SNAP encapsulation and ACKs are 45% of packets)
    - 4.4% for SONET relative to IP over PPP over fiber/WDM
- Bandwidth granularity:
    - In SONET networks, minimum rate is OC1 (~51Mbps)

◦ In WDM networks, issue not at the OXCs but rather at the transmitter; actual rate used could be less than maximum rate possible

- Alternatives for the core network nodes:
  ◦ ATM, MPLS: protocol layer overhead issue
  ◦ SONET/SDH: all three issues
  ◦ IP switches: None
  ◦ WDM OXCs/OADMs: bursty traffic issue + granularity issue
- Answer
  ◦ IP switch based solution seems best
  ◦ If traffic can be shaped to constant rate and delivery of constant-rate traffic at far-end is acceptable, then WDM OXC/OADM based solution is comparable
- Switch costs could offset transmission cost savings

Classification of Optical Networks

- One classification
  ◦ Broadcast and select local optical WDM networks
  ◦ Wavelength routed (wide area) optical networks
- Second classification
  ◦ Optical link networks
  ◦ Single-hop networks
  ◦ Multi-hop networks
  ◦ Hybrid networks
  ◦ Photonic networks

Difference between Optical-Link and Multi-Hop Networks

- Optical-link networks don't use multiple wavelengths while multi-hop networks do.
- Routing problem in optical-link networks is the simple routing problem in packet-switched networks, while in multi-hop networks; this problem is tightly coupled

with the virtual-topology design problem (Agrawal, 2002).

IP/WDM Integrated Routing - Problem Statement

Develop an algorithm for integrated management of routing data in IP over WDM networks.

With SONET cross-connects, it becomes a three-layer problem. With SONET cross-connects and ATM switches, it becomes a four-layer problem (Figure 29).

Two-Layer Routing Problem

- What are the benefits/costs (in terms of network performance and management complexity) of performing traffic/QOS management and survivability at the WDM optical layer instead of at the IP layer
- Is there a hybrid or cooperative approach that is more optimal given a set of realistic performance and complexity constraints (Figure 30)
- If WDM networks are not efficient when used in provisioned mode, do not create a virtual topology by connecting IP routers with light-paths that traverse multiple OXCs

Figure 29. IP/WDM integrated routing problem

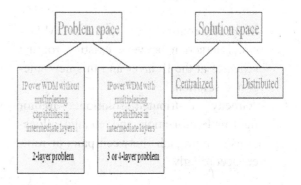

Figure 30. a) Virtual topology. b) Physical topology

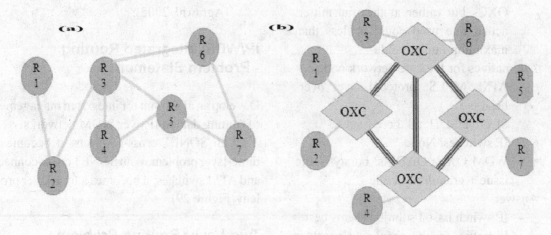

- Above problem not worth solving if packet switches are IP routers - just build a single-layer IP switch based network

What is Particular about This (IP/WDM) 2-Layer Routing Problem?

Limit on the number of optical amplifiers a light-path can traverse before requiring electronic regeneration. All wavelengths amplified equally at an optical amplifier.

Without wavelength changers at OXCs (Optical Cross-Connects), wavelength assignments to light-paths need to ensure availability of selected wavelength on all fibers on the light-path (Figure 31) (Gilbert, 1998).

Solution Strategies

- Integrated routing at the IP and WDM layers: Interaction between existing routing schemes at the IP layer and this new integrated solution.
- "Greedy" distributed solution: Monitor light-path utilization and change allocations of light-paths between pairs or routers accordingly

- Centralized system-wide optimal solution

Generic Integrated Approach (not Specific to IP)

Solve four sub-problems (Stern & Bala, 2008):

- Determine virtual topology to meet all-pairs (source-destination) traffic
- Route light-paths on the physical topology
- Assign wavelengths
- Route packet traffic on the virtual topology
  ○ Sub-problems 1 and 4 are equivalent to a data network design/optimal routing problem
- Capacity assignments between routers are determined for a given traffic matrix
- Flows are determined along with capacity assignments
  ○ Metrics optimized:
  ○ Minimize costs
  ○ Subject to an average packet delay constraint

Figure 31. Wavelength assignment problem

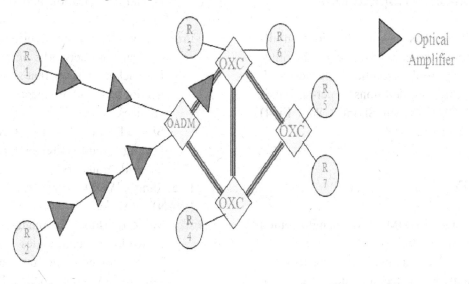

Routing Protocols Used in IP Networks

- Link state based routing protocols, e.g., Open Shortest Path First (OSPF)
  - Currently OSPF Link State Advertisements (LSAs) mainly include operator-assigned link weights
  - Shortest-path algorithms used to determine routing table entries based on these link weights
  - Example: Shortest path from R3 to R7 is via R4 and R5 (Figure 32)

How WDM Wavelength Routed Networks Should be Used for IP Traffic

- Hybrid network: Single-hop and optical-link (Raghuwanshi & Srinivas, 2009)
  - Single-hop: Use WDM circuit switches for large bulk-data transfers
  - Operate WDM network in switched mode
  - Need a routing protocol and signaling protocol

- Dynamic allocation and removal of light paths
- Optical link network: A packet-switched network (allow WDM MUX/DEMUX on links)
  - Packet switched network supports CL and CO services
- In contrast to other hybrid networks, which combine single-hop and multi-hop networks

Figure 32. Routing problem in networks

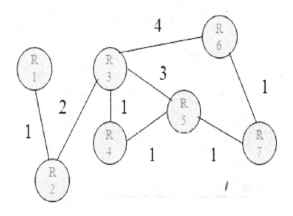

Classification of Applications

Optimal schemes base routing decisions on all-pairs source-destination traffic e.g., the integrated four sub-problem solutions. Shortest-path schemes make routing decisions for per-node pair traffic e.g., OSPF (Open Shortest Path First) (Figure 33 & Figure 34).

SUMMARY

- Regarding WDM wavelength-routed (WAN) networks
  - ○ Value questionable relative to other networking technologies when used in provisioned mode (pre-established lightpaths) to interconnect IP routers
  - ○ In switched mode, ideal for high-bandwidth large file transfers
- Hybrid network: Single-hop and optical-link
  - ○ Single-hop: Use WDM circuit switches for large bulk-data transfers
  - ○ Operate WDM network in switched mode
  - ○ Need a routing protocol and signaling protocol

  - ○ Dynamic allocation and removal of light paths
- Proposed WAN solution: hybrid networks
  - ○ Optical-link networks interconnecting packet switches that support connectionless and connection-oriented services
  - ○ Single-hop networks of OXCs supporting circuit-switched services for large file transfers
- Regarding WDM wavelength routed (WAN) networks
  - ○ Value questionable relative to other networking technologies when used in provisioned mode (pre-established light-paths) to interconnect IP routers
  - ○ In switched mode, ideal for high-bandwidth large file transfers
- Proposed WAN solution: hybrid networks
  - ○ Optical-link networks interconnecting packet switches that support connectionless and connection-oriented services
  - ○ Single-hop networks of OXCs supporting circuit-switched services for large file transfers

Figure 34. Application of real time /non-real time system

Figure 33. Classification of routing schemes

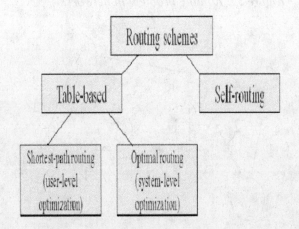

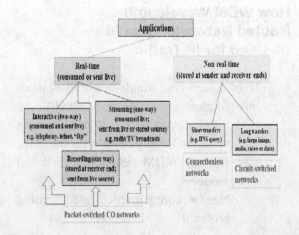

- Current IP over ATM over SONET over WDM network is inefficient and redundant
- Future IP directly over WDM network
  - Advantages
    - Less latency
    - Automatic provisioning
    - Higher bandwidth utilization
- Challenge of packet directly over WDM network
  - Optical buffer
  - Optical burst switch is one of the proposed techniques to IP over WDM network

Optical Networking vis-à-vis Other Technologies

- **Size and Weight**: Since individual optic fibers are typically only 125 µm in diameter, a multiple fiber cable can be made that is much smaller than corresponding metallic cables.
- **Bandwidth**: Fiber optic cables have bandwidths that can be orders of magnitude greater than metallic cable. Low data rate systems can be easily upgraded to higher rate systems without the need to replace the fibers. Upgrading can be achieved by changing light sources (LED to laser), improving the modulation technique, improving the receiver, or using wavelength division multiplexing.
- **Repeater spacing**: With low-loss fiber optic cable, the distance between repeaters can be significantly greater than in metallic cable systems. Moreover, losses in optical fibers are independent of bandwidth, whereas with coaxial or twisted pair cable the losses increase with bandwidth. Thus this advantage in repeater spacing increases with the system's bandwidth.

- **Electrical isolation**: Fiber optic cable is electrically non-conducting, which eliminates all electrical problems that now beset metallic cable. Fiber optic systems are immune to power surges, lightning induced currents, ground loops, and short circuits. Fibers are not susceptible to electromagnetic interference from power lines, radio signals, adjacent cable systems, or other electromagnetic sources.
- **Crosstalk**: Because there is no optical coupling from one fiber to another within a cable, fiber optic systems are free from crosstalk. In metallic cable systems, by contrast, crosstalk is a common problem and is often the limiting factor in performance.
- **Environment**: Properly designed fiber optic systems are relatively unaffected by adverse temperature and moisture conditions and therefore have application to underwater cable. For metallic cable, however, moisture is a constant problem particularly in underground (buried) applications, resulting in short circuits, increased attenuation, corrosion, and increased crosstalk.
- **Reliability**: The reliability of optical fibers, optical drivers, and optical receivers has reached the point where the limiting factor is usually the associated electronics circuitry.
- **Cost**: The numerous advantages listed here for fiber optic systems have resulted in dramatic growth in their application with attendant reductions in cost due to technological improvements and sales volume.
- **Frequency allocations**: Fiber (and metallic) cable systems do not require frequency allocations from an already crowded frequency spectrum. Moreover, cable systems do not have the terrain clearance, multipath fading, and interference problems common to radio systems.

FUTURE TRENDS AND RESEARCH

Recent advances in fiber and optical communications technology have reduced signal degradation so far that regeneration of the optical signal is only needed over distances of hundreds of kilometers. This has greatly reduced the cost of optical networking, particularly over undersea spans where the cost and reliability of repeaters is one of the key factors determining the performance of the whole cable system. The main advances contributing to these performance improvements are dispersion management, which seeks to balance the effects of dispersion against non-linearity; and solitons, which use nonlinear effects in the fiber to enable dispersion-free propagation over long distances. Although fiber-optic systems excel in high-bandwidth applications, optical fiber has been slow to achieve its goal of fiber to the premises or to solve the last mile problem. However, as bandwidth demand increases, more and more progress towards this goal can be observed. In Japan, for instance EPON (Full Service Access Network) has largely replaced DSL as a broadband Internet source. South Korea's KT also provides a service called FTTH (Fiber to the Home), which provides 100 percent fiber-optic connections to the subscriber's home. The largest FTTH deployments are in Japan, Korea, and most recently in China. The speeds of fiber optic and copper cables are both limited by length, but copper is much more sharply limited in this respect. Even in the commercial world, most computers have copper communication cables. But these cables are short, typically tens of meters. Most metropolitan network links (e.g., those based on telephone or cable television services) are several kilometers long, in the range where fiber significantly outperforms copper. Replacing at least part of these links with fiber shortens the remaining copper segments and allows them to run much faster. Fiber is often said to be 'future proof' because the speed of the broadband connection is usually limited by the terminal equipment rather than the fiber itself, Fiber to the node (FTTN), also called fiber to the neighborhood or fiber to the cabinet (FTT Cab), is a telecommunication architecture based on fiber-optic cables run to a cabinet serving a neighborhood. Fiber to the node allows delivery of broadband services such as high speed Internet. High speed communications protocols such as broadband cable access (typically DOCSIS) or some form of DSL are used between the cabinet and the customers. The data rates vary according to the exact protocol used and according to how close the customer is to the cabinet. FTTLA are the initials of Fiber To The Last Amplifier. The network cables being able to use several amplifiers, the FTTLA aims at replacing the coaxial cable to the last amplifier (towards the subscriber) by optical fiber. It acts as a new technology aiming at re-using the network cables existing in particular on the final part while installing of optical fiber more closely to the subscriber while using the coaxial cable of the networks cables for the "last mile" or "last meters" connected with the subscriber. FTTLA is a technology which assists hybrid fiber-coaxial CATV networks to provide to their customers more bandwidth. Fiber to the curb (FTTC) is a telecommunications system based on fiber-optic cables run to a platform that serves several customers. Each of these customers has a connection to this platform via coaxial cable or twisted pair. Fiber to the curb allows delivery of broadband services such as high speed internet. FTTC is subtly distinct from FTTN or FTTP (all are versions of Fiber in the Loop). The chief difference is the placement of the cabinet. FTTC will be placed near the "curb" which differs from FTTN which is placed far from the customer and FTTP which is placed right at the serving location. Unlike the competing fiber to the premises (FTTP) technology, fiber to the curb can use the existing coaxial or twisted pair infrastructure to provide last mile service. For this reason, fiber to the curb costs less to deploy. However, it also has lower bandwidth potential than fiber to the premises.

In the United States of America and Canada, the largest deployment of FTTC was carried out by Bell South Telecommunications. With the acquisition of Bell South by AT&T, deployment of FTTC will end. Future deployments will be based on either FTTN or FTTP. Existing FTTC plant may be removed and replaced with FTTP. Fiber to the premises is a form of fiber-optic communication delivery in which an optical fiber is run from the central office all the way to the premises occupied by the subscriber. Fiber to the premises is often abbreviated with the acronym FTTP.

Active optical networks rely on some sort of electrically powered equipment to distribute the signal, such as a switch, router, or multiplexer. Each signal leaving the central office is directed only to the customer for whom it is intended. Incoming signals from the customers avoid colliding at the intersection because the powered equipment there provides buffering. A passive optical network (PON) is a point-to-multipoint, fiber to the premises network architecture in which unpowered optical splitters are used to enable a single optical fiber to serve multiple premises, typically 32-128. A PON configuration reduces the amount of fiber and central office equipment required compared with point to point architectures. As of 2007, the most common type of active optical networks is called active Ethernet, a type of Ethernet in the first mile (EFM). Active Ethernet uses optical Ethernet switches to distribute the signal, thus incorporating the customers' premises and the central office into one giant switched Ethernet network. Such networks are identical to the Ethernet computer networks used in businesses and academic institutions, except that their purpose is to connect homes and buildings to a central office rather than to connect computers and printers within a campus. Each switching cabinet can handle up to 1,000 customers, although 400-500 is more typical. This neighborhood equipment performs layer 2/layer 3 switching and routing,

offloading full layer 3 routing to the carrier's central office. The IEEE 802.3ah standard enables service providers to deliver up to 100 M-bit/s full-duplex over one single-mode optical fiber to the premises depending on the provider. Speeds of 1 G-bit/s are becoming commercially available.

Business Implications and Applications

Today fiber optic systems are much more cost effective than metallic cable, satellite, and radio for long haul, high bit rate applications. Fiber optic cable is also expected eventually to overtake metallic cable in short haul applications, including metro facilities and local networks. One final cost factor in favor of fiber optics is the choice of material, namely silicon, which of course is one of the earth's most abundant elements, versus copper, which may someday be in short supply, or the radio spectrum, which is already in short supply.

REFERENCES

Agrawal, G. P. (2002). *Fiber-optic communications systems*. John Wiley & Sons. doi:10.1002/0471221147

Baransel, C., Dobosiz, W., & Gewicburzynski, P. (1995). Routing in multi-hop packet switching networks: G-b/s Challenge. *IEEE Network Magazine*, *9*(3), 38–61. doi:10.1109/65.386051

Berry, R., & Modiano, E. (October 2004). The role of switching in reducing the number of electronic ports in WDM networks. *IEEE Journal of Selected Areas in Communication, 22*(8).

Berry, R., & Modiano, E. (2005, August). Optimal transceiver scheduling in WDM/TDM networks. *IEEE Journal on Selected Areas in Communications*, *23*(8). doi:10.1109/JSAC.2005.852240

Brzezinski, A., & Modiano, E. (2005, November). Dynamic reconfiguration and routing algorithms for IP-over-WDM networks with stochastic traffic. *Journal of Lightwave Technology, 23*(10). doi:10.1109/JLT.2005.855691

Chan, V., Hall, K., Modiano, E., & Rauschenbach, K. (1998, December). Architectures and technologies for high-speed optical data networks. *Journal of Lightwave Technology, 16*(12). doi:10.1109/50.736582

Chen, L., & Modiano, E. (2004, December). Dynamic routing and wavelength assignment with optical bypass using ring embeddings. *Optical Switching and Networking (Elsevier), 2004*, 34–42.

Chen, L., Modiano, E., & Saengudomlert, P. (January 2006). Wave band switching in optical networks. *Computer Networks (Special Issue on Optical Networks)*.

Gerstel, O., & Ramaswami, R. (2000, October). Optical layer survivability - An implementation perspective. *IEEE Journal on Selected Areas in Communications, 18*, 1885–1899. doi:10.1109/49.887910

Gilbert, H. (1998). *Deploying optical networking components*. McGraw-Hill. Manchester, J., Anderson, J., Doshi, B., & Dravida, S. (May 1998). IP over SONET. *IEEE Communications Magazine, 36*(5), 136–142.

Modiano, E. (1999, March). WDM based packet networks. *IEEE Communications Magazine*, (March): 130–135. doi:10.1109/35.751510

Modiano, E., & Barry, R. (1999, February). Architectural considerations in the design of WDM-based optical access networks. *Computer Networks*, 1999.

Modiano, E., & Narula Tam, A. (May 2002). Survivable lightpath routing: A new approach to the design of WDM-based networks. *IEEE Journal of Selected Areas in Communication, 20*(4).

Mukherjee, B., Banerjee, D., Ramamurthy, S., & Mukherjee, A. (1996, October). Some principles for designing a wide area WDM optical network. *IEEE Journal on Selected Areas in Communications, 4*(5), 684–696.

Narula, A., Modiano, E., & Brzezinski, A. (October 2004). Physical topology design for survivable routing of logical rings in WDM based networks. *IEEE Journal of Selected Areas in Communication, 22*(8).

Neely, M., & Modiano, E. (2007, June). Logarithmic delay for N x N packet switches under crossbar constraints. *IEEE/ACM Transactions on Networking*, 15.

Raghuwanshi, S. K., & Srinivas, T. (2009). *Numerical study of propagation in optical waveguides and devices*. International VDM Publisher Germany.

Ramaswami, R., & Sivarajan, K. (2002). *Optical networks: A practical perspective* (2nd ed.). Morgan Kaufmann.

Smith, D. R. (2004). *Digital transmission systems* (3rd ed.). Kluwer Academic Publishers. doi:10.1007/978-1-4419-8933-8

Stern, T. E., & Bala, K. (2008). *Multiwavelength optical networks: A layered approach*. Addison Wesley.

KEY TERMS AND DEFINITIONS

Add/Drop Multiplexer: Digital equipment that provides an interface between higher and lower rate signals. A SONET ADM is capable of extracting or inserting lower rate signals from a higher rate multiplexed signal without de-multiplexing the entire signal. Optical add/drop multiplexer. A multiplexer is used in optical networks that can add and drop wavelengths into and out of an optical signal without converting them back to electrical form.

EDFA (Erbium-Doped Fiber Amplifier): Convert the signal back to electric before boosting it. In an EDFA, optical fibers are doped with the rare earth element erbium, which can amplify light in the 1550-nm region when pumped by an external laser.

Optical Line Terminal: A Central Office node that is the interface between the PON and the service providers network services.

Optical Network Terminal: An ITU-T term to describe a single-user case of an *Optical Network Unit* (ONU).

Optical Network: The optical network provides all basic network requirements in the optical layer; namely capacity, scalability, reliability, survivability, and manageability. Today, the wavelength is the fundamental object of the optical network. Currently, basic network requirements can be met through a combination of the optical transport layer (DWDM today), which provides scalability and capacity beyond 10 G-bps, and the SONET/SDH transport layer, which provides the reliability, survivability, and manageability needed for public networks. The long-term vision of an "all optical network" is of a transparent optical network where signals are never converted to the electrical domain between network ingress and egress. The more practical implementation for the near term will be of an opaque optical network, that is, one that works to minimize but still includes optical/electrical/optical conversion. Optical network elements will include terminals, dynamic add/drop multiplexers, and dynamic optical cross-connects.

Passive Optical Network: A point-to-multipoint, passive fiber network architecture in which a single fiber utilizes optical splitters to serve multiple premises.

Physical Layer: The first layer of the OSI reference model. All-optical technologies such as DWDM work at the physical layer

Wavelength-Division Multiplexing (WDM): Allows for a number of optical carrier signals to be put onto a single fiber at different wavelengths, thus enabling bidirectional traffic as well as increased capacity.

APPENDIX: WEB RESOURCES

1. ITU (http://www.itu.int) ITU-T: Telecom sector of the International Telecommunications Union, the United Nations treaty agency that sets telecommunications standards.
2. ANSI (http://www.ansi.org) American National Standards Institute is the national standards body of the United States. It coordinates and accredits standards development across the US.
3. http://www.martindalecenter.com/Calculators4_F_Opt.html. This site has numerous calculators and animations for optical communications.
4. http://optics.byu.edu/animations.aspx. This site also has many animations for optical communications.
5. http://www.ee.buffalo.edu/faculty/cartwright/java_applets/. Another site rich in calculator and animation resources.
6. http://www.cisco.com/en/US/products/hw/optical/ps2011/ products_technical_ reference
7. book09186a0080234230.html Introduction to DWDM from CISCO, although a bit dated (2001).

Chapter 3
The User as a Service

José C. Delgado

Instituto Superior Técnico, Technical University of Lisbon, Portugal

ABSTRACT

The Web has changed a lot since its inception, 20 years ago, now offering dynamic information and services. The users have also evolved and are no longer mere information consumers, but rather active producers. This calls for a paradigm shift, with the user at the center of the information, service, and collaboration networks, taking the role of active services (able to respond to requests), in equal terms with current service providers. This leads to a unified user model, in which both individual and institutional entities are users and providers, although with different emphasis. To support this approach, the authors present a new Web access device, the browserver, which includes a browser and a server working in close cooperation, with the goal of replacing the classical browser but being backwards compatible with it to ease the migration path. The authors show how it can be implemented and its advantages in the case of typical applications.

INTRODUCTION

The web appeared as a universal mechanism of browsing information stored on a universally available server. The browser was an innovation, since until then every application had its specific interface. The technologies (e.g., CGI, HTTP, the browser, HTML) and principles (e.g., stateless servers, sessionless clients, client/server

paradigm) adopted then were tailored for the job (information search and browsing).

Since then, the web has changed a lot. The world has become dependent on the Internet almost as much as on electricity. All sorts of applications now use the web as the main channel, at both consumer and business levels, virtualization and cloud computing are revolutionizing the concept of resource and, above all, users are not mere consumers anymore but are actively contributing to web content and interaction transactions.

DOI: 10.4018/978-1-4666-0203-8.ch003

We are now in the era of consumer-level electronic services, in which users access directly services available online, in a self-service fashion. Many of these services are not limited to consumption, as the highly popular social networks and file sharing sites show. Users also provide services to others (typically involving information sharing).

The underlying technology has evolved as well, spurred in great part by the necessity of improving the end user experience, with more dynamic and interactive pages. Oddly enough, and although the needs and objectives of the Web today are very different from the original ones, most of the technology is based on the same principles that drove the Web at its early stages. Backwards compatibility in technology terms is desirable, but allowing it to influence the Web's model and not providing an evolutionary migration path inevitably leads to problems.

In retrospect, several decisions were taken at the inception of the Web that are understandable in the timeline context but that later hampered the alignment between the Web capabilities and the needs and goals of the society, namely:

- Client/server paradigm, instead of P2P. Users were given a browser and told to browse. Current users do a lot more than browsing and interact seemingly in a direct fashion with other users, but all this is no more than a lot of tweaking with scripts at the browser and support from central servers. It works, but at the cost of the complexity of the entire system. Users are not an integrant part of the Web, but rather separate entities that connect to the Web at browser endpoints. The Web of users doesn't really exist and is no more than a virtualization of the reality;
- A sessionless, stateless, application level protocol (HTTP), when current services require transport level (one OSI level lower,

such as SOAP, strangely enough emulated on top of HTTP) and support for sessions and state, which in practice motivated such tricks as cookies, AJAX and Comet;
- Document oriented information with text as the main information type, with the rest (pictures, videos, animations, sounds, forms, binary data, etc.) as a sort of add-ons. Text markup is still the main information structuring mechanism, but the typesetting model that made HTML be based on SGML is long gone. Today, we no longer have a web of documents, but rather a web of services, with active, not static, information. Web Services, although implementing a service model, are actually (XML) documents. All the behavior is hidden behind the interface and outside the model. The current Web's native entities are still documents, not services.

The main objectives of this chapter are:

- To show that the nature of the Web usage has changed from its inception, 20 years ago, and that there is now a mismatch between that nature and the available technologies that users have at their disposal to access the Web;
- To introduce the idea that a paradigm shift is needed to contemplate the new user semantics and role, from client-server to service-based, decentralized applications. The user is no longer simply a consumer, but an active producer, and needs to be treated as an active service provider, in equal terms with other entities in the Web (namely, current providers);
- To describe the *browserver*, a package comprising a browser and a server, and to justify its need as a new Web access device for human users.

BACKGROUND

Figure 1 presents a simplistic view of the (complex) Web in use today. The Web is server-centric, either explicitly (such as the two servers depicted) or implicitly, with servers hidden inside typical clouds such as search engines (e.g., Google) and collaboration networks, understood here in a broad sense (e.g., social

Networks such as Facebook or LinkedIn, e-mail systems, workflow systems and collaborative packages such as Google Docs).

Users can upload files (F) to a server, where they will be crawled (A) by search engines that can serve users performing information search and retrieval (B). Users can download files (C) directly from a server or obtain them using P2P networks (E). Servers can interact directly (D), using either general specifications such as Web Services or REST, either application specific protocols. Users can interact (G) by means of a collaboration network, most likely a social network, e-mail, instant messaging or some system supporting voice, such as Skype. Most of these cases are based on servers. Even P2P systems resort to servers in several situations.

Table 1 expresses the evolution of the relationship between the user and the Web (letters in parentheses correspond to those in Figure 1):

Figure 1. Simplistic view of Web usage by users. Letters explained in the text

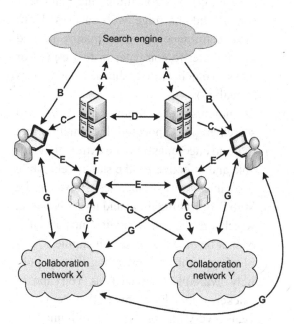

- It all started with users mainly as consumers, browsing through hypermedia information (although naturally some people authored it). This corresponds to an asynchronous communication between the author of a document and the user that reads it and expresses and offline user presence (author and reader never meet). However, this was the first time that users had at their disposal a simple means to author and to

Table 1. Evolution of the Web from the user's point of view (usage and role)

Usage/role	Consumer		Provider	Web type	Evolution
Content	Browsing (C)		Authoring (F)	Web of documents	**Past**
	Search and retrieval (B)		Sharing (E or F+C+D)		
	Instant interaction (message/voice) (F+C+D)			Web of people	**Present**
	Interaction management (G)				
Service	User as a service			Web of services	**Future**

read documents (in fact, person-to-crowd messaging) and constitutes the main reason behind the huge Web success. Until then, communication was mainly limited to computer-to-computer or text e-mail or news (much more limited and less appealing);

- Documents started to grow in number and search engines appeared. Extremely effective and encompassing, are extremely valuable and effective for the static Web, while evolving towards semantics. However, the Web is becoming more and more dynamic, which means that a significant part of it cannot be indexed by search engines;
- Sharing, either by uploading files to publicly available sites such as YouTube or Flicker, either by using P2P systems, reveals a very interesting facet of human nature: the inner satisfaction of having contributed with information that many others can read. The popularity of a file (measured by the number of times it has been viewed/downloaded) is actually used as a metric of success. This unconfessed vanity has indeed fueled much of the Web usage;
- Asynchronous interaction is not as appealing as real-time, so instant messaging and chat rooms soon flourished, as a form of virtual presence. This is a phenomenon that has also happened in cell phones with SMSs. People just love to be connected;
- Collaboration networks, of which social networks are the most popular, combine offline and online presence, together with some form of management of the relationship (friends, followers, group members, and so on).

In terms of final user involvement, collaboration networks constitute the state of the art because they provide the greatest value to the user. As we all know, users want solutions, not technologies, and they always go for the highest level platform that they can access and that is used by the majority of other users (to maximize interoperability). No wonder, then, that users have climbed their evolution ladder through the following platforms, most of the times with a clear winning system/ company:

- **Operating system & office suite:** Microsoft has been dominant;
- **Web (browser):** this is probably one of the best examples of historic non-control by a given system or platform, although many things could be said about this, because the Web was born in a non-commercial context and managed to stay that way. Browsers offer essentially the same functionality and there is no strong reason to favor one or the other;
- **Search engines and associated services:** Google managed to get the lead, by offering great functionality and attracting advertising;
- **Collaboration networks:** Facebook was dynamic enough to attract most of the users in social networks (reportedly surpassing 500 million users in July 2010) (Ostrow, 2010).

The evolution can be better assessed by noting that:

- **Operating system and browser are now omnipresent:** No general purpose computer today lacks them and even embedded systems are getting Internet access based on Web standards;
- According to Dougherty (2010), the weekly share of site visits of Facebook surpassed that of Google in the US for the first time in March 2010, at around 7%. One year before, Google and Facebook had roughly 6.5% and 2.5%, respectively;
- According to comScore (2010), Facebook got 23.1% of the U.S. online display ad-

vertising market in the third quarter of 2010, which was more than the combined share of the sites of the next competitors (Yahoo, Microsoft, Fox Interactive Media and Google – the latter with 2.7%).

The message seems clear. Users want both value and simplicity. Who provides the best value at a single point of entry will have an edge over the competition. One of the main problems, however, is that users have to deal with many systems and collaboration networks that are provider-centric, each with its own set of rules, different from the others. Users need to adapt to the providers, but it would be much better if it could be done the other way around, by designing and building the Web in a user-centric way, instead of provider-centric. How can we do this?

THE SOCIAL NETWORKS EXAMPLE

Given that social networks (SNs) are at the current highest level of user platform evolution and the rate at which Facebook has been growing, which reflects user acceptance, it seems that SNs are a good starting point to start building functionality. For example, in November 2010, Facebook has announced the fusion of messages, chat and e-mail under a single interface, Facebook Messages (Van Grove, 2010). This corresponds to consolidating several collaboration networks into one.

SNs do not really entail new technology, but rather a new use of existing technology. Their added value lies in the applicational level and human interaction. Today, any site with registered users sharing some interest and able to add information (blogs, namely) can be called "social network", but here we distinguish three main types of SNs, according to their primary use:

- **Social Networks (SNs):** This the generic name given to social networks intended primarily for leisure (or at least non-pro-

fessional interests). Facebook, MySpace, Twitter, YouTube and Flickr are examples;
- **Business Social Networks (BSNs):** Special cases of SNs, with professional interests as the primary objective. Some are domain oriented, but most are geared towards as a workforce marketplace (bringing potential employers and employees together), partnership finder and creating communities with similar interests (Skeels & Grudin, 2009). LinkedIn, Ryze, Xing, Plaxo and Ziggs fall into this category;
- **Enterprise Social Networks (ESNs):** Potential successors of Intranets, are used primarily by the employees of a given enterprise and coalesce many of the characteristics of leisure SNs and BSNs. There is a clear professional interest, but they also cherish other interests, culture and leisure oriented, in an attempt to foster additional human links that promote and ease knowledge generation and sharing. Enterprises such as IBM and EMC have found these systems very useful (with Lotus Connections and Jive, respectively).

Current SNs on the market are essentially server based. Many of them have APIs to invoke their services and there is some interoperability at the login level, with some networks allowing users to login with the credentials of another account they might have in another network.

There are currently several proposals for decentralized SNs, platforms and protocols such as OpenSocial, OneSocialWeb, NoseRub, DiSo, Gnu Social, DataPortability, AppleSeed, Diaspora and SocialRiver. In the Workshop on the Future of Social Networking, held by W3C (Hazael-Massieux, 2009), roughly half of the position papers made proposals for decentralizing SNs. Many of these proposals have very limited information available and will likely never have market expression, but the interest and trend towards decentralizing SNs is there. Proposals based on P2P (Seong et al,

2010) and distributed data stores also exist, such as PrPl, PeerSoN and SiFo-Peers.

We establish a simple classification scheme, regarding the nature of the interaction between the users, the providers (the SNs), its combinations and the emphasis on centralization or decentralization. Four main canonic scenarios are considered, as depicted in Figure 2:

• Provider-centric (PC), in Figure 2a. Everything happens at the SN's servers. The user has only a browser, has to register and enter profile information, with no privacy control regarding the SN provider it-

self, and has to deal with each SN separately (duplicate information, with different formats and ontologies and that has to be manually updated), with little or no interoperability;

• Provider-based (PB), in Figure 2b. The user, with just a browser, has to register at a SN and all services are provided at the server side, but that SN can act as a source of information on each user to other SNs (using an API), with information access control policies specified by the user in the primary SN, in a cooperative network in some aspects similar to a single sign on

Figure 2. Different social network organizations

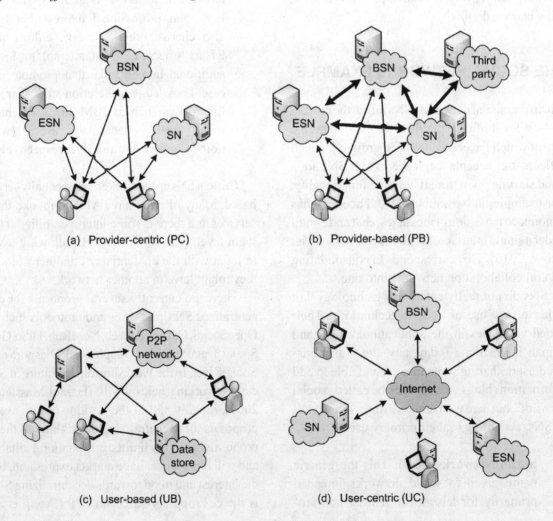

(a) Provider-centric (PC)

(b) Provider-based (PB)

(c) User-based (UB)

(d) User-centric (UC)

arrangement with profile sharing. There is a (limited) transversal view of the user, whose information can also be provided by the SN to third parties, given its marketing value;

- User-based (UB), in Figure 2c. The user does not have to register at a SN and has the capability of publishing his information only once (in a server of his choice) and exchange it with other users by decentralized protocols such as XMPP or P2P techniques. Control over which information is shared and with whom is improved, since the user control where the information resides, but lack of a central provider limits the service set and performance;

- User-centric (UC), in Figure 2d. Although also a decentralized scenario, central SN providers are reinstated, but now as users themselves, in a unified user model, capable of providing both information and services, including mashups of services of other users (people or SNs). Each individual user is now a first class semantic web citizen and his social interface (desktop) is a personalized mashup of other users' services. Each user has his own vision of the web (including the business, enterprise and other social network contexts of interest to that user), not the vision of one or more SN providers. Each user needs to include a server, either in his own laptop or in a proxy server.

There is an inherent evolution from PC (provider-centric) to UC (user-centric). SNs started as isolated systems, information silos, but the main SNs started opening up their APIs, in 2007, when they realized the value they had with user information and which could be used to attract third party companies, more added value and more users. Today, all major SNs, such as LinkedIn, Plaxo and Facebook, offer APIs and this corresponds to the state of the art in SNs available on the market,

with only smaller SNs still closed. Interoperability is now an essential part of a SN.

This doesn't mean that the "walled gardens" are over and there is a range of new SNs and social network platforms currently being proposed and developed, in a much more decentralized model, such as NoseRub, OpenSocial, OneSocialWeb or PrPl, allowing user information to reside in a server chosen by the user, including his own laptop. But the user/provider (client/server paradigm) distinction continues and the user is mainly seen as information.

This chapter goes one step further and proposes the UC scenario as a unification of the two concepts and a means to bring the service paradigm to SNs. The user is no longer a mere account, profile or information producer. The user is now an active, autonomous resource, capable of not only dealing with information but also of providing services and establishing and enforcing his privacy policies. A SN provider enters the scene as simply another user (but with emphasis on the services) and constitutes a means of providing added value on the network, by mashing up services from other users (individual and/or other SN providers).

Each user is responsible for taking care of all his internal information (state) and executing all his services, setting up and carrying out privacy policies under his control (Tootoonchian, Saroiu, Ganjali and Wolman, 2009). However, personal computers are not always connected and have performance or disk space limitations. If this is the case, and a continuous presence or scalable performance is needed, an individual user can delegate transparently part of his responsibilities to a proxy server, of his own choice (choosing exactly which information and services can be transferred). Each user is also able to customize his semantic desktop, so that the most relevant mashups from these networks (from his point of view) can be most easily available.

In fact, there is a model inversion with respect to the original PC (provider-centric) scenario, in which basically an (individual) user has to take the initiative of registering in a SN, to replicate himself across several networks, to take care of multiply updating any changes and to deal with the possible integration. In the UC (user-centric) scenario, the user is at the center and it is up to the provider-based networks to go after him, to crawl his information using a search engine and to ask him to join. If this happens, common profile fields are reused and automatically updated in case of change.

Much like people have become active information producers, when in the past they were passive information consumers, now each individual user is an active service provider and is to able host and control his information (at least the most private one) and even his network contacts. This means that an individual user is now a social network in its own right (representing that user's own vision of the web, a mashup of several business and personal social network domains, not the vision of one or more SN providers).

THE BROWSERVER: A NEW WEB ACCESS DEVICE

The basic Web problem (browsing of remote multimedia contents) has changed substantially since the inception of the Web. From the basic process of putting information on a server that someone else will browse (without any interaction), as depicted by F+C in Figure 1, to the centralized provider-based social networks (Figure 2a) and finally up to the decentralized, user-centric social networks (Figure 2d), in which the centralized social network provider is now a user as any individual user, requirements have changed a lot.

If a problem changes, the solution needs to change as well. Current solutions to the decentralization of social networks typically involve P2P protocols (Yang & Chen, 2008) or decentralized message systems such as XMPP (Saint-Andre, 2005).

However, none of these solutions implements the service oriented paradigm in a clean, transparent way. The message protocols are heavily influenced by the specific objectives of each of these systems. Web Services and REST are better suited to implement the paradigm, but both require servers and not mere browsers. Sitting on top of HTTP, they present their own set of difficulties for symmetric, asynchronous, long-lived communication, required by the user-centric approach, but at least this is a mismatch in the implementation (HTTP was conceived for stateless, sessionless browsing, not for services) and not an impediment of the model. HTML5 (Vaughan-Nichols, 2010) and WebSockets (W3C, 2010), now in the process of standardization, will alleviate this problem.

An implementation best matched to the user-centric approach (Lizcano, Soriano, Reyes and Hierro, 2009), in which the laptop (a personal computing device, in more general terms) must be self sufficient, thus requires both a browser and a server in close cooperation.

This conclusion is general and applies to more than just the social networks domain. Current browsers are full of techniques to support code execution (such as JavaScript) and improved browser-server interaction (such as Ajax), but cannot act as a container for web-enabled applications, since they are not servers. Rich Internet Applications (RIA) (Fraternali, Rossi and Sánchez-Figueroa, 2010), running in the context of the browser or a runtime environment, such as AIR or JavaFX, provide additional features and in fact influenced the HTML5 specification, but they are still conceived as the client side of a client-server application.

To pursue the goal of having active users that are first class Web citizens, supporting new classes of applications or improving existing ones, we need a new approach. The basic unit of interaction of a person with the web should be a browser and a server (not just a browser) deployed as a single unit. The browser started as the universal client for applications. The universal server, on which applications get deployed on the person side, does not yet exist. The operating systems (Windows, Linux), still perform that role, but these were not designed with the web in mind. RIA platforms are web-enabled but were not designed with server semantics.

We have been developing the concept of such a device, which we call the *browserver* (browser +server), with the following main characteristics:

- Designed for a personal computing device, such as a laptop, and not necessarily for a continuous operation server. This means an identification scheme independent of the IP address;

- Fully compatible with all the current characteristics of browsers and capable of normal browser operation;

- Capable of deploying services, as any normal server, and of receiving requests from other browservers, servers or browsers on the Web. These services can be anything, but given the semantics of personal Web access device they will probably be related to the corresponding user (such as making his social network profile available, providing his public cryptographic key, informing his online presence, storing messages sent to the user while he is offline

and so on). Personalization is the strong word here;

- Capable of offline behavior. The presence of a local server enables applications designed with that purpose in mind to work even if no Internet connection is available (with a subsequent synchronization when possible);

- Prepared to automatically and transparently provide a continuous online user presence, even in the absence of an Internet connection or when the user's computer is powered off, by resorting to a remote server (a gateway) that acts as a proxy and provides a minimum set of services. This proxy can be another browserver. When the user goes online again, synchronization takes place;

- Supporting selective roaming, by saving the state of a subset of its services in the gateway, to be recovered at another browserver.

A user with a browserver can publish a service in the Web so that it can be searched, discovered and invoked directly by another browserver or a by a server from some organization. Figure 3 depicts an example, in which a user U_A publishes the descriptions *a1* and *x1* of the services S_a and

Figure 3. The browserver as a personal Web service provider

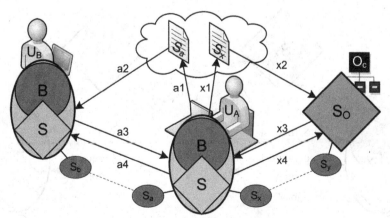

S_x. These are found and retrieved (*a2* and *x2*) by the browserver of user U_B and by the server S_O of the organization O_c. The invocation of services, between S_b and S_a and between S_y and S_x occurs in a direct fashion, with requests *a3* and *x3* followed by replies *a4* and *x4*.

The browserver couples a generic web browser with a generic server which sits between the browser and the web, acts as a proxy server and allows the browser to maintain its normal web browsing behavior. The browser acts as a user interface (UI) for services deployed in the browserver's server or in remote servers.

Local and remote services can interact between themselves or with the user through the browserver UI services. The server and the associated services predefined and deployed in the browserver add the following capabilities:

- Deployment and execution of web services, to support the active behavior of the individual user in a user-centric approach such as that described in Figure 2;
- User interface generation, by generating HTML pages dynamically, according to a predefined mapping between graphical components of the interface of a service and the corresponding components in the browser. This is used to generate user in-

terface pages according to a given interface context of that service, which corresponds to the capabilities of current RIA;

- Continuous presence, by setting up and synchronizing with the gateway.

Figure 4 illustrates the interactions with a gateway, in which *b* is an asynchronous request-reply from server S_X to browserver BS_B, whereas *d* is a request made from BS_B to S_Y, invoking one of its services. Both interactions *a* and *c*, between server S_X and browserver BS_A, involve a service that is proxied at the gateway, which is set as the endpoint for service invocation. In *c*, the reply is sent through the gateway while in *a* it is directly sent to the service that made the original request. To this purpose, *a* defines a ReplyTo endpoint in S_X in such a way that the header is not processed by the gateway and arrives unchanged at the service provider. In *c*, the endpoint is setup so that the gateway is assumed as the endpoint for the reply.

The next section describes our current implementation of the browserver and the following one throws further insight on classes of applications for which it can be useful.

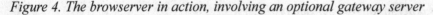

Figure 4. The browserver in action, involving an optional gateway server

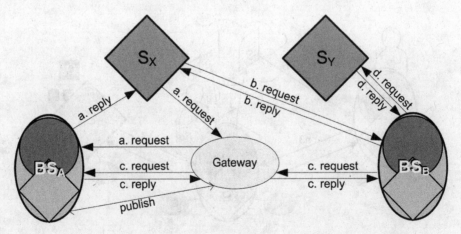

Figure 5. Simplified logical view of the Browserver

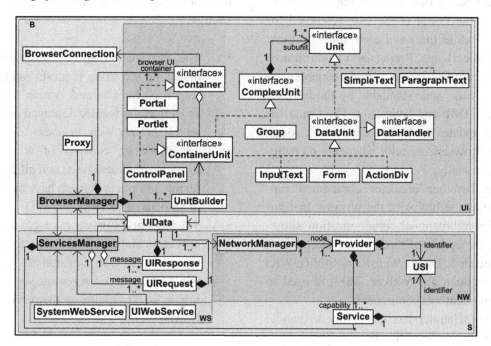

CURRENT IMPLEMENTATION OF THE BROWSERVER

We have used a normal browser coupled with a normal application server to avoid developing the browserver from scratch. A production quality, true browserver would constitute a single, integrated package. In terms of architecture (Figure 5), the browserver has the following main components:

- **Browser Management:** Manages the communication with the browser, updating the displayed interface. Receives UI requests from the Services Management and sends back related user replies;
- **User Interface Management:** Creates, destroys and manages each active user interface (UI) requested by the Browser Management. Converts the internal representation of the UIs to a browser displayable representation using XSLTs or specific converter objects. The components responsible for this are the BrowserManager, the Container and the ContainerUnits;

- **Services Management :** Contains and manages the services that are available for external (local or remote) consumption and handles service's requests and replies;
- **Network Management:** Manages the network which the Browserver is in. Enables service publishing operations on remote service directories and gateways as well as searching the directories for services.

The operation of the browserver can be described as follows:

- The BrowserManager coordinates the creation of Containers and ContainerUnits, and is responsible for sending the full Container UI for the specific browser that requires it through the Proxy, as well as creating new UI units from UIData sent by the ServiceManager, using the UnitBuilder;
- A UnitBuilder takes the XML definition of an UI and builds a ContainerUnit representing that UI. The BrowserManager can then add it to a Container;

- There can be one or more Containers available (the Portal is the base reference for this architecture) and each holds multiple ContainerUnits, Portlets and ControlPanel realizations of these. These elements produce code understandable by the browser like HTML and JavaScript. The Container also updates the UI at the browser through the BrowserConnector whenever it changes internally;
- The BrowserConnector component represents the link with the browser that enables bidirectional communication allowing the update of the browser whenever it is needed. Direct Web Remoting (DWR) (Marginian and Walker, 2009) is used to implement this component;
- A DataHandler has the ability to handle user input from the browser. Its corresponding ContainerUnit handles the data, sending it to the BrowserManager, who then forwards it to the ServiceManager;
- A Interface Unit can be:
  - A SimpleUnit, which cannot hold any other units inside (e.g. a SimpleText is used to present text without any special format);
  - A ComplexUnit, which can hold other units (e.g., in HTML, a <div> element plays this role);
  - A DataUnit, which is a ComplexUnit and DataHandler that collects data from the user (e.g., a <form> element in HTML corresponds to a DataUnit);
  - A ContainerUnit, which is a DataUnit that holds the whole UI for a service and handles input data from the browser, redirecting it to the corresponding service at the Server part;

Different Container, ContainerUnits and/or UnitBuilders implementations enable different graphical frontends. For a mobile device, simply extending an existing Container into a new one that converts the output using XSLT is a feasible solution;

- The ServicesManager is responsible for managing incoming requests and outgoing responses for UIs and system operations, as well as the locally deployed and the remotely known Web services;
- The Network consists of at least one Provider (the local host) and all the known remote providers that can have any number of associated services;
- The NetworkManager manages the known providers and offers a means to remotely register local services and to search for published services. A remote service directory is used to publicize the services of the Browserver.

The browserver has been developed as a Java web application using Java Servlets, Beans, Plain Old Java Objects and Web Services. A GlassFish server and a standard browser have been used for the deployment of the application and display the UIs for the services, respectively. GlassFish supports the deployment of new applications without restarting the server, which allows adding new services as small web applications without restarting the Browserver. Firefox, Chrome, Internet Explorer and Opera have been tested and work with the developed solution.

To exchange data between the browser and server components of the browserver and to update the UI displayed to the user, the implementation uses Ajax techniques (Matthijssen et al, 2010) to actively connect the browserver to the browser, enabling nearly real time update of the UI on any event at the browserver.

The Direct Web Remoting (DWR) library (Marginian and Walker, 2009) has been used for reverse Ajax communication between the browser and the Browserver application and JQuery JavaScript at the browser side to update the DOM structure of the visualized page and gather form

Figure 6. Connection between the browser and the server through DWR

data that is submitted through the DWR. As shown in Figure 6, the browserver communicates (c) with the browser through DWR (b), which consists of a server side Java Servlet in communication with client side Javascript methods through reverse Ajax (a).

It should be noted that this is a solution needed by the current browser technology, with impact in both complexity and performance. If the browser was designed for integration with a server, in a browserver architecture, this could be avoided.

Another feature of the browserver is automatic interface generation when a service needs to obtain an answer from the user (the concept of user as a service), which it can do by sending a UI definition that can contain complex elements such as forms for user data submission or simple informative text to the UIWebService (Figure 5), such as the following example, which requests a name and age:

```
<interface title="Information">
  <form name="informationForm">
    <par>Please fill and submit the following information:</par>
    <text>Your Name:</text>
    <input name="name" type="text"/>
    <text>Your Age:</text>
    <select name="age">
      <option value=""<20"/>
      <option value="20-40"/>
      <option value=""<40"/>
    </select>
  </form>
</interface>
```

The BrowserManager creates (or re-uses) an appropriate ContainerUnit for the Container that targets the browser and further makes use of an appropriate UnitBuilder to parse the UI definition on the request. The UnitBuilder transforms the definition to an internal uniquely identified UI representation user interface Unit. This unit is then added to the ContainerUnit that is further added to the Container. The default Container of the browserver is a Portal which holds Portlets as the ContainerUnits and builds an interface with a desktop-like metaphor (Figure 7a). The portal also includes a control panel that gives the user access to some useful tools. In this case, it is possible to open the list of services (Figure 7b) that are deployed in this browserver and a list of all requests made to the user and not dealt with yet (Figure 7c).

The internal UI representation is transformed into a definition that is interpretable by the browser. The default Portal and Portlet conversion generates HTML, CSS and JavaScript code. To adapt to a different interpreter or to a lower-end device such as a PDA or a mobile phone, the generated interface might either be transformed using XSLTs or new pairs of Containers and Units could be developed to generate specific UIs. Figure 8 summarizes the interface generation for the request example shown above.

When the user submits the answer, the data is gathered and sent to the Container through the BrowserConnector. The Container forwards the data to the corresponding ContainerUnit, which

Figure 7. The browserver portal, showing the interface generated automatically

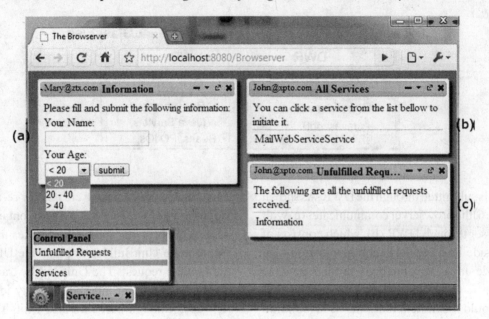

parses and filters the data as needed. The resulting data is sent to the BrowserManager, which forwards it to the ServiceManager to be sent as a data response to the corresponding requester. For the example request above, an example of a response data is:

```
<data>
    <name>informationForm</name>
    <input>
        <name>name</name>
        <value>John</value>
    </input>
    <input>
        <name>age</name>
        <value>20-40</value>
    </input>
</data>
```

Figure 8. User interface generation

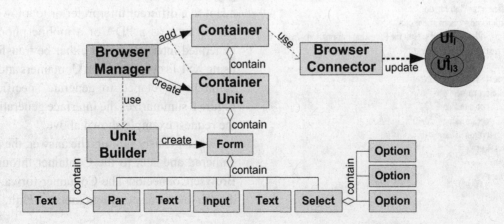

APPLICATION DOMAINS

Any electronic service can be deployed at the browserver, as in any other server. However, the most interesting application domains pertain to the personal use (since this is a device meant to be the connector between a person and the Web) in which a local server presents advantages in respect to a remote server (otherwise there would be no difference between a browserver and a normal browser using a remote server).

Our objective is to exploit the user-centric approach already illustrated by Figure 2 and the capabilities provided by the browserver as a solution to the vision of the semantic desktop (Sintek, Handschuh, Scerri and van Elst, 2009) as the future Web interface of the individual user. Essentially, that vision encompasses:

- The user interface should be customized for each user and fundamentally constitute a mashup of the various contexts relevant to that user;
- The context should be user-centric, in the sense that should reflect the user view of the world, integrating the various roles performed by the user, and not that of individual applications;
- The several types of user interaction (browsing, invocation of electronic services, messaging leisure, professional interests groups, workflow, knowledge management and so on), that up to now have been dealt with separately, with various applications and different rules and policies, should be integrated under one basic but customizable look and feel, to ease user interaction and capitalize on added value that one context can bring to another (for example, a leisure acquaintance can reveal itself very useful in the professional context, or a solution discovered in one context can be very useful in another);

- More than a simple and passive interface, the semantic desktop must be active and implement services that act as a personal assistant (for example, an activity manager integrated with the user's interactions, tracking agenda events, to-do activities and alerts while preserving the user's privacy).

This is nothing new. The best human-computer alignment can only be achieved if the computer-based world, seen from the user interface, is presented to the user in the format and organization that reflect his own context and activities.

Therefore, we strive to lay down the mechanisms necessary not only to implement user interactions with the rest of the world, by browsing, invoking services or performing social interactions, both at the personal or professional levels, but also to integrate the daily activities performed by the user. All these contexts are just different facets of the same user's life.

Current solutions use a mix of server-side and client-side solutions and techniques to be able to deal with the limitations of the client-server model that still rules in a world of browsers and servers. We contend that a service oriented solution is best to solve an entity oriented (user-centric) problem, and the browserver was conceived with that in mind.

As usual, the imagination is the limit and we expect new applications to grow out of this model, in particular if geolocation is available, but we describe here briefly some advantages of the browserver regarding a few application domains.

Social Networks

The two main issues in this domain are:

- Multiple contexts – The user has to deal with several social networks to accommodate all his interests and maintain several copies of the profile and other information;

- Privacy – Information sits on the social network provider's servers and the user has no control over what is being done with it. Privacy policies are usually complex and hard, if not impossible, to verify.

The browserver solves, or at least alleviates, both problems, as described in Figure 2. The user's information is stored in his own computer, and he has control over which parts of it can be disclosed to which provider. Also, providers need to get the information themselves and periodically, if they want to have it updated. This has already been described earlier in greater detail.

Serverless Messaging

The same privacy issue arises in messaging. Messages are stored at the servers that implement the application communication protocol and again there is no control over what is done with them. Direct, browserver to browserver messaging solves this problem, although encryption needs to be used if the message is secret and the channel is not secure.

As a proof-of-concept, we implemented a very simple message application, shown in Figure 9, in which two or more users exchange messages without a server-based protocol. If the user configures the browserver to use a gateway, this will store messages while his computer is offline and will deliver them when the computer goes online again.

Workflow

Decentralized workflow, in which the user is seen as a service that is inserted in a given workflow at the points where action is needed and not at the beginning and end of a given (sub)process (Ricker, 2006), is another area in which the browserver can be very useful. The basic idea is that the user is invoked or notified proactively whenever needed (there is no need to wait for the user to go

to a specific site, since the browserver includes a server of its own) with an interface dynamically and automatically generated (as illustrated by Figures 7 and 8).

The workflow waits for the response of the user and an application deployed at the browserver manages the activities, to-do list and deadlines. This can be done in a universal way (the server is universal, not application specific) and in an integrated manner with other events, activities, to-do list and deadlines. IT should be noted than in many cases e-mail is used for notifications or requests and the deadline management is done manually.

The browserver can also manage responses from other users, generating timeout events and even sending reminders, all in a decentralized way. There are (at least necessarily) servers involved (apart from the browservers themselves), which means that scalability is high. The fact that the user does not have to poll a site to see a to-do list is of crucial importance.

Another advantage is the unification of the software services and human services (Schall, Truong and Dustdar, 2008). This simplifies the design of processes and reduces the effort in changes, allowing to replace a human role by an agent or vice-versa, for tests, to recover from unexpected situations, to collect statistics, and so on.

Figure 10 illustrates a decentralized workflow based on browservers. The inventory system of supermarket Smart Price detects a lower inventory of bicycles and sends a request to the browserver of the manager, Mark. The request pops up in his screen, with a form created automatically, or goes to his to to-do list. Upon approval, a message is sent to the bicycles' manufacturer, Two Wheels. This is not an e-mail message, but an XML message that contains structured data. This company has just in time inventory and this generates a message to the manager, Andy, to approve (if necessary) and order to buy tires from the Rubber Classics company, where the manager, Reno, can

Figure 9. Serverless message exchange

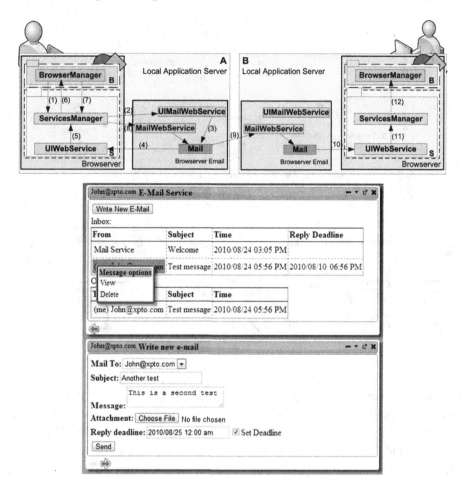

deal with it. All messages are sent directly from browserver to browserver and benefit from the capabilities of the server that allows workflow and activity management applications deal with the users' responsibilities in an active manner.

RELATED WORK

The name *browserver* has already been used in an open source software project (Carvalho et al, 2010), but in a completely different context. This software is a Firefox plugin that enables the storage and retrieval of web browsing data in a remote server (not locally), with the objective to assist in web browsing migration between differ-

ent devices or different users on a single device. This browserver and ours have only the name is common.

Many systems combine a client and a server, but are application specific. All P2P clients are able to answer to requests made by the network, but can only execute the corresponding protocol. In contrast, the browserver is designed with a generic application server, capable of hosting any application.

Colayer (2010) and Google Wave (Trapani & Pash, 2010) contextualize all the communication and shared information into inter-related fully asynchronous flows of information (real time when participants are available). Both of these platforms rely on remote application servers that can have

Figure 10. The user as a service in a simple workflow application

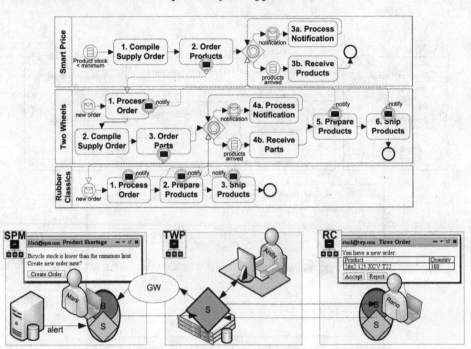

access to the information and offer a limited set of services. Even Google Wave in a Box (North, 2010), which provides a local server, is designed for communication and collaboration, not for generic functionality. In contrast, the browserver turns each user into a generic web service provider, while shifting from client-server to a peer-to-peer paradigm and enabling fully asynchronous communication.

Opera Unite (Opera, 2010) couples a browser to a server, allowing the user to share content directly with another user. However, the communication is always proxied at Opera's servers. If the user shuts down the application, his services also become unavailable. The browserver enables pure P2P communication between entities, promoting information privacy. The presence of its services can be virtualized on remote Gateways, thus allowing to asynchronously request its services even if it is unavailable.

Matsubara (2004) describes a method to get the user to be seen as a web services server to a

business process engine. However, the method results in sending a notification (through email or SMS) to the user, with a URL to follow. Given that the browser is limited to being a client, some external tool must be used to draw user's attention to a task. The browserver enables requests to be sent directly and to notify the user through the browser.

FUTURE RESEARCH DIRECTIONS

The current implementation of the browserver contemplates one user interface (a browser) and one server that can host a number of services. This can be generalized by having only a server, in which the user interface is a service in itself. The underlying model already contemplates this and the automatic user interface generation already assumes a user interface service. But the need to use an off-the-shelf browser has dictated this organization.

Having the interface as a fully featured service is cleaner, closer to the browserver model and even supports several "browsers" (user interfaces) with an associated set of user settings. In other words, a user can have several customized views of the world and different sets of services at his disposal.

Actually, this corresponds, to the concept already preconized by RIAs platforms, onto which Web applications can be deployed. The difference is that, this time, these applications are designed with a service, user-centric and decentralized (no central servers) perspective. The design and implementation of the browserver as a generic, stand-alone service platform is our next goal.

CONCLUSION

The Web landscape changed a lot since its inception, 20 years ago. From basic, passive information browsing, users have evolved to actively produce information today. Naturally, Web technologies have also evolved to make this task easier. However, the basic paradigm (client-server) has remained the same. This forces users to have an indirect presence in the Web, via central servers. If for some cases this is correct, because users want to publish information but not to manage that availability, in many other cases they want privacy and to control what happens when they interact with other users.

The most decentralized systems today are those based on P2P protocols. However, they are not general, in the sense that they implement a predefined set of services and functionality. In our view, the user should have the capability to choose whether to resort to server providers or to provide and manage his own services, in a completely generic and decentralized way.

To support this vision, we proposed to replace the classical browser by a new Web access device, which we designate *browserver*. This is a package of a browser and a server, which permits turning the user into an active entity, offering services.

The current browserver implementation has a rather loose connection between the browser and the server, using an Ajax based solution, but a production quality browserver will be one single application with better performance and capabilities. The architecture and the current implementation of the prototype of the browserver were described, as well as a set of applications which can benefit from the existence of a local server, at the same time that the intermittent nature of user computing devices was not forgotten and contemplated in the design.

ACKNOWLEDGMENT

Credit is due to M. Raposo for his work on the implementation of the browserver.

REFERENCES

Carvalho, L., et al. (2010). Synchronizing Web browsing data with browserver. In *Symposium on Computers and Communications* (pp.738-743). IEEE.

Dougherty, H. (2010). Facebook reaches top ranking in US. *Hitwise Intelligence*. Retrieved November 30, 2010, from http://weblogs.hitwise.com/heather-dougherty/2010/03/facebook_reaches_top_ranking_i.html.

Fraternali, P., Rossi, G., & Sánchez-Figueroa, F. (2010). Rich Internet applications. [IEEE.]. *IEEE Computing, 14*(3), 9–12.

Hazael-Massieux, D. (2009). *Report on the W3C Workshop on the Future of Social Networking*. Retrieved November 30, 2010, from http://www.w3.org/ 2008/09/ msnws/ report.pdf.

Hickson, I. (Ed.). (2010). *The WebSocket API*. W3C Working Draft. Retrieved November 30, 2010, from http://dev.w3.org/ html5/ websockets/.

Lipsman, A. (2010). U.S. online display advertising market delivers 22 percent increase in impressions vs. year ago. *ComScore*. Retrieved November 30, 2010, from http:// www.comscore. com/ Press_Events/Press_Releases/ 2010/11/ U.S._Online_ Display_ Advertising_ Market_ Delivers_22_Percent_Increase_in_Impressions.

Lizcano, D., Soriano, J., Reyes, M., & Hierro, J. (2009). A user-centric approach for developing and deploying service front-ends in the future internet of services. [Inderscience Publishers, Switzerland.]. *International Journal of Web and Grid Services*, 5(2), 155–191. doi:10.1504/ IJWGS.2009.027572

Mah, P. (2010). Facebook unveils new messaging system to rule them all. *FierceCIO*. Retrieved November 30, 2010, from http:// www.fiercecio. com/ techwatch/ story/ facebook-unveils-new-messaging-system- rule-them-all/ 2010-11-16.

Marginian, D., & Walker, J. (2009). *Direct Web remoting - Easy Ajax for Java*. Retrieved November 30, 2010, from http://directwebremoting.org.

Matsubara, D., & Miki, K. (2004). *Method and apparatus for peer-to-peer access*. Patent US 2004/0148434 A1, July 2004.

North, A. (2010). Wave open source next steps: "Wave in a box". Retrieved November 30, 2010, from http:// googlewavedev.blogspot.com/ 2010/ 09/ wave-open- source-next- steps-wave- in-box. html.

Opera. (2010). Opera Unite user guide. *Opera Software*. Retrieved November 30, 2010, from http://unite.opera.com/.

Ostrow, A. (2010). It's official: Facebook passes 500 million users. *Mashable*. Retrieved November 30, 2010, from http:// mashable.com/ 2010/07/ 21/ facebook-500- million-2/.

Ricker, J. (2006). *Human services - Integrating user interfaces into a service oriented architecture*. Retrieved November 30, 2010, from http://www. jeffreyricker.com/ papers/ Human-Services.pdf.

Saint-Andre, P. (2005). Streaming XML with Jabber/XMPP. *IEEE Internet Computing*, 9(5), 82–89. doi:10.1109/MIC.2005.110

Schall, D., Truong, H., & Dustdar, S. (2008). Unifying human and software services in Web-scale collaborations. [IEEE.]. *IEEE Internet Computing*, 12(3), 62–68. doi:10.1109/MIC.2008.66

Seong, S., et al. (2010). *PrPl: A decentralized social networking infrastructure*. In Workshop on Mobile Cloud Computing & Services: Social Networks and Beyond. ACM Press.

Skeels, M., & Grudin, J. (2009). When social networks cross boundaries: A case study of workplace use of Facebook and LinkedIn. In *International Conference on Supporting Group Work* (pp. 95-104). ACM Press.

Takayama, Y., Ghiglione, E., Wilson, S., & Dalziel, J. (2009). Human activities in distributed BPM. In Abramowicz, W., Maciaszek, L., Kowalczyk, P., & Speck, A. (Eds.), *Business Process, Services Computing and Intelligent Service Management, Lecture Notes in Informatics 147* (pp. 139–151). Germany: Gesellschaft für Informatik.

Tootoonchian, A., Saroiu, S., Ganjali, Y., & Wolman, A. (2009). Lockr: Better privacy for social networks. In *International Conference on Emerging Networking Experiments and Technologies* (pp. 169-180). ACM.

Trapani, G., & Pash, A. (2010). *The complete guide to Google Wave*. 3ones, Inc., USA.

Van Grove, J. (2010). Facebook announces new messaging system: "It's Not E-mail". *Mashable*. Retrieved November 30, 2010, from http:// mashable.com/2010/11/15/ facebook-messaging-event/.

Vaughan-Nichols, S. (2010). Will HTML 5 restandardize the Web? *IEEE Computer*, *43*(4), 13–15. doi:10.1109/MC.2010.119

Yang, S., & Chen, I. (2008). A social network-based system for supporting interactive collaboration in knowledge sharing over peer-to-peer network. *International Journal of Human-Computer Studies*, *66*(1), 36–50. doi:10.1016/j.ijhcs.2007.08.005

ADDITIONAL READING

Acquisti, A., & Gross, R. (2006). Imagined communities: Awareness, information sharing, and privacy on the Facebook. In P. Golle & G. Danezis (Eds.), *Proceedings of 6th Workshop on Privacy Enhancing Technologies* (pp. 36-58). Cambridge, UK: Robinson College.

Breslin, J., & Decker, S. (2007). The Future of Social Networks on the Internet: The Need for Semantics. *IEEE Internet Computing*, *11*(6), 86–90. doi:10.1109/MIC.2007.138

Brocke, J., Schenk, B., & Sonnenberg, C. (2009) Organizational implications of implementing service oriented ERP systems: an analysis based on new institutional economics. In Abramowicz, W. (Ed.) *12th International Conference Business Information Systems*, Poznan, Poland (252–263). Berlin, Germany: Springer-Verlag.

Carminati, B., & Ferrari, E. (2008) Privacy-aware collaborative access control in web-based social networks. In V. Atluri (Ed.) *22nd Annual IFIP WG11.3 Working Conference on Data and Applications Security*, Vol. 5094 (pp. 81-96), Heidelberg, Germany: Springer-Verlag Berlin.

Chen, D., Doumeingts, G., & Vernadat, F. (2008). Architectures for enterprise integration and interoperability: Past, present and future. *Computers in Industry*, *59*, 647–659. doi:10.1016/j.compind.2007.12.016

Christidis, K., Papailiou, N., Mentzas, G., & Apostolou, D. (2009) Exploring Gadget-Based Interfaces for the Social Semantic Desktop, In *Panhellenic Conference on Informatics*, (pp. 215-219) Computer Society Press.

Conrad, M., Dinger, J., Hartenstein, H., Schöller, M., & Zitterbart, M. (2005). Combining service-orientation and peer-to-peer networks. In Müller, P., Gotzhein, R., & Schmitt, J. (Eds.), *Lecture Notes in Informatics* (pp. 181–184). Bonn, Germany: Gesellschaft für Informatik.

Crane, D., & McCarthy, P. (2008). *Comet and Reverse Ajax: The Next-Generation Ajax 2.0*. Berkely, CA: Apress, Inc.

DiMicco, J., et al. (2008) Motivations for Social Networking at Work, In *Proceedings of the ACM conference on Computer supported cooperative work* (pp. 711-720), New York, NY: ACM Press.

Earl, T. (2005). *Service-oriented architecture: concepts, technology and design*. Upper Saddle River, NJ: Pearson Education.

Earl, T. (2008). *Principles of service design*. Boston, MA: Pearson Education.

Felt, A., & Evans, D. (2008) Privacy Protection for Social Networking Platforms, In *Workshop on Web 2.0 Security and Privacy*, IEEE.

Grefen, P., Aberer, K., Hoffner, Y., & Ludwig, H. (2000). CrossFlow: Cross-Organizational Workflow Management in Dynamic Virtual Enterprises, *International Journal of Computer Systems. Science & Engineering*, *5*, 277–290.

Grefen, P., Mehandjiev, N., Kouvas, G., Weichhart, G., & Eshuis, R. (2009). Dynamic business network process management in instant virtual enterprises. *Computers in Industry*, *60*(2), 86–103. doi:10.1016/j.compind.2008.06.006

Havey, M. (2005). *Essential business process modeling*. Sebastopol, CA: O'Reilly.

Iannella, R. (2009). Towards E-Society Policy Interoperability. In Godart, C., Gronau, N., Sharma, S., & Canals, G. (Eds.), *Software Services for e-Business and e-Society, IFIP Advances in Information and Communication Technology* (*Vol. 305*, pp. 369–384). Heidelberg, Germany: Springer-Verlag Berlin.

Kim, W., Jeong, O., & Lee, S. (2010). On social Web sites. *Information Systems, 35*(2), 215–236. doi:10.1016/j.is.2009.08.003

Krishnamurthy, B., & Wills, C. (2008) Characterizing Privacy in Online Social Networks, In *Proceedings of the first workshop on Online Social Networks* (pp. 37-42), New York, NY: ACM Press.

Lovelock, C., & Wirtz, J. (2007). *Services marketing: people, technology, strategy*. Upper Saddle River, NJ: Pearson Prentice Hall.

Matthijssen, N., et al. (2010) Connecting Traces: Understanding Client-Server Interactions in Ajax Applications, In *International Conference on Program Comprehension*, (pp. 216 – 225), IEEE.

Mika, P. (2007). *Social Networks and the Semantic Web*. New York, NY: Springer Science.

Petrie, C., & Bussler, C. (2003). Service agents and virtual enterprises: a survey. *IEEE Internet Computing, 7*(4), 68–78. doi:10.1109/MIC.2003.1215662

Ramakrishnan, R., & Tomkins, A. (2007). Toward A PeopleWeb. *IEEE Computer, 40*(8), 63–72. doi:10.1109/MC.2007.294

Schall, D., Dorn, C., Truong, H., & Dustdar, S. (2009). On supporting the design of human-provided services in SOA. In Feuerlicht, G., & Lamersdorf, W. (Eds.), *Lecture Notes in Computer Science* (*Vol. 5472*, pp. 91–102). Heidelberg, Germany: Springer Berlin.

Services, In *IEEE International Conference on Web Services*, pp. 856-863, Los Alamitos, CA: IEEE Computer Society Press.

Sintek, M., Handschuh, S., Scerri, S., & van Elst, L. (2009) Technologies for the Social Semantic Desktop, In Tessaris et al. (Eds.) *Reasoning Web. Semantic Technologies for Information Systems*, Lecture Notes in Computer Science, 5689 (222-254) Springer.

Song, K. & Lee, K. (2007) An Automated Generation of XForms Interfaces for Web.

Spohrer, J., Vargo, S., Caswell, N., & Maglio, P. (2008) The Service System is the Basic Abstraction of Service Science. In Sprague Jr., R. (Ed.) *41st Hawaii International Conference on System Sciences*. Big Island, Hawaii, 104, Washington, DC: IEEE Computer Society.

Uram, M., & Stephenson, B. (2005). Services are the Language and Building Blocks of an Agile Enterprise. In Pal, N., & Pantaleo, D. (Eds.), *The Agile Enterprise*. New York, NY: Springer. doi:10.1007/0-387-25078-6_4

Wu, L., & Park, D. (2009). Dynamic outsourcing through process modularization. *Business Process Management Journal, 15*(2), 255–244. doi:10.1108/14637150910949461

Zdun, U., Hentrich, C., & van der Aalst, W. (2006). A survey of patterns for Service-Oriented Architectures. *International Journal of Internet Protocol Technology, 1*(3), 132–143.

KEY TERMS AND DEFINITIONS

Browserver: A new web access device that extends the browser by adding a local server in close cooperation. The main idea is that the individual user can now become a first class web actor, capable of not only placing requests but also to satisfy requests from other actors, either server applications or other browservers. This frees the user from many of the limitations of the browser, while maintaining the sandboxing principle.

Collaboration Network: A set of people and/or organizations interlinked and sharing some common interests or activities. In the context of this chapter, the communication platform is some form of web based system, most commonly today supported by servers belonging to a single organization (the collaboration network provider). This term is also used to designate the platform itself or even the provider, but the collaboration network is really the complete set of all the actors involved.

Continuous Presence: Capability of a user to maintain a minimum set of services and/or information available to other users when that user is not connected to the network. This involves some server and works in close cooperation with the browserver, which upon reconnecting synchronizes with it and takes over in a completely transparent way.

Decentralized Collaboration Network: A collaboration network in which interaction is done directly between the collaborating entities, without the need of intermediaries such as applications residing on servers. Note that this definition pertains to the applicational level, not the network platform level.

Provider-Centric: The paradigm associated with the client/server model. All the services are provided by central servers. Users are mere clients of those servers, usually accessing services by a client program such as a browser.

Resource: Any entity implementing at least one service. Resources interact by sending each other messages. Reception of a message by one resource causes a reaction that depends on the message and the services that resource implements.

Service: A set of related functionalities that define a meaningful concept in a resource interaction context.

Social Network: A kind of collaboration network with emphasis on human interaction and information sharing, for personal or professional purposes.

User-Centric: Collaboration network paradigm in which the user is the main network player, not the provider. The user is seen by his peers as a service, with server capabilities, not as a mere client of some server. The browserver is a fundamental web access device in this paradigm.

Chapter 4
Web Services for Healthcare Management

Lucio Grandinetti
Università della Calabria, Italy

Ornella Pisacane
Università della Calabria, Italy

ABSTRACT

Nowadays, Health Care Organizations (HCOs) are interested in defining methodologies of Information Technology (IT) for providing high quality services at minimum cost. Through modern software and hardware, they can process data and manage the three important phases: diagnosis, prognosis, and therapy. In this scenario, Web Technologies (WTs) can: provide advanced Information Systems that combine software applications; offer a heterogeneous connectivity to users; allow costs reduction; improve the delivery of the services; guarantee an interactive support of the doctors, interconnectivity between the HCOs, and effective information sharing. In this chapter, first it is described how to provide the services of a HCO through the WTs, and then it is shown how Operations Research makes it more effective, to deal with, for example, clinical data classification problem, clinical predictions, clinical what-if analysis, and Web services composition process.

INTRODUCTION

Health Care is *"The prevention, treatment, and management of illness and the preservation of mental and physical well-being through the services offered by the medical and allied health professions"* (*American Heritage Medical Dictionary*).

DOI: 10.4018/978-1-4666-0203-8.ch004

The main actors are: *Healthcare Administrators* (overseeing various healthcare departments and personnel and sometimes administrating some healthcare facilities or managing a small group of nurses); *Medical Specialties* (including respiratory care, medical imaging, health information technology, clinical research administration and more); *Medical Assistants* (performing clerical tasks in hospitals and physician's offices, including billing, filing, scheduling and helping patients fill out necessary forms. They sometimes also assist with basic medical work); *Physical Therapists* (treating patients with injuries, diseases or age-related problems that impair their physical well–being).

The *patients* represent the users and thus the final consumers of the health services. That being so, a HCO could be modeled like a *Supply Chain*, with suppliers and customers, offering its services at specific costs.

Each actor (supplier or customer) performs specific activities. For example: a supplier, on the base of the specific role, could take care either of the therapies (Physical Therapists) or of the administrative aspects (HC Administrators). On the other hand, a customer could require some suggestions, therapies and analyses. It is worth noting that there is no rigid and fix classification because, sometimes, a supplier could also become a customer.

In the literature, different models of supply chain for HC are proposed even though a lot of them are more focused on the classical supply chain perspective of a major manufacturer. This approach could not be valid for a general HC network because it has to offer specific services. In Hübner (2008), it is proposed a supply chain model for HC considering the customer's point of view. This proposal integrates a *process model*, a *document model*, and a *functional model* because they combine the view of clinical and economic issues related to the procurement, provision, and use of medical supplies. The first model is divided in two main components: the strategic part and the operational one. The second model, instead, is more focused on the data and information related to all the clinical and economic aspects occurring in HCO. Finally, the third model is a natural integration of the first two ones. Its functions are divided into layers (*Content, Contract, Order-to-payment, Service, Clinical Outcome,* and *Knowledge*) organized and managed like a stack. The main goal of this stack is to follow the product's path from the supplier to the customer

(patient) in which its information and knowledge is accumulated in order to use it without problems.

Figure 1 shows a schematic example of a health supply chain where: the first node represents the set of HC components (doctors and administrative personal); the second is the set of the customers (patients) and the two arrows represent the flow through the network. These flows could be information, data, therapies, suggestions and results of clinical analyses, but also medical products, medicines and payments for health services. Moreover, the two loops represent the internal actions performed by both HC personnel (to transfer, for example, the test tubes from a medical department to the specific laboratory) and patients, respectively.

The advantage of representing a HCO as a supply chain is to track products and information. This also assures the safety of patients; a saving of production, procurement and logistics costs; a facility of itemized billing and maintenance of regulatory compliance. In the efficient management of a HCO as a supply chain it is introduced the role of the *manager* who generally has to: supervise the human resources departments in the hospitals; oversee the medical assistants and the billers in physician's offices; manage the support staff in rehabilitation facilities and fill many other roles.

Moreover, because HC is considered one of the largest industries in the world (Marsh et al.

Figure 1. A schematic example of a health supply chain

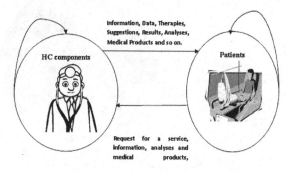

(1998)), a manager is also interested in reducing the total expenditures and managing efficiently the supply chain.

In fact, the health costs represent the most critical aspect in managing a HCO. For example, in 2008, U.S. health care expenditures were about $7,681 per resident and accounted for 16.2% of the nation's GDP. In fact, some analysts pointed out that the total health care expenditures grew at an annual rate of 4.4% in 2008. The expenditures in the United States on health care surpassed $2.3 trillion in 2008, more than three times $714 billion spent in 1990, and over eight times the $253 billion spent in 1980 (*Source: Centers for Medicare and Medicaid Services, Office of Actuary, National Health Statistics Group, National Health Care Expenditures Data, January 2010*). These high costs in HC management could be due to different factors: introduction of new technologies and medicines; treatment of chronic diseases (requiring long-term cares and cutting into the total costs for about 75%); aging of population and increment of administrative costs (cutting into the total costs for about 7%). For this reason, by the years, different proposals have been presented to control, as possible, these expenditures: investing on new technologies; improving quality and efficiency (decreasing the unwarranted variation in medical practice and unnecessary care cutting

into the total costs for about 30%) and increasing the prevention degree.

Hospital care and physician/clinical services combined account for half (51%) of the nation's health expenditures (Figure 2 --*Source: Centers for Medicare and Medicaid Services, Office of Actuary, National Health Statistics Group, National Health Care Expenditures Data, January 2010*). As shown, HC expenditures represent a large percentage of the total amount spent by a Country and thus it becomes very important to investigate for reducing them.

That being so, the HC managers are always interested in funding the most effective HC system (i.e., the most effective supply chain) using a limited number of resources and minimizing the total costs. On one side, this aspect is more related to the use of mathematical models and solving approaches provided by *Operation Research* (OR). On the other side, nowadays, the HCOs are also interested in defining methodologies of the *Information Technology* (IT) and in using them for satisfying their users' requirements. In particular, they are focused on providing the services at high quality and minimum cost by using the modern software and hardware technologies in order to process the clinical data and to manage the three main phases: *Diagnosis*, *Prognosis* and *Therapy*.

Figure 2. National health expenditures (2008)

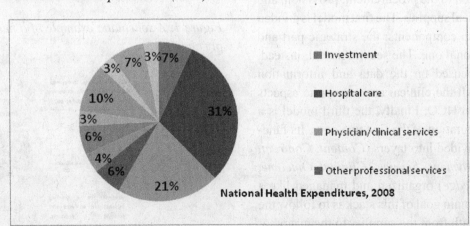

The result is open network architecture supporting the *access, classification, process* and *analysis* on data. In fact, because some deficiencies exist in the current *HC* organization (for example, inadequate and/or superfluous and/or incorrect cares; high costs and so on), *IT* can help *HCO* to acquire; manage; analyze and spread information and knowledge to provide a healthier and safer life to each individual.

For example, in July 2003, the Japanese government promoted the so called "*e-Japan strategy II*" for a more advanced implementation of *IT*, such as a new clinical policy for improving the quality of the health services, guaranteeing the authentication infrastructure in the medical treatment field; disclosing information of medical institutions to patients and establishing the online billing system of medical service fees (Mayumi et alt. (2005)). However, other main reasons exist for promoting the use of *IT* in the *HC* management:

- A more effective information for the clinical practice in order to improve the cares and the preventive therapies. This also implies a relevant development of the rural countries. There are some examples: *Satellife* that, using handheld computers(*Personal Digital Assistants* (PDAs)), delivers local reference material and medical journal content to rural health clinics; *On-Cue Compliance*, that using *Short Messaging Service* (*SMS*), helps to decrease some medical problems due to non-compliance by sending patients timely reminders via their personal cellular(it is currently used in South Africa, with almost a 100% success rate); *Jiva's Teledoc*, that using Java-enabled cellular, is providing village-based healthcare workers with real-time ability to transmit diagnostic information in India.

- An interconnection between the clinicians thanks to the access to the digital information about the medical cures and an improvement of the population health thanks to the continuous information sharing.

- A cost reduction, avoiding possible overheads and at the same time guaranteeing an improvement in delivering the health services.

Figure 3. Investment of the industries in defining information systems

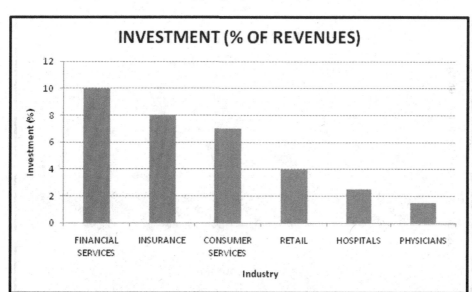

Although there are some relevant advantages, the *HCOs* are behind the other industries in investing their own revenues in using *IT* (only about 4% of its revenues: Figure 3 (*Source: Lewin Group, Forrester Research, LEK analysis*).

Nowadays, for an easier integration of IT inside HC management, digital information is universally used, containing the health data of an individual: *Personal Health Record* (*PHR*). The users can maintain and manage their own personal health information in a *PHR* created by the experts or by the individual. It is maintained in a private and protected way and the individual has to decide who can access it. For this reason, it constitutes an informative scheme and it is different from the ones provided by the single expert. Together with PHR, the *Electronic Health Record* (*EHR*) is also used. However, the main difference between a *PHR* and an *EHR* is that the former is controlled by the user; while, the latter is mainly controlled by the doctors and/or general experts. In any case, to access to both of them, a computer has to be used and often connected to the web.

In 2002, *Harris Interactive* has estimated that Sweden is investing more than the others in the use of the *EHR* by general and primary care physicians (as shown in Figure 4).

Recently, the *Center for Information Technology Leadership* (*CITL*) has completed an analysis estimating that the cost for investing in the use of an *EHR* will be about 278$ billion in the next ten years. But, this investment provides a relevant saving of the total annual expenses of a country in the *HC* industry.

Although the costs reduction represents one of the major reason to invest in advanced information systems, they also allow users to have an interactive support of the doctors; an interconnectivity between the various *HCO*, all over the world, and, consequently, an effective information sharing.

However, it is worth noting that the use of *IT* in *HC* management generates a set of relevant problems, as explained later, related to *data security* and *transmission*; *network limitation*; *system and language interoperability*. In particular, the latter is an important aspect to be addressed in order to allow and guarantee the integration of the different functionalities and data, usually coming from different sources.

Figure 4. Use of EHR by care physicians (in %)

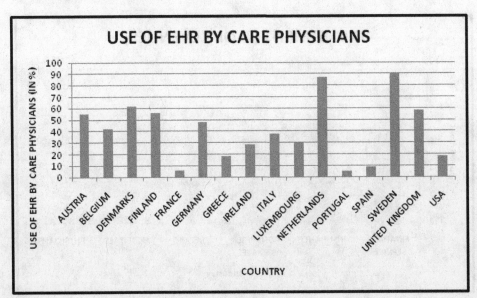

In fact, the systems could be developed in different programming languages (*Java*, *C++* and etc.); on different platforms (*Microsoft Windows*, *Linux* and etc.) and using different *Database Management Systems* (*Microsoft SQL Server*, *Oracle* and etc.).

Thus the *Web Services* (*WSs*) can be seen like innovative instruments able to successfully address, for example, the issue of the system and language interoperability, through the standard web browser utilities (as shown later). Moreover, through Internet, they can also offer a heterogeneous connectivity to all the users. For example, a web-based system could be effective to provide services to both doctors and patients, especially the ones that need a continuous support during the therapy (the diabetics, for example).

In this context, OR provides an effective set of optimization techniques and mathematical models that could be offered to the final users through user-friendly interfaces thanks to the *WSs*.

The aim of this Chapter is to show how to model and define Medical Web Services (MWSs), taking into consideration the relative challenges and also integrating the optimal models and methodologies of OR. In particular, we especially show how OR provides a valid set of methodologies, to deal with classical operative problems (i.e., clinical data classification, medical predictions, what-if analysis, medical resources management), that can be easily used by the final users through WSs. As a practical example, we describe a web based software tool for the diabetes treatment (Grandinetti and Pisacane (2008), Grandinetti and Pisacane (2011)) able to: perform both predictions on the future glycaemia level of the patients in a specific time horizon and what-if-analysis(showing how the glycaemia level could vary if some parameters are changed either in the diet of the patient or in the clinical treatment); share information and suggestions, creating a virtual community between specialists and patients; inform users about their health condition by using a data classification algorithm; allow the patient to maintain a daily diary about the personal health condition; know about the evolution of the health condition. Finally, we also show how OR mathematical models can support and help the MWSs composition process.

Medical Web Services

Even seeing towards different directions, both industries and academia are by now recognizing the importance of the Web Services. In fact, the formers are more interested in a modularization of the service layers; whereas, the latter in an expressiveness of the services descriptions.

In any case, whatever the goals are, the Web Services are defined as "*self-contained, self-describing modular applications*" (Martin (2001)) and they can also be seen like modular software describing a set of operations accessible through some specific standards (*OAP*, *UDDI*, *WSDL*, *.NET*).

They are actually used in different fields with huge success and vast consensus (*Ebay* and *Amazons* are just two examples).

The general model of a WS provides an ideal platform to its own users allowing an integration of different applications representing competitive standards. As known, in fact, a WS can be seen like a set of objects and different operations accessible through the protocols and the Internet services. It is invoked on-demand either by the business processes or by the applications or by the users. Then, its main goal and role can vary from a simple calculation to a complex transaction. Some of its key components are: *eXtensible Markup Language* (*XML*), an universal standard for the documents and data structure on the web; *XML schema*, providing means for defining the documents structure individuating the specific tags to be used; *Web Service Flow Language* (*WSFL*), a XML-based specification for representing the business workflow across the WS required for a specific business process; *Universal Description, Discovery and Integration* (*UDDI*), representing a specification for registering business partners offering WS, the offered WS and the technologies supported by it; *Web Services Description Language (WSDL),* an XML-based specification for describing the implementation details of a WS and also allowing a service provider to show the abstract service interface and to describe the service implementation; *Simple Object Access Protocol (SOAP),* allowing and guaranteeing the communication mechanism between two or more systems by using XML (for its goal, it can use *HTTP*, *SMTP* and other protocols for message passing).

This Chapter focuses attention on how to define, model and implement a *Medical Web Service* (*MWS*). At first, the medical domain and the relative requirements are introduced; second, it is shown how to model these health services on the base of *IHE* (*Integrating* the *Healthcare Enterprise*) administrative process flow; third, it is explained how the recent protocols of the WSs and the relative efforts in this field can help to solve the application integration.

Using and defining WSs in the medical domain is relevant and important to improve the quality of delivering health services. Recent statistics, in U.S., for example, show that adults receive only the half of the recommended cares and especially more than 98,000 adults died each year due to some avoidable medical errors. One of the most recommended solutions to this problem is to use software and to define advanced information systems for transferring suggestions and specific evaluations to patients and doctors.

Nowadays, there are three types of *Medical Information Systems* (*MIS*): *Hospital Information System* (*HIS*), used for administrative purposes (i.e., the patient and visit management, the billings, etc.); *Radiology Information System (RIS)*, used for the images in the radiology department and taking care of the patient registration, the examination scheduling, etc.; *Picture Archiving and Communication System (PACS)*, used for the management of all the types of clinical images. It also takes care of the transfer of the patients' data

to the different medical department; announces when a procedure ends; stores, prints, archives all the images and their data generated during a clinical process.

HL7 for RIS and *DICOM* for PACS are the most common and relevant protocol standards for these services. The latter manages the Client/Server communications used and established for the exchange of the information about the patients and the examination. Usually, it also manages what is concerned with the patients, the visits and the medical and clinical procedures. *HL7*, instead, takes care of the clinical data exchange between the different medical providers.

IHE represents an ambitious effort for integrating the two above standards by using a common framework. The need for defining *IHE* as a common standard is inducted by an incompatibility problem especially when some medical software products are implemented by using *LH7* and others by *DICOM*. By using *IHE* as a standard, the messages are sequenced in order to represent real-life scenarios and the flows are made up by a complete and well defined set of transactions performed by various and different actors. It allows the applications to be strongly integrated also in different and various scenarios.

It is worth noting that to design a MWS some aspects have to be taken into account: *Transportation mechanism* (for example, SOAP-over-HTTP communication); *Reliability and security requirements* (for example, WS-Security or WS-ReliableMessaging); *Composite language* for transforming the workflow representing the business process into a service-oriented environment (for example, BPEL); *Transactional behavior* for guaranteeing the processes quality (for example, WS-Transaction).

The Transportation mechanism is very important when a MWS is implemented by using the WS technology. Usually, the messages transfer is performed by using XML or SOAP and there are three different possibilities: to convert the messages and the data into XML format; to attach the original messages to the SOAP ones and to use some specific identifiers for executing the workflow; to separate the workflow domain from the communication mechanism even this possibility requires establishing a new and distinct communication channel. Many HL7 messages and some DICOM messages contain a little amount of data to be transferred and then they can easily be translated into XML messages. In some cases, a DICOM message could also contain some images. Thus, it is necessary to use attachments for the original messages and integrate a specific identifier inside the same message. The images can be compressed by using *JPEG 2000 Compressor*, for example. For the attachments, instead, some techniques like *WS-Attachments* based on DIME and *SOAP-Messages with Attachments* can be used.

The first step in defining and modeling a MWS is the clear identification of the messages and the data. The simplest way to do that is to use some specific identifiers. Thus, the data exchange is identified by the system identifiers. For example, the DICOM objects and the HL7 messages use some identifiers (patient ID, visit ID, image ID, etc.). Moreover, because the two above standards use different identifiers, IHE tries to create a mapping between them in order to define a unique identification for data and services.

The second step is related to the coordination of the business partners of a process that is necessary especially in a MWS. Unique identifiers are usually required and they are used by coordinators to properly define the context for the participants.

The third important aspect is related to the Web Services Transactions. The use of specific transactions protocols increases the quality of the WSs. The most common standards are *WS-Transaction* and *WS-TransactionManagement* and the relative models are distinguished on the base of the transaction type: *Direct transaction*, useful for short transactions; *Queued transaction*, for middle term transactions and *Compensation-based transactions*, for long term transactions, e.g., IHE adopts the compensation-based transactions.

About the security aspect, IHE defines a Secure Node Actor. Each of these nodes requires its own certificate and thus, a set of secure nodes creates a security domain. *WS-Security* is a security model supporting the username/password security, *X.509* certificates and Kerberos or SSL for authentication. Power et alt. (2006) propose an approach for facilitating the system-wide security for guaranteeing a fine-grained access control inside the systems in which web services are deployed. Their first step is the development of *health grids*. The authors discuss about the need of the web services to be secure especially because they remotely access to the medical data. Moralis et alt. (2009) describe a web services based security architecture for improving security performance maintaining interoperability with legacy *Grid Security Infrastructure* (GSI). Their architecture uses GSI X.509 Certificates or Proxy Certificates (RFC3820) for the initial authentication of a user and it subsequently maps this identity to a Kerberos one. Thus, it uses WS Security Kerberos Token Profile for embedding user credentials within WS mechanisms. Wang et alt. (2004) give an overview on the security problems. They argue that solving them is a crucial step for guaranteeing the success of web services.

For the WS registration and binding, the *Universal Description Discovery and Integration (UDDI)* standard is used. It provides some yellow pages (for searching a service implementing specific transactions) and green pages (to bind to the service at run-time). For the WSs composition, it is necessary to consider the structure and granularity of the WS itself as a part of the executed workflow.

The variables of a workflow in a MWS are of four different categories: *attributes for the participants and for the transactions*; *attributes for the messages*; *attributes for the information state*; *remaining attributes*.

Then, the whole infrastructure is made up by: a central and core workflow using a database; a workflow engine and a *Business Process Execu-*

tion Language (*BPEL*) engine. BPEL is a XML-based language used for formally describing the business processes in order to allow a task subdivision between the actors. A BPEL application is invoked as a WS and interacts with the world invoking other WSs. For this reason, it could also be seen as a web-services coordination, allowing a recursively composition. The runtime environment in which the generic process is executed is called BPEL engine.

The process for defining and modeling a MWS can be described and divided in some points, as follows:

1. To provide the model defining the IHE framework: the use-case UML diagrams (Fowler and Scott, 1998) are required. In fact, by them, it is possible to individuate the various layers. Each layer defines *profiles*, *flows*, *transactions* and *messages*. The profiles are subdivided into flows and each flow has to be supported by an application implementing the profile. In general, the flows are represented by specific sequence diagrams and each of them specifies a transaction. Each transaction is defined by HL7 and DICOM messages to be sent and/or received. The buildup model has a four levels: the first three levels represent the workflow; whereas, the last one the domain.

2. To define the process flow: the UML activity diagram where an IHE actor defines the public process and the transactions are converted into BPEL activities is required.

3. To define the transactions: starting from the UML sequence diagram, defined at step 2, each transaction is split into two pairs of invocations and receives activities.

4. To integrate the security requirements: a security domain contains one or more IHE actors that could be either authentication-free or encryption-free. Usually, the medical security domain requires at least 128bit key-length and an asymmetric encryption.

As known, the asymmetric encryption requires two keys: a secret private key and a published public key. Using them, it is possible a protection of the message creating a digital signature of a message through the private key that could be verified by the public one.

5. To integrate the transactional requirements: at this step, it is necessary to define the scopes inside the activities and the compensation activities themselves. Usually, the transactions are rectangular and the scopes are curly braces. The compensation activities are below the scopes inside the rectangular.

6. To define the BPEL process: at this step, it is necessary to specify the types, the variables, the messages and the correlations deriving from DICOM and HL7.

According to the six above points, an important requirement for modeling and defining MWS is the electronic data integration actually obstructed by the attempts to connect different applications to the clinical networks and to the information systems. The lack of standards has caused a huge increment of costs for integrating various health organizations. For this reason, recently, some industries have developed some possible standards with the aim to realize a low-cost integration. An example is *Health Level 7 Clinical Document Architecture* (*HL7 CDA*). It defines how the clinical documents, usually containing all the patients' data, can be exchanged between the different information systems. Its new version is *HL7v3* that describes how the clinical information could be exchanged between the various point-of-care devices, laboratory information systems and hospital information systems. A CDA can be seen as a document markup standard for the architecture and semantics of exchanged clinical documents and information and represents a complete information object including images, text, sounds. All the documents that are compliance to this standard must have a header section containing patients' data, the author and the date of creation etc. There is also a free section that could be divided in other subsections. At the end of the document there must be a signature. A CDA is always human readable and machine processable and could represent a Discharge Summary, a Referral, a Clinical Summary Report, a Diagnosis Report, etc. It is characterized by three different levels (as also shown in figure 5): *Level one*, the most general architecture and supporting CDA semantics including the sections and the structured entities; *Level two*, providing added constraints by introducing new templates at Section level; *Level three*, providing added constraints by introducing new templates at Entry Level and sometimes also at Section Level.

Together with the HL7v3 message passing standard, it evocates a XML document markup standard specifying the general structure and the intrinsic semantic of the clinical documents in order to guarantee and allow the exchange and

Figure 5. The three CDA levels

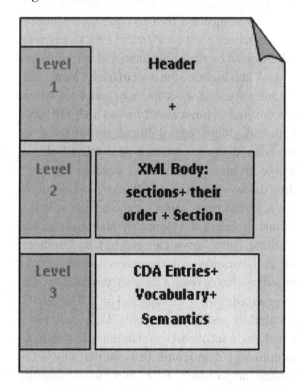

the sharing. A CDA document satisfies the following characteristics: persistent (it continues to exist in an unaltered state for a period fixed by some local requirements); human readability; potential for authentication (it is an assemblage of information that are supposed to be legally authenticated); context (it fixes the default context for its contents); wholeness (the authentication is applied to the whole document and not only to single portions) and stewardship. The definition of a CDA has allowed the easy development of new standards that guarantee more stability to the WSs and at the same time have extended their application fields.

Related Work

In literature, some references address the problems related to modeling and defining MWS. Anzböck et alt. (2005) present all the details for implementing a MWS; Perminov et alt. (2008) present a web service application for remote medical consults where the architecture is made up by two main components: a server and a client. Their base model has three levels: a client, a server application and a data base server. The server application of the system allows a client to be connected to the data base server and it is implemented by a web service. The client establishes the dialog between a generic user and the system. The data base server, instead, processes the requests of the server application written in *SQL* language. Kooper et alt. (2008) address the problem of 3D medical volume reconstruction by using WSs, implemented as additional layer to the dataflow framework. Koulouzis et alt. (2010) compare two transport models of workflow execution for data medical visualizations. A service based approach for constructing distributed visualization pipelines in order to allow the experts a view and an interaction with medical data sets is proposed.

Useful information related to the MWSs can be found in the documents on the standards HL7, DICOM and IHE.

In Anzböck and Dustdar (2003), the authors present an inter-organizational workflow in the medical imaging domain even a first work related to this topic is already described in Anzböck and Dustdar (2003(a)).

Useful references on WSDL and BPEL can be found at the relative web sites.

An earlier work on modeling MWSs is found in Anzböck and Dustdar (2004). In Von Berg et alt. (2001), the authors compare the classical workflow models for the clinical imaging with Biztalk. This work is referred to the middleware paradigm in an Internet environment and it does not take into consideration mixed environments. However, this is an important contribute for introducing the MWSs requirements.

In Ratib et alt. (2003), the authors describe the KIS/RIS/PACS integration and IHE framework without focusing the attention on modeling the medical services by using the web services technology.

In Hludov et alt. (2000), the authors consider the issues related to the compression technologies and to the transfer of compressed images over http. In Breu et alt. (2004), the authors provide a different approach for the security workflow infrastructure focusing on a subset of the security requirements for the medical services. In Lundberg (2000), the author analyzes the impacts on work practices and interdependencies in radiological work by PACS. In addition, he illustrates how detailed workplace studies may identify substantial social changes, emerged from initially insignificant technical solutions that rapidly grows and becomes central in complex health care networks.

By the years, some important and relevant MWSs have been defined. For example: Siemens Medical Web Services (http://www.medical.siemens.com) that merges systems for innovative diagnostic imaging, IT solutions, management consults and services for supporting the customers in order to reach excellent clinical results and a substantial costs reduction; GE Medical Systems (http://www.gemedicalsystems.com) provides innovative technologies and medical services in order to improve healthcare by using its own experience in the medical imaging, software technologies, clinical diagnostic products, patients monitoring systems and etc.; Agfa Healthcare (http://www.agfa.com/healthcare/) provides an extensive set of solutions, including *Hospital Information Systems* (HIS), *Clinical Information Systems* (CIS), RIS, PACS, *Laboratory Information Systems* (LIS), *Cardiology Information and Image Management Systems*, for reporting, enterprise scheduling, decision support, and data storage and, finally Philips Healthcare (http://www.medical.philips.com). *Atbrox* (http://aws.amazon.com/solutions/case-studies/atbrox) defines a software to assist individuals with dyslexia and to improve their written ability; *Pathwork Diagnostics* (http://pathworkdx.com) is a molecular diagnostics company using machine learning algorithms for helping oncologists during the delicate phase of diagnosis; *Nimbus Health* (http://www.nimbushealth.com/corporate/Index.html) assists doctors and hospitals to save money by enabling healthcare providers for sharing medical records with patients in an easy and online way; *Wellness checkpoint* (http://wellnesscheckpoint.com) *Health Risk Assessment* (HRA) used by many multinational corporations to track and improve the overall health metrics of organizations; *Medical Imaging and Computing for Unified Information Sharing* (MEDICUS-http://dev.globus.org/wiki/Incubator/MEDICUS) provides different services like teleradiology, image archiving, distributed warehousing and drug discovery and using *Globus Toolkit* (http://www.globus.org/); *caBIG* (cancer Biomedic Informatics Grid), developed by National Cancer Institute (http://www.cancer.gov/), to promote the collaboration with the cancer research community and to develop a standard terminology for representing data in this medical field. The caBIG vocabulary and Data Elements Workspace have developed a set of criteria for defining the medical terminology's structure. In a similar way, EU-funded project *neuGRID* (http://www.neugrid.

eu/) guarantees to the neuroscientists an advanced e-infrastructure in order to clinically assess new imaging markers of neurodegenerative diseases.

In Cimino et alt. (2009), the evolution of the criteria and results in evaluating and analyzing four specific standards (Gene Ontology, NCI Thesaurus, Common Therminology for Adverse Events (CTCAE) and Logical Objects, Identifiers, Names and Codes (LOINC)) are described.

In Sloot et alt. (2009), *ViroLab* is described. It provides the researchers with an appropriate tool and interactive framework for personalized drug ranking, integrating tools, modules, protocols and interfaces in a virtual manner. In Rajasekarana et alt. (2010), a wireless sensor grid architecture for monitoring and controlling the health status of patients is described and detailed. In Marović and Jovanović (2006), an interactive analysis tool for 3D medical and clinical images (named *VIVE-Volumetric Image Visualization Environment*) is proposed and described. Its aim is to support and assist during the diagnosis, surgical planning, therapy evolution and remote 3D examination. In Dong et alt. (2006), the authors describe and define a Grid solution for the simulation and visualization of the human arterial system. In Marsh et alt. (1998), an alternative technique to visualize the inner mucosal surface of the colonic wall is described and proposed. They also argue about the adoption of high performance computing and networking in order to support and facilitate virtual medical applications. Foster et alt. (1998) analyze the need requirements for a telemedical computing infrastructure and show how it is possible to use metacomputing environments for telemedicine. Finally, in Polemi (1998), *EUROMED-ETS* is described and presented for securing telemedicine applications over the web. In Hashmi et alt. (2005), the authors describe a scalable emergency medical response system that couples the efficient data collection of sensor networks with the flexibility and interoperability of a web services architecture.

Challenges in Modeling Medical Web Services

Defining and modeling MWSs present some important and relevant issues and challenges. In general, a model should be as simple as possible and contain the right level of details. Furthermore, on the base of the specific requirements of the system in exam, the *completeness*, the *extensibility* and the *ability* to represent security are the most important criteria. These are more relevant especially in the healthcare systems. For this reason, different and important challenges have to be considered in modeling MWSs:

- **Processes complexity:** the healthcare delivery usually involve multiple types of providers with different knowledge levels that often reside in various physical locations. The complexity is usually measured on the base of the number involved units and the number of transactions between the collaborative parts of the processes. However, by the years, a lot of efforts have be conducted for modeling the collaboration between the parts of a process by research in this field has shown that it is usually difficult.

- **Privacy and security requirements:** privacy and security requirements represent important aspects especially in the healthcare systems because they usually collaborate with other organizations (i.e., financial and insurance companies requiring some details on the patient's data). For this reason, the models have to take into account both the aspects.

- **User understandability:** the used models have to improve the comprehension of the parts involved in the processes. The process redesign and reengineering reform process inefficiencies reduce cycle time and remove no-value-added tasks. In particular, the models in the healthcare environment have to be clearing as much as possible because they could also be used for staff training.

- **Optimized models:** more detailed models could be confusing. For this reason, they usually represent the processes at high level. However, in some specific healthcare context, some important details are required. Thus, the models have also to be flexible as much as possible.

- **Processes evolution:** the constant evolution and the dynamic nature of the healthcare systems increase the complexity degree of the relative processes. The systems should also be able to adapt themselves to the different and dynamic scenarios and requirements. In this context, the modularity becomes an important and relevant feature of the models. In fact, modular models are simple to read and less resistant to the various changes. Moreover, they are also able to increase the reusability degree.

- **Integration and nested processes:** nested healthcare processes create inherently nolinear relationships and remove the boundaries between the sub-systems. This aspect increases the complexity in modeling the processes. Different sub-systems could have different requirements and features. For this reason, it is often necessary to use different modeling languages for various departments.

In addition to the above cited issues, an important and relevant challenge to be considered in modeling MWSs is *interoperability* of the *Healthcare Information System* (*HIS*). It can be defined as the "*capacity and ability of two or more programs to share and process information without considering the implementation language and platform*". Medical and clinical applications are often defined on various software platforms that are independent and heterogeneous and a lot

of them also use different and specific hardware supports.

Moreover, a lot of large scale telemedicine systems can be also provided by different vendors using different standards and formats. These are some of the primary causes for the interoperability problem that could be examined and analyzed from different points of view:

- **Language interoperability:** usually, the various HISs are developed and designed by different IT providers and the developers could use different languages. This could cause an hard reuse and sharing of the applications;

- **Semantic interoperability:** the various components of a HIS could assign different meanings to the data. Currently, one of the main efforts is to try to overcome the semantic interoperability by using a common clinical dictionary;

- **Database system interoperability:** the patients' data are often memorized in different databases and it means that they can be hardly shared and exchanged among the applications. For this reason, usually, the HISs prefer to use a single database even this solution does not guarantee the flexibility of the distributed application.

- **System-platform interoperability:** the HISs could be developed using different platforms. For example, a HIS could be developed using Windows platform and it is not always guaranteed that the same application is able to run under Linux platform.

The above four points remark that the interoperability problem concerns different aspects. Thus, it could be solved by applying different strategies at different levels.

Typical solutions involve the development of middleware applications to allow no interoperable applications to communicate to each other using the message paradigms. For example, *CORBA* and *DCOM* are two of the most used middleware technologies. Nevertheless, both of them require advanced software knowledge.

Nowadays, WSs are increasing its importance and relevance also as a new generation for the applications integration. They, in fact, allow the applications to communicate to each other simply using the standardized *XML* messaging system.

The WS technology is based on open standards and common infrastructures. The framework is divided in three areas: *communication protocols*; *service descriptions* and *service discovery*.

The use of standard *XML* protocols guarantees that the WSs can be platform-language and vendor independent and thus an optimal solution for the applications integration and the interoperability problem.

In general, in fact, the applications send and receive requests and responses to and from the WSs by using *SOAP*. When a program invokes a WS method, the relative request and all the needed information are packed into a *SOAP* message and sent to the final destination. When a WS receives the *SOAP* message, it processes the content in which the method and its input parameters are specified. After that, the method is invoked and the response is sent to the client in another *SOAP* message. This is the general mechanism used by the WSs for putting into communication different applications.

With the increased development of the medical technologies, new techniques for the clinical treatments have been experimented. For example: for the amputee's treatment, new osseointegration techniques have been discovered and for the diabetes's one, new therapies and insulin control techniques have been introduced. Thus, the definition of a web service based system is fundamental for collecting, for example, all the needed patients' information before, during and after the therapy. But, such system requires the integration of different applications and points of view (doctors, patients and administrative personal) that could use also different systems to

access to the WS. For this reason, the system has to assure the capability to interact with different operative systems (*Microsoft Windows, Linux* etc.). Moreover, some patients' records could be produced by already existing systems used by the doctors or by already existing healthcare management environment. Thus, the system has also to assure the interaction with different Database Management Systems (*Microsoft SQL server, Oracle* and *Microsoft Access*). In order to overcome the language interoperability problems among the applications, the system has also to assure the interaction and the compatibility with different implementation languages (*Java, Visual Basic, C++, C#* and so on).

Two are the major platforms: *Microsoft .Net* and *Java 2 Enterprise Edition*. The former is considered as the major platform because it could guarantee more features like the interoperability, scalability and cost. In general, the web service based system is built upon one of these platforms and the WS plays the main role of middleware. Because the WS extrapolates data from different databases, they could be written in *XML* messages and consequently *SOAP* could act as *XML* envelop to warp these *XML* databases into specific *SOAP* messages. Then, these *SOAP* messages are transmitted back to the applications by using *HTTP* protocol. *Miscrosoft .Net* platform is a neutral language and represents an open programming platform in which different and various languages can be plugged.

The source code is firstly converted into an *Intermediary Language* (*IL*) analogous to the *Java bytecode*. Then, the *IL* code is transformed into a native executable language (*Common Language Runtime-CLR*) analogous to the *Java Runtime*

Figure 6. Conversion mechanism

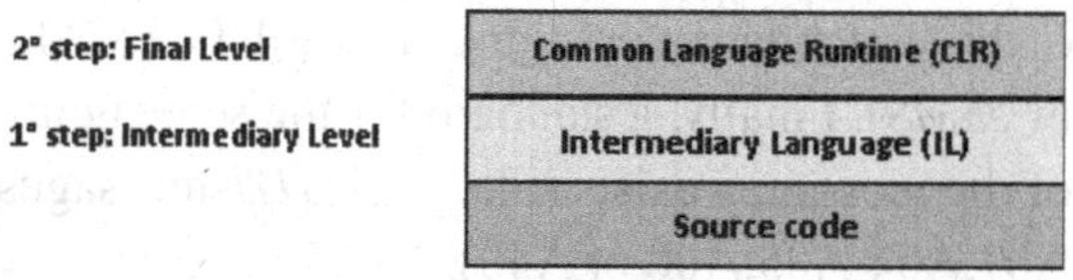

2° step: Final Level	Common Language Runtime (CLR)
1° step: Intermediary Level	Intermediary Language (IL)
	Source code

Environment (*JRE*). The methodology, typically, used for verifying if a WS and the platform could be really able to overcome the interoperability problems, is as follows:

- **Assessment of language interoperability:** managing to integrate the system with applications built in different programming languages;
- **Assessment of system interoperability:** Testing the system on different web browsers; Testing the system on different DBMSs; Testing the system on different operating systems.

For example, the interoperability problem of an HIS manly concerns the messages exchanged among the applications; the interoperability of the EHRs; the interoperability of the patients' identifiers; coding terms; clinical guidelines and healthcare business processes.

It is possible to distinguish two main layers: *syntactic* and *semantic layer*. The former concerns the ability of the system to share and exchange information and it is related to different layers: network and transport layer (*Internet*); application protocol layer (*HTTP* or *email*); messaging protocol and message format layer (*ebXML messaging* or *SOAP*) and sequencing of the messages. The syntactic layer guarantees that the message is correctly delivered but not that its content will be correctly processed by the machine that receives it. This last aspect, instead, is related to the semantic interoperability representing the ability of the system to correctly understand the information at the level of formally defined domain concepts.

Nowadays, for the syntactic interoperability, *TCP/IP* (*Internet*) represents the de-facto online communication standard; on the top, an application standard protocol (*HTTP* or *SMTP*) and on the top of this, a standard messaging protocol (like *SOAP* or *ebMS*). Finally, a standard for the sequencing of the messages exists (like *HL7 ADT* messages A01,A04,A05,A08 or A40).

Because the semantic interoperability concerns the data description, it is defined by *ontology*. Ontology is "*a formal, explicit specification of a shared conceptualization*" (Gruber (1993)). "Formal" means that it is described by a specific language called *ontology language*; "explicit", instead, means that the concepts and the relationships are defined by specific and clear names and definitions. In general, it provides a common vocabulary and together with a set of concrete instances constitutes a knowledge base. For example, *Web Ontology Language* (*WOL*) is considered one of the most important and popular ontology language.

About, finally, the *HER* interoperability, different standards exist: *Health Level 7 (HL7) Clinical Document Architecture (CDA)*; *CEN EN 13606 EHRcom* and *openEHR*. The reader can find a detailed survey in Eichelberg (2005). The general technical characteristics that have to be satisfied by them are: mapping of the patients' identifiers among the different healthcare applications; authenticating the users across the enterprises; guaranteeing that all the computers involved have a consistent time (i.e., system clocks and time stamps well synchronized) and, finally, authenticating nodes and obtaining audit trail.

OPTIMIZING MEDICAL WEB SERVICES

In this section, we discuss on how to introduce Operations Research (OR) methodologies and approaches inside the MWSs. Especially for the medical field, OR can support the process of composing WSs and can help to provide optimized healthcare services to the final users. These are just two of the other aspects that can be successfully managed by OR.

Optimal Web-Based Health Services

From a healthcare services point of view, OR and its optimization techniques can be used in managing a HCO at different levels: *Strategic* deciding how to divide the resources; what percentage of the total costs has to be paid by the government; how to optimize the costs due to services (for example the patients transportation to the hospital) and the ones due to the drugs and vaccines; *Tactical* deciding how to plan the selection of the goods and services and the allocation of the resources and finally, *Operational* deciding how to design the HC supply chain; to allocate and schedule the medical equipment and how to perform previsions on the demand. IT can also provide techniques and methodologies for addressing the criticisms at each of the above three levels, for example:

- **Demand forecasting:** OR provides quantitative and qualitative methods. The former are more used because more accurate than the latter requiring the availability of good historical data. In Finarelli and Johnson (2004), for example, a nine-step quantitative demand forecasting model is described in detail for healthcare management; in Cote and Tucker (2001) four methods for forecasting in healthcare are proposed whose accuracy is discussed and analyzed in Jones et al. (2008). In Beech (2001) a market-based forecasting model for healthcare service is derived and in Myers and Green (2004) a two-step approach is presented. Finally, in Xue et al. (2001) forecasts on the trend of the renal disease in the United States by using autoregressive and exponential smoothing models are performed.
- **Location selection:** it is a typical OR problem whose goal is the selection of the best location for a site. In HC management, the selection concerns the medical sites (either hospitals or clinical centers) taking into ac-

count different factors (for example, the times required by the most disadvantaged users to reach it). For example, in Bruni et al. (2006) a mathematical formulation considering the time in the transplant process and of the spatial distribution of the transplant centers is proposed.

- **Capacity planning:** it concerns the capacity of the clinical centers for treating. For example, in Adan et al. (2009) a mixed integer mathematical model with stochastic lengths of stay for optimizing the resource utilization in a cardiothoracic surgery centre is proposed.
- **Scheduling:** it is related to patients and resources scheduling. The former finds the optimized patients-clinical site/patients-clinical staff schedule in order to minimize the costs. For example, in Persson and Persson (2009), a scheduling problem is solved considering economic, medical and time constraints. The resources scheduling problem is related to the staff and the internal resources (beds, instruments and etc.). For example, in Pato and Moz (2008) a nurse rerostering problem by using a genetic algorithm is addressed.
- **Other issues:** in Aktin and Ozdemir (2009), a two-stage approach for coronary stent manufacturing from a one-dimensional cutting stock problem is proposed; in Flessa (2003), a linear-programming model for the best budget allocation to a set of healthcare resources in Tanzania is formulated; in Bortfeld et al. (2008), the uncertainties problem of the radiation therapy for the cancer patients is addressed; in Wake et al. (2009), the problem of the minimization of the total treatment time in cancer radiotherapy using multi-leaf collimators is analyze; in Nigmatulina et al. (2009), some solving strategies for global pandemic influenza taking into account prevention aspects are designed. Recently,

also some new simulation techniques are integrated in OR methods in order to address specific HC problems like *hospital admission* and *services*, *patient recovery*, *resource planning*, *facility utilization* and *vaccination*.

However, some relevant challenges exist and occur. For example, one is not sure whether the data used is relevant and valid or if the models defined are a correct representation of goals and constraints. Especially the accuracy of the data is a relevant and important issue in a clinical decision making process made up by the three most important phases: *Diagnosis*, *Prognosis* and *Therapy*. Each of this moment is based on identification, measure and interpretation of patients' data.

In this specific scenario, a *Clinical Decision Support System* (CDSS) becomes a fundamental part of the clinical knowledge management technologies. Thanks to the ability of supporting the three above steps, it can be seen as a computer system able to provide reminders, advice and/ or interpretation to a user at a specific time. In Perreault and Metzger (1999), the four functions of a CDSS are listed: *administrative* (concerning clinical coding and documentation, authorization of procedures, and referrals); *managing clinical complexity*; *cost control* (concerning medication orders and avoiding duplicate or unnecessary tests); *decision support* (concerning clinical diagnosis and treatment plan processes). For all the above reasons, a CDSS could also be considered as significant part of the clinical knowledge management technologies (Grandinetti et al. (1998)) supporting the clinical processes and use of knowledge for diagnosis and investigation through treatment and long-term care.

From a generic point of view, a CDSS has to be based on a *Medical Knowledge Based Decision Support Systems* (MKBDSS). A MKBDSS is made up by two main components: a *Medical Knowledge Base* (MKB) and an *Inference Engine* (IF). The former constitutes a relevant set of well known clinical experiences and cases that can be accessible electronically by computers. Thus, it also constitutes a source of possible and relevant data to be used by users and to be constantly updated considering new clinical disease and experiences. Doctors and experts update it with new diseases, therapies, preventions and cares. A *MKBDSS* receives information and patients' data. These inputs are efficiently processed by the *MKB* and by the *IF* to provide in output decisions on diagnosis, prognosis and therapy. It is worth noting that the more the clinical experts update the *MKB*, the more accurate the outputs are.

In Shahsavar et al. (1995), the authors describe a *MKBDSS* (*VentEx*) supporting the decision-making in ventilator therapy. They use real data coming from 12 patients for validating the *MKB*. In Haux (1989), the author describes how and to what extend patients' data in expert systems in order to create clinical knowledge and to perform statistical analysis. Firstly, the pitfalls of goal-oriented mechanisms for the multiple usability of data are described; then, a mechanism for the data acquisition and inference (together with a procedure in order to control the selection bias) is proposed. In Peleg and Tu (2006), the authors review the literature and give some directions and suggestions in order to develop and create usable *MKBDSS*.

In this chapter, we focus the attention on a subset of the services offered by a MWS that could be optimized and efficiently managed by OR: the *Clinical Data Classification*; the *Clinical Predictions* and the *Clinical What-if Analysis*. These issues are correlated to each other and can be seen as three sequential processes.

Data Classification Problem

Firstly, in fact, the patients 'data have to be acquired and consequently classified. It implies the so called *Data Classification Problem* that represents the *Data Categorization* to use them properly. This process optimizes the way for storing data taking into consideration technical, administrative, legal and economic purposes. Data classification can be performed on the base either of the most critical or of the most importance or of the most use value. Modern mechanisms consider the content, the operating platform, the average file size (in megabytes or gigabytes), the last update and reading. The more accurate and advance the classification mechanism is, easier and faster the finding process becomes. This optimization process is very important in medical field where the practice is guided by the empirical observations and then, by the years, a lot of data, also coming from different databases and sources, have been collected. In order to develop usable medical databases, specific classification methods are required. For example, *Artificial Intelligence*, together with specific techniques, is able to manage efficiently the data to obtain knowledge. Moreover, because the data are also characterized by uncertainty, by the years, a set of paradigms have been designed and developed for better managing them. Some strategies belong to the *Supervised Classification* whose goal is to decide, on the base of the information obtained analyzing the previous cases (for example, the symptoms), the more appropriate classification (i.e., establishing the specific disease of a patient).

In Sierra et al. (2001), an overview of different classification approaches is proposed. In particular, the Supervised Classification is applied and a learning algorithm for obtaining a classifier is designed. This approach, in general, needs a data set of N samples, each of them characterized by n different features and symptoms. This learning algorithm, starting from the data set, inducts the classification that will be used in a second step for predicting the class of the next samples. The input data belong to the *training set* and consist of a set of records. Each record has specific attributes and/or multiple features and has also a label identifying its class.

One of easier classification methods is the *Classification Tree (CT)*. A CT is built subdivid-

ing iteratively the records in homogenous subsets in regard to the output variable. This subdivision produces a tree hierarchy, where the subsets of records are called *nodes* and the final ones *leaves*. The nodes are labeled as *attributes*, the arcs (i.e., the branches of the tree) become the possible values for the above attributes and a leaf represents the final class. Thus, the classification mechanism follows a path along the tree from the root to a leaf. The different possible paths are represented by the branches of the tree and they provide a set of *decision rules*.

In the medical area, the attributes represent the patients' data (for example, *age*, *weight*, *blood pressure* and so on); the internal nodes are tests on the attributes; the branches are possible results for these tests performed on the parent node and finally, the leaves represent a specific probability distribution for that class (for example, is the patient affect by a disease? If yes, what is the disease?). Thus, a CT built for medical data is called *Clinical Classification Tree* (CCT).

Figure 7 shows an example of a CCT. The attributes are made up by the value of the blood pressure over the initial 24 hour period; the age and the heartbreak. The initial set of patients is divided on the base of their blood pressure measured over the initial 24 hour period. A first subset is made up by patients whose blood pressure is greater than a threshold; the second whose blood pressure is lower. This last subset belongs to the high risk patients. The first subset is again divided into two subsets on the base of their age. The first subset is made up by patients whose age is greater than 63 years old; the second whose age is lower. This last subset belongs to the low risk patients. The first subset is instead divided into two other subsets: the first has tachycardia; the second has not. The former belongs to the high risk class; the latter to the low risk patients. Through this CCT, an initial set of patients has been classified as either high risk or low risk patients.

In Kershaw et al. (2007), a CCT for indentifying individuals at risk of sexual transmitted disease

(STD) during pregnancy is proposed. It is also showed that this CCT can identify risk factors usually not individuated by some traditional risk screenings. For this reasons, it can be used for the STD treatment, care and prevention.

Once a CT is built, the next step is to prune it, as much as possible in order to easily classify the data even coming from different medical and clinical sources.

One of the most used classification algorithms is the *ID3* algorithm. It is a greedy algorithm because, at each step, performs the move maximizing the good quality of the tree. The tree is built through a top-down policy (the *divide et impera* method): dividing the problem in a finite number of littler sub-problems that usually are easier to be solved. Thus, the algorithm starts from a tree with just the root node and assigns to it all the training instances; then, it selects an attribute and creates as many nodes as the possible values of the selected attribute. Thus, it recursively proceeds using the new nodes as roots for the next iterations. The stooping criterion checks both all the instances of a node belong to the same class (i.e., the node becomes a leaf with the assigned class) and there are no attributes to be used for dividing the tree (i.e., the node becomes a leaf whose

class is the most common among its instances). The algorithm improves the *Concept Learning System* (*CLS*) algorithm.

Let's be *S* the set of training instances (whose cardinality is equal to *c*). The goal is to find the attribute that better divides this set. In the following, a pseudo-code of the algorithm is presented:

An alternative way to proceed is to assign not only a class but a probability distribution for this class.

For example, let's assign 5 values to the last node of a tree: *yes, yes, yes, no* and *no*. To this node it is possible to assign the following probability distribution p(*yes*)=3/5 and p(*no*)=2/5. In this case, the tree is *probabilistic* and not *deterministic*.

A crucial step in building a CT by using the *ID3* algorithm is the *Attribute Selection* that could also distinguish the various implementations. Three are the most common procedure for selecting an attribute: *Information Gain* (typically used by the ID3 algorithm); *Gain Ratio* and *Gini Indices* (used by IBM Intelligent Miner).

The former is mainly based on two concepts: *Entropy (E)* and *Information Gain (G)*:

$$E(S) = \sum (-p(I) \log_2 p(I)) \qquad (1)$$

Figure 7. A CCT example

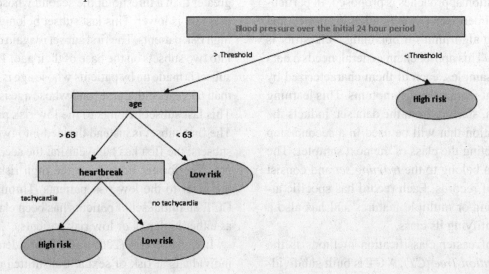

where $p(I)$ indicates the portion of S belonging to the class I and the sum is defined over c. $E(S)$ is equal to 0 if all the components of S belong to the same class (i.e., perfectly classified data). If $E(S) = 1$, the data are totally random. The *Information Gain G*, instead, is defined on a couple *(S,A)*, where A is an attribute:

$$G\left(S, A\right) = E\left(S\right) - \sum \frac{\left|S_v\right|}{\left|S\right|} E\left(S_v\right) \qquad (2)$$

where the sum is over all the possible values v assumed by the attribute A and $S_v \subseteq S_v$ contains all the instances for which the attribute A assumes value v. Among all the attributes, the procedure selects the one whose gain is the greatest. But, this approach prefers the attributes with more different values and this implies the possible risk of *overfitting*.

The *Gain Ratio*, instead, modifies the *Information Gain* technique by taking into account the number of values of the attributes. It introduces the so called *Intrinsic Information* of an attribute that can be seen like the entropy of this specific attribute. The problem related to this approach is an *over-compensation* (an attribute is selected just because its intrinsic information is low).

However, a CCT is not the only method for solving the Data Classification Problem. In Xu and Papageorgiou (2009), a mixed integer linear mathematical model for the multi-class data classification is proposed. A hyper-box representation able to capture disjoint data regions is used. The model minimizes the total number of misclassified data and for this reason a solution approach for assigning potential multiple boxes to each single class is implemented. The computational results show that the approach is competitive in terms of accuracy. In Lu and Han (2003), an overview of different already proposed cancer classification approaches are described and their features in terms of required computational times, accuracy and ability to reveal biologically mean-

ingful gene information are analyzed. Some gene selection methods to be integrated in the cancer classifiers are also introduced. In Desper et alt. (2004), phylogenetic methods to both class discovery and class prediction problems are applied in tumor classification context. In Sharma and Paliwal (2008), the Gradient LDA technique for avoiding the singularity problem related to the within-class scatter matrix is used and its usefulness for cancer classification problem is shown. In Abdel-Aal (2005), it is shown how to use the adductive network classifier committees trained on various features for increasing the accuracy important and necessary in medical diagnosis. Finally, in Piclin et alt. (2004), a *Adaptive Fuzzy Partition* (AFP) algorithm is proposed for classifying an anticancer data set.

Once data are correctly collected and classified, they can be successfully used also for performing predictions on the future information.

Clinical Predictions Problem

The *Clinical Predictions Problem* could be present at different steps in managing HC requirements, for example: to predict either the number of patients arriving in a next period of time to a clinical department or the trend of a clinical value of a specific patient following a specific care. Thus, it could be seen like a problem related to both administrative and organizational aspects and clinical long term cares. The prediction process assumes a very important role in HC management and usually it is performed by the managers who often require the availability and analysis of the historical clinical data. Performing predictions in the clinical environment is not simple at all, for many and relevant aspects: *Data availability* because both the quantitative and qualitative techniques need a consistent historical report for performing reliable predictions in the future and it is a crucial aspect in the clinical field because patients' data are often reserved by privacy law; *Data dynamism* because the clinical data need to be constantly update and consequent arrangements are required for both the internal and the external variables (demography, new technologies and so on); *External factors* because all the methods assume that the external and internal factors remain the same during the predictions and it is generally not true at all. Thus, the manager expertise is required for a right interpretation of the results. For example, in a given clinical department, a manager could be interested in knowing either the future number of patients of a new doctor or if it is advisable that a senior doctor with a large number of patients leaves the department. During the prediction process, the manager has to take into account also external factors that in some case could influence the internal organization of the department. In literature, there are both quantitative and qualitative methods for performing predictions. But, it is worth noting that a manager, before using them, has to analyze all the possibility and then choices the best one (i.e., in general the one that minimizes the presence of errors). The qualitative methods require the ability, experience of the experts and do not exclude the use of simple quantitative instruments (like graphs and simple mathematical operations). They are usually used for the middle-long term predictions and in the case in which the experts have not a sufficient quantity of data in the historical report. Instead, the quantitative ones require the intensive use of mathematical models and instruments and they are typically used for the predictions in the cases in which the experts have a sufficient quantity of data in the historical report.

The notation used in the following is the one introduced in Ghiani et al. (2004). In particular, in the following, with the generic term *demand* is assumed either a demand of the patients for obtaining a health service or a clinical value of a patient/group of patients and it is denoted by d_t (at period t) and T is the current period. By $p_t(\tau)$, $\tau = 1, 2, ...$, the prediction at period $t+\tau$ is denoted. Moreover, in the following, it is assumed the use of quantitative methods and thus they are

described with more details. In general, the trend of the demand could be: *Constant* (a patient has almost the same value of a clinical parameter); *Linear* (the value of a clinical parameter of a patient increases over the horizon); *Periodic* (the value of a clinical parameter of a patient periodically repeats itself).

On the base of an accurate analysis of the trend, a specific prediction method has to be selected and used. In Ghiani et al. (2004), some methods for the above three cases are presented and usually the manager, after analyzing the historical report, has to select the method to be used. For the constant trend, the main prediction methods are:

- The *elementary technique*: it is assumed that the prediction for a period in advance p_{T+1} is equal to the historical data at this period (i.e., $p_{T+1}=d_T$)
- The *exponential smoothing technique*:

$$p_{T+1} = \alpha d_T + \left(1 - \alpha\right) p_T \tag{3}$$

where α is an empiric parameter usually set to either 0.2 or 0.3;

The *moving average technique*

$$p_{T+1} = \sum_{k=0}^{r-1} \frac{d_{T-k}}{r} \tag{4}$$

where r is a parameter and identified the last r-data in the historical report.

For the linear trend, the general computational schema, common to the methods, is the following:

$$p_T\left(\tau\right) = a_T + b_T\tau \quad \tau = 1,2 \tag{5}$$

and the main prediction methods are:

- The *elementary technique* sets $a_T = d_T$ and $b_T = d_T - d_{T-1}$ in Formula (5);

- The *Holt method* sets $a_T = \alpha d_T + \left(1 - \alpha\right)\left(a_{T-1} + b_{T-1}\right)$ and $b_T = \beta\left(a_T - a_{T-1}\right) + (1 - \beta)b_{T-1}$ in Formula (6), choosing $a_1 = d_1$ and $b_1 = 0$;

- The *linear regression* sets

$$b_T = \frac{\dfrac{-(r-1)}{2}\displaystyle\sum_{k=0}^{r-1} d_{T-k} + \sum_{k=0}^{r-1} k d_{T-k}}{\dfrac{r(r-1)^2}{4} - \dfrac{r(r-1)(2r-1)}{6}} \tag{6}$$

$$a_T = \frac{\displaystyle\sum_{k=0}^{r-1} d_{T-k} + b_T \dfrac{r(r-1)}{2}}{r} \tag{7}$$

where r represents the last r-data in the historical report.

the *moving average* sets

$$a_T = 2\gamma_T - \eta_T, \tag{8}$$

$$b_T = \frac{2}{r-1}\left(\gamma_T - \eta_T\right) \tag{9}$$

where γ_T is the average value over the r more recent values and it is computed:

$$\gamma_Y = \sum_{k=0}^{r-1} \frac{d_{T-k}}{r} \tag{10}$$

and η_T is the average value over the r more recent average values and it is computed:

$$\eta_T = \sum_{k=0}^{r-1} \frac{\gamma_{T-k}}{r} \tag{11}$$

For the periodic trend, it is important to identify, before performing predictions, the length of cycle after that the trend repeats itself. This length is denoted by M. In this case the prediction methods usually used are:

The *elementary technique*: it computes the prediction in advance as follows

$$p_T(\tau) = d_{T+\tau-M}, \tau = 1, 2, ..., M. \tag{12}$$

- The *revised exponential smoothing*.
- The *Winters method*.

For the revised *exponential smoothing* method and the *Winters method*, the reader is remanded to Ghiani et al. (2004).

Because of the presence of some prediction errors, the manager has also to take into account the accuracy of a method before selecting it. Usually, the accuracy is evaluated applying a method in the past in order to compute the errors that could be done. Starting from these observations, some measures could be estimated and derived: the *mean absolute deviation*; the *mean absolute percentage deviation* and finally the *mean squared error*. They are usually used for making comparisons between the different prediction methods that a manager could consider.

However, in Schachter et Ramoni (2007), a *Bayesian* network model is built and it is validated on a dataset of 503 new clinical entities with an accuracy of about 78%.

As also reported in Grobman and Stamilio (2006), an efficient clinical prediction system has to satisfy two main characteristics: to be able to perform predictions in an accurate way; to be easy used in the medical setting.

The common prediction methods are not able to satisfy both the characteristics and thus recently, the researchers have to be involved and interested in funding and designing new and more advanced methods.

The nomograms represent advanced methods used for predictions and visualization of results. They are often used also in medical field and for the treatment of some diseases with the main function to visualize clinical results as shown in (Lubsen et alt. (1978)). They have been also used to present probabilistic classification models in clinical field and oncology (Kattan et alt. 1998) because using simpler graphical presentation, easy to be read and interpreted, and may be used to predict outcome probabilities without the computer or calculator.

In Shabsigh and Bochner (2006), the current status of outcome predictive models for bladder cancer is summarized and the focus is particularly on the ability of nomograms to predict disease recurrence, progression, and patient survival. The authors argue that the nomograms have emerged as excellent tools providing improved predictive accuracy compared to standard categorical models and have proven to be easily adapted for clinical use. In fact, they facilitate patient counseling, treatment decision, and risk stratification for clinical trials. However, the authors also individuate and remark the most relevant and important points for some future works in using nomograms for treating specific diseases.

In Cho et al. (2008), a new nonlinear localized radial basis function (LRBF) kernel and a new visualization system for risks analysis are developed. In particular, the latter applies a nomogram and LRBF kernel to visualize the results improving the interpretability of results maintaining high prediction accuracy.

In Sandhu et alt. (2010), the prognostic accuracy of fracture risk assessment tool (FRAX™) and Garvan nomograms in an independent Australian cohort are evaluated.

In literature, some examples of using nomograms for diabetes treatment exist. In Wells et al. (2008), a tool for predicting the risk of mortality in patients with 2-type diabetes is developed. The analysis is manly based on a Cox proportional hazards regression model defined by using medication class and predictor variables selected on the base of their relation with mortality. The nomograms are here used for predicting, for example, 6-year probability of survival. In Chant et al. (2005), the nomograms are used for an intensive blood glucose control.

However, in Grobman and Stamilio (2006), a detailed overview of the most useful methods for clinical predictions is proposed. The attention is mainly focused on the *predictive nomograms*. These methods are able to take into consideration the effects of some independent multiple variables and consequently present graphically their interactions. However, the statistical methods underlying them may use very complicate multivariable techniques that do not assume distributions of the data. Despite their intrinsic complexity, the final prediction model is very clear because each independent variable is associated to a number of points that are summed to each other in order to detect the total score representing the prediction of interest.

In Kattan et alt. (2003) and in Kattan et alt. (2006), the clinical value of the predictive nomograms is shown by performing evaluations on patients affected by prostate cancer. The authors develop predictive nomograms allowing, for example, a 5-years survival predictions after either a surgical procedure or radiotherapy. They conduct a nonrandomized analysis of 1,677 patients treated with three dimensional conformal radiation therapies and that have been followed until their deaths, and the time at which they have developed metastasis has been noted. Thus, a nomogram for predicting the 5-year probability of developing metastasis is defined and validated. It has also shown an excellent ability to discriminate among patients in an external validation data set.

The predictive nomograms can be also easily implemented on a computer, entering the required input factors. By specific algorithms, in fact, the probability outcome can be automatically computed. It is usually assumed to have three scales ("*points*", "*total score*" and "*outcome probability*", whose values are shown in Figure 8). If, for example, the aim is to evaluate the probability that a patient has a specific pathology, then the method can be computerized as follows.

1. For each factor that influences the prediction, evaluates the relative values after patient's test;

2. For each of these values, associates the bigger value in the" *points*" scale;
3. Computes the total score in the relative scale;
4. Draws a black line from the value at step 3 until the "*outcome probability*" scale.

The example in Figure 8 represents a specific case in which three factors (*A*, *B* and *C*) influence the prediction that a patient has pathology. The patient's test has registered the following values: 30 for A, 20 for B and finally 80 for C. The relative points in the correspondent scale are 40, 40 and 60 and thus the total score is 140. The value 0.15 corresponds at 140 total score in the "*outcome probability*" scale. It means that the patient has pathology with 15% of probability.

The second advanced prediction method is based on the *Cart Analysis*. It is mainly based on building a specific tree and the specialists can easily predict following the paths on the tree. It is predictive method that uses no parametric techniques for evaluating the data and the initial population (historical report) is divided in subgroups considering the critical factors. The way used for selecting these factors and the order of the splitting data in subgroups are both the result of a mathematical algorithm that maximizes the accuracy of the prediction. Considering the example illustrated in Figure 8, the relative tree, in this case, is shown in Figure 9.

This method is simple to be implemented because it does not require complex mathematical formulas and the building of the tree is immediate. Usually, the built tree is coherent with the methods already used by the physicians. For example, for better understanding and analyzing the tests and the clinical analysis of a specific patient, the clinicians use specific characteristics in order to individuate the most appropriate therapies and then the most likely outcomes. The Cart Analysis is already used with success for predicting: the death of immunodeficiency syndrome and decompensate heart failure patients; the ectopic pregnancy.

In Guzick et al. (2001), the Cart Analysis is used for distinguishing men with sub fertility with the use of semen analysis variables. Some topics and general reviews can be found in Zhang and Singer (1999) and in Lemon et al. (2003).

Clinical What-if Analysis

The *What-if analysis*, instead, consists in evaluating the performances of a real system under specific conditions and assumptions that cannot be immediately applied in a low-cost way. For example, it is a valid tool to be used for the systems management because it provides predictions on the future trends of the most significance variables. The goal is to find the best conditions for the system in exam (for example, the best

Figure 8. An example of predictive nomograms

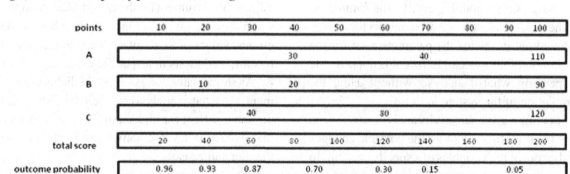

Figure 9. An example of using cart analysis

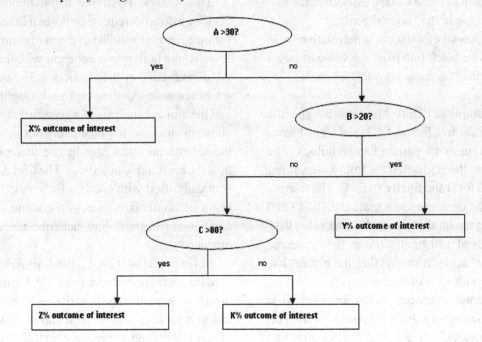

resources allocation at minimum cost). Usually, the conditions of a system are modified and controlled directly by varying some parameters. Thus, the what-if analysis (or alternately *sensitivity analysis*) directly acts on the parameters and their possible values.

At being so, this type of analysis is usually able to give an appropriate answer to the following question: *What happens to the system (in terms, for example, of its stability) if some parameters are modified?*

To obtain an answer to this question, the manager could use either mathematical models or the processes simulation. Especially, the simulation of the models uses the what-if analysis for changing without problems the parameters set for the execution of the system. In fact, it is not possible to perform what-if analysis without using the simulation of the system in exam.

For this reason, sensitivity analysis can be seen like the investigation of all the possible changes and errors of the variables of a specific system. In

Clemson et al. (1995); Hamby (1994) and Lomas and Eppel (1992), some reviews are proposed. However, they are more focused on the mathematical aspects rather than the theoretical ones. In Pannell (1997), a theoretical and methodological review is proposed and described. It is argued that an understanding of *Bayesian probability* revision could help to interpret a sensitivity analysis. Moreover, some approaches of sensitivity analysis are proposed. In the medical field, because the data are more affected by randomness, the what-if analysis helps to better analyze the system in exam and to understand how it could vary. It represents an important instrument for the experts, for example, when they are interested in analyzing how some clinical values of a patient can vary consequently to some variations in a specific care.

As shown later, for example, in diabetic treatment, the what-if analysis can help the expert and the same patient for understanding how can vary the glycaemia level if something is changed in the diet and/or care.

A Web-Based System for Diabetes

In this section, a concrete example of a MWS for diabetes treatment (developed and detailed in Grandinetti and Pisacane (2011)) is described and analyzed taking into consideration all the aspects discussed in this Chapter. The specific medical field concerns diabetes because the patients need continuous and usually long-term cares and supports and because this pathology requires specific therapies. At being so, it could be useful to have an automatic web-based system for providing the most important services to patients and doctors.

The web based system developed in Grandinetti and Pisacane (2011) provides a continuous and interactive support to the patients during the delicate process of the therapy and a common platform to the doctors and specialists for sharing information and news in this specific clinical field.

For example, this software tool performs predictions on the future glycaemia level of the patients over a specific time horizon and what-if analysis (showing how the glycaemia level could vary after some changes into the therapy and/or diet); allows an effective information and suggestions sharing (creating a virtual community among the specialists); informs users about their health condition (througha specific classification algorithm based on the *CT*) and, finally, allows patients to plan a daily diary.

The main motivation for describing this system in this Chapter concerns the merge of two different aspects (discussed above): software engineering (i.e., web services) and Operations Research methods for optimizing the healthcare processes. Thus, it could be seen like a valid interactive software instrument for supporting the patients and the doctors, at the same time and with different specific functionalities.

In Grandinetti and Pisacane (2011), after a detailed overview of the literature, solutions for the different aspects, already described in this Chapter, are proposed: the *Data Classification*, in the system, is treated by using the Classifica-

tion Trees and implementing the *ID3* algorithm; the already cited *Prediction* techniques are all implemented in a software library available to the users; the *What-if analysis* is implemented by a specific compartmental model; the *patient's daily diet* is addressed by a mathematical model planning the diet taking into account constraints on the lower and upper bounds imposed on the nutrients and foods and minimizing the presence of sugar. It is worth noting that the web service application becomes the best way to easily provide all the above functionalities offered by Operations Research.

After the authentication phase, the system proceeds to recognize the user as either a new patient or a diabetic or a doctor. In the first case, the patient registers herself; inserts the personal clinical values and waits for an answer from the system (and consequently in this phase the specific data classification algorithm is invoked). In the second case, the patient inserts the personal current glycaemia level and the system updates the electronic diary and decides whether or not the user needs an insulin dose or some changes in the diet. In the last case, the doctor can create and use new knowledge by using specific diagnosis models (for example, the classification models for the predicting and establishing presence/absence of diabetes in a new clinical case). The doctor, moreover, can view detailed data for a specific model (accuracy evaluations, parametric values and so on); eliminate a model; use a model for forecasting; save a diagnosis for a specific clinical case and provides online support for patients during emergency events.

About the implementation aspects: *SOA* and *Data Mining* are used and the application is adapted to be deployed on a *Web Services Resource Framework* (an implementation of Open Grid Services Architecture) container within the *Globus* toolkit framework.

The system in exam reaches the interoperability and the other interesting features of service oriented computing and it could be deployed on any system in an easily way. The application can be also used in a grid environment like a consumer or a producer with very little changes. A database system for storing patients' and doctors' information is implemented and the *JDBC* library is used for accessing the operations. Finally, *WEKA* library is also used for the data mining operations.

In figure 10 (Source: Grandinetti and Pisacane, (2011)), the whole architecture of the application in exam is shown and presented. The blue level is related to the user interface and represents the external and visible part of the web based application. It is what the user (patient or doctor) can directly use and through it the same user can interact with the different functionalities of the system. It also represents the visible integration of the Operations Research methodologies with the Web Services functionalities. The red level, instead, represents the aspects related to Operations Research. Finally, the green level represents the implementation aspects related to Web Services and Optimization problems. For this reason, the more effective way to read and analyze the

Figure 10. Architecture

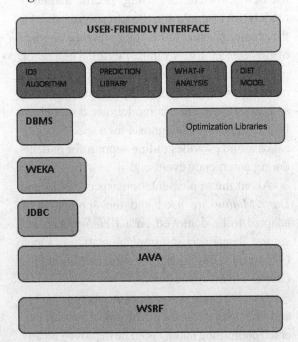

architecture depicted in figure 10 is to use a top-down approach: the visible part is only the interface and the internal parts represent the various engines used for aiming the goals. By using this application, the users can communicate to each other with a relevant decrement over all the costs and medical expenses due to the diagnosis, prognosis and therapy for the long-term diabetes treatment and care. It could be seen like the result of merging software engineering aspects with Operations Research methods and thus like an interactive support for the worldwide users.

Optimal Medical Web Services Composition

The automated composition of WSs or the process of forming new value added WSs is one of the most relevant and important challenges in the semantic WS research area.

Semantics is able to describe capability and processes of WSs. However, the functional description of WSs needs using formal models. In Claro et alt. (2005) and in Constantinescu et alt. (2004), the authors describe two different approaches using matrices to represent the Web services domain. In particular, in the former, an AI planning problem is solved where actions are viewed as tasks. An action is formally described with their preconditions and effects and a task is executed by concrete WSs, according to a service/task (row/column) matrix. In the latter, instead, a method to store WS (using an input/output (row/column) matrix) is proposed. Both matrix models do not propose reasoning about those matrices and, consequently, matrices are simply considered as representation models. From Health Telematic Networks (in Wu et alt. (2003)) to regression planning based on extensions of PDDL (Dermott (1997)), different planning approaches have been proposed for the composition of WSs. In Narayanan et alt. (2002), a situation calculus is proposed to represent WS and Petri nets for describing its execution behaviors.

In Benatallah et alt. (2002), a planner is declared as a state chart, and the resulting composite services are executed by replacing the roles in the chart by selected individual services. Mao et alt. (2001) propose a composition path, a sequence of operators that compute data, and connectors that provide data transport between operators. Zhang et alt. (2003) propose a forward chaining approach to solve a planning problem.

In Freddy and Alain (2006), the authors a formal model (i.e. Causal link matrix) as a necessary starting point to apply problem-solving techniques such as regression-based search for WSs composition. The suggested model is innovative and it is also able to support a semantic context, on the contrary of the above cited models, for finding a solution for an AI planning-oriented WS composition. They also motivate the validity of defining formal and mathematical models for WSs composition considering a specific healthcare scenario in which six different WSs exist and communicate to each other. This scenario is focused on the telemedicine collaboration in order to reduce the added consulting, examination and fees and for improving the patients flow management. Obviously, a complete and exhaustive clinical observation in a hospital is not a realistic issue for some reasons related to costs (especially in the case of elderly). A possible solution to this problem could consist in the implementation and definition of a WS that automatically follows-up the patients by a reliable WS interoperation. For the specific scenario made up by six WSs: *WS1* could return the blood pressure of a patient; *WS2* and *WS3* could return the supervisor and a physician of an organization, respectively; *WS4* could return a warning level given a blood pressure; *WS5* could return the Emergency department given a warning level and, finally *WS6* could return an organization given a warning level. In this scenario, the optimization algorithms and techniques of OR, defined for the WSs composition, have to be able not only to find the feasible plans but also the best one considering specific

optimization criteria. Because, on the other hand, a user request could correspond not only to one specific service but also to a set of WSs, the composition process becomes relevant for obtaining the expected result. Moreover, because, usually, there are many services with the same goal but different features, non-functional criteria have to be defined for distinguishing them. In this way, the final user is able to choose the optimal solution.

For example, in Claro et alt. (2005), service quality variables as non-functional criteria for making an optimal service composition for a goal are introduced. The authors propose multi-objective optimization techniques to find a set of optimal Pareto solutions from which a user can choose the most interesting tradeoff.

CONCLUSION

Nowadays, the main goal of the HCOs is to provide their services to the final users improving the quality and at the same time reducing the total costs (in part due to the clinical and medical expenses). In this Chapter, we have shown how *Web Services* (new and advanced software technologies) can provide information systems combining different software applications. They can also guarantee a heterogeneous connectivity to users, an interactive support of the doctors, interconnectivity between the *HCOs* and an effective information sharing; allow a costs reduction and improve the quality of the services.

We have firstly described how to model Medical Web Services for providing the healthcare services taking into consideration the relative challenges; then, we have demonstrated how Operations Research can optimize the healthcare services, dealing with the major aspects: *Data Classification*, *Medical Predictions* and *What-if Analysis*. At this level, we have provided a concrete example describing a web based software for the diabetes treatment (Grandinetti and Pisacane, (2011)). This application shows how it is also possible to combine two different subjects: the Operations Research methodologies to optimize the Healthcare processes and the Web Services technologies for providing their services in a user-friendly way. Finally, we have also shown how the optimal mathematical models of OR can also support the important and relevant WS composition process, especially in the medical field.

REFERENCES

W3C. (2001). Web services description language (WSDL) 1.1. Retrieved from http://www.w3.org/TR/wsdl.html

Abdel-Aal, R. E. (2005). Improved classification of medical data using abductive network committees trained on different feature subsets. *Computer Methods and Programs in Biomedicine, 80*(2), 141–153. PubMed doi:10.1016/j.cmpb.2005.08.001

Ackerman, E., Gatewood, L. C., Rosevear, J. W., & Molnar, G. D. (1965). Model studies of blood-glucose regulation. *The Bulletin of Mathematical Biophysics, 27*, 21–37. PubMed doi:10.1007/BF02477259

Adan, I., Bekkers, J., Dellaert, N., Vissers, J., & Yu, X. (2009). Patient mix optimization and stochastic resource requirements: A case study in cardiothoracic surgery planning. *Health Care Management Science, 12*, 2. doi:10.1007/s10729-008-9080-9

Aktin, T., & Ozdemir, R. G. (2009). An integrated approach to the one-dimensional cutting stock problem in coronary stent manufacturing. *European Journal of Operational Research, 196*, 737–743. doi:10.1016/j.ejor.2008.04.005

Ankolenkar, A., Burstein, M., Hobbs, J., Lassila, O., Martin, D., & McIlraith, S. … Zeng, H. (2001). DAML-S: A semantic markup language for Web services. In *Proceedings of SWWS'01* (pp. 411-430). Stanford, USA.

Anzböck, R., & Dustdar, S. (2003). Interorganizational workflow in the medical imaging domain. In *Proceedings of the 5th International Conference on Enterprise Information Systems (ICEIS)*. Angers, France: Kluwer Academic Publishers.

Anzböck, R., & Dustdar, S. (2003a). *Medical Web services workflows with BPEL4WS*. Retrieved from http://www.infosys.tuwien.ac.at/Staff/sd/papers/MedicalServicesWorkflowsWithBPEL4WS.pdf

Anzböck, R., & Dustdar, S. (2004). Modeling medical Web services. *BPM 2004, Conference on Business Process Management, LNCS 3080*, (pp. 49–65). Springer.

Anzböck, R., & Dustdar, S. (2005). Modeling and implementing medical Web services. *Data & Knowledge Engineering, 55*(2), 203–236. doi:10.1016/j.datak.2005.03.009

Balakrishnan, S., Narayanasamy, R., & Savarimuthu, N. (2009). Feature subset selection using Nomogram in Type II Diabetes databases. *Indian Journal of Medical Informatics, 4*(1), 5-5. ISSN 0973-9254

Beech, A. J. (2001). Market-based demand forecasting promotes informed strategic financial planning. [PubMed]. *Healthcare Financial Management, 55*(11), 46–56.

Benatallah, B., Sheng, Q. Z., Ngu, A. H. H., & Dumas, M. (2002). *Declarative composition and peer-to-peer provisioning of dynamic Web services* (pp. 297–308). ICDE.

Bergman, R. N., Phillips, L. S., & Cobelli, C. (1981). Physiologic evaluation of factors controlling glucose tolerance in man: measurement of insulin sensitivity and beta-cell glucose sensitivity from the response to intravenous glucose. *The Journal of Clinical Investigation, 68*(6), 1456–1467. PubMed doi:10.1172/JCI110398

Bortfeld, T., Chan, T. C. Y., Trofimov, A., & Tsitsiklis, J. N. (2008). Robust management of motion uncertainty in intensity-modulated radiation therapy. *Operations Research, 56*(6), 1461–1473. doi:10.1287/opre.1070.0484

Breu, R., Hafner, M., Weber, B., Alam, M., & Breu, M. (2004). *Towards model driven security of inter-organizational workflows. Institut for Informatics.* University of Innsbruck.

Bruni, M., Conforti, D., Sicilia, N., & Trotta, S. (2006). A new organ transplantation location-allocation policy: A case study of Italy. *Health Care Management Science, 9*(2), 125–142. PubMed doi:10.1007/s10729-006-7661-z

Chant, C., Wilson, G., & Friedrich, J. O. (2005). Validation of an insulin infusion nomogram for intensive glucose control in critically ill patients. *Pharmacotherapy, 25*(3), 352–359. PubMed doi:10.1592/phco.25.3.352.61594

Cho, B. H., Yu, H., Lee, J., Chee, Y. J., Kim, I. Y., & Kim, S. I. (2008). Nonlinear support vector machine visualization for risk factor analysis using nomograms and localized radial basis function kernels. *IEEE Transactions on Information Technology in Biomedicine, 12*(2). PubMed.

Cimino, J. J., Hayamizu, T. F., Bodenreider, O., Davis, B., Stafford, G. A., & Ringwald, M. (2009). The caBIG terminology review process. *Journal of Biomedical Informatics, 42*(3), 571–580. PubMed doi:10.1016/j.jbi.2008.12.003

Claro, D. B., Albers, P., & Hao, J. K. (2005). *Selecting Web services for optimal composition.* In ICWS: International Workshop on Semantic and Dynamic Web Processes.

Clemson, B., Tang, Y., Pyne, J., & Unal, R. (1995). Efficient methods for sensitivity analysis. *System Dynamics Review, 11*, 31–49. doi:10.1002/sdr.4260110104

Conforti, D., & Guido, R. (2005). Kernel-based support vector machine classifiers for early detection of myocardial infarction. *Optimization Methods and Software, 20*(2-3), 401–413. doi:10.1080/10556780512331318164

Constantinescu, I., Faltings, B., & Binder, W. (2004). Type based service composition. In *WWW Conference Alternate Track Papers & Posters,* (pp. 268-269).

Cote, M. J., & Tucker, S. L. (2001). Four methodologies to improve healthcare demand forecasting. [PubMed]. *Healthcare Financial Management, 55*(5), 54–58.

Deci, E. L., & Ryan, R. M. (1991). A motivational approach to self: Integration in personality. In R. Dienstbier (Ed.), *Nebraska Symposium on Motivation, vol. 38: Perspectives on motivation* (pp. 237-288). Lincoln, NE: University of Nebraska Press.

Dermott, D. M. (1997). *PDDL - The planning domain definition language.*

Desper, R., Khan, J., & Schäffer, A. A. (2004). Tumor classification using phylogenetic methods on expression data. *Journal of Theoretical Biology, 228*(4), 477–496. PubMed doi:10.1016/j.jtbi.2004.02.021

Dong, S., Insley, J., Karonis, N. T., Papka, M. E., Binns, J., & Karniadakis, G. (2006). Simulating and visualizing the human arterial system on the teragrid. *Future Generation Computer Systems*, *22*(8), 1011–1017. doi:10.1016/j.future.2006.03.019

Eichelberg, M., Aden, T., Riesmeier, J., Dogac, A., & Laleci, G. (2005). A survey and analysis of electronic healthcare record standards. *ACM Computing Surveys*, *37*(4). doi:10.1145/1118890.1118891

Finarelli, H. J. Jr., & Johnson, T. (2004). Effective demand forecasting in 9 steps. [PubMed]. *Healthcare Financial Management*, *58*(11), 52–58.

Flessa, S. (2003). Priorities and allocation of health care resources in developing countries: A case-study from the Mtwara region, Tanzania. *European Journal of Operational Research*, *150*(1), 67–80. doi:10.1016/S0377-2217(02)00786-5

Foster, I., von Laszewski, G., Thiruvathukal, G. K., & Toonen, B. (1998). A computational framework for telemedicine. *Future Generation Computer Systems*, *14*(1–2), 109–123. doi:10.1016/S0167-739X(98)00013-2

Fowler, M., & Scott, K. (1998). *UML distilled: Applying the standard object modeling language (M. Fowler with K. Scott* (Addison, W. L. O. T. S., Ed.).

Freddy, L., & Alain, L. (2006). *A formal model for semantic web service composition* (pp. 385–398). ISWC.

Ghiani, G., Laporte, G., & Musmanno, R. (2004). *Introduction to logistics systems planning and control*. Wiley.

Grandinetti, L., Conforti, D., & De Luca, L. (1998). CAMD and TeleEEG: Software tools for telemedicine applications. In Sloot, P., Bubank, M., & Hertzberger, B. (Eds.), *High Performance Computing and Networking* (*Vol. 1401*, pp. 64–73). Lecture Notes in Computer Science Berlin, Germany: Springer–Verlag.

Grandinetti, L., & Pisacane, O. (2008). Web services for optimal clinical support systems. In *Proceedings of the 2008 International Conference on Semantic Web and Web Services*, Las Vegas, Nevada, USA.

Grandinetti, L., & Pisacane, O. (2011). Web based prediction for diabetes treatment. *Future Generation Computer Systems*, *27*(2), 139–147. doi:10.1016/j.future.2010.08.001

Grobman, W. A., & Stamilio, D. M. (2006). Methods of clinical prediction. *American Journal of Obstetrics and Gynecology*, *194*(3), 888–894. PubMed doi:10.1016/j.ajog.2005.09.002

Gruber, T. (1993). A translation approach to portable ontology specifications. *Knowledge Acquisition*, *5*, 199–220. doi:10.1006/knac.1993.1008

Guzick, D. S., Overstreet, J. W., Factor-Litvak, P., Brazil, C. K., Nakajima, S. T., Coutifaris, C., et al. (2001). Sperm morphology, motility, and concentration in fertile and infertile men. *The New England Journal of Medicine*, *345*, 1388–1393. PubMed doi:10.1056/NEJMoa003005

HL7 Organization. *Health Level 7*. (2000). Retrieved from http://www.hl7.org

Hamby, D. M. (1994). A review of techniques for parameter sensitivity analysis of environmental models. *Environmental Monitoring and Assessment*, *32*, 135–154. doi:10.1007/BF00547132

Harrell, F. E. (2001). *Regression modeling strategies: With applications to linear models, logistic regression, and survival analysis*. New York, NY: Springer.

Hashmi, N., Myung, D., Gaynor, M., & Moulton, S. (2005). A sensor-based, Web service-enabled, emergency medical response system. In *Proceedings of the Mobisys 2005 Workshop on End-to-End Sense and Respond Systems.*

Haux, R. (1989). Knowledge-based decision support for diagnosis and therapy: On the multiple usability of patient data. [PubMed]. *Methods of Information in Medicine, 28*(2), 69–77.

Hludov, S., Meinel, C., Noelle, G., & Warda, F. (2000). *PACS for teleradiology*. Retrieved from medicineonline.de.

Hübner, U. (2008). The supply chain model of ebusiness in healthcare. In *eBusiness in Healthcare, Health Informatics, Part IV*, (pp. 299-318). DOI: 10.1007/978-1-84628-879-1_14

Jaques, P. A., & Viccari, R. M. (2006). Considering students' emotions in computer-mediated learning environments. In Ma, Z. (Ed.), *Web-based intelligent e-learning systems: Technologies and applications* (pp. 122–138). Hershey, PA: Information Science Publishing.

Jones, S. S., Thomas, A., Evans, R. S., Welch, S. J., Haug, P. J., & Snow, G. L. (2008). Forecasting daily patient volumes in the emergency department. *Academic Emergency Medicine, 15*(2), 159–170. PubMed doi:10.1111/j.1553-2712.2007.00032.x

Kattan, M. W., Eastham, J. A., Stapleton, A. M., Wheeler, T. M., & Scardino, P. T. (1998). A preoperative nomogram for disease recurrence following radical prostatectomy for prostate cancer. *Journal of the National Cancer Institute, 90*, 766–771. PubMed doi:10.1093/jnci/90.10.766

Kattan, M. W., Zelefsky, M. J., Kupelian, P. A., Cho, D., Scardino, P. T., & Fuks, Z. (2003). Pretreatment nomogram that predicts 5-year probability of metastasis following three-dimensional conformal radiation therapy for localized prostate cancer. *Journal of Clinical Oncology, 21*, 4568–4571. PubMed doi:10.1200/JCO.2003.05.046

Kershaw, T. S., Lewis, J., Westdahl, C., Wang, Y. F., Rising, S. S., Massey, Z., & Ickovics, J. (2007). Using clinical classification trees to identify individuals at risk of STDs during pregnancy. *Perspectives on Sexual and Reproductive Health, 39*, 141–148. PubMed doi:10.1363/3914107

Kooper, R., Shirk, A., Lee, S. C., Lin, A., Folberg, R., & Bajcsy, P. (2008). 3D medical volume reconstruction using Web services. *Computers in Biology and Medicine, 38*(4), 490–500. PubMed doi:10.1016/j.compbiomed.2008.01.015

Koulouzis, S., Zudilova-Seinstra, E., & Belloum, A. (2010). Data transport between visualization web services for medical image analysis. *Procedia Computer Science, 1*(1), 1721–1730. doi:10.1016/j.procs.2010.04.194

Lemon, S. C., Roy, J., Clark, M. A., Friedmann, P. D., & Rakowski, W. (2003). Classification and regression tree analysis in public health: Methodological review and comparison with logistic regression. *Annals of Behavioral Medicine, 26*, 172–181. PubMed doi:10.1207/S15324796ABM2603_02

Lomas, K. J., & Eppel, H. (1992). Sensitivity analysis techniques for building thermal simulation programs. *Energy and Building, 19*, 21–44. doi:10.1016/0378-7788(92)90033-D

Lu, Y., & Han, J. (2003). Cancer classification using gene expression data. *Information Systems, 28*(4), 243–268. doi:10.1016/S0306-4379(02)00072-8

Lubsen, J., Pool, J., & Van der Does, E. (1978). A practical device for the application of a diagnostic or prognostic function. [PubMed]. *Methods of Information in Medicine, 17*, 127–129.

Lundberg, N. (2000). *Impacts of PACS on radiological work*. Department of Informatics, University of Gothenburg.

Mao, Z. M., Randy, H., Katz, E., & Brewer, A. (2001). *Fault-tolerant, scalable, wide-area Internet service composition*.

Marović, B., & Jovanović, Z. (2006). Web-based grid-enabled interaction with 3D medical data. *Future Generation Computer Systems, 22*(4), 385–392. doi:10.1016/j.future.2005.10.002

Marsh, A., Simistirab, F., & Robb, R. (1998). VR in medicine: Virtual colonoscopy. *Future Generation Computer Systems, 14*(3-4), 253–264. doi:10.1016/S0167-739X(98)80025-3

Martin, J. (2001). Web services: The next big thing. *XML Journal, 2*. Retrieved from http://www.sys-con.com/xml/

Mayumi, H., & Masakazu, O. (2005). Applying XML Web services into health care management. In *Proceedings of the 38th Annual Hawaii International Conference on System Sciences (HICSS'05): Vol. 06.* Washington, DC: IEEE Computer Society.

Moralis, A., Pouli, V., Papavassiliou, S., & Maglaris, V. (2009). A Kerberos security architecture for Web services based instrumentation grids. *Future Generation Computer Systems, 25*(7), 804–818. doi:10.1016/j.future.2008.11.004

Myers, C., & Green, T. (2004). Forecasting demand and capacity requirements. [PubMed]. *Healthcare Financial Management, 58*(8), 34–37.

Narayanan, S., & McIlraith, S. (2002). *Simulation, verification and automated composition of Web services*. In: Eleventh International World Wide Web Conference. NEMA and Global Engineering Group. (1998). *DICOM 3 standard*. Retrieved from http://www.nema.org

Nigmatulina, K. R., & Larson, R. C. (2009). Living with influenza: Impacts of government imposed and voluntarily selected interventions. *European Journal of Operational Research, 195*(3), 613–627. doi:10.1016/j.ejor.2008.02.016

Oosterwijk, H. (2005). *DICOM basics*. OTech Inc/Cap Gemini Ernst and Young.

Pannell, D. J. (1997). Sensitivity analysis of normative economic models: Theoretical framework and practical strategies. *Agricultural Economics, 16*, 139–152. doi:10.1016/S0169-5150(96)01217-0

Pato, M. V., & Moz, M. (2008). Solving a bi-objective nurse rerostering problem by using a utopic pareto genetic heuristic. *Journal of Heuristics, 14*(4), 359–374. doi:10.1007/s10732-007-9040-4

Peleg, M., & Tu, S. (2006). Decision support, knowledge representation and management in medicine. IMIA Yearbook of Medical Informatics 2006. *Methods of Information in Medicine, 45*(1), 72–80.

Perminov, V. V., Perepelitsina, E. Y., Antsiperov, V. E., & Nikitov, D. S. (2008). Remote medical consultations over the Internet: An implementation based on Web-service technologies. *Journal of Communications Technology and Electronics, 53*(1), 104–112. doi:10.1134/S1064226908010130

Perreault, L., & Metzger, J. (1999). A pragmatic framework for understanding clinical decision support. *Journal of Healthcare Information Management, 13*(2), 5–21.

Persson, M., & Persson, J. A. (2009). Health economic modeling to support surgery management at a Swedish hospital. *Omega, 37*, 853–863. doi:10.1016/j.omega.2008.05.007

Piclin, N., Pintore, M., Wechman, C., & Chrétien, J. R. (2004). Classification of a large anticancer data set by adaptive fuzzy partition. *Journal of Computer-Aided Molecular Design, 18*(7), 577–586. PubMed doi:10.1007/s10822-004-4076-0

Polemi, D. (1998). Trusted third party services for health care in Europe. *Future Generation Computer Systems, 14*(1–2), 51–59. doi:10.1016/S0167-739X(98)00008-9

Power, D. J., Politou, E. A., Slaymaker, M. A., & Simpson, A. C. (2006). Securing Web services for deployment in health grids. *Future Generation Computer Systems, 22*(5), 547–570. doi:10.1016/j.future.2005.09.003

Rajasekarana, M. P., Radhakrishnana, S., & Subbarajb, P. (2010). Sensor grid applications in patient monitoring. *Future Generation Computer Systems, 26*(4), 569–575. doi:10.1016/j.future.2009.11.001

Ratib, O., Swiernik, M., & McCoy, J. M. (2003). From PACS to integrated EMR. *Computerized Medical Imaging and 1020 Graphics,* 2003, (pp. 207–215).

Revet, B. (1997). *DICOM cookbook.* Retrieved from ftp:// ftp-wjq.philips.com/ medical/ interoperability/ out/ DICOM_Information/

Sandhu, S. K., Nguyen, N. D., Center, J. R., Pocock, N. A., Eisman, J. A., & Nguyen, T. V. (2010). Prognosis of fracture: Evaluation of predictive accuracy of the FRAX™ algorithm and Garvan nomogram. *Osteoporosis International, 21,* 863–871. PubMed doi:10.1007/s00198-009-1026-7

Schachter, A. D., & Ramoni, M. F. (2007). Clinical forecasting in drug development. [PubMed]. *Nature Reviews. Drug Discovery, 6,* 107–108. doi:10.1038/nrd2246

Shabsigh, A., & Bochner, B. H. (2006). Use of nomograms as predictive tools in bladder cancer. *World Journal of Urology, 24,* 489–498. PubMed doi:10.1007/s00345-006-0122-y

Shahsavar, N., Ludwigs, U., Blomqvist, H., Gill, H., Wigertz, O., & Matell, G. (1995). Evaluation of a knowledge-based decision-support system for ventilator therapy management. *Artificial Intelligence in Medicine, 7*(1), 37–52. PubMed doi:10.1016/0933-3657(94)00025-N

Sharma, A., & Paliwal, K. K. (2008). Cancer classification by gradient LDA technique using microarray gene expression data. *Data & Knowledge Engineering, 66*(2), 338–347. doi:10.1016/j.datak.2008.04.004

Sierra, B., Inza, I., & Larrañaga, P. (2001). Lecture Notes in Computer Science: *Vol. 2199. On applying supervised classification techniques in medicine* (pp. 14–19).

Sloot, P. M. A., Coveney, P. V., Ertaylan, G., Müller, V., Boucher, C. A. B., & Bubak, M. T. (2009). *HIV decision support: From molecule to man. Philosophical Transactions of the Royal Society of London. Series A: Mathematical and Physical Sciences, 367, 2691–2703.* PubMed.

Systems, B. E. A. IBM, Microsoft, SAP AG and Siebel Systems. (2003). *Business process execution language for Web services,* version 1.1. Retrieved from http:// www-106.ibm.com/ developerworks/ library/ ws-bpel/

Von Berg, J., Schmidt, J., & Wendler, T. (2001). *Business process integration for distributed applications in radiology.* Philips Research. In Third International Symposium on Distributed Objects and Applications (DOA_01), Rome, Italy, 2001.

Wake, G. M. G. H., Boland, N., & Jennings, L. S. (2009). Mixed integer programming approaches to exact minimization of total treatment time in cancer radiotherapy using multileaf collimators. *Computers & Operations Research, 36*(3), 795–810. doi:10.1016/j.cor.2007.10.027

Wang, H., Huang, J. Z., Qu, Y., & Xie, J. (2004). Web services: Problems and future directions. *Web Semantics: Science. Services and Agents on the World Wide Web, 1*(3), 309–320. doi:10.1016/j.websem.2004.02.001

Wells, B. J., Jain, A., Arrigain, S., Yu, C., Rosenkrans, W. A., Jr., & Kattan, M. W. (2009). Predicting 6-year mortality risk in patients with type 2 Diabetes. *Diabetes Care, 32*(5), e60. PubMed doi:10.2337/dc09-0327

Wu, D., Parsia, B., Sirin, E., Hendler, J. A., & Nau, D. S. (2003). *Automating DAML-S Web services composition using SHOP2* (pp. 195–210). ISWC.

Xu, G., & Papageorgiou, L. G. (2009). A mixed integer optimisation model for data classification. *Computers & Industrial Engineering, 56*(4), 1205–1215. doi:10.1016/j.cie.2008.07.012

Xue, J. L., Ma, J. Z., Louis, T. A., & Collins, A. J. (2001). Forecast of the number of patients with end-stage renal disease in the United States to the year 2010. [PubMed]. *Journal of the American Society of Nephrology, 12*, 2753–2758.

Zhang, H., & Singer, B. (1999). *Recursive partitioning in the health sciences*. New York, NY: Springer-Verlag.

Zhang, R., Arpinar, I. B., & Aleman-Meza, B. (2003). *Automatic composition of Semantic Web services* (pp. 38–41). ICWS.

KEY TERMS AND DEFINITIONS

Decision Support System: "*A computer-based system that enables management to interrogate the computer system on an ad hoc basis for various kinds of information on the organization and to predict the effect of potential decisions beforehand. Abbreviated DSS.*" from *Sci-Tech Dictionary* (*McGraw-Hill Dictionary of Scientific and Technical Terms*, 6th edition, published by The McGraw-Hill Companies, Inc.)

Medical Information Systems: "*Standardized methods of collection, evaluation or verification, storage, and retrieval of data about a patient.*" from *Sci-Tech Dictionary* (*McGraw-Hill Dictionary of Scientific and Technical Terms*, 6th edition, published by The McGraw-Hill Companies, Inc.)

Optimization: "*The procedure or procedures used to make a system or design as effective or functional as possible, especially the mathematical techniques involved.*" from *Answers.com* (http://www.answers.com).

Chapter 5
The Physical Layer Aspects of Wireless Networks

Neetesh Purohit
Indian Institute of Information Technology, India

ABSTRACT

The modern era belongs to wireless communication systems. The cellular networks, which were originally designed for voice services, have now been upgraded to accommodate Internet services. Wi-Fi and Wi-Max systems have been explicitly developed for delivering data services over wireless channels. Just like wired systems, wireless systems also follow the layered architecture for developing or accessing various Internet services; still, there exist significant differences between the technologies used at various layers for the similar purpose. Special design requirements of physical layer due to distinct properties of wireless channel have caused these differences. Low bandwidth supported by the channel, poor equipment capabilities, et cetera, features require special attention in developing various Internet services intended to be accessed by wireless devices. This chapter addresses various aspects of the physical layer of a wireless channel for developing a basic understanding of the problems, existing solutions, and proposals for future networks.

INTRODUCTION

The breakthrough in the physical layer technologies over the last few decades enables portable mobile terminals to achieve very high data rates and avail any kind of Internet based service be- sides traditional voice services. Increased data rate and anytime anywhere service feature of wireless networks are used by modern society in reframing its existing business and social activities besides creating several new activities. Data rate of wireless networks is still incomparable with wired network technology but the freedom of moving and doing the work simultaneously gives them

DOI: 10.4018/978-1-4666-0203-8.ch005

an upper edge. Significant modifications in upper layers of Internet protocol stack has been done for accessing Internet services using wireless devices but without solving the bottlenecks associated with physical layer technologies, it would not have been possible. The evolution of physical layer technologies for wireless systems took more than a century. Over this period many ups and downs have been observed in radio technology. Specifically it underwent a golden age during 1890-1940. It had attracted best engineers for developing new technologies for building efficient and robust wireless communication systems. The popularity of amplitude modulation (AM) based systems, the struggle of Armstrong in establishing superiority of frequency modulation (FM) based systems, Invention of television (TV) etc. are some of the memorable happenings belonging to this golden age (Calhoun, 2003). At the same time several simplex type (one way) and stationary duplex type (two ways) wireless communication systems were deployed for different applications. Development of a mobile duplex communication system was a dream for wireless engineers of that era. Realization and commercialization of this dream took a long time due to two major reasons. First was the transfer of wireless technologies to military during Second World War, thus leaving no technical development was available in commercial domain. Second reason lies in the fundamental limitations of available technologies at that time. Specifically physical layer technologies of that era were not able to overcome the typical characteristic features of the wireless channels. First generation cellular network (1G) was frequency modulation (FM) based analog system which had very poor spectral efficiency and service performance. Deployment of second Generation (2G) cellular network in 1990 brings another golden age for wireless communication which is also known as 'digital radio revolution'. It is still continuing, by getting boosted from the deployment of third generation (3G) and emergence of fourth generation (4G) wireless networks. 2G networks are optimized for voice traffic but perform poorly on data traffic. A new air interface called radio transmission technology (RTT) was defined as 3G - a cellular system which is equally good for both voice as well as data traffic. But the supported data rate is still not sufficient for running some applications. Since wireless LAN technology has been improved to support very high data rates, thus a common platform has been defined where different air interfaces should converge and is now called 4G networks. This chapter addresses the evolution of various physical layer technologies from 1st generation to 4th generation cellular networks. The physical layer of other modern wireless networks has also been covered in this chapter.

Fundamentals of Communication Systems

The channel, transmitter and receiver are the three essential modules of any electrical communication system. If conducting wires or optical fiber cables are used as a channel, then it is called wired communication systems, when space itself is used as channel then it is called wireless communication system. Channel is the most important part of a communication system because it connects source with destination units and governs their design specifications. These units are required for overcoming the undesired effects produced by the channel and achieving efficient communication. The wired channels are engineerable because appropriate manufacturing technology may be used and at least in principle a given set of characteristic features can be easily achieved. On the other hand, wireless channel is known to be nonengineerable because we can't do any modification in characteristic features of the channel itself. Thus all the engineering intelligence should be applied in transceiver designing for getting faithful communication over wireless channel. Higher transmission power requirement due to unguided power spreading, fading and interference due to extreme environment conditions, etc.

limitations complicate the designing of wireless communication systems. Being hand held device the mobile station must be low weight, small sized and highly power efficient. These requirements add further constraint in developing transceivers for wireless systems. So it is quite understandable, why it takes a long time for developing a mobile duplex communication system.

A copper wire channel carries electric current or voltage and its performance is mainly governed by the thermal noise. The optical fiber channel carries light and its performance is governed by dispersive and attenuation characteristics of the fiber. The space carries electromagnetic (EM) waves whose transmission involves several propagation mechanisms like scattering, diffraction, etc which causes multipath propagation. Doppler Effect is observed with the communication of both EM as well as sound waves whenever there exist some relative motion between transmitter and receiver or the environment contains moving objects. These effects cause dispersion in time domain as well as in frequency domain. These dispersions define the channel characteristics and govern the performance of wireless systems. Fading, which is defined as fluctuation in the power levels of received signal at the receiver, is an additional feature associated with wireless channels. When both transmitter and receiver are stationary (e.g. microwave link used in telephone system) then line of sight communication at large height above the ground should be used for minimizing the degradation due to the above mentioned effects. In modern wireless mobile networks, the mobile station is always located close to ground i.e. in the vicinity of large number of objects like trees, buildings, vehicle, human, animals, etc. which create significant multipath component thus spreading as well as fading. Since these effects cannot be avoided thus these are required to be explicitly considered while designing the system.

A wireless transceiver should contain source coder, channel coder, modulator, amplifier, signal estimator, equalizer, etc. as sub modules. The circuit realization of various sub-modules in wireless systems is significantly different as compared to wired system due to scarcity of bandwidth, scarcity of power etc. The techniques like source coding, channel coding, modulation etc primarily govern the bandwidth requirement where as diversity, equalization, type of amplifier along with a particular modulation technique etc factors govern the power efficiency associated with a transceiver. Choice of the bandwidth efficient or the power efficient technique is a major issue in transceiver design which depends upon several factors like computational complexity, latency, implementation complexity etc. This chapter describes various design technologies and tradeoffs between them. Starting from classical design approach, Shannon theory based design and the modern design concepts (which have been moved well beyond the framework of communication systems laid down by Shannon) have been summarized. The characteristic features of a wireless channel, the theoretical framework for quantifying them and their implication in transceiver designing are summarized in section II. Depending upon several other limitations, either transmitter oriented or receiver oriented strategies or some time a combination of both may be used for improving the performance of wireless communication systems. These strategies are discussed in section III and section IV respectively.

THE WIRELESS CHANNEL CHARACTERISTICS

The space provides an unguided wireless channel, thus making the transmitted EM waves spread in several directions, including the direction of receiver. The reflection, refraction, diffraction and scattering phenomenon generate several copies of the transmitted signal. Many of them reach their destination by a different path, thus each one has different phase and power level. These components may or may not be resolvable depending

Figure 1. General view of a wireless channel with various propagation mechanisms

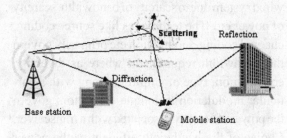

upon the structure of wireless channel and the data rate. This process produces time domain dispersion and is known as multipath propagation. Additionally the Doppler Effect observed in mobile environment causes spectral dispersion too. Besides dispersion both the mechanisms are also responsible for generating heavy fluctuation in received signal strength. This phenomenon is known as fading. Dispersion and fading are unavoidable features of wireless systems which are required to be dealt at physical layer. Thus proper understanding of dispersion and fading is needed.

Time Domain Dispersion

Broadening of pulses or time domain dispersion is an important effect produced by multipath propagation. Dispersion introduces inter symbol interference (ISI) in the transmitted symbols which degrades correlation between received symbols and the standard set of symbols, hence creating the chances of introducing error. Higher dispersion causes more ISI thus resulting in higher error rate. It defines a fundamental limitation on the data rate that can be supported by the wireless channel making the estimation of dispersive characteristics of a wireless channel a very important part of wireless system design. Following parameters have been defined for the quantification of fading generated by multipath propagation.

- **Power delay profile:** Due to multipath propagation, several echoes of transmitted signals are observed at the receiving point over a span of time. The pictorial representation of power of all echoes Vs their time delay with respect to first arriving signal is called power profile of the channel. Figure 2 shows power profile of a typical channel.

- **Mean excess delay:** It is the normalized first moment of the power profile which can be defined as

$$\bar{\tau} = \frac{\Sigma_k a_k^2 \tau_k}{\Sigma_k a_k^2} = \frac{\Sigma_k P(\tau_k)\tau_k}{\Sigma_k P(\tau_k)} \tag{1}$$

- **rms delay spread:** It is the normalized standard deviation of power delay profile which is defined as

$$\sigma_\tau = \sqrt{\overline{\tau^2} - (\bar{\tau})^2} \tag{2}$$

$$\overline{\tau^2} = \frac{\Sigma_k a_k^2 \tau_k^2}{\Sigma_k a_k^2} = \frac{\Sigma_k P(\tau_k)\tau_k^2}{\Sigma_k P(\tau_k)} \tag{3}$$

- **Maximum excess delay spread (X dB):** It is defined as the maximum delay associated with an echo which is X dB below the maximum value of echo received at any

Figure 2. The power delay profile of a typical channel

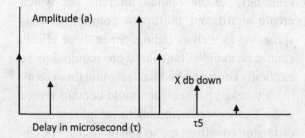

instant of time. In figure 2 it is the fifth received pulse ($\tau 5$).

- **Coherence bandwidth:** Various propagation mechanisms like scattering, diffraction etc are frequency dependent phenomenon i.e. time delay associated with each multipath component and thus the rms delay spread is a function of frequency contents of the transmitted signal. The exact dependence is a function of the structure of wireless channel i.e. location, shape and size of various objects causing scattering, diffraction, etc. Low value of rms delay spread assures low ISI, so higher correlation will exist between the transmitted and the received symbols which in turn ensures lower error rate. The range of frequency over which significant correlation between transmitted and received signal exists is called coherence bandwidth. It means that two tones separated by coherence bandwidth or more will produce uncorrelated signals at the same receiving point. Depending upon 50% or 90% correlation level following expressions have been estimated for the same.

$$B_c \approx \frac{1}{5\sigma_t} \text{ for } 50\% \text{ and } B_c \approx \frac{1}{50\sigma_t} \text{ for } 90\%$$

(4)

Experimental measurements are used for estimating coherence bandwidth. Either channel sounding techniques should be used for finding power profile from which coherence bandwidth should be estimated or it may be directly measured by increasing data rate of transmitter till received symbol shows 50% or 90% correlation in statistical sense. Error rate will be lower if the bandwidth (BW) of transmitted signal is less than the coherence bandwidth. If a communication system requires higher BW than coherence bandwidth of the channel then additional processing of received signal e.g. equalization should be used. This issue will be elaborated in section 2.3.2

Doppler Spread

The relative motion between the transmitter and receiver or the movement of other objects in the close vicinity of stationary transmitter and stationary receiver causes Doppler Effect. Thus, new frequency contents are generated which cause the broadening of spectral contents of transmitted signal at the destination. The amount of broadening is directly proportional to the relative velocity and dependent upon direction as well.

If single tone signal having frequency f_c is transmitted from transmitter and it is received by the receiver having maximum relative velocity v m/sec, moving at an angle θ from transmitter then the deviation from f_c in either direction will be $=(v.f_c.cos\theta)/c$, where c is the velocity of light. The maximum deviation $f_d = v.f_c/c$ will define the bandwidth of received signal. Instead of single tone, if the transmitted signal has bandwidth $= W$ then BW of received signal will be $= W + 2f_d$ (from $W - f_d$ to $W + f_d$). The spectral broadening automatically alters the time domain properties of received signal too as compared with transmitted signal thus the correlation between transmitted and received signals is reduced. Higher velocity results in more broadening in frequency domain, more distortion in time domain resulting in low correlation, which may lead to higher error rate. There exists maximum correlation at the start of transmission, afterwards it becomes smaller and smaller over the time till they become totally uncorrelated. Coherence time has been defined as the time duration for which sufficient correlation exists between the transmitted and the received symbols. After expiration of coherence time the channel characteristics should again be estimated for faithful recovery of transmitted signal from received signal. Thus it is generally desired that at least one complete packet should be transmitted within coherence time of the channel. Following expression is generally used for the coherence time (T_c) (Rappaport, 2006)(Oestges & Clerckx, 2007).

$$T_c = \sqrt{\frac{9}{16\pi f_d^2}} = \frac{0.423}{f_d} \quad (5)$$

Effects of Fading on the Performance of Communication System

The fading is defined as the fluctuation in the power levels of received signal at the receiver. When both the transmitter and the receiver are stationary e.g. microwave link used in telephone system, then these affects are minimized by using line of sight communication at a height much greater than the ground. It is not possible in cellular mobile system where mobile stations are always located close to the ground. In the vicinity of ground large number of objects like trees, buildings, vehicle, human, animals, etc. exists which create significant multipath components. In this scenario there should exist fading along with time and frequency dispersions. Following four channel types have been defined for classifying the wireless channels-

1. Flat slow fading channel (Ts<<Tc i.e. Bs>>B_D, and Bs<<Bc i.e. Ts>>σ)
2. Flat fast fading channel (Ts>Tc, Bs<B_D, and Bs<<Bc i.e. Ts>>σ)
3. Frequency selective slow fading channel (Ts<<Tc i.e. Bs>>B_D, and Bs>Bc i.e. Ts<σ)
4. Frequency selective fast fading channel (Ts>Tc, Bs<B_D, and Bs>Bc i.e. Ts<σ)

Each category title has 3 segments, the first segment defines the nature of time domain dis-

persion offered by the channel, second segment defines the frequency domain dispersion offered by the channel and third segment invariably contains the word 'fading' which is in accordance with the fact that the dispersion may or may not cause distortion but fading always exists in all channels. Dispersions and associated parameters have already been discussed in the last section which plays the main role in defining the above classes as indicated in the bracketed terms. Several models have also been proposed for estimating the fading characteristics of a wireless channel like Rayleigh, Ricean, Nakagami, Weibull etc. In case of non fading channels, all coefficients of the channel may be assumed to be the same (unity) but depending upon environmental conditions one of above model will give better approximation of the same. The output signal produced by channel (i.e. the input signal to receiver) should be given as

$$y = \sqrt{E}.h + n \quad (6)$$

where n is the complex AWGN. The Rayleigh fading model is generally used when no line of sight component exists between a transmitter and receiver pair whereas Ricean fading model is more suitable whenever there exists a line of sight component between the two.

Probability density function (pdf) for Rayleigh channel is given by

$$p(r) = \begin{cases} \dfrac{r}{\sigma^2} \exp\left(-\dfrac{r^2}{2\sigma^2}\right) & (0 \leq r \leq \infty) \\ 0 & r < 0 \end{cases} \quad (7)$$

For Recian channel the pdf is given by

$$p(r) = \begin{cases} \dfrac{r}{\sigma^2} e^{-\frac{(r^2+A^2)}{2\sigma^2}} I_0\left(\dfrac{A_r}{\sigma^2}\right) & for\,(A \geq 0, r \geq 0) \\ 0 & for\,(r < 0) \end{cases} \quad (8)$$

The additive white Gaussian noise (AWGN) channel model is used in studying the conductive wired channels. If polar line coding format is employed with symbol energy (E) and power of white noise (N_0) then the bit error rate,

$$BER = Q\left[\sqrt{2p}\right] \tag{9}$$

where $\rho = E/N_0$ and the Q function is defined as the area under the Gaussian tail. Hence BER decreases exponentially with increase in signal to noise ratio. This result can be used as a reference for comparative performance analysis of wireless channels in various fading types. The received signal level fluctuates as $h.\sqrt{E}$ where h is predicted by the specific fading model thus modified BER for a channel having probability density function p(h) can be evaluated as

$$BER = \int Q\left[\sqrt{2.p}\right] hp(h)\, dh = \frac{1}{4p} \text{ (for Rayleigh fading channel)} \tag{10}$$

Strikingly, in non fading AWGN channel, BER decreases exponentially however, the decrease varies inversely in Rayleigh fading channel. It should now be clear that in wireless channels fading will cause very high error rate as compared to the wired channels. This may be further enhanced if certain conditions on data rate and speed of mobile station (MS), in comparison to coherence bandwidth and coherence time of the wireless channel, are not satisfied (Oestges & Clerckx, 2007)(Molisch, 2003)(Lu, 2002).

The Constraints in Designing Transceiver for Wireless Networks

The typical characteristics of wireless channel and many other features associated with the practicability of the overall system create several constraints in the transceiver design for wireless networks. These can be summarized as follows:

- Being a hand held device, the mobile unit must be small in size and should have low weight too. These features restrict the display size, input capabilities, storage capacity and above all the computational power of such devices. For real time applications computationally complex technologies cannot be used with them. These features not only affect the physical layer design but are very important in designing upper layers too.

- Antenna is an integral part of every wireless system. The antenna theory suggests that the physical length of antenna should be at least 1/10 of the wavelength at which it is supposed to work. It requires that mobile devices must operate on very high frequency so that the antenna length should remain within few inches. With restriction on size, choosing a high gain antenna is a typical task.

- Mobile systems are getting power from battery i.e. they have limited power supply. Thus power efficient techniques are required to be used at all levels specifically in power amplification of transmitted signal. It is the main issue behind the development of cellular systems although many authors have emphasized on its frequency reuse feature.

- Wireless channels are nonclonable. Thus bandwidth is another precious commodity. Heavy cost is associated with getting the license of a single radio frequency (RF) channel. It requires the selection of bandwidth efficient technologies for source coding, channel coding, modulation etc.

- The wireless channel is dynamic in nature due to adverse environmental conditions, multipath propagation and Doppler Spread. Wireless systems are required to overcome their effects and minimize the error rate. Extra efforts are needed for avoiding the occurrence of error by improving signal reception using the diversity technique and controlling the inter symbol interference by using the equalization technique. Efficient error control coding techniques should also be used for rectifying the errors. These techniques are discussed in the following sections (Calhoun, 2003)(Giannakis et al., 2001)(Gu, 2008).

TECHNIQUES FOR EFFICIENT TRANSMISSION ON WIRELESS CHANNEL

Communication involves the transmission of information bearing signal from the source point to a distant point. All such signals inherently possess analog nature but the analog communication systems are highly inefficient systems thus these have been replaced by the digital communication systems. All the modern wireless communication systems are digital and they invariably contain a source coder which is responsible for efficient representation of message signal generated by the end user. The channel coder provides error control capabilities but the nature of signal is still baseband which cannot be efficiently transmitted. Thus modulator is another integral part of transmitter which places the desired compressed information into appropriate frequency band. In order to meet the attenuation offered by the channel, signal amplification is needed before it is radiated by the antenna.

Source Coding and Data Compression

The bandwidth is a scarce resource in wireless networks, hence source coding and data compression are very important building blocks. These techniques define exact number of bits to be transmitted and govern the quality of regenerated signal at destination. The basic idea of source coding can be traced back to Information theory suggested by Shannon. The probability of occurrence of a particular message governs its information content. The source coding involves efficient representation of source symbols. Large number of lossless compression techniques like Huffman coding, Lemple-Ziv coding, run length encoding etc. are based on the source coding principle. Large compression may be achieved by combining digital signal processing techniques with some basic source coding techniques but such compressions techniques involves loss of some information when uncompressed. The complex algorithms may reduce the bandwidth requirements to a large extent but they need more computational power and create more latency. Settling this tradeoff towards lower bandwidth side along with satisfactory signal quality, at receiving end, is the main criterion in wireless transceiver designing.

Speech is the most important commodity in communication engineering. There exist several methods for digitizing the speech signal e.g. pulse code modulation (PCM), a nondifferential time domain technique, requires 64kbps data rate for generating toll quality voice but it may be reduced to about 32 kbps when frequency domain sub band coding (SBC) technique is used. Even 32 kbps is too high for wireless channels. Thus the approach of coding has been changed from waveform coding to the source coding. The linear predictive coders are developed which analyze the voice segment and generate a report which is transmitted to destination. The decoder is able to synthesize the voice signal from the received report. Power spectral density, autocorrelation, voiced, unvoiced, etc. properties of speech signal and various digital signal processing schemes are exploited by the linear predictive encoder (LPC) used in modern cellular mobile system for achieving low data rate e.g. the data rate requirement is reduced to less than 14kbps for GSM (Rappaport, 2006)(Proakis, 2001).

Channel Coding

Channel coding refers to the systematic addition of redundant bits at transmitter side and their removal at receiver side such that a finite number of transmission errors can be detected. The correction of errors may be done either by asking for retransmission or by appropriately processing the received codeword. The former technique is known as backward error correction (BEC) where as latter is known as forward error correction (FEC) systems. In correcting same number of errors FEC code length is more (more bandwidth) than the required BEC code length. But the retransmission mechanism enhances the effective bandwidth requirement of BEC. Low error rate requires very few retransmissions so BEC is suitable, but the error prone wireless systems need FEC. The wireless channel has dynamic characteristics; therefore it demands optimization in FEC protocol. It is done by introducing the concept of incremental redundancy, which enhances the bandwidth efficiency at the cost of computational complexity. The EDGE technology supports incremental redundancy scheme and 9 different data packets, called modulation and coding formats (MCS). MCS-1 has highest error correcting capabilities (lowest data rate) where as MCS 9 has highest data rate (lowest error correcting power). Radio block is the basic unit of transmission, which is divided into four parts and transmitted in four consecutive slots of designated packet data channel (PDCH) i.e. length of a frame is 4 time slots. The structure of a radio block depends upon MCS selected by Link Adaptation (LA) protocol depending upon current radio condition. On unsuccessful transmission, IR will incrementally transmit redundancy using same or different MCS of same family (MCS 9/6/3 or MCS 7/5/2) till decoding is successful (Glisic, 2007).

Just like source coding schemes the bandwidth requirement of error control coding schemes can also be traded for the computational complexity involved in generating the code words at the transmitter and regeneration of message from the received codeword at the destination. The features of convolution coding like simple generation mechanism, very high error correcting capability etc enable it to be preferred in several wireless systems over other coding schemes. The convolutional encoder is represented by (n, k, L) where k is number of message bits used to generate a code word, n is the length of the code word and L is the number of codewords that can be influenced by a message bit during its stay in the encoder (It depends upon the length of encoder). The code trellis and the state diagram are alternative ways of representing a convolutional encoder. These representations show the contents of encoder before and after generation of codeword defined as the current and the next state of the encoder respectively. Each possible input bit string along with the respective output codeword should be mentioned in showing the transitions from the current to the next state. Thus given a code trellis and input bit stream, respective codeword stream can be easily generated. If the code trellis and a stream of received codeword (may be affected by channel noise) are known at the receiving end, then the respective input bit stream can be generated with significantly low BER. Viterbi, sequential and feedback decoding techniques have been widely used for decoding purpose. Viterbi decoding technique possesses maximum error correction capability but high latency, storage and computation requirements limit the use of Viterbi method. Sequential Decoding is an alternate way in which output is generated after each received codeword but it has very high error rate. The Feedback Decoding is a compromise between Viterbi and sequential decoding in which first output is available after predetermined number of steps (e.g. 3), so it possesses moderate delay and moderate error correction capability (Proakis, 2001)(Carlson et al., 2010). Development of various computationally efficient systems has allowed the designers of wireless systems to use more robust codes like turbo codes which need complicated iterative decoders.

Modulation

Baseband transmission of signal is highly impracticable. The signals are required to be converted into bandpass format for efficient transmission which is the primary job of a modulator at the transmitting side. Modulation is a nonlinear process which generates new frequency components out of which some are desired and others are undesired. The range of desired frequency components directly governs the RF bandwidth requirements of the system where as the properties of undesired components create new problems like adjacent channel interference, choice of power amplifier, etc. Hereunder a few widely used modulation techniques in wireless communication systems are discussed.

Phase Modulation Techniques

The phase modulation techniques offer great saving in terms of bandwidth but it has a trade-off with increased bit error rate. Generation of abrupt phase shifts is another limitation of PSK systems. It may trigger generation of out of band components by the amplifier section. BPSK possesses highest possible phase shift of π which is retained by QPSK system with added advantage of enhanced bandwidth efficiency at the same BER. The merits of QPSK can be availed along with a maximum possible instantaneous phase shift of $\pi/2$ by introducing a delay element in one of the input lines of QPSK modulator. It is called offset QPSK system (Proakis, 2001).

Frequency Modulation Techniques

The frequency shift keying uses two orthogonal frequencies for representing logic 0 and logic 1. It requires higher bandwidth than PSK technique. When the frequencies are chosen such that there exist smooth transition of phase with any arbitrary change of input symbol then it is called continuous phase FSK (CFSK). The minimum shift keying (MSK) is a CFSK type technique which possesses the minimum separation between the orthogonal frequencies so that the continuous phase shift characteristic can be achieved. Although it requires more bandwidth than QPSK system but offers low out of band components thus giving rise to adjacent channel interference. The Gaussian minimum shift keying (GMSK) forces the input stream to pass through a Gaussian shaped low pass filter then uses an MSK modulator. The filter causes spreading of pulses and results in intersymbol interference (ISI) but it generates the constant envelope waveforms with significantly low out of band components (Carlson et al., 2010).

Coherent and Non Coherent Detection

There exist two alternate ways of data reception in digital communication systems. The coherent reception system uses matched filters or correlators which are optimum filter thus minimizing BER. It needs tight synchronization control between the transmitter and the receiver and hence are employed in forward link in cellular system where separate synchronization channels are available. The non coherent system does not need the synchronization overheads but they have high BER. It uses envelope detectors and locally estimated bit sync signal for data regeneration (Carlson et al., 2010).

Power Amplification

A power amplifier draws DC power from the battery of mobile devices and boosts the RF power of transmitted signal. Gain, Bandwidth, noise figure, slew rate, stability etc are some important parameters associated with the amplifier design. Significant amount of battery power, which is highly precious, is consumed by the power amplifier as compared to any other operation done by the wireless device. Thus power efficiency is the most important concern for wireless systems. The linear amplifiers like class A, Class B, etc. produce very low distortion produced and at the same time they possess poor power efficiency. Thus they may be suitable for downlink transmission (BTS to MS) but not good for mobile terminals. The non linear amplifiers provide very high power efficiency but the cost is required to be paid in terms of heavy distortion. The distortion may be kept under some level by designing the characteristics of input signal to non linear amplifiers such that non linear distortion should be minimized. The abrupt phase characteristic of modulated signal is primarily responsible for non linear distortion. The modulation techniques which produce continuous phase in modulated signal are needed for using power efficient amplifiers which ensures longer lifetime thereby reducing the effective cost of mobile terminals. Discussion in last section shows that greater phase continuity requires more transmission bandwidth enhancing the operational cost. This tradeoff has been settled down in favor of former in GSM system by adopting continuous phase GMSK technique where as in favor of later in CDMA based IS-95 systems by using abrupt phase QPSK technique. The reason lies in the capability of CDMA technique which needs very low transmission power but very high bandwidth making bandwidth efficiency more important than the power efficiency. Thus linear amplifiers are better.

There exist two designing approaches for power amplifiers viz analog design and the switching design. Class A, Class B, Class AB and Class C power amplifiers belong to the former category where as Class D belongs to switching category. In analog design approach the transistors

operate in their active region and produce linear output if configured as class A, class B or class AB. Nonlinear output will be produced if class C configuration is used. The efficiency of class C amplifier is 75% as compared to 65% in class B and 50% in class A which is in reverse order of the non linear distortion produced by them. Switching amplifiers possess 100% power efficiency thus these have brought a phenomenal change in communication system design. The transistors in switching amplifiers operate in either saturation state (full current but no voltage drop across it) or cutoff state (full supply voltage across it but no current). In both states the net power consumption in terms of heat is zero which explains the 100% efficiency tag associated with it. It has a comparator in which the signal is accepted on one terminal and the other terminal is connected to a high frequency reference waveform. It generates PWM as output waveform, the switching output stage does the amplification and the final LC lowpass filter does the needful reconversion which does not consume any power in removing high frequency contents. The reference frequency should be at least 10 times higher than the highest frequency of the signal which is needed to be amplified. This generates pulse width modulated signal and the switching output stage gives the desired amplification to this PWM signal. The LC low pass filter regenerates the amplified version of input signal without consuming any power. The Switching amplifiers have emerged after introduction of class C amplifiers. Thus these have been designated as class D. Some people are incorrectly calling it digital amplifiers by observing 'D' in its class and use of switching elements in the circuits, but it should be clear that switching amplifiers basically amplify the analog signals (Tasic et al., 2009)(Glisic, 2007).

The Antenna

No wireless communication is possible without an antenna. Thus it is an integral part of all wireless communication systems. The antenna converts the electrical energy into EM waves at the transmitting end which is carried by the space to the receiving end where another antenna performs the inverse task. Both, the acceleration and the deceleration of charge in a conductor cause radiation of EM wave from it. The transmission lines are designed such that the radiation should be minimized because useful power is required to be delivered to the load connected at the end of the transmission line. But antenna is a specially designed structure which maximizes the radiation so that a distant load may be energized by capturing these radiations. There exist several electric (E) and magnetic field (H) components in the close vicinity of transmitting antenna but most of them die out as the distance increases. Above a distance of $2L^2/\lambda$ (L is largest dimension of antenna and λ is the wave length) following Maxwell's equations, a time varying electric field generates a time varying magnetic field which in turn regenerates similar electric field and so on. This mechanism causes the propagation of EM waves. The power associated with EM waves is described by a poynting vector in terms of radiation density

W *(in Watt/(meter². steradian)) = E (in Volt/(meter². steradian)) x H (in Ampere/(meter². steradian))*
(11)

It may be integrated over a spherical surface (infinitesimal area $dA = r^2 sin\theta d\theta d\varphi$) for obtaining total radiated power if the source of the EM wave is assumed to exist at its centre. Alternatively radiation intensity which is defined as the power radiated by an antenna per unit solid angle, it may be used for finding total radiated power by integrating it over the total solid angle. Essentially the radiation intensity

$(U) = W.r^2$ Watt/steradian
(12)

Antenna Parameters

Following are the important parameters associated with an antenna

- **Radiation pattern:** Distribution of radiated power around the antenna is defined as radiation pattern which depends upon several antenna design parameters like length/aperture, feeding mechanism etc. The highest area lobe is called major lobe, other lobes are called the minor lobe or the side lobe. The minor lobe just opposite of major lobe and is called the back lobe. The side lobe levels and the front to back lobe power level govern the interference, hence playing a very important role in selecting the antenna for a particular application. The radiation pattern can be divided into three categories and accordingly antennas can be classified. The spherical pattern (Isotropic antenna) is the first category which is used for reference purposes for accessing various characteristic features of a practical antenna but no physical antenna have precisely spherical radiation pattern, although it can be approximated. Doughnut pattern (Omnidirectional antenna) is the second category which has equal radiated power in a particular plane (the circular patter) but it reduces to zero in moving away from this plane. This is a desirable in public broadcasting applications like terrestrial TV, radio etc. The third category radiation pattern is known as directional pattern (Directional antenna). Large number of practical antennas falls into this category. It is desirable in fixed point to point links like telephone microwave towers, geostationary satellite links etc.

- **Half power and first null beamwidth:** The angle between half power points on either side with reference to the maximum point of main lobe is called half power beamwidth, whereas the angle between the nulls adjacent to main lobe is called first null beamwidth. These are used to estimate the directional characteristics of an antenna. Lower beamwidth indicates highly directional antenna.

Directivity and Gain: The ratio of radiation intensity in the direction of major lobe to the radiation intensity when same antenna is assumed to have isotropic radiation pattern is defined as directivity.

$$D = U/U_0 = 4\pi \, (U/Prad) \tag{13}$$

Since it is defined in terms of radiated power, it does not take antenna losses into account. There may exist some reflection whenever the characteristic impedances of adjoining devices do not match, the ohmic losses invariably remain with conductors etc. The total input power requirement is a more useful quantity in designing the complete system. Thus the gain of an antenna is defined as the ratio of radiation intensity in the direction of major lobe to the radiation intensity corresponding to input power when same antenna is assumed to have isotropic radiation pattern.

$$Gain = U/(U_0 \, corresponding \, to \, Pin) = U/(Pin/4\pi) = 4\pi \, (U/Prad)(Prad/Pin) = (Directivity)(efficiency) \tag{14}$$

Antenna is definitely a passive device thus radiated power (*Prad*) will always be smaller than the input power (*Pin*). But in a specific direction it is much higher than the uniform radiation thus reducing the transmission power requirement which is equivalent of achieving amplification. Thus the antenna gain is precisely known as directive gain.

- **Radiation Resistance:** It is a fictitious quantity defined for accounting the power radiated by an antenna. If a current I_g is flowing in the transmission circuit and is radiating P_{rad} amount of power, then the radiation resistance R_r should be defined such that $P_{rad} = (1/2)|I_g|^2.R_r$. Higher value of radiation resistance is equivalent to more radiated power for same value of transmitter current. On the other hand the ohmic resistance of transmitter circuitry should be kept as low as possible so that losses can be minimized. At the receiving end the power delivered to the load is the desired power and the power dissipated in the radiation resistance represents the scattered or reradiated power.

- **Polarization:** The orientation of electric flux lines defines the polarization of EM wave. It may be either linear (vertical or horizontal with respect to earth) or elliptical (clockwise or counterclockwise). Circular polarization is a special type of elliptical polarization. The polarization of an antenna is defined in terms of the polarization of EM wave produced by it i.e. a vertically polarized antenna means the antenna produces or receives vertically polarized waves. It is especially important at receiving side where the polarization of antenna should be matched with the desired EM wave. The polarization loss factor defined as the square of the magnitude of the dot product between the unit vectors in the direction of the antenna and the incident wave governs the amount of power intercepted by the receiving antenna.

- **Effective length and Effective Aperture:** Effective length is a vector quantity which gives the open circuit voltage at the receiving side on multiplication with the incident electric field. It may be more or less than the physical length of the antenna. Similarly the ratio of power delivered to the load at the receiving side to the incident power density is called the effective area (aperture) of antenna. The ratio of effective area to the physical area is known as the aperture efficiency of an antenna. The effective aperture of an antenna is directly proportional to its directivity and the square of wavelength of the signal to be transmitted.

- **Bandwidth:** Bandwidth is defined as the frequency range of input electric signal over which various characteristic features of an antenna remains under satisfactory limits. Radiation resistance, input impedance, gain, etc. are the parameters of interest which can be monitored for defining the bandwidth. Most of the parameters are interrelated i.e. the change in frequency changes the current distribution hence the input impedance of wire antenna resulting in a mismatch with the feed line. This causes more reflection which in turn reduces the radiated power. The radiation resistance is also reduced.

- **Antenna array:** In modern wireless communication systems strict shaping of radiation pattern is required for controlling the cochannel and adjacent channel interferences. Sometimes it requires dynamic adjustment too. An array of antenna simplifies such kind of jobs. Thus it is preferred to be used at base station. When two or more number of antenna elements are placed in close vicinity and similar signals are fed to them then the overall radiation pattern is the vector addition of the individual radiation patterns. Various features of antenna array like mechanical characteristics of each element, spacing between them, feeding amplitude and phase difference etc, can be used for obtaining desired characteristics of radiation pattern.

- **Reciprocity:** The reciprocity theorem states that the relationship between an oscillating current and the resulting electric field is unchanged if one interchanges the points where the current is placed and where the field is measured. The admit-

tance between a pair of wireless devices remains same in both directions. Thus the power delivered will remain same if anyone of these two systems used as transmitter and other as receiver. It also justifies the notion that the properties of an antenna remain same irrespective of its use as a transmitting or a receiving antenna.

Mobile Station Antenna Design

Being a battery operated hand held device it needs an antenna having features like high gain, low weight, low size, mechanical robustness etc. Small antennas have limited aperture and therefore poor gain. The manufacturing cost must be low as these are required to be produced in large numbers. Many user terminals now operate over a wide range of frequencies. Thus, higher bandwidth is an additional requirement for modern devices. Input impedance matching with the source is very difficult over a wide range of frequency specifically when there is a constraint on the size too. Thus gain and bandwidth cannot be increased simultaneously. The cellular mobile and other systems which are using frequency division duplexing (FDD) requires 8-17% antenna bandwidth for faithful working on the uplink as well as the downlink band. The 10% system bandwidth can be achieved by inducing current on the handset chassis and designing the antenna element just as a coupling element instead of radiating element. (Rappaport, 2006) The problem in this method arises from the fact that these devices are required to operate in close proximity of the user's hand, head and other body parts and effect of such designs on health need to be addressed as per the guidelines laid down by world health organization.

In early age mobile devices helical antennas were used for availing advantages associated with circular polarization, two different set of helix were used for different frequency bands. Later on the retractable whip antenna was built with the helix. The required impedance bandwidth can be very easily obtained by extending this whip antenna and the normal helix may be used for normal operations. The whip size = $3\lambda/8$ is used for ensuring the shift of maximum current farther away from the user and reduce the current on the phone chassis. Since the dominant radiation direction of monopole is along the ground plane, its length is required to be kept several wavelengths for producing stable input impedance which is impractical in mobile devices. The inverted F antenna removes this drawback because it has the radiation pattern in a direction normal to the ground plane. Thus one side of the terminal case may be used for creating ground plane whose length is several order more than what was available for a whip antenna. Planar inverted F antenna (PIFA) has been used in many mobile devices which has 14% more bandwidth and can be further increased by adding parasite conductor layers. The radiation pattern is similar to uniform current dipole in the space above the ground plane. The modern mobile devices are equipped with either microstrip patch or chip antennas. Usually a $\lambda/2$ or $\lambda/4$ metallic square patch is built with the conducting chassis of mobile device acting as ground. Its radiation pattern and other characteristics are similar to PIFA with an added advantage in easy manufacturing because it does not require vertical short circuit that was needed in PIFA. With the development in VLSI fabrication technology the chip antenna, also known as semiconductor antenna, are also increasingly used in mobile devices (Kraus et al., 2007)(Saunders & Zavala, 2007).

Base Station Antenna Design

Power, size and the computational capabilities does not impose any constraints at the base station. Thus very efficient antenna assembly should be created for transmission as well as reception purpose at the base station for compensating the poor ability of mobile stations and enhancing the overall quality of transmission between them.

Macro cells used in cellular networks require well planned antenna assembly because it is going to govern the frequency reuse factor which in turn will decide the maximum traffic capacity of the cellular network and hence the revenue generated by the cellular operator. Antenna arrays, Diversity techniques, mechanical or electrical downtilting, beamforming, etc. techniques are required to be used for controlling the cochannel interference, improving the reception quality and achieving performance improvement. The macro cell is divided into sectors and a directive antenna array having vertical as well as horizontal elements is used for illuminating each sector. Strict control on the radiation pattern is desired making careful evaluation of feed current inevitable. The downtilting should also be separately evaluated for each sector. Adaptive antenna techniques like switched beam antenna, beamforming, adaptive arrays are used for further fine tuning the radiation pattern and enhancing the capacity by lowering cochannel interference. Both polarization and antenna diversity may be used for data reception. The microcell covers a particular street or similar area which is comparatively much smaller than macro cell. Some shaping to radiation pattern is still needed but resources are comparatively limited. The interaction between antenna and its surroundings becomes more important for finding the practical antenna pattern. Yagi uda, shrouded omnidirectional, etc. antennas are generally used in microcell. The picocell occurs indoor and it covers very small area. It requires very wide beamwidth for providing uniform coverage but substantial delay spread is observed with high beamwidth which imposes a tradeoff. Universally linear polarization is in use by overlooking the benefits of circular polarization due to easy manufacturing of linear patterned antenna. At higher frequencies patch antennas are used in Pico cells where as wire antennas are preferred for lower frequency band (Kraus et al., 2007)(Saunders & Zavala, 2007).

TECHNIQUES FOR IMPROVED RECEPTION FROM WIRELESS CHANNELS

Earlier communication systems possess very simple receiver e.g. analog radio systems, 1G cellular network etc. The transmitter was responsible for achieving faithful transmission. No additional help was available at the receiver side. Keeping the cost and size of the receiver at lower end may be the reasons behind it. This philosophy has been changed in modern system designs, now the receiver is also contributing towards the successful data transfer. The receiver possesses the received signal which has travelled through the channel, containing the current state of channel. The multipath propagation effect of wireless channel has also created multiple copies of the transmitted signal at the destination. If it is properly processed then the quality of the received signal can be enhanced to many folds. Huge reduction in production costs enables wireless engineers to design highly sophisticated receivers which have the needful capabilities of running complex algorithms within a short period of time. Following techniques are used in modern wireless receivers for better reception

Synchronization

The faithful operation of a digital communication system needs proper bit synchronization, frame synchronization as well as carrier synchronization. The closed loop bit synchronizers use voltage controlled clock. Associated circuitry like zero crossing detectors, early-late circuit, etc. forces the clock to match with the transmitter side clock. The pseudo noise sequences are used for frame synchronization purposes. The valid frame has a PN sequence for marking start of frame. Same sequence is stored in the tap-gains of a tapped shift register. The received symbols are passed through this shift register. Due to auto-correlation property of an PN-sequence a high signal is generated whenever a valid frame arrives. The carrier synchronization channels are generally established in forward link of cellular systems. Otherwise traditional techniques may be used for carrier synchronization (Carlson et al., 2010) (Kraus et al., 2007).

Diversity

A diversity technique uses multiple copies of the transmitted signal at the receiving end such that the overall received signal strength should be enhanced. Multiple copies may be available in time domain, frequency domain, space domain and the polarization domain. The RAKE receivers of modern code division multiple access (CDMA) systems use multiple time delayed copies of the transmitted signals and coherently combine them for better power reception. Orthogonal frequency division multiple access (OFDM) is an example of frequency diversity which utilizes discrete Fourier transform (DFT) principles and several subcarriers data transmission for availing diversity. Multiple input multiple outputs (MIMO) is the latest example of utilizing space domain diversity which observes the multipath propagation as an advantage and may increase throughput in presence of heavy multipath propagation scenario. Multiple polarization signals are available at the base station in cellular systems which may be easily collected and processed for better signal strength (Wang & Poor, 2004).

Channel Estimation and Equalization

The channel estimation method accesses the amount of amplitude and phase distortion that has been generated by the wireless channel. The equalization is responsible for removing these ill effects and regenerating the symbol after demodulation. Following any particular algorithm like zero forcing, least mean squares, recursive least squares, etc. the equalizer generates final symbol from the received symbol. If this final symbol is again given as feedback to equalizer in taking subsequent decisions then it is called nonlinear equalizer otherwise it is a linear equalizer. Equalization operation is able to mitigate the effect of intersymbol interference (ISI). GSM standard uses 26 bit training bit sequence in each frame for the purpose of channel estimation which is then used by the equalizer.

Sophisticated Decoding of Channel Codes

The hard decision decoders were used in the early age of digital communication systems. The development of 3-bit soft decision decoder brought huge improvement but its performance was also much beyond the Shannon's estimate. Recently iterative decoders have been suggested which have ensured improvement in the BER with enhancement in the number of iterations. Turbo codes and its variants have achieved closeness with the Shannon limit when decoded iteratively for large iterations. The latency is the primary concern in such receivers (Lee, 1998).

Spreading Techniques

Traditional systems need guard space in time, frequency and space domains for un-interfered operation but modern research says that spreading the signal in frequency, time or the space domain is advantageous for better communication. The autocorrelation, balance, run, etc. properties of pseudonoise (PN) sequences have been utilized in bits and pieces in several systems. When it is combined with the concept of orthogonality which exists between various signal sequences then a new multiuser system called spread spectrum or the code division multiple access (CDMA) system is evolved. The orthogonal codes are assigned to individual users and they are allowed to transmit the assigned code (for logic 1) or its complement (for logic 0) at the same time and on the same carrier frequency. If all users are perfectly

synchronized and the specific orthogonal code is known at the destination then the data can be extracted from the fully interfered signals even if transmission takes place well below the thermal noise level. It is due to the de-spreading property of PN sequences. Instead of single pulse it needs to transmit a long sequence of pulses within same time. Thus bandwidth expansion takes place. The major advantage of spread spectrum technique lies in huge power saving, combating noise and interference etc. The advantages of time domain spreading has been very well illustrated by the OFDM and multi carrier CDMA systems. The OFDM allows the transmitted signal to take a shape, in terms of power bandwidth spectrum, which matches with that of channel thus accomplishing low distortion communication. The signal spreading in space is a natural process in wireless communication. Multiple antennas may be used at the destination for getting the diversity benefits at receiving end. MIMO technique has established that if more spreading is done by putting multiple antennas at the transmitting end then better quality signal will be received and even there may be some improvement in net data rate. V-BLAST and D-BLAST projects have generated significant results. Alamauti and other space-time code based MIMO system have already been recommended by various standardization agencies (Oestges & Clerckx, 2007)(Lau & Wok, 2006) (Paulraj et al., 2006).

SUMMARY

The physical layer concerns with putting data over the channel at transmitting side and recollecting it at the destination. It has to take care of various features of the channel so that faithful transmission can be accomplished. The primary question, 'What is so different in designing wireless system as compared to wired system?' has been addressed. Fundamental concepts of various subsystems of a physical layer of a wireless communication system have been introduced.

The layered architecture in data communication assumes the independent working of various layers but it has been observed that the performance of standard TCP over wireless system degrades several folds. The distinct nature of wireless channel is the main reason behind it. Several variant of TCP are now available which account for various features of wireless channel and improve its performance. Similarly the database management systems are also dependent upon several physical layer aspects of wireless systems thus understanding the working principles of physical layer may be very helpful for all wireless system professionals.

FURTHER READING

Only the tip of an iceberg has been touched in this chapter. Thorough understanding of the various aspects of physical layer needs further reading. Fortunately huge literature is available in this field. A very brief survey of same is presented hereunder. The book authored by G. M. Calhoun (Calhoun, 2003) has fluency similar to that what exists in novel. It does not contain any mathematical expression or the numerical example still it possesses great depth in explaining various pre Shannon and post Shannon signal architectures. The books authored by Rapport (Rappaport, 2006) and Lee (Lee, 1998) are good enough for undergraduate level students. Several essential concepts associated with wireless channels and systems have been introduced in these books. Mathematical modeling of wireless channels and various signal processing techniques have been summarized in (Molisch, 2003), (Giannakis et al., 2001) and (Wang & Poor, 2004). In depth explanation of most recent wireless systems is presented in (Lu, 2002) and (Glisic, 2007). Fundaments of antenna engineering (Kraus et al., 2007)(Saunders & Zavala, 2007) and the complete design of RF

sections of an transceiver (Gu, 2008)(Tasic et al., 2009) are very important topics for the people who are interested in developing new circuits and systems for wireless applications. Modern wireless systems are essentially digital communication systems following the fundamental laws of communications engineering (Carlson et al., 2010) and the more advanced theory of digital communication systems (Proakis, 2001). The emergence of the concept of multiple input and multiple output (MIMO) has converted the role of multipath propagation phenomenon from enemy to friend of communication (Oestges & Clerckx, 2007). Multiple antennas are required at transmitting as well as receiving terminals and the introduction of space time coding may generate huge diversity and multiplexing gain (Paulraj et al., 2006). The concept of cross layer design with multiple antennas (Lau & Wok, 2006) further extends the benefits of multiple antenna systems.

REFERENCES

Calhoun, G. M. (2003). Third generation wireless systems: *Vol. 1. Post Shannon signal architecture*. Boston, MA: Artech House.

Carlson, A. B. (2010). *Communication systems* (5th ed.). Singapore: McGraw Hill International.

Giannakis, G. B. (2001). *Signal processing in wireless and mobile communications* (*Vol. 1*). Prentice Hall.

Glisic, S. G. (2007). *Advanced wireless communications* (2nd ed.). UK: Wiley.

Gu, Q. (2008). *RF system design of transceivers for wireless communications*. New Delhi, India: Springer.

Kraus, J. D. (2007). *Antennas for all applications* (3rd ed.). New Delhi, India: Tata McGraw Hill.

Lau, V. K. N., & Wok, Y. K. R. K. (2006). *Channel adaptive technologies and cross layer designs for wireless systems with multiple antennas*. Wiley.

Lee, W. C. Y. (1998). *Mobile communications engineering* (2nd ed.). Singapore: McGraw Hill.

Lu, W. W. (2002). *Broadband wireless mobile*. UK: Wiley.

Molisch, A. F. (2003). *Wideband wireless digital communications*. New Delhi, India: PE.

Oestges, C., & Clerckx, B. (2007). *MIMO wireless communications*. UK: Elsevier.

Paulraj, A. (2006). *Introduction to space time wireless communications*. Cambridge, UK.

Proakis, J. G. (2001). *Digital Communications* (4th ed.). Singapore: McGraw Hill.

Rappaport, T. S. (2006). *Wireless communications* (2nd ed.). New Delhi, India: PHI.

Saunders, S. R., & Zavala, A. A. (2007). *Antenna and propagation for wireless communication systems* (2nd ed.). UK: Wiley.

Tasic, T. (2009). *Circuits and systems for future generations of wireless communications*. New York, NY: Springer.

Wang, X., & Poor, H. V. (2004). *Wireless communication systems: Advanced techniques for signal reception*. New Delhi, India: PE.

KEY TERMS AND DEFINITIONS

Antenna: An integral part of wireless systems which converts electrical energy into EM waves and vice-versa.

CDMA: Code division multiple access implements the spread spectrum concept.

CFSK: Continuous frequency shift keying minimizes the abrupt phase change in an arbitrary symbols sequence.

Channel Coding: Technique of undoing the errors caused by channel during data transmission.

Fading: Fluctuation in the strength of received signal due to multipath propagation or Doppler Effect.

ISI: Inter Symbol Interference occurred due to overlapping of a few consecutive symbols due to channel dispersion.

MIMO: Multiple input multiple output system uses multiple antennas at transmitting and receiving ends and generated diversity gain or the multiplexing gain.

Physical Layer: Bottom layer of OSI model which concerns with data transmission.

Source Coding: Technique of converting raw data supplied by user into transmission efficient format.

Chapter 6
Internet Security Using Biometrics

Shrikant Tiwari
Institute of Technology, Banaras Hindu University, India

Aruni Singh
Institute of Technology, Banaras Hindu University, India

Ravi Shankar Singh
Institute of Technology, Banaras Hindu University, India

Sanjay K. Singh
Institute of Technology, Banaras Hindu University, India

ABSTRACT

Internet security is a big challenge for Internet users, and passwords are the primary means of authenticating users. Establishing identity is becoming difficult in this vastly interconnected society. The need for reliable Internet security techniques has increased in the wake of heightened concerns about security and rapid advancements in networking, communication, and mobility. Biometrics is the science of identifying an individual based on his physical (static) or behavioral (dynamic) characteristics, and it is beginning to gain acceptance as a legitimate method for determining an individual's identity. Biometrics has been used for many years in high security government and military applications, but the technology is now becoming affordable for use as an authentication methods and general security feature. In this chapter, the authors provide an overview of Internet security using Biometrics.

INTRODUCTION

Internet security is concerned about the protection and access of information elements (e.g. multimedia data) thereby ensuring that only authorized users are able to access the contents available in digital media. Hackers and impostors are posing threat to a country (by hacking sensitive documents) and the society (by economic fraud and accessing secret information). Internet users such as military, intelligence, organizations, authors, authorized distributions or individual users are losing billions of dollars or their secret information.

DOI: 10.4018/978-1-4666-0203-8.ch006

Earlier, security was synonymous with secrecy and the shared secret between two business parties was a worldwide approach. But secret passwords require a great deal of trust between secret sharing parties. It is difficult to trust the administrator or other users of the internet network service provider that we access.

Most computers hacking today are due to compromise by system users or hackers using legitimate accounts to gain access to security. The identity of a person is becoming challenging in vastly connected information society. A large number of biometric-based identification systems are being deployed for many civilian and forensic applications invoking considerable interest.

It is difficult to ignore the presence of the internet economy or its future potential growth. It is always been suggested that there is no way of making the internet 'hundred percent safe and secure. Therefore, organizations and Government are forcing to implement high security policies to prevent unauthorized access into corporate networks to overcome risk. (Reid, 2003)

INTERNET SECURITY

Existing Security Primitives and Their Limitations

The existing security primitives use a generic cryptographic system, the user authentication method is possession based. It means the possession of the decrypting key is sufficient to establish the authenticity of the user. Since cryptographic keys are long and random they are difficult to member. So, these keys are stored and released based on some alternative authentication mechanism i.e. password. As shown in Figure 1 if internet users use simple password then it is easy to guess, and they compromise security and complex password which are difficult to remember, and are costly to maintain. Most internet users use the same password across different application, as hacker

or impostor after getting a single password can now access multiple applications. So in a multiuser account case, passwords are unable to provide no repudiation.

Password Survey (Nov. 2006)

1. 26%- use common words, dates, phone, address numbers
2. 38%- recycle old passwords
3. 62%- change password only if perceiving a security threat
4. 17%- keep password list on monitor, keyboard or desk drawer.

Need for Security

Security is a major concern with internet users and system administrators find it difficult to protect confidential information in individual files, for which they lock a computer system to unauthorized users. To control access to an intranet or extranet, or conduct business on the Internet, one needs to determine an appropriate level of security and the effective means to achieve the objectives. The threat to internet security is one of the main barriers to electronic transaction.

Internet uses Simple Mail Transfer Protocol (SMTP) to transmit electronic mail and most business transactions. These transmissions have as much privacy as a postcard and travel over insecure, untrusted lines. Anyone anywhere along the transmission path can obtain access to a message and read the contents with a simple text viewer or word processing program. Because the transmission lines are insecure, it is easy to forge e-mail or use another person's name. Theft of identity is becoming the nation's leading incidence of fraud due to which a person can even claim that someone else have sent a message.

Organizations in both the public and the private sectors are well aware of the needs of Internet security that is why they are protecting their Internet data and corporate systems. To provide a secu-

Figure 1. Different methods to remember passwords

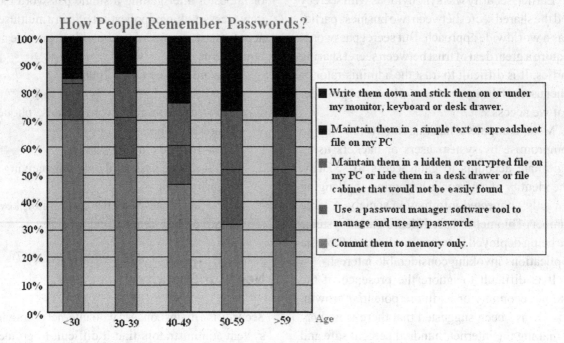

rity wall between the intruder and the corporate network is the best way to keep an intruder from entering the network. Since the intruders enter the network through software program, such as a virus or worm etc. In direct connection, firewalls, data encryption, and user authentication can restrain a hacker up to some extent.

The first objective to improving security is to control physical access by limiting it to authorized individuals. The principle is that the fewer people who can get physical and administrative access to sensitive files or to server systems, the greater the security will be. Most applications rely on passwords, personal identification numbers, and keys to access restricted information or confidential files. Passwords, cards, personal identification numbers and keys can be forgotten, stolen, forged, lost or given away. Moreover, these devices serve primarily to identify the person. They cannot verify or authenticate that the person really is who he or she claims to be.

Security Requirement in the Internet Environment

The design of trustworthy and robust Internet security systems, with built-in security, privacy and trust is a challenging task. Educating users to understand security, privacy and trust in the Internet by providing usable and credible support protecting their data and privacy needs lots of effort. Thus helping them to make informed and reliable decisions on the trustworthiness of information, services, social contacts and services is part of the internet security.

Following are the security requirement in the Internet environment.

- Securing and maintaining the identity of billions of networked persons, devices, things, services and virtual entities connected in the Internet;
- Managing the interactions and interfaces between heterogeneous ICT systems and

engineering scalable security policies across the Internet;

- Increasing the level of security of critical infrastructures that are interdependent and controlled through vulnerable networks;
- Design and implementation of scalable, dependable and resilient open systems and composite services;
- Evaluating expected security, dependability and resilience properties at design stage or during dynamic evolution at runtime;
- Monitoring, forecasting and managing dependable behavior, evolution and adaptation to changing contexts, operating conditions, regulations or practices of use, while guaranteeing service level provision or best trade-off between conflicting factors based on business oriented risk analysis;
- Enhanced security of highly distributed virtual entities and trusted infrastructures based on virtualized communication, computing and storage resources;
- Requirement of new crypto schemes both in the core networks, to cope with ever increasing data transfer rates (crypto at Gbits/sec or even Tbits/sec), and at network edges.

The above issue and challenges for security provisioning on the internet address both core dependability and security technologies needed to allow creation of a secure and trustworthy Internet, or technologies that need to be addressed in conjunction with those developed.

Security at Network level must address the issue of new network architectures and communication protocols that incorporate security, user accountability and privacy-protection. We must work on secure and auditable service platforms and middleware; trustworthy end-to-end services; virtualization and secure management of resources; taking account of application and domain specific needs at the software and service level.

Internet Security Issues

Virus and other malicious soft attacks appeared with the spread of the software-based Internet nodes, network and "cyber-security".

The key differences between the synchronous Public-Switched Digital Network (PSDN) and Internet are that which transports packets in an asynchronous manner in contrast to the former that transports byte-size information in a continuous and synchronized manner.

Thus, in order to eliminate the risk and assure data security and privacy, highly complex, difficult, and sophisticated algorithms are necessary for the generation of the security codes and their distribution. Moreover, the network itself should be sophisticated and be able to detect malicious attackers and outsmart them by adopting sophisticated countermeasure strategies (Eschelbeck, 2000).

In general, security assurance is concern with many dimensions that aims to ensure a level of trust to the client and by the client up to extent of expectations. Such expectations include information or data protection during its creation, use, transformation, storage, transport, and deletion at the application layer, at the layer boundaries of the reference model such as the ISO, ATM, and TCP/IP at the transport layer, and in a computation environment *(Magazine,* 1999).

Internet Security Services

Cryptography with strong encoding is the mechanism that ensures message confidentiality. The network also provides an *accountability* function that monitors and ensures that actions of any entity on the network security can be traced back to it(Kartalopoulos, 2008).

Cryptography performs several important information security services: source and destination *authentication, authorization,* data *integrity,* message *confidentiality,* and *non-repudiation.*

- *Authentication* is the process that verifies the identity of the source that a received message that was sent by the rightful sending entity and detects if the message has been altered (FIPS Pub, 1994, 1997, 2002). Authentication is accomplished with cryptographic checksums the *authentication code*, which are calculated according to an approved cryptographic algorithm. It is difficult to forge without knowing the secret code.

- *Authorization* is the process that grants access privileges to an entity such as the intended destination or to a third party. Authorization to the destination is granted after verification of the destination. To a third party, access is granted after the official and justified request to access a message and perhaps modify the message. Access is under the control of an *access authority* (or function), which is responsible for monitoring and granting privileges to other authorities that request access.

- *Data integrity* pertains to identifying possible unauthorized alterations in the transported information.

The question asked - Is the data received exactly the same data that was sourced, or some of it or all of it has been altered? In communications, one of the mechanisms that secure data integrity is watermarking, that is invisible text superimposed to the original text that only the rightful recipient knows how to remove. Thus, when part or all of the text is altered by an unauthorized entity, the watermarking has been altered as well.

- *Message confidentiality* is the service that warranties that information during its transport from source to destination will not be disclosed.

- *Non-repudiation* provides proof of the integrity and the origin of a message to a third party. Non-repudiation also prevents an entity from denying involvement or receipt of a message. For example, a signed message provides undeniable proof that the message was received. In communications, this is accomplished using a digital signature that is calculated with a secret key.

In cryptography, the term *key escrow system* or *escrow* means that the two components that comprise a cryptographic key are entrusted to two key component holders called *escrow agents*. The escrow agents provide the components of the key to a *grantee* entity only upon fulfillment of specified conditions. When the grantee entity obtains the key component, it reconstructs the unique key and obtains the session key which is then used to decrypt the cipher text that is sent to it (FIPS Pub 1994). The cryptographic process includes a secure mechanism for transporting the special knowledge to the rightful recipient. It also includes a process for transforming the cipher text back to its original form. The cryptographic process that changes the form of the original data (the *plain text*) to unintelligible is called *encoding* or *ciphering*. The result of encoding is the *cipher text*. The process of restoring the original form of data is called *decoding* or *deciphering*. Because the cipher text may contain sensitive or secret information intended to the rightful recipient only, a malevolent or bad actor may want to know the content of the cipher text, gain unauthorized access to the cipher text, and by trying different possible keys may be able to *break* the cipher text. This is known as *brute attack* (Kartalopoulos, 2008).

Internet Security Developments

Every industry has its own specific needs and requires certain security measures to protect its data from hackers. The public and private sectors have their own strengths and weaknesses on Internet security. Each industry requires certain security measures to protect its data while in transit. Developing a plan that has proportionately more strength than weakness is always the goal of any organization. However, the Internet is an uncontrolled frontier that is still growing. It may take some time to develop stronger methods for data security.

Protecting an organization from the perils of the Internet is similar to the job of a security guard working during the night shift: As long as he stays awake and keeps his eyes open, the chances are that nothing will happen. While companies arm themselves with the latest IDS and virus software, there is still a chance that someone from the outside can get in and wreak havoc on the company's system. Software and hardware configurations keep most of the intruders at bay, but being able to recognize abnormal activity when it occurs seems to be the best method. This requires a well trained IT staff to constantly monitor the network for deviants, using the system software to set up audits in all the right places. As technology continues to evolve and software and hardware improvements are implemented, there may come a time when hackers not only will be forced to stay outside the company walls, but also will be exposed by law enforcement during the process. (Eschelbeck, 2000)

The future of Internet security, therefore, resides in human intervention and innovation. Implementing hardware and software solutions, as well as using human intervention to continually monitor the network, are two of the best ways to keep abreast of attacks from the outside.

In addition, SSL, the standard for secure Internet transmissions used by credit card companies, may get a face-lift in the near future. To improve the security between themselves and their customers, the credit card companies have been developing another standard called the secure electronic transaction (SET) standard, which may have an effect on the security of Internet transaction. SET focuses on confidentiality and authentication. SET-compliant software will not only make sure that thieves cannot steal a credit card number, but also keep a merchant from seeing the number while still providing assurances that the card is valid. The transmission will pass through the merchant's hands directly to the credit card user, which will then decrypt it and credit the merchant's account (*Magazine*, 1999).

The possibility of the back-end authentication process (in a networked situation) being compromised by the passing of illegal data may represent a point of vulnerability. The authentication engine and its associated interface could be fooled. It is necessary to suggest a measure of risk to the biometrics system in use, especially when the authentication engine may not be able to verify that it is receiving a bona fide live transaction data (and not a data stream from another source). Even a highly accurate biometrics system can reject authorized users, fail to identify known users, identify users incorrectly, or allow unauthorized person to verify as known users. In addition, if a third-party network is utilized as part of the overall biometrics system -- for example using the Internet to connect remotely to corporate networks --the end-to-end connection between host controller and back-end application server should be carefully considered.

However, in most cases, biometrics system cannot determine if an individual has established a fraudulent identity, or is posing as another individual during biometrics enrollment process. An individual with a fake passport may be able to use the passport as the basis of enrollment in a biometrics system. The system can only verify that the individual is who he or she claimed to be during enrollment, unless a large-scale identification system is built in which all users are matched against all other users to find duplicates or individual attempts to enroll more than once.

AUTHENTICATION METHODS

There are three main ways to authenticate an identity of a person: (Reid, 2003)

Something We Know: This refers to anything that needs to be remembered to prove our identity. The information remembered could be of the following types:

- Passwords
- Pass phrases
- Personal Identification Numbers(PIN)
- Secret handshakes

Passwords are the most frequently used to authenticate a person that only he knows. Passwords, however, have the following problems: They can be stolen, written down in easily accessible locations, shared, or guessed. To strengthen passwords, they are normally implemented with a supporting policy. Sharing passwords, writing them down, or not changing them frequently violates most password policies. Automated methods can be used for enforcing a password policy.

Something We Have: Anything that the user is required to possess can be used as an authenticating token. A token is generally issued to one user. A token is registered to a user, and when it is presented for authentication, that unique token is verified as being legitimate. That is also used to verify its registration, if it has been lost or stolen,

and if the user ID presented with it matches. If matched, the user is authenticated. Otherwise, the authentication request is rejected. Tokens fall into two general categories:

1. Storage tokens
2. Dynamic tokens

Something We Are: Any physiological (static) or behavioral (dynamic) trait that can be reliably measured can be used to authenticate a person is called a biometric.

Physiological characteristics include fingerprints, iris and hand geometry, ECG signals, retina, facial characteristics, thermal images etc. and behavioral characteristics include signature, voice, keystroke, gait etc.

BIOMETRICS

Why Biometrics?

The limitation of password can be overcome by the use of better methods of authentication. The main use of Biometric network security will be to replace the current password system. Maintaining

Figure 2. Biometric traits

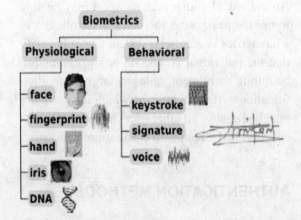

Figure 3. Figure representing the graph of increase of security level vs. authentication methods

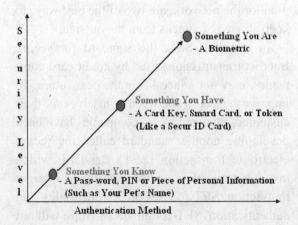

password security can be a major task for even a small organization. Passwords have to be changed every few months and people forget their password or lock themselves out of the system by incorrectly entering their password repeatedly. Very often people write their password down and keep it near their computer. This completely defeats the purpose of network security.

Biometric refers to recognizing an individual based on the physical and behavioral characteristic (traits as identifiers) such as face, fingerprint, iris, hand geometry, voice, signature, gait etc. Biometric system has several advantages over traditional authentication techniques. It is more reliable than password-based authentication as biometric traits cannot be lost or forgotten (where as password can be forgotten or lost); Biometric identifiers are difficult to share, copy and exchange. In case of Biometrics the person being authenticated is required to be present at the time and place of authentication. It is very difficult for hackers or impostor to forge Biometrics (as it requires more experience, time, memory, access privileges). As a result these key are stored somewhere (for example, on a computer or a smart card) and released based on some alternative authentication mechanism (e.g. password).

Finally a biometrics based internet security scheme is a better alternative to traditional authentication schemers. Biometrics can also be used in conjunction with password (or tokens) to increase the level of internet security.

Biometric System Technology

A biometric system acquires biometrics data (physiological, behavioral) from an individual, extracts a salient feature set from the data, compares this feature set against the feature set stored in the database and executes an action based on the matching of features. There are four major modules of biometric system (Jain, Flynn and Ross (2008) as shown in Figure 4.

1. Sensor module
2. Quality assessment and feature extraction module
3. Matching module
4. Database modules

- **Sensor modules:** A biometric reader or scanner is required to acquire the raw biometric data of an individual. A digital representation of biometric characteristic needs to be sensed and captured for quality assessment and feature extraction. A biometric sensor such as fingerprint scanner, digital camera is one of the central pieces of a biometric capture module.
- **Quality assessment and feature extraction module:** To determine the quality and suitability of biometric data acquired by the sensor in assessed. The acquired data is subjected to a signal enhancement algorithm in order to improve its quality. In

Figure 4. Biometric system technology

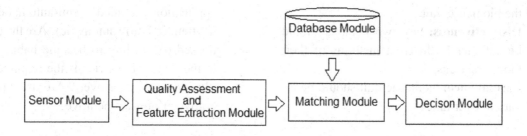

order to facilitate matching or comparison of the raw digital representation is usually further processed by feature extractor to generate a compact but expressive representation called feature set. For example the position and orientation of minutiae points in a fingerprint image would be computed in feature extraction module.

- **Matching module:** the matching (or comparison) stage (also known as a matcher) takes a feature set and an enrollment template as inputs and computes the similarity between them. The matcher module also includes a decision making modules, in which the match scores are used to either validate a claimed identity or provide ranking in order to identify individual. For example, in this module the number of matching minutiae between the query and the template can be computed and treated as matching score.
- **Database module:** Is devoted to storing templates and other demographic informatics about the user. The data captured during the enrollment process may or may not be supervised by human depending on the application.

Comparison of Various Biometric Traits

Any human anatomical or behavioral trait can be used as a biometric identifier to recognize a person as long as it satisfies the following requirements: (Maltoni, Maio, Jain, Prabhakar, 2009)

- **Universality:** each person should possess the biometric trait.
- **Distinctiveness:** any two persons should be sufficiently different in terms of their biometric traits.
- **Permanence:** biometric trait should be invariant over time.

- **Collectability:** biometric trait can be measured quantitatively. However, in a practical biometric system, there are a number of other issues that should be considered in selecting a trait, including:
- **Performance:** recognition accuracy, speed (throughput), resource requirements, and robustness to operational and environmental factors.
- **Acceptability:** up to large extent users are willing to accept the biometric identifier in their usual lives.
- **Circumvention:** ease with which the biometric system can be circumvented by fraudulent methods.

A number of biometric traits are in use in various applications. Each biometric trait has its own strengths and weaknesses and the choice typically depends on the application. No single trait is expected to effectively meet the requirements of all the applications. The match between a biometric trait and an application is determined depending upon the characteristics of the application and the properties of the trait. Some of the issues that need to be addressed in selecting a biometric trait for a particular application are: (Maltoni, Maio, Jain, Prabhakar, 2009)

- What are the application need, a verification or identification system? If an application requires an identification of a subject from a large database, it needs a very distinctive biometric trait (e.g., fingerprints or iris).
- Which are the implementation characteristics of the application? For example, is the application attended (semi-automatic) or unattended (fully automatic)? Are the users trained (or willing to become habituated) to the given biometric? Is the required application covert or overt? Are users cooperative or non-cooperative?

- What is the storage size requirement of the application? For example, an application that performs the recognition on a smart card may require a small template size.

- What are the accuracy requirements? As application requires very high accuracy needs a more distinctive biometric.

- What types of biometric traits are acceptable to the target user population? Biometric traits have different degrees of acceptability in different demographic regions depending on the cultural, ethical, social, religious, and hygienic standards. The acceptability of a biometric in an application is often a compromise between the sensitivity of the targeted population to various perceptions or taboos and the value or convenience offered by biometrics-based recognition.

A brief introduction to the most common biometric traits is provided below. Figure 2 displays several biometric traits that have been either adopted in commercial systems or are being investigated.

- **Iris:** Visual texture of the human iris is determined by the chaotic morphogenetic processes during embryonic development and also distinctive for each person's eyes. An iris image is typically captured using a noncontact imaging process, which often involves cooperation from the user, both to register the image of iris in the central imaging area and to ensure that the iris is at a predetermined distance from the focal plane of the camera. Even iris recognition technology is extremely accurate. (Daugman, 1999)

- **Face:** Face is one of the most acceptable biometric traits because it is one of the most common methods of recognition that humans use in their daily visual interactions. Acquisition of face images is nonintrusive. It is very easy to develop face identification and recognition techniques.

- **Hand and finger geometry:** It is features related to the geometry of human hand are relatively invariant and peculiar to an individual. The image acquisition system requires cooperation of the subject to capture frontal and side view images of the palm flatly placed on a panel with outstretched

Figure 5. Examples of biometrics traits: a) ear, b) face, c) facial thermogram, d) hand thermogram, e) hand vein, f) hand geometry, g) fingerprint, h) iris, i) retina, j) signature, and k) voice

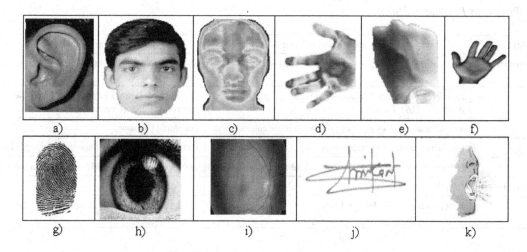

fingers. Due to its distinctiveness, hand geometry-based systems are only used for verification and do not scale well for identification applications. Finger geometry systems (which measure the geometry of at most two fingers as opposed to the whole hand) may be preferred because of their compact size.

- **Hand or finger vein:** Near-infrared imaging is used to scan the back of a clenched first to determine hand vein structure. Veins could also be detected in a finger using infrared or near-infra-red sensing. Systems for vein capture use inexpensive infra-red light emitting diodes (LEDs), leading to commercial systems for hand and finger vein biometrics.

- **Voice:** Voice capture is unobtrusive and may be the only feasible biometric in applications requiring person recognition over a telephone. Voice is not expected to be sufficiently distinctive to permit identification of an individual from a large database of identities. Moreover, a voice signal available for recognition is typically degraded in quality by the microphone, communication channel, and digitizer characteristics.

- **Signature:** The way a person signs his name is known to be a characteristic of that individual. Signatures have been acceptable in Government, legal, and commercial transactions as a method of verification for a long time. Signature is a behavioral biometric that changes over time and is influenced by physical and emotional conditions of the signatories.

The biometric identifiers described above are compared in Table 1 Note that fingerprint has a nice balance among all the desirable properties. Every human being possesses fingers (with the exception of hand-related disability) and hence fingerprints. Fingerprints are very distinctive and they are permanent; even if they temporarily change slightly due to cuts and bruises on the skin, the fingerprint reappears after the finger heals. They do not suffer from the problem of segmenting the fingerprint from the background.

The deployed fingerprint recognition system is most mature biometric technologies and a offering good performance and fingerprint scanners have become quite compact and affordable. Because fingerprints have a long history of use in forensic divisions worldwide for criminal investigations (Jain, Ross and Pankanti, 2006).

Table 1. Examples of commonly used representation and matching scheme for different biometrics traits (Jain, Ross and Pankanti, 2006)

Modality	Representation of Scheme	Matching Algorithms
Fingerprints	Minutiae distribution, Ridge and Valleys analysis	String Matching, Correlation techniques, Hough Transfo- rmation
Face	Principal Component Analysis (PCA), Linear Discriminant Analysis(LDA), Eigenfaces	Euclidian Distance, Elastic Bunch graph, Neural Networks, Support Vector Machine SVM
Iris	Texture analysis, Key point extraction, Contour enhancement	Hamming Distance
Voice	Linguistic and acoustic acquisition	Hidden markov Model, Phonotactic recognition
Ear	Helix and lobe analysis, PCA, Force Field Transform	Euclidean distance, Local Surface patch(LSP), ICP
Hand Geometry	Length/width of fingers/palm, Texture analysis	Euclidean distance
Gait	Foot forward strides, PCA & LDA	Stance period matching, Silhouettes template matching

FUNCTIONALITIES OF BIOMETRIC SYSTEM

Biometrics is not only a fascinating pattern recognition research problem but, if carefully used, could also be an enabling technology with the potential to make our society safer, reduce fraud, and lead to user convenience (user friendly man-machine interface) by broadly providing the following three functionalities.

Verification

Biometrics can verify with high certainty the authenticity of a claimed enrollment based on the input biometric sample. For example, a person claims that he/she is known as Mr. X within the authentication system and offers his/her fingerprint; the system then either accepts or rejects the claim based on a comparison performed between the offered pattern and the enrolled pattern associated with the claimed identity. Commercial applications, such as computer network logon, electronic data security, ATMs, credit-card purchases, physical access control, cellular phones, personal digital assistants (PDAs), medical records management, and distance learning are sample authentication applications

Identification

Given an input biometric sample, identification determines if the input biometric sample is associated with any of a large number (e.g., millions) of enrolled identities. Typical identification applications include welfare-disbursement, national ID cards, border control, voter ID cards, driver's license, criminal investigation, corpse identification, parenthood determination, missing children identification, etc. These identification applications require a large sustainable throughput with as little human supervision as possible.

Screening

Screening applications determine whether a person belongs to a watchlist of identities. Examples of screening applications could include airport security, security at public events, and other surveillance applications. The screening watchlist consists of a moderate number of identities. By their very nature, the screening applications:

1. Do not have a well-defined "user" enrollment phase
2. Can expect only minimal control over their subjects and imaging conditions
3. Require large sustainable throughput with as little human supervision as possible.

Table 2. Comparison of various traits. High, medium, and low are denoted by H, M, and L, respectively. (C. Soutar, Available: http://www.bioscrypt.com)

Biometric identifier	Universality	Distinctness	Permanence	Collectability	Performance	Acceptability	Circumvention
Face	H	L	M	H	L	H	H
Fingerprints	M	H	H	M	H	M	M
Hand Geometry	M	M	M	H	M	M	M
Iris	H	H	H	M	H	L	L
Key Strokes	L	L	L	M	L	M	M
Signature	L	L	L	H	L	H	H
Voice	M	L	L	M	L	H	H

Screening cannot be accomplished without biometrics by using token-based or knowledge-based identification.

Biometric systems are being increasingly deployed in civilian applications that have several thousand enrolled users.

Biometrics Error

Biometric system is not error free system. The critical promise of the ideal biometric trait is that when a sample is presented to the biometric system, it will offer the correct decision. In practice, a biometric system is a pattern recognition system that inevitably makes some incorrect decisions. Let us first try to understand why a biometric system makes errors and then discuss the various types of errors. We also encouraged the readers to refer to ISO/IEC 19795-2 (2007) and to the other sections of ISO/IEC 19795 for a comprehensive treatment of biometric system errors.

Reasons behind System Errors

There are three primary reasons that explain the errors made by a biometric system (Maltoni, Maio, Jain and Prabhakar 2009)

- **Information limitation:** the invariant and distinctive information content in the biometric samples may be inherently limited due to the intrinsic signal capacity of the biometric identifier. For instance, the distinctive information in hand geometry is less than that in fingerprints. Consequently, hand geometry measurements can differentiate fewer identities than fingerprint even under ideal conditions. Information limitation may also be due to poorly controlled biometric presentation by the users or inconsistent signal acquisition. Differently acquired measurements of a biometric identifier limit the invariance across different samples of the pattern. For example, information limitation occurs when there is very little overlap between the enrolled

Figure 6. Biometric enrolment & authentication system

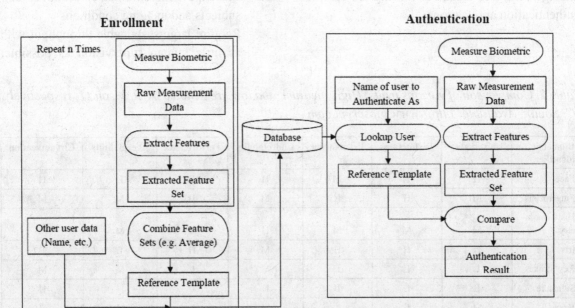

and sample fingerprints (e.g., left and right half of the finger). In such situations, even a perfect matcher cannot offer a correct decision. An extreme example of information limitation is when the person does not possess or cannot present the particular biometric needed by the identification system (e.g., amputees with missing hands and fingers).

- **Representation limitation:** the ideal representation scheme should be designed to retain all the invariance as well as discriminatory information in the sensed measurements. Practical feature extraction modules, typically based on simplistic models of biometric signal, fail to capture the richness of information in a realistic biometric signal resulting in the inclusion of erroneous features and exclusion of true features. Consequently, a fraction of legitimate pattern space cannot be handled by the biometric system, resulting in errors.

- **Invariance limitation:** finally, given a representation scheme, the design of an ideal matcher should perfectly model the invariance relationship among different patterns from the same class (user), even when imaged under different presentation conditions. Again, in practice (e.g., due to non-availability of sufficient number of training samples, uncontrolled or unexpected variance in the collection conditions) a matcher may not correctly model the invariance relationship resulting in matcher errors.

The challenge is to be able to arrive at a realistic and invariant representation of the biometric identifier from a few samples acquired under inconsistent conditions, and then, formally estimate the discriminatory information in the signal from the samples. This is especially difficult in a large-scale identification system where the number of enrolled users is huge (e.g., in the millions).

BIOMETRICS IN NETWORKS

The use of biometrics for network security is for secure workstation access for a workstation connected to a network. Each workstation requires some software support for biometric identification of the user as well as, depending on the biometric trait being used, some hardware device. Hardware device such as computer mice with built in thumbprint readers, voice recorders etc. would be the next step up. These devices would be more expensive to implement on several computers, as each machine would require its own hardware device. A biometric mouse with its device drivers (Chadwick, Good, Kerr, McGee and O'Mahaonv, 2001).

One way that biometrically verified identifications would be implemented is using a centralized system (particularly using voice biometrics). Such a system would be ideal for implementing secure remote logons by mobile users. Remote network access enables tale working, which has been promised by the 'e' community for a long time, especially with the arrival of broadband access from the home. It is also important for field employees who travel all over for the company, yet need access to company resources. Biometric identification used along with a secure connection (a problem that is entirely separate to that of Biometrics) to the network makes this once vulnerable aspect of networking more secure.

Passwords are the primary means of authenticating network users. However, network administrators are becoming concerned about the limited security provided by password authentication. Many network administrators are now of the opinion that their password-based security systems are not all that secure. User passwords are routinely stolen, forgotten, shared, or intercepted by hackers. A recent example of the limitations of passwords, a group of hackers from Europe broke into the e-mail system at Stanford University, stole thousands of student and staff passwords, and went undetected for three weeks (Bloomberg News,

1998). Another serious problem is that computer users have become too trusting or careless. They routinely use the same password to enter both secure and insecure Web sites as well as their networks at work.

In response to the proven lack of security provided by password authentication, network administrators are, in growing numbers, replacing network passwords with smartcards, biometric authentication, or a combination of the three. Smart cards are credit card-size devices that generate random numbers about every minute, in sync with counterparts on each entry point in the network. To log on to a computer, users enter a password and the number that appears on the smart card's LED window. Smart cards work well as long as the card isn't stolen. A better choice to ensure network security is the use of biometrics.

Biometric verification provides a much higher level of security vs. traditional solutions such as passwords, smart cards, or tokens by verifying that the user is who he claims to be and not merely the holder of a card, token or password.

Integrating Internet Security with Biometrics

Last ten years has witnessed drastic changes in business processes. The number of organizations that store and access confidential data in digital form on computer networks or over the Internet has increased exponentially. The importance of Internet security will therefore become an important aspect as the threat-level of electronic crime is rapidly increasing. The internet community has gained numerous benefits from using new computing technologies, these technologies have at the same time made the wired community more valuable to attacks in electronic information transfer security (Oppliger, 2002).

The use of Biometrics has been for years in high-security Government and military applications, but the technology is now becoming affordable for use as a network authentication method

and general security feature. It is tempting to think of biometrics as being sci-fi futuristic technology that we should in the near future use together with solar-powered cars, food pills, and other fiendish devices. There are many references to individuals being formally identified via unique soft-biometric features such as scars, measured physical criteria or a combination of features such as complexion, eye color, height, etc.

The existence of automated biometrics has been for more than 30 years now. Fingerprint has been used to identify criminals and is acceptable in court of law. The manual process of matching is very tedious and time-consuming. Now a days good number of automatic finger-scanning systems is being installed in many of the security systems. The system measured the shape of the hand and looked particularly at finger length. Its use pioneered the application of hand geometry and set path for biometric technologies as a whole (Zhang, D.D., 2000).

Figure 7 illustrates how common Internet security technologies such as a firewall or remote access service (RAS) server with biometrics user authentication can be used to protect against data intrusion from the outside and within. If a user tries to access this server with combined biometrics and is not authorized to do so, the IDS will alert information technology (IT) staff of that entry, even though the user may or may not have the right biometrics user authentication.

Since the IDS use both static and dynamic monitoring systems to monitor direct attacks and abnormal network accesses.

Data encryption is also used throughout the network. Users calling in from a switched telephone network can use data encryption via Point-to-Point Tunneling Protocol (PPTP) to exchange data from their laptop or home computer to the Internet through the corporate network and vice versa. User connects to the network through a RAS server, is given the same access right as any other user in the company. The RAS server sends encrypted data to another computer or server

Figure 7. Integrating common Internet security technologies with biometrics

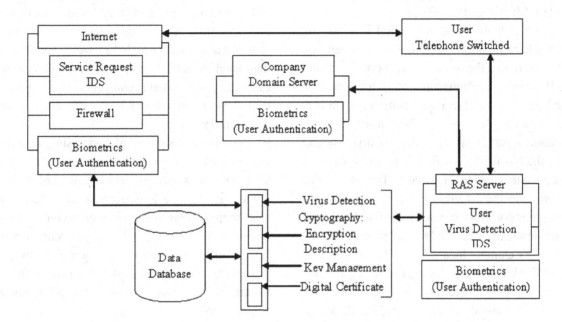

using PPTP. The RAS server also has its own safeguards, such as user call-back to a specific phone number to establish a connection and user authentication, encrypted passwords and user permissions (Shoniregun, 2002).

The implementation of data encryption can be in between a corporate server and a vendor or supplier through an extranet. If data security is necessary on an extranet, both parties could use encryption to ensure privacy and data protection. By incorporating a virtual private network (VPN) on an extranet, both a company and its supplier can ensure maximum data protection on the Internet.

In addition to extranets and VPN, digital certificates and key management are two other alternatives for data security. If a company has an enterprise network that spans a large geographical area, corporate officials could use this technology to protect sensitive data from unauthorized access. For example, if the human resources and finance departments need to share sensitive data, they could communicate through the corporate intranet and use key management to protect the

data and digital certificates to verify the accuracy of transmission (Shoniregun, 2002).

Virtual Private Networks (VPN) and extranets provide some type of security; key management and digital certificates are simply two additional locks and keys that could be set in place for peace of mind. Setting up a secured network is a challenging task. It requires careful design, thought, adequate planning, perspectives and recommendations of technologist. The Internet service provider network should be configured so that it is scalable and flexible to handle additional hardware and software as the network grows with combined Internet security technologies and biometrics.

Much attention has been paid to biometrics in recent months as a means to increase security for public places and businesses. Biometrics technology is superior to other identification solutions because it verifies a person's identity based on a unique physical attribute rather than some paper or plastic ID card, and as such, the number of biometric implementations is on the rise. Public awareness and acceptance of biometrics is increasing steadily as well. People realize the improved safety this technology offers us collectively as a society (Shoniregun, 2002).

The Newham Borough Council is a case in point where biometric technology has been adopted to combat the frequent street crimes within the Borough. The Newham Borough Council in east London uses a facial recognition system in a closed-circuit television (CCTV) control-room application as part of an anti-crime initiative. FaceIt, from the US firm Visionics, is part of a CCTV-based system called Mandrake. The Mandrake system uses the FaceIt software in conjunction with other control-room software and hardware to automatically scan the faces of people passing 144 CCTV cameras located around Newham. The system's objective is to reduce crime in Newham by searching for matches in a video library of known criminals stored in a local police database (Clinton, 1997).

The use of Biometrics provides greater security of our personal data and financial assets, which is more essential than ever before and using as a safeguard to our most critical data that could cause us the most harm if accessed by the wrong person. Some of the biggest potential applications include the use of biometrics for access to Automated Teller Machines (ATM), credit or debit cards. Many types of financial transactions are also potential applications e.g., banking by phone, banking by Internet, and buying and selling securities by telephone or by Internet.

With the application of biometrics several countries have saved significant amounts of money by implementing biometric verification procedures. The numbers of benefits claims has dropped dramatically in the process, validating the systems as an effective deterrent against multiple claims.

Criminals can use the Internet to find out all kinds of personal information about an individual like driver's license number or bank account number, even in some US prisons, visitors are subject to verification procedures in order that identities are not interchanged during the visit. Criminals can obtain the necessary data to get new credit cards issued in our names, print fake checks in our name, obtain bank loans in our name, and perpetrate other creative scams in our name to profit at our expense. When we find what has happened, serious damage can be done. Victims of identity theft often spend years and thousands of dollars clearing their names and credit reports (Clinton, 1997).

Implementing payment processing systems that utilize biometrics with private account management can easily prevent credit card crime. Biometrics can be incorporated at the point of sale, thereby enabling consumers to enroll their payment options e.g., checking, credit, debit, loyalty, etc., into a secure electronic account that is protected by, and accessed with, a unique physical attribute such as a fingerprint. Cash, cards or cheques are not needed to make purchases, so there is no need to carry them in a purse or wallet. Not carrying a purse or wallet eliminates the chances of it being stolen or lost while shopping (Oppliger, 2002).

Biometric transaction-processing systems allow consumers to manage point-of-sale payment easily and securely. This solution is particularly well suited for personal check use. Biometrics can also offer increased protection for check-cashing services, whether personal or payroll. By requiring biometric identity verification before allowing a check to be cashed, the possibility of it being presented by anyone other than the intended payee is eliminated.

Biometrics technologies have been provided a security solution that can improve the collective safety of society, and it is undoubtedly useful in this manner. Since the September 11 terrorist attack on US (World Trade Tower) many questions have been raised concern with airport security. Biometrics can be implemented as one of the main component of security system. A biometrics verification and identification can ensure that a person is who claims to be and prevent the suspect individuals. If the identity of a traveler or employee is a merit of question, biometrics can be a highly effective solution. An individual using a forged or stolen ID card, if required to verify biometrically before entering in a secure area, would likely be detected if his or her biometric does not matched the biometric on file. An individual claiming a fraudulent ID can be identified from a database of known criminals and linked to biometric identification systems, which may prevent him/her from boarding an airplane (Liu, 2001).

ATTACKS ON A BIOMETRIC SYSTEM

There are seven main areas where attacks may occur in a biometric system:

- Presenting fake biometrics or a copy at the sensor, for instance a fake finger or a face mask. It is also possible to try and resubmitting previously stored digitized biometrics signals such as a copy of a fingerprint image or a voice recording.

- Producing feature sets preselected by the intruder by overriding the feature extraction process.
- Tampering with the biometric feature representation: The features extracted from the input signal are replaced with a fraudulent feature set.
- Attacking the channel between the stored templates and the matcher: The stored templates are sent to the matcher through a communication channel. The data traveling through this channel could be intercepted and modified - There is a real danger if the biometric feature set is transmitted over the Internet.
- Corrupting the matcher: The matcher is attacked and corrupted so that it produces pre-selected match scores.
- Tampering with stored templates, either locally or remotely.
- Overriding the match result.

Figure 8. Vulnerabilities in a biometric system (Ratha, Connell, and Bolle, 2001)

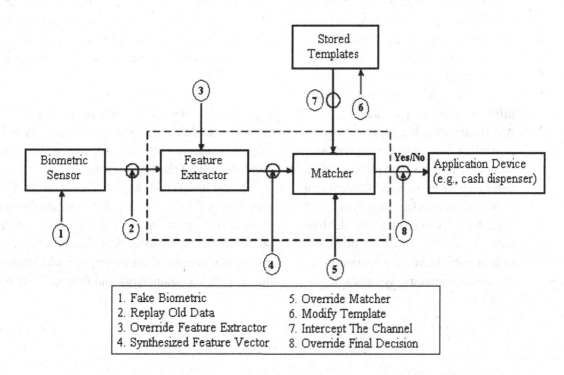

1. Fake Biometric
2. Replay Old Data
3. Override Feature Extractor
4. Synthesized Feature Vector
5. Override Matcher
6. Modify Template
7. Intercept The Channel
8. Override Final Decision

The security afforded by a biometric system can be undermined due to a variety of reasons: (Ratha, Connell, and Bolle, 2001).

- Administration: The administrative capability of the system can be abused to compromise the integrity of the system.
- Intrinsic: The inherent limitation in information content, and the representation/matching schemes may result in the erroneous acceptance of an intruder.
- Infrastructure: A denial-of-service attack can disable system functionality.
- Non secure processing: A hacker could exploit the nature of processing adopted by the system to fraudulently gain access into the system.
- Patent: Biometrics identifiers are not secrets and, hence, an intruder, though unaware of the intricacies of the system, could create physical or digital artifacts to fool the system.
    1. **Zero-effort attacks:** The biometric traits of an opportunistic intruder may be sufficiently similar to a legitimately enrolled individual, resulting in a False Match and a breach of system security. This event is related to the probability of observing a degree of similarity between templates originating from different sources by chance.
    2. **Adversary attacks:** This refers to the possibility that a determined impostor would be able to masquerade as an enrolled user by using a physical or a digital artifact of a legitimately enrolled user. An individual may also deliberately manipulate his or her biometric trait in order to avoid detection by an automated biometric system.

Zero-Effort Attacks

What is the probability that the biometric data originating from two different individuals will be sufficiently similar? This question leads to the issue of individuality in biometrics. The individuality of a certain biometric trait is a function of the interclass similarity and the intra class variability associated with the trait. In order to address this issue, one could model the source that generates the biometric signal or model the parameters constituting the template (i.e., feature set). The individuality problem, in the context of, say, fingerprints, can be formulated in many different ways depending on which one of the following aspects of the problem is under examination:

1. Determine the probability that any two (or more) individuals may have sufficiently similar fingerprints in a given target population;
2. Given a sample fingerprint, determine the probability of finding a sufficiently similar fingerprint in a target population;
3. Given two fingerprints from two different fingers, determine the probability that they are sufficiently similar. A scientific basis for fingerprint comparison can establish an upper bound on the performance of fingerprint systems.

Given a representation scheme (*minutiae distribution*) and a similarity measure (*string matching*), there are two approaches for determining the individuality of the fingerprints.

In the empirical approach, representative samples of fingerprints are collected and using a typical fingerprint matcher, the accuracy of the matcher on the samples provides an indication of the uniqueness of the fingerprint with respect to the matcher. (Jain, Ross and Pankanti, 2006)

Adversary Attacks

Biometrics are not "secrets." Physical traits, such as face and fingerprint, can be surreptitiously obtained from an individual (e.g., covert acquisition of face images or lifting latent prints from an object) for creating digital or physical artifacts that can then be used to spoof the identity of a legitimately enrolled individual. Besides this, there are other attacks that can be launched against an application whose resources are protected using biometrics (Gorman, 2003, Uludag and Jain 2004).

1. **Circumvention:** An intruder may fraudulently gain access to the system by circumventing the biometric matcher and peruse sensitive data such as medical records pertaining to a legitimately enrolled user. Besides violating the privacy of the enrolled user, the impostor can modify sensitive data including biometric information.
2. **Repudiation:** A legitimate user may access the facilities offered by an application and then claim that an intruder had circumvented the system. A bank clerk, for example, may modify the financial records of a customer and then deny responsibility by claiming that an intruder must have spoofed her (i.e., the clerk's) biometric trait and accessed the records.
3. **Collusion:** An individual with super-user privileges (such as an administrator) may deliberately modify biometric system parameters to permit incursions by a collaborating intruder.
4. **Coercion:** An impostor may force a legitimate user (e.g., at gunpoint) to grant him access to the system.
5. **Denial of Service (DoS):** An attacker may overwhelm the system resources to the point where legitimate users desiring access will be refused service. For example, a server that processes access requests can be bombarded with a large number of bogus requests, thereby overloading its computational resources and preventing valid requests from being processed.

STATISTICAL MEASURES OF BIOMETRICS

To know how well something performs, we must be able to quantify the performance. For our purposes, the statistical measures to be used for biometrics are: (Reid, 2003)

- FAR (False Acceptance Rate)
- FRR (False Rejection Rate)
- FTE (Failure to Enrol)
- EER (Equal Error Rate)

A discussion of each statistical measure follows.

FAR

Definition

The FAR is defined as the probability that a user making a false claim about his/her identity will be verified as that false identity. For example, if X types Y' user ID into the biometric login for Y' PC, X has just made a false claim that he is Y. X presents his biometric measurement for verification. If the biometric system matches X to Y, then there is a false acceptance. This means that X's biometric feature could be is very similar to Y' or matching threshold is set too high. Anyway, a false acceptance has occurred (Reid, 2003).

Evaluation of FAR

When the FAR is calculated. Using our example, it is equal to the number of times that X has successfully authenticated as Y divided by his total number of attempts.

In this case, we refer as

$$Y \rightarrow \text{"Match User"}$$

X→ "Non Match User."
Where n is enrolled user

N	Value
1	Y
2	X

Non Match User'(n) = Number of Non Match
  User Successful Authentications
Non Match User (n) = Number of Non Match
  User Attempts To Falsely Authenticate
FAR (n) = Non Match User'(n)/Non Match
  User (n)

n = 1

$$\frac{FAR(Y)}{X(Y)}$$

This gives us the basis for X and Y. Another user Z X and Y are represents user population. Assume that the FAR will be the same for Z.

Statistically, the more times something is done, the greater the confidence in the result. Thus, to ensure a high probability that the FAR we calculate is statistically significant, we would need to do this for every combination of users we have. Calculate FARs for each user's attempt to falsely authenticate as another, sum them up, and divide by the total number of users.

Thus we have

$$FAR(Y) = \frac{\left(\dfrac{X'(Y)}{X(Y)} + \dfrac{Z'(Y)}{Z(Y)}\right)}{2}$$

If we generalize the formula, we get:
  n = enrolled user
  N = total enrolled user population
  Non Match User'(n) = Number of Non Match
    User successful Authentication
  Non Match User (n) = Number of Non Match
    User Attempts To Falsely Authenticate

N	Value
1	Y
2	X
3	Z
4	K
5	P
.	.
N	T

FAR(n) = Non Match User'(n) / Non Match
  User(n)

$$FAR = \frac{1}{N}\sum_{n=1}^{N} FAR(n)$$

FRR

Definition

The FRR is defined as the probability that a user making a true claim about his/her identity will be rejected as him/her. For example, if Y types his correct user ID into the biometric login for his PC, Y has just made a true claim that he is Y. Y presents his biometric measurement for verification. If the biometric system does not match Y to Y, then there is a false rejection. This could happen because the matching threshold is set too low, or Y' presented biometric feature is not close enough to the biometric template. Anyway, a false rejection has occurred.

Evaluation of FRR

It is equal to the number of times that Y unsuccessfully authenticated as Y divided by his total number of attempts. In this case, Y is referred to as the "Match User":
  n = enrolled user
  N = total enrolled user population

N	Value
1	Y
2	X

Match User'(n) = Number of Match User Unsuccessful Authentications

Match User (n) = Number of Match User Attempts To Authenticate

FRR (n) = Match User'(n)/Match User (n)

n = 1

$$FRR(Y) = \frac{Y'(Y)}{Y(Y)}$$

This gives us the basis for Y' FRR. Another user X Y represents user population Assume that the FRR will be the same for X.

Statistically, the more times something is done, the greater the confidence in the result. Thus, if we want to ensure a high probability that the FRR we calculate is statistically significant, we would need to do this for every user. We would then need to take all the calculated FRRs for each user's attempt to authenticate as himself/herself, sum them up, and divide by the total number of users. The result is the mean (average) FRR for all users of a system.

Thus we have

$$FRR(N) = \frac{\left(\dfrac{Y'(Y)}{Y(Y)} + \dfrac{X'(X)}{X(X)} \right)}{2}$$

If we generalize the formula, we get:

n = enrolled user

N = total enrolled user population

Match User'(n) = Number of Match User Unsuccessful Authentication

Match User'(n) = Number of Match User Attempts To Authenticate

N	Value
1	Y
2	X
3	Z
4	K
5	P
.	.
N	T

FRR(n) = Non Match User'(n) / Non Match User(n)

$$FRR = \frac{1}{N} \sum_{n=1}^{N} FRR(n) \ (\text{Paul Reid, } 2003) \ \text{FTE}$$

Definition

The FTE is defined as the probability that a user attempting to biometrically enroll will be unable to. For example, K goes to the group in his company responsible for biometric enrollments. He is quickly instructed on the use of a biometric device, and then he attempts to have his biometric trait enrolled. At this time, he is unable to be enrolled. What defines his FTE can influence this measure. If the FTE is defined as a single-attempt failure, then the FTE will likely be higher than what would be seen over a larger group of people.

The FTE is normally defined by a minimum of three attempts. This is justified by the Rule of Three. The Rule of Three in this case provides us with a confidence level for a given error rate for our FTE. It also assumes that each attempt to enroll is independent, identically distributed, and that the user population size is significantly large enough. For example, if K is part of a population of 300 people, then using the Rule of Three for a 95% confidence level, we would obtain an FTE of 1%. Thus, if K is still unable to be enrolled after three attempts, he has had an FTE.(A.J.Mansfield and J.L.Wayman, 2002). (Paul Reid, 2003)

Evaluation of FTE

When the FTE is calculated by a biometric vendor, it is generally calculated with three attempts for enrollment. Since multiple attempts may need to occur before a decision is made on a success or failure, the three or fewer attempts will be called an enrollment event. In this case, a successful enrollment event occurs if K can be enrolled in three or fewer attempts. An unsuccessful enrollment event occurs if K, on his third attempt, is still unsuccessful. Thus, the FTE is calculated as the number of unsuccessful enrollment events divided by the total number of enrollment events.

n = Enrollment Candidate N = Total Number of Enrollment Candidates

N	Value
1	K
2	X

Event'(n) = Number of Unsuccessful Enrollment Events

Event (n) = Total Number of Enrollment Events

FTE (n) = Event'(n) / Event (n)

n = 1

FTE (K) = Event'(K) / Event (K) It gives us the basis for K's FTE.

If we have another user, X? K represents user population Assume that the FTE will be the same for X.

Statistically, the more times something is done, the greater the confidence in the result. Thus, if we want to have a high confidence that the FTE we calculate is statistically significant, we would need to do this for every user. We would then need to take all the calculated FTEs for each user's attempt to biometrically enroll, sum them up, and divide by the total of all biometric enrollment attempts to determine the mean (average) FTE.

For example, we could take the above formulas and do them over again for each user. We would eventually get something that looks like the following:

$$FTE\left(N\right) = \frac{\left(\dfrac{Event'\left(K\right)}{Event\left(K\right)} + \dfrac{Event'\left(X\right)}{Event\left(X\right)}\right)}{2}$$

If we generalize the formula, we get:

n = Enrollment Candidate

N = Total Number of Enrollment Candidates

Event'(n) = Number of Unsuccessful Enrollment Events

Event(n) = Total Number of Enrollment Events

N	value
1	Y
2	X
3	Z
4	K
5	P
.	.
N	T

FTE(n) = event'(n) / Event(n)

$$FTE = \frac{1}{N}\sum_{n=1}^{N} FTE\left(n\right) \text{ (Paul Reid, 2003.)}$$

EER

Definition

The EER is defined as the crossover point on a graph that has both the FAR and FRR. It can also be calculated from a ROC curve, which plots FAR against FRR to determine a particular device's sensitivity and accuracy. The choice of using the crossover point of the FRR/FAR or using a ROC is a question of significance. An EER calculated using the FRR and FAR is susceptible to manipulation based on the granularity of threshold values. A ROC-based EER is not affected by such manipulations because the FRR and FAR are graphed together. Thus, the EER calculated using a ROC is less dependent on scaling. (Bromba, http://www.bromba.com/faq//biofaqe.htm)

Evaluation of EER

To calculate the EER using the FRR/FAR crossover, the following is done: For any given threshold value from 0 to 1, respective FAR and FRR are calculated and plotted on the same graph. Since the granularity used for the values between 0 and 1 can be selected, this introduces the pos-

Figure 9. Calculating EER from FAR – FRR intersection

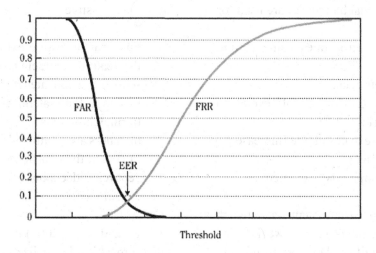

sibility of manipulating the results. A sample graph would look like Figure 10. (Paul Reid, 2003) As we can see from the graph, the EER occurs where the two lines cross.

To calculate the ROC of a biometric system, each corresponding FAR and FRR point is plotted on a logarithmic scale (Figure 10-2). The EER is then found by extending a 45-degree line from the point of origin (0, 0). Where this line crosses the ROC is the EER. This happens because when the FRR has a value of 1, the FAR has a value of 0, and when the FRR has a value of 0, the FAR has a value of 1. (Paul Reid, 2003)

WHY MULTIMODAL BIOMETRICS?

The strength and weakness of each Biometric trait depends on the application. A single biometric is not sufficient to meet all the requirements (e.g. accuracy, acceptability, cost, uniqueness etc.). The use of biometric for internet security is determined depending upon the requirements of the

Figure 10. Calculating EER from a ROC curve

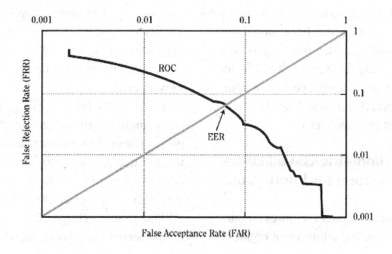

application and the properties of Biometrics traits. Therefore, multimodal biometrics are used for-

- Unacceptable error rates using a single biometric
- Noisy biometric data
- Flexibility to provide one of several possible biometrics
- Reduce failure to enroll rate (increase population coverage)
- Difficult to employ fake biometric

Multimodal Biometric System is a system that uses more than one independent or weakly correlated biometric identifier taken from an individual (e.g., fingerprint and face of the same person, or fingerprints from two different fingers of a person). Multimodal biometrics use a combination of different biometric recognition technologies In order for the biometrics to be ultra-secure and to provide more-than-average accuracy, more than one form of biometric identification is required. Hence the need arises for the use of multimodal biometrics. This uses a combination of different biometric recognition technologies.

- Multimodal biometrics systems improve performance
- A combination in a verification system improves system accuracy
- A combination in an identification system improves system speed as well as accuracy
- A combination of uncorrelated modalities (e.g. fingerprint and face, two fingers of a person, etc.) is expected to result in a better improvement in performance than a combination of correlated modalities (e.g. different fingerprint matchers.)

A Multimodal Biometric-Based User-Identification System for Internet use

A multimodal biometric system requires an integration scheme to fuse the information obtained from the individual modalities. Various levels of fusion are possible:

1. Fusion at the feature-extraction level, where the features extracted using two or more sensors are concatenated;
2. Fusion at the matching-score level, where the matching scores obtained from multiple matchers are combined;
3. Fusion at the decision level, where the accept/reject decisions of multiple systems are consolidated.

(Jain and Ross, 2001) described an interesting approach to the realization of a multimodal biometric verification system that uses fusion at the matching-score level based on learning user-specific matching thresholds as well as the weights of individual biometric traits (Ross, Nandakumar, and Jain, 2006).

DISCUSSION AND FUTURE WORK

The future of internet security using biometrics depends upon the application, requirement (threat model) and return on investment (ROI). The biometric industry must first shed the negative media perceptions of the technologies. It must change the perceptions of an immature and standards developing market. It must improve the engineering of biometric applications and show a better return on investment to corporations. And most importantly, it must improve its growth by eliminating the privacy perceptions and legal issues that exist.

In most of the businesses organization consumers are increasingly recognizing the limitations of passwords and PIN numbers, as computer hacking identify theft become more common, Biometrics devices offer a higher level of security because they verify biological characteristics which are difficult to attack (forge). Biometrics devices also relieve security personnel, network managers and customer service representatives of the difficult job. PIN was one of the first identifiers to offer automated recognition and this also applies to cards and other tokens. We may easily recognize the token, but it could be presented by anybody.

A biometric, however, cannot be easily transferred between individuals and represents a unique identifier as compared with the traditional PIN. Biometric devices are not easily spoofed. In the context of travel and tourism, for example, one immediately thinks of immigration control, boarding gate identity verification and other security related functions. Everyday questions following questions are asked.

Who should be given access to a secure system?

Who has the authorization to perform a given transaction?

Biometrics also presents important technical policies and system challenges that must be solved because there is no substitute for this technology for addressing many critical internet security problems. There are no guidelines to integrate biometric authentication mechanisms into existing applications. However, the early implementers of biometric technology have found themselves limited to single application implementations based on single vendor product offerings. A single biometric trait is not sufficient to meet all the requirements (e.g. accuracy, acceptability, cost, uniqueness etc.). The use of multi modal biometric for internet security is determined depending upon the requirements of the application and the properties of Biometrics traits. Soft Biometric traits like gender, height, weight, age, and ethnicity to complement the identity information provided by the primary biometric identifiers. Although soft biometric characteristics lack the distinctiveness and permanence to identify an individual uniquely and reliably yet they provide some evidence about the user identity that could be beneficial.

Internet users want to control what personal information is disclosed about them to others and how that information is used and further distributed and shared. The state of the art technology for internet security has been addressed and pointed out the imminent integration of business self-regulation and the consumer's ability to enhance individual privacy protection through the use of biometrics. There is a need of biometric technologies to protect privacy on the Internet. A company has the choice of using virtual private networks, digital certificates, data encryption, and network operating systems to protect their data while in transit, ensure the identity of a user, and mask the data from unauthorized eyes.

The future of internet security is not all rosy, because as the Internet technology continues to become more complex, the safeguards used today may be severely out of date tomorrow. Biometric will be most effective when it is integrated with other security measures. Strong encryption is not the answer to every security issue.

The technology of Internet security using biometrics cannot be predicted to the rate technology is advancing. The ethical issues related to biometrics technologies are of major concern. With the advancement of the time society is growing more complex and people becoming more interconnected in every ways? While biometric technology appears to be well suited to provide a user convenient component of secure person identity linkage, there may be cultural, societal, and religious resistance towards acceptance of this technology. Community needs the privacy, dignity and autonomy of each individual. We must develop new protection for privacy in the face of new technological reality.

A poorly implemented biometric system can be the cause of disaster, and further basis of resistance by the user. On the other hand a well implemented biometric system will be sufficient to safeguard the privacy of user. More attention is needed for general education of the end users, system administrators, integrators and most important public policy makers.

One of most problematic vulnerabilities of biometrics is that once a biometric image of template is stolen, it is stolen forever and can't be reissued, updated, or destroyed. The solution to this problem is cancelable (reusable) biometrics. A cancelable template stored in a database of certain application can't be used in another application. A cancelable template can be produced by transforming either the biometric image or features into another representation space by using a noninvertible transform.

The factor that is going to drive the Internet security is the set of applications and level of security required. The future of internet security will possibly be similar to an immune system. The immune system fights off attacks and builds itself to fight tougher enemies. In the same way, the network security will be able to function as an immune system. The trend towards biometrics implementation could have taken place a while ago, but it seems that it isn't being actively pursued. Many security developments that are taking place are within the same set of security technology that is being used today with some minor adjustments

CONCLUSION

It is important to understand that foolproof internet security systems simply do not exists, and perhaps never in near future. Security is the risk management strategy that identifies controls, eliminates, or minimizes uncertain events that may adversely affects system resources and information assets. The security requirement of a system depends upon the requirements (threat modal) of an application and cost benefit analysis.

Selecting the right biometric is a complicated problem that involves more factors than just accuracy. It depends on cost, error rates, computational speed, acquit ability, privacy and easy of use. A research is needed into anti-spoofing techniques

aiming at making biometrics authentication and identification systems, which is intelligent in distinguishing between presented real and fake data. Special techniques that are applied at the time and place the person tries to gain access to the biometric system are to be developed performing liveliness checking and thus trying to detect cases of biometrics provided from artificial equipment.

The practical challenges in security and privacy are extended into the social, political and economic sphere and triggered by the technological artefacts themselves. It is certain that biometric based internet security system will have a profound influence on the way we conduct our daily business because of the inherent potential for effectively linking people to records, thereby ensuring internet security. There are no cause-and effect relations amongst technological implementations and the resulting infrastructures, as a variety of contextual elements influences the implementations themselves. Sustained efforts in designing techniques for information protection are essential to streamline the proliferation of convenient and efficient biometric systems. Therefore, more research concerning biometric implementations is needed to incorporate aspects of biometric security and privacy that go beyond the purely technical domain with its rational-logical solutions. Issues such as data protection, new opportunities for criminality and the handling of false positives and false negatives should be treated under a new perspective of a broader internet security; a perspective that will recognize both the validity of such an approach and of advancing biometric security and privacy beyond the scope of strictly technical solutions.

REFERENCES

Bolle, R., Connell, J., Pankanti, S., & Ratha, N. (2003). *Guide to biometrics*. New York, NY: Springer.

Bromba, M. (n.d.). *Bio-identification frequently asked questions.* Retrieved from http://www.bromba.com/ faq/ biofaqe.htm

Chadwick, K., Good, J., Kerr, G., McGee, F., & O'Mahaonv, F. (2001). *Biometric authentication for network access and network application.*

Clinton, W. J. (1997, 18 May). *Commencement Address at Morgan State University, 1997.*

Cukic, B., & Bartlow, N. (2005). Biometric system threats and countermeasures: A risk based approach. In *Proceedings of the Biometric Consortium Conference* (BCC 05), Crystal City, VA, USA, Sept. 2005.

Daugman, J. (1999). Recognizing persons by their iris patterns. In Jain, A. K., Bolle, R., & Pankanti, S. (Eds.), *Biometrics: Personal identification in a networked society.* Norwell, MA: Kluwer.

Eschelbeck, G. (2000). Active security: A proactive approach for computer security systems. *Network and Computer Application, 23*, 109–130. doi:10.1006/jnca.2000.0103

Jain, A. K., Flynn, P., & Ross, A. A. (2008). *Handbook of biometrics.* New York, NY: Springer.

Jain, A. K., Nandakumar, K., & Nagar, A. (2008). Biometric template security. *EURASIP Journal on Advances in Signal Processing, 8*(2), 1–17. doi:10.1155/2008/579416

Jain, A. K., & Ross, A. (2001). *Learning user-specific parameters in a multibiometric system.* Retrieved from http:// www.rossarun.jain. cse. msu.edu

Jain, A. K., Ross, A., & Pankanti, S. (2006). Biometrics: A tool for information security. *IEEE Transactions on Information Forensics and Security, 1*(2), 125–143. doi:10.1109/TIFS.2006.873653

Kartalopoulos, S. V. (2008). Network security. *Conference on Next Generation Intelligent Optical Networks,* (pp. 191–251).

Liu, Y. (2001). *E-commerce agents, marketplace solutions, security issues, and supply and demand.* Springer.

PC Magazine. (1999, March). *The future of Internet security.*

Maltoni, D., Maio, D., Jain, A. K., & Prabhakar, S. (2009). *Handbook of fingerprint recognition.* New York, NY: Springer.

Mansfield, A. J., & Wayman, J. L. (2002). *Best practices in testing and reporting performance of biometric devices,* (version 2.01, p. 11). Middlesex, UK: Centre of Mathematics and Scientific Computing National Physical Laboratory.

O'Gorman, L. (2003). Comparing passwords, tokens, and biometrics for user authentication. *Proceedings of the IEEE, 91*(12), 2019–2040. doi:10.1109/JPROC.2003.819605

Oppliger, R. (2002). *Internet and Intranet security* (2nd ed.). Artech House Publishers. FIPS Pub. (1994, September 28). *FIPS Pub 190: Guideline for the use of advanced authentication technology alternatives.* FIPS Pub. (1994, February 9). *FIPS Pub 185: Escrowed encryption standard.* FIPS Pub. (1997, February). *FIPS Pub 196: Entity authentication using public key cryptography.* FIPS Pub. (2002, March). FIPS Pub 198: The keyed-hash message authentication code (HMAC).

Ratha, N., Connell, J. H., & Bolle, R. M. (2001a). An analysis of minutiae matching strength. In *Proceedings of the International Conference on Audio and Video-based Biometric Person Authentication,* Halmstad, Sweden, June 2001, (pp. 223–228).

Ratha, N. K., Connell, J., & Bolle, R. (2001b). Enhancing security and privacy in biometrics-based authentication systems. *IBM Systems Journal*, *40*(3), 614–634. doi:10.1147/sj.403.0614

Ratha, N. K., Connell, J., & Bolle, R. M. (1999). A biometrics-based secure authentication system. In *Proceedings of the Workshop on Automatic Identification Advances Technologies*, 1999.

Ratha, N. K., Connell, J. H., & Bolle, R. M. (2003). Biometrics break-ins and band-aids. *Pattern Recognition Letters*, *24*(13), 2105–2113. doi:10.1016/S0167-8655(03)00080-1

Reid, P. (2003). *Biometrics for network security*. Prentice Hall PTR.

Roberts, C. (2007). Biometric attack vectors and defenses. *Computers & Security*, *26*(1), 14–25. doi:10.1016/j.cose.2006.12.008

Ross, A. A., Nandakumar, K., & Jain, A. K. (2006). *Handbook of multibiometrics*. New York, NY: Springer.

Schneier, B. (1999). Attack trees. *Dr. Dobb's Journal*, *24*(12), 21–29.

Shoniregun, C. A. (2002). The future of Internet security: Should common Internet security technologies be blended with biometrics for accuracy and reliability. *ACM: Ubiquity, 3*(37).

Soutar, C. (n.d.). *Biometric system security White Paper*. Bioscrypt (Online). Retrieved from http://www.bioscrypt.com

Tistarelli, M., Li, S. Z., & Chellappa, R. (2009). *Handbook of remote biometrics*. New York, NY: Springer.

Uludag, U., & Jain, A. K. (2004). Attacks on biometric systems: A case study in fingerprints. In *Proceedings of SPIE-EI Security, Steganography and Watermarking of Multimedia Contents VI*, San Jose, CA, January, (pp. 622–633).

Zhang, D. D. (2000). *Automated biometrics technology and systems*. Kluwer Academic.

Chapter 7
Quality of Service (QoS) in WiMAX

Kashinath Basu
Oxford Brookes University, UK

Sherali Zeadally
University of the District of Columbia, USA

Farhan Siddiqui
Walden University, USA

ABSTRACT

The WiMAX technology provides wireless QoS-enabled broadband access for fixed and mobile users at the metropolitan level. It is end-to-end IP based and provides a rich set of QoS support for multimedia-based ubiquitous computing. The main contribution of WiMAX in terms of technology has been over its radio interface, which is based on the IEEE 802.16-2004 and 802.16e protocols. It is a two layer protocol stack, which provides a very robust QoS framework. At the physical layer, it focuses on optimising the use of radio resources. In the MAC layer, the main focus is on efficient scheduling and allocation of bandwidth to meet the QoS requirements of IP sessions. This chapter investigates the WiMAX architecture, its components, and the QoS support provided by the IEEE 802.16 protocol stack. It also examines mobility management issues, end-to-end QoS, and current and future application areas of the technology.

INTRODUCTION

With the rapid proliferation of ubiquitous computing devices along with them hosting multimedia applications, it has become important to facilitate an infrastructure to support both mobility and QoS over a wireless environment. There have been many attempts to address either of them,

but few attempts to address both goals (i.e., mobility and Quality of Service (QoS)) together. For example, the WiFi solution based on IEEE 802.11 provides bandwidth up to 300 Mbps, but is limited in range to less than 100 metres and does not provide any inherent QoS support. On the contrary, most 3G mobile technologies can offer mobility and coverage over a wide area but have bandwidth limited to 20 – 40 Mbps depending on the specific technology. Moreover, it is not fully

DOI: 10.4018/978-1-4666-0203-8.ch007

IP based and is therefore an expensive solution for the long term. In this context, the Worldwide Interoperability for Microwave Access (WiMAX) network offers a solution by providing broadband wireless access with QoS and full mobility at the metropolitan level. A single WiMAX base station (BS) can cover a cell radius of up to 30 miles and speed up to 128 Mbps. Typically, as with any wireless technology, a compromise is made between distance and bandwidth based on the channel condition and load.

The WiMAX spectrum ranges from 2 – 66 GHz and covers both licensed and unlicensed bands. Different countries and operators use different subsets of these bands based on local government policies and usage requirements. The radio interface is based on Orthogonal Frequency Division Multiple Access (OFDMA) and the individual channel sizes range from 1.5MHz – 20 MHz. WiMAX supports both Line-Of-Sight (LOS) and Non-LOS (NLOS) communication. The LOS transmission uses the higher frequencies range up to 66 GHz while the NLOS uses frequencies in the range 2-11 GHz. The LOS set-up is used to provide wireless backhaul for telephony and data services as a replacement of existing copper, fiber and satellite-based backbone infrastructure. It could also be used to connect tall office towers with the BS as an alternative to high bandwidth leased line. The NLOS set-up acts as a wireless access network for home and office users. However, unlike WiFi it is not restricted to only hotspots but supports full mobility with QoS over the entire coverage area. With its efficient handover and roaming support, WiMAX is also a candidate for 4G mobile technology.

The WiMAX standard was first introduced in late 2001. After a few ratifications, a comprehensive document covering the various aspects of the technology was produced in 2004 as 802.16-2004 (IEEE 802.16, 2004). An extension to the standard covering mobility and enhanced QoS support was included in the IEEE 802.16e (IEEE 802.16e, 2005). Till this point, WiMAX only supported point-to-point and point-to-multipoint communications. Another extension covering mesh and ad-hoc model of communication was included in IEEE 802.16j.

This chapter focuses on the QoS support provided in the WiMAX technology. It is based on IEEE 802.16-2004 and 802.16e addendum. It presents an analysis of the end-to-end WiMAX protocol stack, the QoS provisions available over each layer and in each segment of the stack and how it is integrated to provide an end-to-end QoS solution.

WIMAX ARCHITECTURE

The WiMAX architecture defines a framework for end-to-end IP-based QoS-enabled multiservice for fixed and mobile users. It is based on the IETF standardized IP protocols and the network specification was developed by the WiMAX Forum's Network Working Group (NWG) with input from the Service Provider Working Group (SPWG) about the service requirements.

The WiMAX network reference model is made of three logical components (Figure 1). This includes the Mobile Station (MS), the Access Service Network (ASN) and the Connectivity Service Network (CSN). Each component is characterized by a set of related functionalities and are interconnected with other components by a clearly defined set of standardized interfaces. This allows smooth interoperability between different types of vendor equipments operating at different levels of the network.

The MS is generic mobile equipment providing connectivity between the mobile host and the ASN. The host could be a notebook, a WiMAX-enabled smart phone or a wireless backhaul point for example. The MS is connected to the ASN via the R1 radio interface based on the IEEE 802.16 MAC and Physical layer (PHY) standards. This interface is used both for data and control plane messages. The ASN consists of Base Stations

Figure 1. WiMAX network reference model

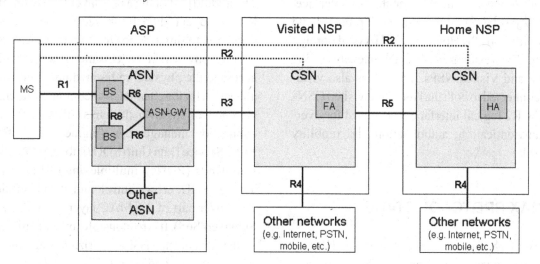

(BS) and ASN Gateways (ASN-GW). The BSs are connected to the MS via the R1 interface and implements the PHY and MAC features of IEEE 802.16. These include the MAC level uplink and downlink schedulers for MAC level QoS management. Several BSs are connected to an ASN gateway via the R6 interface. This path is used to transport layer 2 control messages from the ASN-GW and also for tunneling layer 3 control information and data from the CSN via the R3 interface. The ASN-GW is responsible for radio resource management between the base stations and supports ASN anchored mobility between the BSs connected to the same ASN-GW. ASN-GWs are also inter-connected via the R4 interface for mobility between the ASNs/ ASN-GWs. A BS can also be connected to more than one ASN-GW for load balancing and redundancy purposes. The recently revised implementation profile of ASN (ASN Profile C) also includes a logical R8 interface directly between the BSs for fast handovers between the BSs and could be used for both control information and data transport. Several ASNs interconnected via the R4 interface are managed by a Network Access Provider (NAP). These infrastructure services are used in turn by a Network Service Provider (NSP). A NSP may use the

access infrastructure of several NAPs and a NAP may also share its infrastructure with several NSPs. The NSP is a business entity providing IP connectivity and operator-managed services to the WiMAX subscribers. Each NSP has a separate CSN that implements a range of layer 3 functionalities. These includes IP address management and resolution through Dynamic Host Control Protocol (DHCP) and Domain Name Service (DNS), support for IP mobility, QoS management based on admission and usage control, user and device authentication and authorization via the Authentication Authorization Accounting (AAA) proxy/server, subscriber billing, internetworking gateways for connectivity with other types of network such as the Internet, Public Switched Telephone Network (PSTN) and mobile networks, connectivity to managed WiMAX services such as IP Multimedia services (IMS), location-based services, peer-to-peer, multicast and broadcast services and lawful intercept services. The CSN is connected to the ASN via the R3 interface which is used to tunnel both data and control information between the two components. The CSN also plays an important role in mobility. These include intra CSN mobility between the ASNs via the R3 and R4 interfaces and inter CSN mobility between the NSPs via IP tunnels over the R5 interface. Mobility is based on the mobile IP protocol and is facilitated by the Home Agent (HA) and Foreign Agent (FA) residing in the CSN gateways of the Home and Visited NSPs. The MS is also virtually connected to both the Home and visited CSNs via the R2 logical interface that is used for overlay authentication, authorisation and mobility control.

WIMAX PROTOCOL STACK

The WiMAX network provides end-to-end IP connectivity between the MS and the CSN. Operation on the WiMAX network model is facilitated by an end-to-end WiMAX protocol stack. The protocol stack isdifferent for each of the communication interfaces between the components (Figure 2). Some of the interfaces also have a separate stack for the control plane (Figure 3). The R1 interface between the mobile and the base station provides the radio access for WiMAX and is based on the IEEE 802.16e protocol stack. It is a two-layered stack covering the physical and the MAC layers. The physical layer is based on the Scalable OFDMA to transport data and control over the air interface. The WiMAX MAC layer is connection-oriented and is made up of three sublayers. The topmost section is the Convergence Sublayer (CS). The CS sublayer is responsible for mapping higher layer protocols and their QoS requirements over the MAC layer. There are two types of CS: The Asynchronous Transfer Mode (ATM)-CS and the packet CS. The ATM-CS maps different types of ATM services and the packet CS maps different types of packets of different protocolssuch as IPv6, IPv6, PPP, etc. The QoS parameters of the higher layer service flow is characterized by a unique Service Flow Identifier (SFID) which is mapped to a unique MAC level logical connection through a Channel Identifier (CID). The CS sublayer may also compress repetitive parts of the higher layer encapsulated protocol for efficiency.

The middle part of the MAC layer is the Common Part Sublayer (CPS). It provides all the functions necessary to support the QoS of the service flows over the physical layer. This includes controlling access to the physical radio medium, bandwidth allocation for the channels, scheduling of the channel connections over the physical layer frames, connection management, fragmentation of the MAC Service Data Unit (SDU) into MAC Protocol Data Units (PDUs), multiplexing of SDUs into a single PDU, error control, and retransmission. The lower part of the MAC layer is the Security Sublayer (SeS). It is responsible for authentication of the SS and the BS, authorization against the theft of service and encryption for data integrity. The Private Key Management (PKM) protocol could be used to exchange of digital certificates for authentication and authorization and for the distribution of keys for encryption. The payload could be encrypted using encryption algorithms such as Rivest Shamir Adleman (RSA), Data Encryption Standard (DES), Advanced Encryption Standard (AES), etc.

The R6 and the R3 interface between the BS and the ASN-GW and the ASN-GW and the CSN are generally based on a wireline IP network. The IP data packets received at the BS over the IEEE 802.16e MAC connections could be mapped onto (need to define all these acronyms Kashi) GRE, MPLS, VLAN or IP tunnels by mapping the CIDs on to Generic Routing Encapsulation (GRE) keys, MPLS labels, VLAN tags or IP tunnel address respectively.

Control information in the WiMAX network is generally encapsulated within User Datagram Protocol/Internet Protocol (UDP/IP). These include the exchange of ASN control messages between BSs or between ASN-GWs or between BS and ASN-GW at the R8, R4 and R6 interfaces respectively (Figure 3). Similarly at the R3 interface, mobility management protocols such as Mobile IP (MIP) and authentication, authorisation and accounting (AAA) protocol named Remote Authentication Dial In User Service (RADIUS)

Figure 2. End-to-end protocol stack of the WiMAX network model

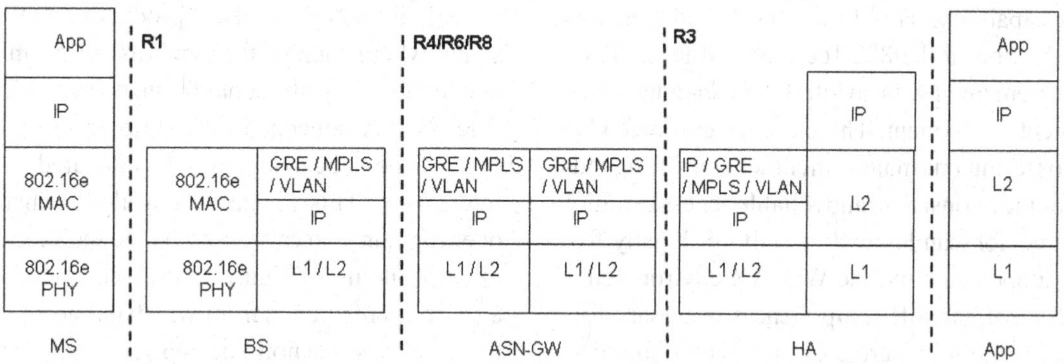

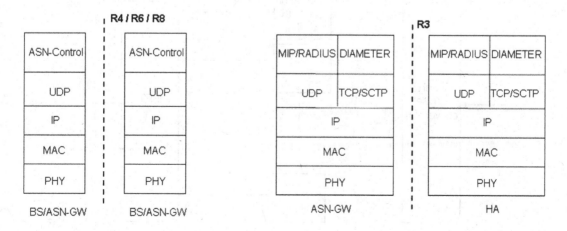

are encapsulated over UDP/IP. The only exception is if AAA is done using the (define acronym) DI-AMETER protocol which is based on connection-oriented TCP or Stream Control Transmission Protocol (SCTP) over IP.

QOS AND WIMAX

QoS Support in the WiMAX Protocol Stack

The goal of the WiMAX protocol stack (Figure 2) is to provide a consistent and reliable QoS over the WiMAX network from the MS to the CSN. The connection between the BS to the CSN is typically

wireline and is based on established connectivity protocols. On the other hand, the connectivity between the MS and the BS is radio-based. Providing consistent and reliable connectivity over this section of the network is essential to support end-to-end QoS. This radio network is based on the IEEE 802.16e protocol stack and includes the physical and the MAC layers.

QoS in the IEEE 802.16e Physical Layer

The QoS support in the physical layer of the IEEE 802.16e protocol stack is based on the coordination of a number of components. The main component in this layer is the Scalable OFDMA technique

Figure 3. Control protocol stack of the WiMAX network model

with its inherent efficient radio resource management capability. This forms the foundation for QoS support at the 802.16e physical layer. This is supplemented with an intelligent antenna management component. There are several recently proposed antenna management schemes designed to provide a consistent and reliable access to radio resources for seamless end-to-end QoS. Finally, for QoS support in a mobile WiMAX environment, an efficient handoff component is necessary for seamless mobility across cells. This section discusses the QoS support offered by each of these components in detail.

Scalable OFDMA

The scalable OFDMA technique used over the radio interface has several inherent QoS support mechamisms. It is based on the OFDM principle which has three main stages for generating the radio signals (Figure - 4) (Johnston & Yaghoobi, 2004). In the first stage, the source signals are converted from the serial to the paralleldomain. After this each of the parallel signal stream is modulated and coded into symbols to increase the efficiency of the channels. Finally, the parallel symbol streams are passed to an Inverse Fast Fourier Transform (IFFT) module. The OFDM

theory shows that when an IFFT of magnitude N is applied on N symbols, it produces an OFDM signal where each of the symbols is transmitted in one of the N orthogonal frequencies. OFDMA extends this concept to multiple access where each of the subcarriers may be allocated to different users. This allocation may also be changed over regular intervals based on the QoS requirement of the user (Figure 5). Sub-channelization also offers resilience from wideband noise since the users who are notallocated the effected channels will only suffer from minimal or no impact. Moreover, during the modulation and coding phase, each of the channels may be coded with a different modulation and coding scheme based on the channel condition at that point of time. For example, a highly efficient 64-Quadrature Amplitude Modulation (QAM) coding scheme could be used when the channel condition is good, whereas a more robust Binary Phase Shift Keying (BPSK) scheme is suitable when the channel condition is poor. In intermediate conditions, 16-QAM or Quadrature Phase Shift Keying (QPSK) may be more suitable. The efficiency of an encoding scheme is determined by the number of bits it can encode in each symbol. For example, 64-QAM can encode 6 bits per symbol whereas BPSK can only encode 1 bit per symbol. Therefore a

Figure 4. OFDM stages

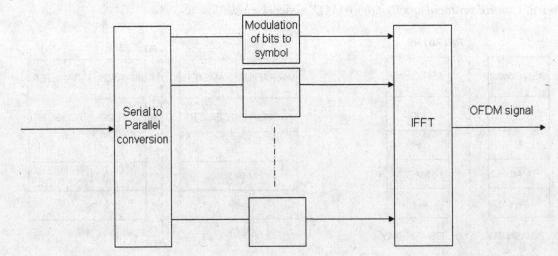

Figure 5. OFDMA multiple access

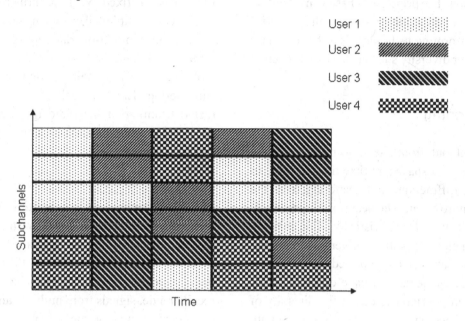

channel coded with 64-QAM will provide much higher bit level throughput than one coded with BPSK, even though their frequency bandwidth may be the same (Bestetti, Giambene, & Hadzic, 2008).

Using scalable OFDMA the carrier bandwidth can be divided into 128 to 2048 subcarrier channels with each subcarrier bandwidth in the range 1.25 to 20 MHz. This scalability in the number of subcarriers optimizes the usage of radio resources. The frequency bandwidth of the carrier can be adapted based on the number of subcarriers. When the demand for radio resource increases, the number of subcarriers is increased with spare radio resources from neighbouring cells. Similarly, when the demand decreases, the number of subcarriers is reduced and resources are released. In addition, these OFDMA subcarrier channels are orthogonal to each other; therefore there is minimal interference between the subcarriers. As a result, the subcarriers can be very closely spaced minimizing the wastage of unused frequency bands between them leading to an increase in the effective frequency bandwidth of the carrier. Another

advantage of using OFDMA with the single carrier frequency modulation technique is that the source symbols are now spread across several subcarriers thereby increasing the symbol duration. In contrast, when using a single carrier the symbol duration has to be a fraction of this time to achieve the same overall symbol transmission rate. This long symbol period along with some additional guard band can completely eliminate Inter Symbol Interference (ISI) from multipath fading. These characteristics of scalable OFDMA have made it the ideal candidate for QoS provisioning for IEEE 802.16 physical layer.

Antenna Management in WiMAX

Intelligent antenna management techniques can significantly improve the QoS offered by the radio resources at the physical layer. The IEEE 802.16e standard provides several advanced antenna technologies that can improve the quality of the received signals, increase the throughput of the channel, the range of coverage and capacity and also reduce the amount of interference and power consumption. The principle is based on either the receiver diversity at the BS site as is the case with most beamforming technologies or both (sender and receiver diversity such as in MIMO) (Lehne & Pettersen, 1999).

Beamforming

Signal sent out from the transmitter over the radio undergoes space and time diversity due to reflection, diffraction, and scattering over the cellular environment. The beamforming technology exploits this characteristic by using an array of antenna element at the receiver to capture the signal. The same signal captured by the different antenna elements will have different levels of noise and interference due to the diversity of their path. These signals are then combined with different weights based on their reception quality to generate the final output signal with a high Carrier to Interference and Noise Ratio (CINR). While combining, signals received with high noise and interference are weighted down whereas good quality signals are weighted up. This approach helps to achieve interference diversity gain. Moreover, since beamforming produces output signal with a high CINR, therefore more efficient modulation and coding schemes could be used to increase the effective capacity of the channel.

On the downlink side, based on the information received from the uplink side, the Direction Of Arrival (DOA) can be estimated and then power can be allocated to the different transmission path accordingly. In this case the goal is to ensure that the beam from the resulting antenna system focuses towards the direction of the MS. This approach has several advantages over a traditional sectored antenna system. In this case, since the beam is focused only towards the direction of the user and not throughout the sector, any interference is only restricted to a small angle. Moreover, by concentrating the energy only within a small region significant antenna gain can be achieved and the coverage area of the BS can be increased.

In the case of fixed WiMAX further spatial diversity can be exploited by reusing the same radio resource in two non-overlapping regions of the same sector. This however, is not possible for mobile users where their positions may change and overlap. This approach of adaptive and directed beaming of the radio resource also reduces the power consumption of the system.

MIMO

The MIMO technology uses multiple antennas at the sender and receiver ends. During transmission, these antennas exploit the spatial and temporal diversity by sending signals on different radio paths over the same subcarrier channel. At the receiver side, signals from multiple antennas are combined to increase the receiver sensitivity or the capacity of the subcarrier or both.

The WiMAX Forum has adopted two out of the several MIMO technologies proposed in the IEEE 802.16e standard for downlink. These are the Space-Time Transmit Diversity (STTD) and the Spatial Multiplexing (SM) schemes. The STTD scheme is based on exploiting the spatial

Figure 6. Beamforming

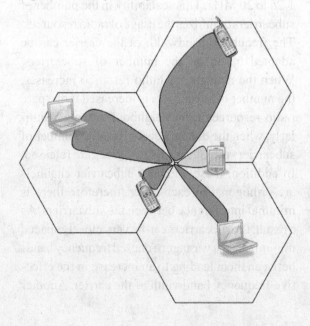

diversity by using several antennas separated over space to transmit the same information separated over space and time with a space-time encoding scheme. For example matrix A is a two antenna system with two symbols X_1 and X_2 to be

$$A = \begin{bmatrix} X_1 & -X_2 \\ X_2 & X_1 \end{bmatrix} \quad \begin{array}{l} \text{Antenna - 1} \\ \text{Antenna - 2} \end{array}$$
$$t = 1 \quad t = 2$$

transmitted. Using space-time encoding, at time $t = 1$ symbols X_1 and X_2 will be transmitted and at time $t = 2$ symbols $-X_2$ and X_1 will be transmitted from the two antennas respectively. Using this scheme, the theoretical diversity gain is the product of the number of transmitters and receivers. Therefore the received signal quality can be improved by increasing the number of transmit/receive antennas.

The SM scheme uses multiple antennas to transmit different signals in parallel on separate independent streams over the same subcarrier. Using this scheme, the theoretical capacity of the subcarrier can be increased up to a maximum which is proportional to the minimum between the total number of transmit and receive antennas.

Therefore using MIMO, the receiver can benefit from diversity gain or/and increased throughput. In situations where the channel condition is poor and the received signal is weak, STTD scheme could be used to increase the robustness of the signal whereas when the receiver's channel is well conditioned and the received signal is strong, the SM scheme could be used to improve the throughput. A combination of these two schemes will provide a more flexible and robust QoS to the receiving MSs. The two schemes can be combined using a two tier hierarchical antenna system. At the top level, antennas may be grouped into a number of SM sets. Each of these sets may transmit different signals in parallel. At the next level, the antennas within each SM set can use STTD to transmit the same information

over separate time and space. So for example, when the channel condition deteriorates, the size of the SM sets could be increased and therefore the number of such sets decreased leading to more redundant transmissions at the expense of reduced throughput. During good channel conditions, the number of sets could be increased and therefore the size of such sets decreased to provide a higher throughput. The channel condition could be estimated based on the feedback obtained from the MSs to the BS using a closed-loop feedback scheme. In theory, it is possible that the different antennas in the antenna system are located at different BSs. However, that will create additional complexity in synchronization and scheduling among the different BSs.

In the uplink direction, WiMAX standard uses only the collaborative SM MIMO scheme. In this scheme, several mobile stations equipped with a single antenna transmit to the BS on the same channel using different sets of pilot signals. This could significantly improve the capacity of the channel depending on the channel condition.

The WiMAX forum adopted MIMO schemes that are based on two antennas at each end at the BS and MS for downlink and one antenna at the MS for uplink. This trade-off is mainly to optimize the amount of additional hardware, processing overhead, and power consumption at the MS. In future releases of the WiMAX standard, as equipment size and energy usage reduces, MIMO technologies will be further exploited.

Handover Support in WiMAX

Beamforming and MIMO technologies can extend the cell coverage, increase the signal to noise ratio or cell capacity up to a certain threshold that may be suitable for fixed or nomadic subscribers. However, in order to support full mobility of the MS, these antenna schemes have to be supplemented with an efficient handover scheme to facilitate smooth and transparent migration between different cell regions. Handover in WiMAX is based on the mobility support schemes proposed in the IEEE 802.16e extension. There are two main categories of handover: Hard and soft handover. Hard handover, also called break-before-make, involves the mobile station disconnecting with the current serving BS before making a new connection with a neighbouring BS. This process has a large overhead by repeating the entire network re-entry phase with the new target BS. These include the additional control and delay overheads in the initial ranging negotiation phase, authentication, authorization, and registration phases with the new BS and encryption key exchange. Due to these reasons hard handover is only suitable for simple mobility and non-real-time applications.

The other category of handover is soft handover, also known as make-before-break. In this scheme, a radio connection to a target BS is first made before disconnecting from the current serving BS. In this type of handover, the MS maintains a diverse set of potential BSs for future handovers. This list is prepared by a MS by scanning the neighbouring BSs (by inspecting the Uplink Channel Descriptor (UCD) and Downlink Channel Descriptor (DCD) sections of their frames) or in collaboration with the current serving BS (by inspecting the neighbourhood advertisement messages from the BS) (Becvar & Zelenka, 2006). In either case, initial ranging has to be conducted by the MS with the BSs in the list. The radio resource used in the ranging process can be optimized with the BSs sending their ranging responses over the Access Service Network (ASN) backbone to the current serving BS. The serving BS may then coordinate with the MS to decide on the target BS. During the actual handover, the re-entry phase can be shortened by transferring the current state information of the connection over the backbone network from the serving BS to the current BS. Using this soft approach, re-connection is only required in layer 1 and the existing connections of layer 2 and upward can be maintained. Therefore the MAC connection Identifiers (IDs) and the IP connectivity above it can be maintained. This al-

lows maintaining a homogeneous transparent QoS even for real-time applications. This is in contrast to the hard handover approach where the entire network re-entry phase has to be repeated and reconnection is required at each layer of the stack thereby introducing delay and control overheads.

There are two variations of soft handovers. These are the Macro Diversity Handover (MDHO) and Fast BS Switching (FBSS). In the MDHO, the MS transmits and receives from all the BSs in the diversity set. Data is combined in the downlink direction from the BSs to the MS using diversity combining and in the uplink direction from the MS to the BSs using selection diversity. In the FBSS mode, data is transmitted and received from a single anchor BS at any one time. This anchor BS may however change within the diversity set from one frame to another based on the signal quality (Chammakhi Msadaa, Câmara, & Filali, 2010).

The various components of layer 1 can synchronize with each other to provide a reliable and consistent QoS over the physical radio layer. For example, when intelligent antenna management techniques such as beamforming and MIMO are used to improve the receiver sensitivity, then less robust but more efficient modulation and coding scheme such as 64-QAM could be used to send a higher number of bits per symbol without the loss in quality. Similarly, using beamforming, the size of a cell could be increased and the usage of radio resource optimized. Likewise, MIMO can help both to increase the signal quality and the capacity of the sub-carrier channel. The physical bandwidth of the radio medium can also be increased by scaling up the number of subcarriers using scalable OFDMA. All these techniques provide a robust framework for QoS support at layer 1.

802.16e Physical Layer Frame Structure

The frame is divided into two sections: the downlink and the uplink subframe. In the TDD mode, these two sections are separated over time.

The frame is of fixed length but the size of the individual sections can vary from one frame to another based on the demand on the downlink and uplink side. In the FDD mode, the two subframes are of fixed length and are separated over different frequency channels.

An IEEE 802.16e frame is made up of a fixed number of physical slots where a slot is the duration of four OFDM symbols. Each of the uplink and downlink regions of the frame is divided into a number of sections for control and data transport between the serving BS and the MSs in the cell. The structures of an OFDM TDD downlink and uplink subframe sare shown in Figure 7. The downlink subframe from the BS to the MSsconsists of one PDU shared by the different MSs. The frame begins with a preamble which is used for synchronization between the listening MSs and the BS. This is followed by the Frame Control Header (FCH), the Downlink Map (DL-MAP) and the Uplink Map (UL-MAP) fields. These fields provide an index to the location, profile, and the Channel Identifiers (CID) associated with the different downlink and uplink bursts in the frame. The CID field is used to identify the MS(s) associated with a MAC layer channel and the profile describes the size and modulation and coding scheme used for the bursts. Occasionally, some of the frames also contain the downlink and the uplink channel descriptors (DCD and UCD) fields which contain the descriptions of burst profiles available at the downlink and uplink direction along with information about the chan-

nel conditions under which they could be used. For the uplink side, the MS could use it as a reference to encode the bursts it sends to the BS. For the downlink side, if the quality of the received signal lies outside the lower or the upper threshold of the particular encoding scheme used, then the mobile station could request the BS to use a more or a less robust modulation and coding scheme. The control fields themselves are always encoded with a robust encoding scheme to protect them from transmission noise. The remainder of the downlink subframe is filled with downlink bursts for MSs in the cell.

The uplink subframe begins with the contention slots used for initial ranging during the network entry phase. MSs joining a network use these slots to synchronize physical layer parameters such as power level, frequency and timing offset. The slots are also used to request for dedicated non-contention-based basic, primary and possibly secondary management MAC channels. This field is followed by another range of contention slots used for bandwidth request. These slots are used by the MSs to requests uplink bandwidth from the BS. The remainder of the uplink subframe is filled with burst from the different MSs based on the bandwidth allocation in the UL-MAP.

In the case of OFDMA physical, the logical structure of the frame is identical; however the physical structure is different since the frame is now extended over both time and subcarrier domain (Figure 8). The burstto/from a frame is spread over a number of subcarriers and several slot

Figure 7. TDD OFDM physical frame

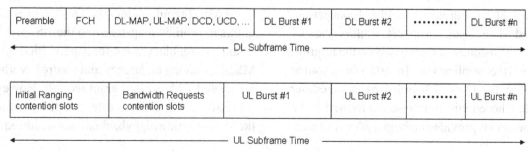

Preamble	FCH	DL-MAP, UL-MAP, DCD, UCD, ...	DL Burst #1	DL Burst #2	··········	DL Burst #n

←————————————————— DL Subframe Time —————————————————→

Initial Ranging contention slots	Bandwidth Requests contention slots	UL Burst #1	UL Burst #2	··········	UL Burst #n

←————————————————— UL Subframe Time —————————————————→

Figure 8. TDD OFDMA physical frame

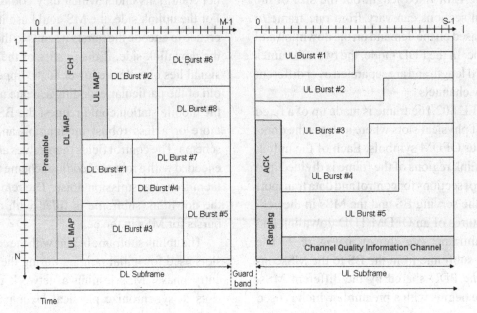

intervals. The robustness of the frame could be improved by dividing the frame into a number of permutation zones and then using different combination of non-adjacent subcarrier frequencies to encode adjacent regions of the frame. Each permutation zone could use a different permutation algorithm such as PUSC or FUSC, AMC, (need to define all these acronyms) etc. to select the subcarriers. This frequency diversity within a frame provides protection against frequency selective fading. This physical layer frame provides the foundation over which the IEEE 802.16e layer 2 QoS provisioning schemes could be deployed.

QoS in MAC Layer

The IEEE 802.16e protocol stack has a connection-oriented MAC layer. It supports multiservice by providing customized QoS based on the requirement of the application. In 802.16e resource allocation for QoS is handled by a scheduler module whose main component is located at the BS. The QoS is provided at the granularity of each

individual flow identified by a Unique Channel Identifier (CID) and characterized by a QoS class and its set of QoS parameters.

IEEE 802.16e QoS Classes

There are five different QoS classes in 802.16e to cater for different categories of application. These are the: Unsolicited Grant Service (UGS), Extended real-time Polling Service (ertPS), real-time Polling Service (rtPS), non real-time Polling Service (nrtPS) and Best Effort (BE). These QoS classes vary in their QoS parameter set (Table 1) and have different types of bandwidth request and allocation schemes.

The UGS class provides a constant bit rate service by allocating fixed sized bandwidth grants to the MS at regular intervals. The MS uses these grants to send data upstream to the BS. There is no explicit regular request for bandwidth from the MS, thus saving on latency and control overhead associated with explicit grant request. However, if the queue size exceeds a certain threshold then the MS can send a piggybacked bandwidth request to the BS by setting the Slip Indicator (SI) bit in the grant management subheader. This type of service is suitable for real-time constant bit rate traffic such as T1/T3 circuits and uncompressed voice and video.

The ertPS is based on the flexibility of the UGS and rtPS class. In this case, the BS sends unsolicited bandwidth grants to the MS at regular intervals similar to UGS. However, unlike UGS here the grant sizes could be variable and request to change the grant size could be piggybacked in the grant management subheader of upstream MAC frames. This type of service class is suitable for delay and rate sensitive variable bit rate traffic such as compressed voice.

The rtPS class is suitable for rate sensitive traffic with less stringent and flexible delay requirements (such as encoded streaming video and audio) compared to the ertPS class.. In rtPS, the BS provides uplink slots at regular intervals for sending grant requests. The MS could use these slots to request bandwidth dynamically based on the characteristic of the service flow. The size of the grant request is variable and is based on the state of the flow at that point of time. Unlike the UGS and ertPS, in this case there is a delay overhead between the request and the allocation of the transmission slot (Belghith; Nuaym, & Maill'e, 2008).

The nrtPS QoS class is suitable for delay-tolerant, variable bit rate, bursty traffic such as telnet, ftp, etc. In this class, the BS provides slots for request grants based on only the minimum data rate of the traffic. Any additional bandwidth request has to be made using shared contention-based request handling channel.

The BE class is suitable for connectionless IP traffic (such as email and http). This class does not offer any bandwidth guarantees. The service flow uses mainly the contention slots to request uplink grant opportunities. During lightly loaded network conditions, the BS may also send unsolicited grant opportunities.

IEEE 802.16e QoS Parameters

The MAC layer of 802.16e provides a rich set of QoS parameters similar to many other multiservice QoS based networks such as Asynchronous Transmission Mode (ATM) or Integrated Services (Intserv). The QoS parameters quantify the QoS class at a detailed level of granularity. The main parameters include the following:

- Maximum data rate: The peak rate of the service flow.
- Minimum data rate: The minimum bandwidth that has to be assigned to the flow even at times of network congestion.
- Maximum burst size: The maximum size of the data block transmitted at peak rate.
- Maximum jitter: The maximum delay variation in the arrival of the MAC PDUs of the connection.
- Maximum latency: The maximum end to end delay between the MS and the BS.
- Priority: Prioritize between two flows sharing identical QoS parameters.

The particular service flow may use a subset of these QoS parameters based on its QoS class (Table 1).In addition to these there are several other parameters. These include parameters to specify whether the PDUs are of fixed or variable length, size of fixed length PDUs, restrictions on uplink bandwidth request options, etc (Nuaymi, 2007).

Admission Control and Scheduling in IEEE 802.16e

Admission control in a WiMAX network is based on the availability of resources to meet the QoS of the new service flow without affecting the existing service flows. There are two categories of service flows based on which there are two variants of admission control schemes. One of the categories is the pre-provisioned service flow. Under this

Table 1. Key parameters of the IEEE 802.16e QoS classes

QoS Class	Maximum data rate	Minimum data rate	Maximum jitter	Maximum latency	Priority
UGS	x		x	x	
ertPS	x	x	x	x	
rtPS	x	x		x	
nrtPS	x	x			x
BE	x (optional)				x

category, a subscriber has a static provisioned list of service flows and its associated QoS parameters. Admission control is carried out when subscribers join the network. All the associated service flows in the pre-provisioned list are admitted and resources reserved on successful admission control even though they may not be all active. The QoS level of the service flows are static and cannot be changed. The service flows are only deleted when the user leaves the network. This approach of admission control may overprovision resources since inactive service flows and other flows that are transmitting below their provisioned QoS levels may not use their allocated resources optimally.

The other category of service flows is the dynamic service flow where a service can be created by an existing user at any time and the QoS parameters of the service can be changed in the middle of a session. Similarly a user may delete any of its current flows without disconnecting from the network. A dynamic admission control scheme is required to deal with this type of service flow. In this approach, resources could be used more optimally as service flows are added, deleted, and modified on an ad hoc basis based on the current requirement level (Wood, 2010).

The admitted flows in a WiMAX network share the resources between them. The resource sharing between the flows is handled by a scheduler module which has two components. The main scheduler is based in the BS and it handles all downlink and uplink traffic. In the uplink side, it allocates bandwidth grants either at the granularity of individual channels, a group of channels or to the entire MS. In the latter two cases, a second scheduler at the MS schedules the bandwidth between contending channels.

The job of the scheduler is to allocate bandwidth to a service flow based on its QoS class and QoS parameters. As discussed earlier, for the UGS and ertPS class unsolicited bandwidth grants are sent based on their QoS requirements. For the remaining classes, bandwidth is allocated based on grant requests. A scheduling algorithm may also consider several other factors to provide the required level of QoS with the most optimal and efficient usage of resources. Traditional packet scheduling algorithms such as priority-based queuing, weighted round robin, deficit round robin, weighted fair queuing, etc could be used (Rashwan, ElBadawy & Ali 2009). In addition, many scheduling schemes have been proposed exclusively for WiMAX to cater for multiservice scheduling over the radio interface. These schemes have their own advantages and disadvantages. One of the schemes is the Temporary Removal Scheduler (TRS) that uses the quality of the radio signals of the transmission requests to prepare the scheduling list. Channels whose signals are above a certain threshold are only included in the list. In this scheme, channels with good quality signals will be rewarded at the expense of poor and noisy channels. Therefore the noisy channels may suffer from delay and jitter and could be unsuitable for real-time service. The Opportunistic Deficit Round Robin (O-DRR) scheduler addresses this drawback by also considering delay (by using queue length) along with signal strength as metrics to make scheduling decision. Another interesting approach is the Frame Registry Tree scheduler (FRTS) in which the MAC PDUs are organized as a tree structure based on their latest acceptable arrival deadline. A tree is made up of subtrees which consist of PDUs that are part of the same physical frame. A packet is placed in the tree based on its latest acceptable arrival deadline (Belghith & Nuaymi, 2008). If there are not enough PDUs in a subtree to fill up a frame, then PDUs from the subtree with the next closest deadline may be chosen. The tree configuration may change based on the variation in the QoS level and burst profiles. Another scheduling scheme is the Adaptive rtPS scheduler in which the scheduler predicts the future bandwidth requirements of the rtPS channels and allocates resources in advance accordingly. This reduces the delay associated in waiting for the next request opportunity. In general, an efficient WiMAX specific scheduling scheme will use at least a service flow's QoS parameter list, bandwidth requests, and signal quality to decide on the bandwidth allocation and burst profile for the flow.

End-to-End QoS

Applications require consistent and reliable QoS on an end-to-end basis. The end-to-end path may include different types of wireline and wireless networking technologies. In order to provide QoS on an end-to-end basis it is important that each of these intermediate networks has support for QoS provisioning. In addition, there has to be a well defined policy for mapping the QoS requirements from one type of network to another. In the context of WiMAX, the path between the MS and the IP core network needs to provide a guaranteed end-to-end QoS. This path encompasses the IEEE 802.16e protocol stack over the radio interface between the MS and BS and different types of mainly IP-enabled QoS technologies across the ASN and CSN up to the core.

In the radio segment of the path, a session is identified by a CID and characterized by a traffic class and its associated set of QoS parameters (Table 1). Across the ASN and CSN these sessions can be mapped on a one-to-one basis over other identical QoS-enabled multiservice technologies such as IP based integrated services (Intserv) paths or Asynchronous Transmission Mode (ATM) network's virtual circuits. In the case of Intserv, the 802.16e QoS class and its associated parameters could be mapped to an Intserv traffic class and its associated Traffic Specification (TSpec) parameters (Chen, Jiao & Guo, 2005, p. 3335). Similarly, in the case of ATM the QoS parameters could be mapped over an ATM QoS class and its associated traffic descriptors and QoS parameters (Table 2) (Basu, 2010). In other types of IP based networks such as MPLS, Differentiated services network (Diffserv), IP tunnels, etc., the CID could

Table 2. Mapping of IEEE 802.16e QoS parameters over Intserv and ATM

Traffic Category	IEEE 802.16e MAC classes	Intserv class	ATM class
Leased Line (E1/T1), PCM voice	UGS	Guaranteed Service (GS)	Constant bit rate (CBR)
VoIP	ertPS	Guaranteed Service (GS)	CBR/ Real-time Variable Bit Rate (rt-VBR)
Compressed video (Video-on Demand (VOD), IPTV)	rtPS	Guaranteed Service (GS)	rt-VBR
High bandwidth file transfer and downloads	nrtPS	Controlled Load Sharing Service (CLS)	Non rt-VBR/ Available bit rate (ABR)
Http, normal ftp, etc.	Best Effort (BE)	BE	UBR

also be mapped directly to a GRE key, MPLS label, DSCP or a VLAN tag configured appropriately with an equivalent set of QoS parameters.

A one-to-one mapping can preserve the QoS granularity of the flows; however this approach is not scalable. At the core of the network flows have to be aggregated based on similarity of QoS requirements and the nature of applications and serviced at the aggregated class level.

SUMMARY AND CONCLUSION

One of the strong characteristics of WiMAX is its rich set of inherent QoS. At the physical radio layer, the OFDMA technique provides optimized utilisation of the radio resources and partitions sub-carriers dynamically based on demand. This is supplemented with a rich set of intelligent antenna management and handover techniques. At the MAC layer, WiMAX provides a rich set of QoS classes and parameters and provides the facility to serve traffic at the granularity of individual sessions. The QoS offered at the radio part could be mapped onto existing QoS-enabled wireline technologies up to the IP core network.

The WiMAX technology has a wide variety of applications and is continuously evolving to cater for emerging application and service requirements. The initial fixed WiMAX version provided a good alternative to Asymmetric Digital Subscriber Line (ADSL) and cable modem at the access level and T1/ATM links at the backhaul. It provided a solution for fast deployment with limited set-up and running cost compared to the wireline alternatives. Mobile WiMAX provided the opportunity to cater to different types of ubiquitous devices and multimedia applications and an opportunity to provide a full end-to-end QoS-enabled IP based 4G mobile infrastructure. The most recent IEEE 802.16j addendum includes support for mesh networking enabling support for sensor and ad-hoc networking infrastructures (Kuran & Yilmaz,

(2006). This tremendous potential for adaptability with the WiMAX technology will play a significant role in its future success and viability.

REFERENCES

Basu, K. (2010). *QoS mapping of IP flows over ATM cell streams: Models for mapping variable length IP packets over fixed length ATM cells* (pp. 54–63). Saarbrücken, Germany: Lambert.

Becvar, Z., & Zelenka, J. (2006). Handovers in mobile WiMAX. *Research in Telecommunication Technology, 1*, 147–150.

Belghith, A., & Nuaymi, L. (2008). Comparison of WiMAX scheduling algorithms and proposals for the rtPS QoS class. In *14th European Wireless Conference, 2008* (EW 2008) (pp. 1-6). Prague.

Belghith, A., Nuaymi, L., & Maille, P. (2008, September). *Pricing of real-time applications in WiMAX systems.* IEEE 68th Vehicular Technology Conference (VTC2008), Calgary, Canada.

Bestetti, A., Giambene, G., & Hadzic, S. (2008). WiMAX: MAC layer performance assessments. *3rd International Symposium on Wireless Pervasive Computing (ISWPC 2008),* (pp. 490-494).

Chammakhi Msadaa, I., Câmara, D., & Filali, F. (2010). Mobility management in WiMAX networks. In Tang, S.-Y., Müller, P., & Sharif, H. R. (Eds.), *WiMAX security and quality of service: An end-to-end perspective* (pp. 179–210). Chichester, UK: John Wiley & Sons, Ltd. doi:10.1002/9780470665749.ch7

Chen, J., Jiao, W., & Guo, Q. (2005). An integrated QoS control architecture for IEEE 802.16 broadband wireless access systems. In *Global Telecommunications Conference, 2005 (IEEE GLOBECOM),* vol. 6 (pp. 3335-3340). St. Louis, MO.

IEEE802.16. (2004). IEEE standard for local and metropolitan area networks-Part 16: Air interface for fixed broadband wireless access systems.

IEEE802.16e. (2005). IEEE standard for local and metropolitan area networks-Part 16: Air interface for fixed and mobile broadband wireless access systems.

Johnston, D., & Yaghoobi, H. (2004). *Peering into the WiMAX spec: Part 1 & 2.* Intel Corp. Retrieved October 22, 2010, from http:// www. eetimes.com/ design/communications-design/ 4009277/ Peering-Into-the- WiMAX-Spec-Part-1

Kuran, M. S., & Yilmaz, B. (2006). Quality of service in mesh mode IEEE 802.16 networks. *International Conference on Software, Telecommunications and Computer Networks (SoftCOM)* (pp. 107-111). Split, Croatia.

Lehne, P. H., & Pettersen, M. (1999). An overview of smart antenna technology for mobile communications systems. *IEEE Communications Surveys, 2*(4).

Nuaymi, L. (2007). *WiMAX: Technology for broadband wireless access.* Wiley. doi:10.1002/9780470319055

Rashwan, A. H., ElBadawy, H. M., & Ali, H. H. (2009). Comparative ASSESSMENTS FOR Different

WiMAX scheduling algorithms. In *World Congress on Engineering and Computer Science 2009 (WCECS 2009)* vol. I. San Francisco.

Wood, M. C. (2010). *An analysis of the design and implementation of QoS over IEEE 802.16.* Retrieved October 18, 2010, from http:// www. cs.wustl.edu/ ~jain/cse574-06/ftp/ wimax_qos/ index.html

ADDITIONAL READING

Ahmadi, S. (2009). An overview of next-generation mobile WiMAX technology (WiMAX update). *IEEE Communications Magazine, 47*(6), 84–98. doi:10.1109/MCOM.2009.5116805

Ai, B., Yang, Z. X., Pan, C. Y., Ge, J. H., & Lu, Z. (2006). On the synchronization techniques for wireless OFDM systems. *IEEE Transactions on Broadcasting, 52*(2). doi:10.1109/ TBC.2006.872990

Andrews, G., Ghosh, A., & Muhamed, R. (2007). *Fundamentals of WiMAX: Understanding Broadband Wireless Networking.* Prentice Hall.

Balachandran, K., et al. (2007.), Design and Analysis of an IEEE 802.16e-Based OFDMA Communication Sysetem, *Bell Labs Technical Journal, Issue 4,* (pp. 53–73).

Bingham, J. A. C. (1990). Multicarrier modulation for data transmission: An ideal whose time has come. *IEEE Communications Magazine, 28*(5), 5–14. doi:10.1109/35.54342

Chakraborty, M., & Bhattacharyya, D. (2010). Overview of End-to-End WiMAX Network Architecture. In Tang, S.-Y., Müller, P., & Sharif, H. R. (Eds.), *WiMAX Security and Quality of Service: AN End-to-End Perspective* (pp. 3–22). Chichester, UK: John Wiley & Sons, Ltd. doi:10.1002/9780470665749.ch1

Chang, B. J., Chen, Y. L., & Chou, C. M. (2007). Adaptive Hierarchical Polling and Cost-based Call Admission Control in IEEE 802.16 WiMAX, *Wireless Communications and Networking Conference (WCNC 2007)* (pp. 1954 – 1958), Hong Kong.

Cicconetti, C., Lenzini, L., Mingozzi, E., & Eklund, C. (2006). Quality of service support in IEEE 802.16 networks. *IEEE Network, 20,* 50–55. doi:10.1109/MNET.2006.1607896

Eklund, C. (2006). *WirelessMAN: Inside the IEEE 802.16 Standard for Wireless Metropolitan Networks*. IEEE Press.

Etemad, K. (2008). Overview of mobile WiMAX technology and evolution. *IEEE Communications Magazine*, *46*(10), 31–40. doi:10.1109/MCOM.2008.4644117

Etemad, K., Lee, J., & Chang, Y. (2010). Overview of WiMax network architecture and evolution. In Etemad, K., & Lai, M.-Y. (Eds.), *WiMax Technology and Network Evolution* (pp. 147–178). Piscataway, NJ: IEEE Press. doi:10.1002/9780470633021

Jain, R., So-In, C., & Tamimi, A. (2008). *System Level Modeling of IEEE 802.16e Mobile WiMAX Networks: Key Issues* (*Vol. 15*, p. 5). IEEE Wireless Communication.

Kumari, K., Narasimha, S., & Sivalingam, K. M. (2010). QoS Issues and Challenges in WiMAX and WiMAX MMR Networks. In Tang, S.-Y., Müller, P., & Sharif, H. R. (Eds.), *WiMAX Security and Quality of Service: AN End-to-End Perspective* (pp. 261–308). Chichester, UK: John Wiley & Sons, Ltd.doi:10.1002/9780470665749.ch10

Lee, H., Kwon, T. & Cho,cD. (2006). *Extended-rtPS Algorithm for VoIP Services in IEEE 802.16 systems," IEEE Int. Conference on Communications, vol. 5* (pp. 2060-2065). Istanbul, Turkey.

Li, Y. G., & Stuber, G. L. (2006). *Orthogonal Frequency Division Multiplexing for Wireless Communications*. Springer. doi:10.1007/0-387-30235-2

Liberti, J., & Rappaport, T. S. (1999). *Smart Antennas for Wireless Communications: IS-95 and Third Generation CDMA Applications*. Prentice Hall.

Nee, R. V., & Prasad, R. (2000). *OFDM for Wireless Multimedia Communications*. Norwood, MA: Artech House Inc.

Ni, Q., Vinel, A., Xiao, Y., Turlikov, A., & Jiang, T. (2007). WIRELESS BROADBAND ACCESS: WIMAX AND BEYOND - Investigation of Bandwidth Request Mechanisms under Point-to-Multipoint Mode of WiMAX Networks. *IEEE Communications Magazine*, *45*, 132–138. doi:10.1109/MCOM.2007.358860

Rastin, P., Dirk, S., & Daniel, M. (2007). Performance Evaluation of Piggyback Requests in IEEE 802.16, *IEEE Vehicular Technology Conference* (pp. 1892-1896), Baltimore, MD.

So-In, C., Jain, R., & Tamimi, A. (2009). *Scheduling in IEEE 802.16e Mobile WiMAX Networks: Key Issues and a Survey* (*Vol. 27*, p. 2). IEEE JSAC.

Tran, M., Doufexi, A., & Nix, A. (2008). Mobile WiMAX MIMO performance analysis:Downlink and uplink. In *IEEE 19th International Symposium on Personal, Indoor and Mobile Radio Communications (PIMRC 2008)* (pp. 1–5), Cannes.

Yaghoobi, H. (2004). Scalable OFDMA Physical Layer in IEEE 802.16 WirelessMAN, *Intel Tech. Journal, vol. 8(3)* (pp. 201–12.).

Yang, X., Venkatachalam, M., & Mohanty, S. (2007). Exploiting the MAC layer flexibility of WiMAX to systematically enhance TCP performance, *IEEE Mobile WiMAX Symposium* (pp. 60-65).

Zheng, L., & Tse, D. N. C. (2002). Diversity and freedom: A fundamental tradeoff in multiple antenna channels. In *IEEE International Symposium on Information Theory (ISIT)* (p. 476), Lausanne, Switzerland.

APPENDIX: LIST OF ACRONYMS

AAA	Authentication, authorisation and accounting
ASN	Access Service Network
ATM	Asynchronous Transfer Mode
BPSK	Binary Phase Shift Keying
BS	Base station
CID	Connection Identifier
CINR	Carrier to Interference and Noise Ratio
CSN	Connectivity Service Network
DCD	Downlink Channel Descriptor
FA	Foreign Agent
FRTS	Frame Registry Tree scheduler
GRE	Generic Routing Encapsulation
HA	Home Agent
IFFT	Inverse Fast Fourier Transform
IMS	IP Multimedia services
ISI	Inter Symbol Interference
LOS	Line-Of-Sight
MDHO	Macro Diversity Handover
MIMO	Multiple Input/Multiple Output.
MPLS	Multiprotocol Label Switching
MS	Mobile Station
NSP	Network Service Provider
O-DRR	Opportunistic Deficit Round Robin
OFDMA	Orthogonal Frequency Division Multiple Access
PSTN	Public Switched Telephone Network
QAM	Quadrature Amplitude Modulation
QoS	Quality of Service
RADIUS	Remote Authentication Dial In User Service
SCTP	Stream Control Transmission Protocol
SFID	Service Flow Identifier
STTD	Space-Time Transmit Diversity
TRS	Temporary Removal Scheduler
UCD	Uplink Channel Descriptor
WiMax	Worldwide Interoperability for Microwave Access

Chapter 8
Analysis of the High–Speed Network Performance through a Prediction Feedback Based Model

Manjunath Ramachandra
Philips Innovation Campus, India

Pandit Pattabhirama
Philips Innovation Campus, India

ABSTRACT

Performance modeling of a high speed network is challenging, especially when the size of the network is large. The high speed networks span various applications such as the transportation, wireless sensors, et cetera. The present day transportation system makes uses of Internet for efficient command and control transfers. In such a communication system, reliability and in-time data transfer is critical. In addition to the sensor information, the present day wireless networks target to support streaming of multimedia and entertainment data from mobile to infrastructure network and vice versa. In this chapter, a novel modeling method for the network and its traffic shaping is introduced, and simulation model is provided. The performance with this model is analyzed. The case-study with wireless networks is considered. The chapter is essentially about solving the congestion control of packet loss using a differentially fed neural network controller.

DOI: 10.4018/978-1-4666-0203-8.ch008

INTRODUCTION

In a wireless network, the reflections and multi path transmission result in increased self similarity for the signal at the receiving end. The self similarity of the network refers to the invariance of the shape of the autocorrelation function when observed over multiple time scales. The self similarity imparts long-range dependency in to the traffic. As a result of long range dependency, the traffic turns bursty resulting in under or over utilization of the resources, increased packet loss etc.

In order to reduce the loss of multimedia data over the wireless medium, it is required to pump-in less data by controlling the degree of compression (and improving the channel coding) when the channel is more noisy. The importance of signal strength over the delays in a wireless channel are provided in (Beatriz Soret, M. Carmen Aguayo Torres, and J. Tomás Entrambasaguas, 2010).

When command and control data is to be exchanged, the data needs additional protection with an appropriate channel coding mechanism. It reduces the further deterioration of the signal to noise ratio (SNR) over the disturbed channel. In order to make it possible, a feedback on the channel status in terms of percentage loss of the data packets over the channel is required to be transferred to the source. Based on this input, a decision on the data transmission rate over the channel may be done.

For a perfect synergy between the forward and the feedback path, the properties of forward path that impart aberrations to the signal have to be annulled by generating appropriate signals in the feedback path. Ideally, the controller generating the feedback signal should have the same characteristics of the network. I.e., it should be a network in its own sense.

A good controller is required to foresee the trends in the network traffic variations and provide inputs to the traffic source well in advance. The source would get sufficient time to adjust the traffic rate or provide sufficient redundancies with appropriate channel coding schemes so that it would not flood the resources when it is disturbed. In this work, a neural network based controller is proposed. When a portion of the output of the neural network is tapped and provided as the additional input, it starts exhibiting the important characteristics of the data network such as self similarity, long range dependency, abstraction and so on and behaves as a miniaturized data network.

BACKGROUND

Independent of its origin, the internet traffic has a few know characteristics in common. It includes

- A few Predictable parameters in statistical sense
- Traffic follows poisson distribution
- Internet traffic is bursty. This is because packets of various size are involved Burstiness of one flow affects the other adaptive flows. This property is useful for the traffic control
- Overlapping of the independent on-off data sources leads to the arrival pattern distribution with heavy-tailed autocorrelation function. The long-range dependancy in the traffic leads to no "flattening" towards a mean when zoomed out. The same structures may be found at different time scales; hence the traffic is self similar
- TCP is known to propagate bottleneck self-similarity to the end system. The work-around is to use a model to predict traffic instead of guessing

The other features of the internet traffic include jitter, packet losses, delay, large buffer requirements, less data for decision, time varying characteristics and congestion.

Network Congestion

A network is said to be in a congested state if the aggregate demand for the bandwidth exceeds the available capacity of a link. It results in performance Degradation. Typically, congestion leads to congestion. As a result of congestion, there will be multiple packet loss, Low link utilization (low Throughput), High queuing delay, 'Congestion collapse', failure to meet the agreed quality of service and increased requirement of the resources. There are two common approaches for the congestion control:

- **Window-based:** Here the sources limit the number of unacknowledged packets in the network by reducing the window size. The window represents the maximum number of packets that can remain un-acknowledged at a given point of time. The features of window based control include
  - Window size gets increased and decreased based on the network status.
  - Implicit congestion signal based on packet loss
  - Slow-start
  - Fast-retransmit, fast-recovery
  - Congestion avoidance
- **Rate-based:** Here the rate of the traffic is varied based on the congestion status of the network. e.g., token bucket algorithm. It limits the transmission rate at the source

Random Early Detection (RED)

The RED provides a mechanism to detect incipient congestion in the network (J Padhye, V. Firoiu, D. Towsley and J Kurose, 2000). The goal of this algorithm is to minimize packet loss and queuing delay, avoid global synchronization, maintain high link utilization and remove the bias against the bursty source.

A traffic Controller shall have bursty and non bursty components, shall incorporate previous his-

tory. In RED, it is achieved by randomized packet drop and queue length averaging. It targets to keep mean of queue length (Q_{ave}) constant. Increase from the mean value triggers the random drops.

The basic algorithm of RED works as a low-pass filter (exponential weighted moving average). The filter parameters are to be small enough to filter out the transient congestion, and large enough for the average to be responsive.

Feedback Controller Architecture

A conventional neural network may be used to generate the requisite control signals in line with RED. Neural networks are used to relate non linearly connected input and output (Aarts, E.H.L. and Korst, J.H.M., 1989). They learn the input output pattern and start predicting the output after the training period. The architecture of a neural network is shown in Figure 1.

In the ex-or function learning rule, the output is 1 if $W_0 *I_0 + W_1 * I_1 + W_b > 0$ and 0 if $W_0 *I_0 + W_1 * I_1 + W_b <= 0$. The weights get updated through the back propagation of the error algorithm as $\Delta w = \xi.(error).i$

Figure 1. Artificial neural network

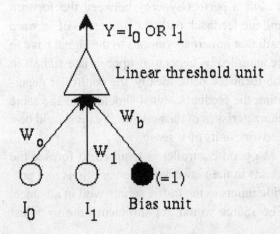

Differentially Fed Artificial Neural Network (DANN)

The output of a neural network but for the non-linearities is given by

$$y = \sum w_i x_i + w_j x_j \qquad (1)$$

Here x_i, x_j and y are the inputs and array of outputs at different time instants, w_i and w_j the corresponding weights. The space spanned by the weight vector for different inputs is a hyper plane (Amari.s, 1982, 1995, 1998, 2000). The linearity of the output is expressible as ARMA (Auto Regressive Moving Average)

$$y(n+1) = b_0 y(n) + b_1 y(n-1) + \ldots + a_0 x_n + \ldots \qquad (2)$$

Here b_0 and a_0 are constants. The auto regressive terms b_0 b_n are realized using differential feedback. The architecture of a DANN is shown in Figure 2.

The properties of a DANN(Manjunath.R, Gurumurthy.K.S., 2002, 2002a) are provided in Listing 1.

Listing 1. Properties of DANN relevant of network traffic shaping

- It makes use of historical inputs

- For a given number of iterations, the square error decreases with the order of the differential feedback. For infinite feedback, the square error is zero

- The output with different orders of feedback forms a manifold of hyper planes (M.Frazier and B.Jawerth, 1985) each of which is self similar to the other. The self similarity originates due to long range dependency in the data.

- The self similar outputs have varying degrees of abstraction (B. Jawerth and G. peters, 1993) each of which may be generated through the other by convolving with a Gaussian pulse.

- It works as a Bayesian estimator (D.J.C.Mac Kay, 1992, 1992a). It may be used for learning rules or equations when the input output relationship is probabilistic (Radford Neal, 1996) and the output is the degree of belief in a specific hypothesis (Zhu, H. Rohwer, R., 1995) or rule associated with a model.

- The combined effect of a large set of models or estimators (Rao, C. R., 1962) shifts towards the ideal estimator, replacing the set by a single model.

- DANN output resembles the data network signals at the receiver in statistical sense.

Figure 2. Architecture of DANN

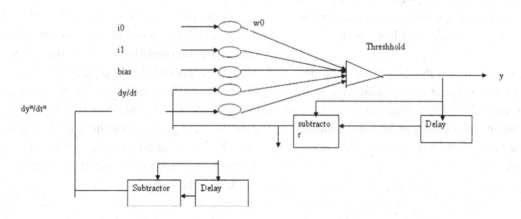

DANN FOR TRAFFIC SHAPING

Here, the neural network model that satisfies the aforementioned requirements of the controller is provided. Reliable transfer of data over the network requires network performance modeling. The performance model of the network also helps in the measurement of parameters and supports the experiments to improve the performance. The model has to imitate all the characteristics of the network in the statistical sense.

It is used as a predictor of the traffic status (or the RED signal) a few time steps ahead so that the data sources will have sufficient time to adjust the data rates and reduce the congestion. In a DANN, the usage of previous samples results in long range dependency. The dependency is a result of pileup due to previous transmission rates (the output of DANN) and previous resource allotments (the input of DANN) as shown in Figure 3.

This architecture implies a differential (delayed) feedback from the output to the input. Thus the proposed architecture better catches the dependencies. The abstract levels of higher order feedback correspond to self similarity of the network traffic over different time scales. As an ideal estimator, the model can replace multiple congestion control algorithms. It replaces the conventional neural networks to provide better results. As a tailored system, it reflects the properties of the computer network. Insertion of a DANN in the traffic loop makes the network to behave as a DANN exhibiting all the properties in a counter balancing fashion, depending up on the amount of feedback. The traffic input has 2 parts:

- Deterministic, high resolution, low pass component contributing for the bias of the variations of buffer utilization
- Random, low resolution, high pass component controlled or reduced by differential feedback

In a packet buffer of the network, the queue consists of a fixed part and the variable fluctuations. The impulse and Gaussian parts; Gaussian part (McKenzie, P. and Alder, M., 1994) is the aggregation of many connections and impulse part arises as a result of a few dominant connections. The DANN output also contains 2 components- one Gaussian component and one impulsive component.

Prediction Based Feedback

Here, the future traffic pattern is predicted through a shifted ECN (or RED signal).It is a multiple timescale control where the packet loss rate p(t) is predicted using a neural network.

The predicted value is used to adjust the data transmission rates from the source. It reduces the congestion & delays. The effect of shift is to provide

- Sufficient time to adjust the rates
- Global learning by merging QOS rules
- Stable system
- Reduced RTT & loss rate
- Reduced buffer size
- Reduced Queue variance & jitter
- Reduced flooding & timeouts
- More throughputs. Goes well with the real time traffic

Properties of the Model

The properties of the network are reflected in to this model. The model of controller provides a mechanism to control the behavior of the network. The traffic model helps to identify key properties of network traffic affecting performance and aid in the simulation. The model is indicative of channel dynamics and provides methods for traffic shaping. The longer time scales are used to control the data rates while the smaller time scale are used to modulates the same.

Figure 3. Traffic shaping with DANN

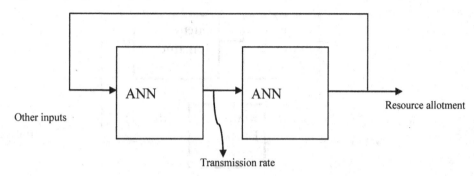

The effect of providing differential feedback in the model is to shift or scale the time. Shift or prediction reduces the delay: It is as though the effective bandwidth increases. Finally it boils down to adjusting the bitrates and reduces the self similarity (counter the fading & multi path) to meet the delay bounds. The features of quality of service (QoS) controller model include:

- Match with the traffic characteristics.
- Produce output similar to the network.
- Prediction of trends
- Shift the prediction.

The QoS is very important and often difficult to support over a wireless medium. The relevance of QoS is highlighted in (S. Chen, J. Cobb, 2006).

Features of the Proposed Model

The proposed information feedback model goes well with the characteristics of the network that support the distributed components. The traffic over the network, be it LAN or the WAN, turns out to be self-similar. I.e., the shape of the autocorrelation function of the traffic observed over different time scales remain the same. The status signal such as the probability of packet loss sampled from the network, spans several time scales (S. Mallat and W.L. Hwang, 1991). i.e. It

Figure 4. Equivalent architecture with delayed feedback

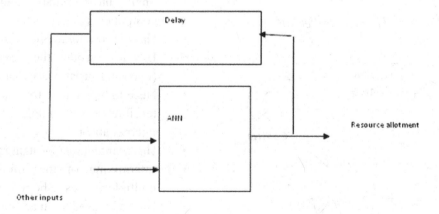

Figure 5. Control system

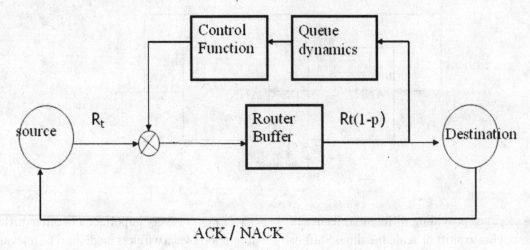

ACK / NACK

happens to be the resultant of the events taking place at different timescales. The controller model precisely has all these characteristics, making it look like the network. If it sits in the feedback path, it should be easy to control the network as shown in Figure 6.

QoS is related to buffer dynamics. Though the large buffers reduce the packet loss, the packet delays increases. On the other hand, small buffers could result in reduced delay at the risk of increased packet loss. It calls for different enforcements i.e. packet discard rules to ensure the QoS adaptively depending up on buffer size, growth, rate

Figure 6. Feedback based controller in the network

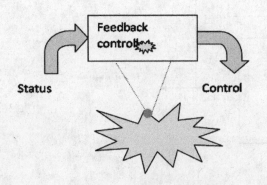

of the growth etc. These parameters are considered as the inputs of the DANN that predicts the traffic at different time scales. As a result of the differential feedback used in the controller, the control signal spans multiple time scales. This important feature provides additional advantage of 'multiple time scale control" for the inter component communication. The requirements of a DANN based feedback controller are provided in listing 2.

Listing 2. Requirements of the controller
- Shall address delay, jitter etc
- Has to consider self similarity of the traffic
- Shall have bursty and non bursty components
- Has to incorporate the previous history
- Has to consider the components- mean (bias) and variations(variance) of the traffic
- Need to be scalable for unknown sizes, extensible over technologies that the growing internet absorbs
- Has to maintain Constant rate traffic.
- Intermixing of the information among multiple classes to be reflected
- Has to be used as an add-on

The usage of previous values in the feedback control is equivalent to sieving the traffic through multiple time scales. Hence, when a DANN is used, it is equivalent to scale the time by a factor that is a function of the order of the feedback. DANN produces the same results of scaling. The time shift provided for the predicted samples amounts to generating the samples with future and past values.

Derivative action generally reduces the oscillations. So, proportional derivative with prediction may be used to reduce the queue variance. The idea here is to use the shifted versions of the 'near future' prediction of the loss probability as the control signal that is fed back to the input. Shift provided to the feedback signal is equivalent to scaling the network with increased number of components.

Performance with Multiple Scales of Congestion Control

The dynamics of a network congestion control strategy can span multiple time scales. On the fastest time scale, congestion control should provide protection against the sudden surges of the traffic by a quick reaction to the buffer overloads. The reaction time in this type of control is, at the best in the order of one round-trip time, since, that is how fast news of the congestion can reach a source node and the response to it propagates back to the troubled spot. This type of congestion control is referred as dynamic and the corresponding time scale is taken as short term. On a slower time scale, congestion control could mean gradual but steadier reaction to the build-up of the congestion as perceived over a period involving tens or hundreds of round-trip times. It is on this time scale that the notions such as the average transmission rate of a session, rate allocation, and fairness become meaningful.

The terms quasi-static and medium term are used to refer to this type of congestion control and the corresponding time scale, respectively. Still,

on the slower time scales, congestion control can include long-term activities such as the service scheduling on the network switches and network reconfiguration wherever possible.

Now, a window scheme for the end-to-end congestion control is considered. A window scheme keeps the amount of outstanding data for a given session limited to a maximum, referred as the window size. The window size may be changed in response to the changing network conditions. It is important to see what type of congestion control can be accomplished by the window scheme if the window size is held constant.

Let 'S' be a session with a window size w_s. An infinite source for the session is assumed so that the window is always fully utilized. Denoting by θ_s and ρ_s the round-trip time and the transmission rate of this session, averaged over some short term interval, Little's formula gives,

$$\rho_s \approx \frac{\omega_s}{\theta_s} \qquad (3)$$

Even with a fixed ω_s as the traffic increases and network links approach congestion, the round-trip time θ_s will increase, resulting in a proportionate reduction in the rate ρ_s. The reaction to the increased queuing delay takes place within one round-trip time. Therefore, window scheme provides a form of dynamic congestion control even if the window size is not adjusted according to the network conditions. If the window size is modified in response to the dynamic network conditions, the window scheme combines the advantages of the dynamic and quasi-static congestion control.

The controller provided here is for the adaptive allocation of the average session rates in the Internet, based on the quasi-static network conditions. These allocated rates, may be applied in two ways: directly by controlling the instantaneous transmission rate, or indirectly by a window scheme with the window size set in-accordance with the allocated rate.

Let r_s denote the average rate allocated to the session S. In the direct, i.e., rate-based approach, in order to apply r_s, the minimum spacing between the packet transmission times may be either set to $1/r_s$ or more. It is typically determined through a leaky bucket mechanism. Alternatively, to apply r_s by means of window scheme, the window size ω_s should be set to $\omega_s = r_s\tau_s$ where τ_s is the average round-trip time of the session S.

The above approach combines the fast dynamics of the window scheme with the quasi-static rate adjustments, provided τ_s is the average round-trip time of the session S. Consider θ_s and ρ_s the round-trip time and the transmission rate of session S, averaged over a window. It follows that:

$$\rho_s \approx \frac{\omega_s}{\theta_s} = r_s\frac{\tau_s}{\theta_s} \qquad (4)$$

It clearly shows that, with the increase of the short term roundtrip time θ_s, the short term rate ρ_s decreases, providing the quick reaction to the congestion. If τ_s allowed to be dominated by the short term fluctuations of the round-trip time, then it gives $\tau_s \approx \theta_s$, and $\rho_s \approx r_s$, resulting in neutralizing the dynamic component of the window congestion control. An exponentially weighted running average algorithm is used to update the estimation of τ_s upon observing the round-trip time $\theta^{(p)}$ of each new packet p from S

$$\tau_s \leftarrow (1-\beta)\tau_s + \beta.\theta^{(p)} \qquad (5)$$

If β is in the order of $1/\omega_s$, then the averaging interval in (5) is roughly one round-trip time (i.e., the time it takes to send ω_s packets), which is not what is required. For averaging to take place over the medium term, β in (5) should be at least one or two orders of magnitude smaller than $1/\omega_s$.

The basic principle of the proposed active queue management scheme is to avoid congestion within a network by predicting the future input rate via the predictability of the LRD processes.

The objective is to maintain an upper bound on the average queue size and reduce the jitter as much as possible by keeping the aggregated input rates at or just below the service rate at a congested router all the time. In addition, it is required to protect well-behaving flows from the ill-behaving ones by allocating the bandwidth among flows in an approximately fair manner. The additional goals include the avoidance of the global synchronization and of a bias against bursty traffic.

A congestion avoidance mechanism maintains the network in a region of low delay and high throughput. The proposed scheme uses the predicted future input rate to detect the incipient congestion at a large time scale. If it detects the potential congestion, it marks incoming packets randomly according to the corresponding marking probabilities that are determined as a function of the severity of an incipient congestion. By considering input rate variations, the proposed scheme can adjust to the rapid input rate variations.

Because the proposed scheme detects an incipient congestion at a large time scale, senders can react for network conditions more rapidly. They can receive the congestion signal and reduce their sending rates before the network goes into severe congestion. As a result, the aggregated input rate at a congested router is kept at or just below the service rate. So, the amount of buffer space required accommodating an applied load greater than the link capacity can be reduced. It also reduces the end-to-end delay and delay jitter.

The second key component of a congestion avoidance gateway is to decide which flows to notify of congestion at the gateway. If congestion is detected before the gateway buffer becomes full, it is not necessary for the gateway to drop packets to notify sources of congestion. In this case, gateways can notify sources to reduce the sending rate without packet drops. Thus, the proposed scheme can support various congestion control mechanisms at the end systems and can be easily combined with gateway mechanisms such as ECN and TCP rate schemes. Because the packet marking probability is set in proportion to the predicted input rate, the more a flow sends packets during congestion, the more packets from the flow are marked. Thus, the probability of marking a packet from a particular flow becomes roughly proportional to its fair share of the bandwidth through the gateway. By doing so, the proposed mechanism can protect well-behaving flows from misbehaving ones and does not have bias against the bursty traffic.

The proposed scheme uses randomization in choosing which arriving packets to mark to avoid global synchronization. The proposed scheme is scalable because it can provide QoS mechanism without maintaining the per-flow states. It is evolutionary because it can be easily deployed in current routers merely upgrading the software and it is economic in that it does not require large buffer space.

Relevance of the Congestion Detection Interval

The congestion detection interval is a critical point in the design of the proposed congestion avoidance algorithm. If the interval is too long, the controller cannot adapt fast for the changes in the traffic input rate, making the difference between the predicted input rate and the actual input rate very large. As a result, packets get dropped in the network. On the other hand, if the interval is too short, the prediction error would be too large and the network would be left with near congestion state.

The controller handling short timescales are to account for the bursty traffic from a single dominant or a limited number of data sources that tend to flood the buffers along the path. Such a source can be contained the earliest after RTT and adequate buffer space has to be reserved to handle the same.

Higher order feedback translates to linear shifts. When a time shift is given to the control signal such as from RED, it is as though a PI, PD or PID controller is placed in front of RED. Using a combination of the PI controller and PD controller, it is possible to improve both the steady-state and transient responses. One can either first improve the transient response by using PD control and then the steady-state error of this compensated system by applying PI control or vice versa.

In the Closed loop control system, meddling with the RTT will have a profound impact on the stability of the system. Time shifts of the feedback signal improve the stability and achieve it quickly. The amplitude of transients of the packet queue i.e. queue fluctuations get reduced with increase in the shift. The settling time gets reduced and the stability is achieved faster. Small value of N, the number of data sources or large value of C, the channel capacity decreases the stability and increases the amplitude of oscillations.

As RTT decreases, the frequency of limit cycle oscillations increases. The amplitude reduces. Their product roughly remains constant. When RTT is nearly equal to the propagation delay, packet drops become aggressive. It calls for reduced window size or more NAK to maintain the agreed rate. With the use of shifted predicted feedback signal, the RTT and loss probability deceases simultaneously. The loop can afford to have larger gain at the cost of reduced delay or shifted feedback. The buffer dynamics affect the QoS. Small buffer reduces the delay at the cost of increased packet loss. The paper (Homero Toral, Deni Torres, Leopoldo Estrada, 2009), provides an insight for packet loss and delay in VOIP traffic.

Performance Results

Performance improvement as a result of this controller model (as well as the network model) is provided here. For the simulation, the default parameters shown in listing 3 are considered. The simulink blocks generate TCP source to resemble the background ftp kind of traffic and two http sources to resemble the on-off traffic. The various scopes provide the file dumps and the wave forms to observe the output. RED controller has been implemented with Floyd equation. The packet loss probability is predicted a few steps ahead of time using a neural network.

Listing 3. Simulation parameters
- The buffer size of the gateway is 200 packets.
- 120 sources are considered in the experiment.
- The simulation has been carried out with Simulink version 6 releases 12.
- The traces up to 70 ms are considered.
- Prediction is done with a DANN.
- The loss rate reduces with increase in the prediction step or order of the feedback.

The simulation results are provided in table 1. The important features are highlighted in Listing 4.

Table 1. Performance with different shifts

S1. No.	Shift	Loss. probability	Queue variance
1	0	7.4%	136.8258
2	1	6%	133.3290
3	2	5%	133.9068
4	4	0.725%	135.5478
5	6	0.55%	136.1364

Listing 4. Simulation results
- The packet loss ratio has been reduced with feedback.
- The input consists of 20 sources supporting FTP that exist over the entire simulation time.
  ○ The total packet loss ratio without prediction or shifts is found to be 7.4%.

Figure 7. Simulink setup

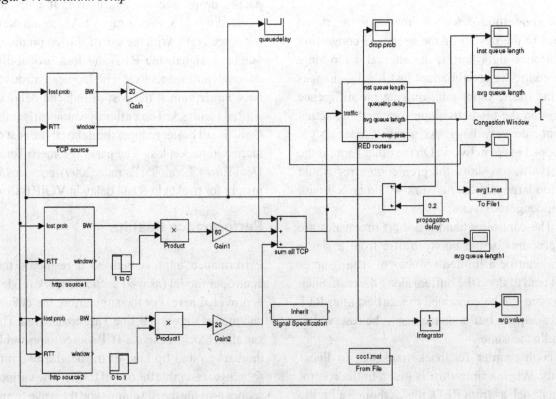

- With a neural network prediction, it has been reduced to 6%
- With a sixth order differentially fed neural network, it is reduced further to 0.55%.

In this experiment the maximum buffer size was varied to determine the relationship between the maximum buffer size and the equilibrium backlog performance of RED and the proposed method. 60 TCP sessions over 150 seconds were initiated for each queue size. Utilization, packet loss and delay were measured. The delay and loss performance are shown in table 2 and table 3. The maximum buffer size is measured in ms, which is the number of bits backlog over the link capacity.

With increase in the prediction step, the peak delay reduces and remains better than RED. The same is shown for buffer size 250. Interestingly, as the buffer size increases, the signal gets compressed and advanced; a similar phenomenon is observed with increase in the prediction step

ISSUES AND SOLUTIONS

This section explains how the proposed model addresses the problems in simulation of the performance. The example of wireless adhoc network has been considered for the case-study.

A wireless adhoc networks with multi hop transmissions and Rayleigh fading suffers with a set of issues that drastically reduce the throughput if not addressed properly.

Unlike a fixed infrastructure network, in a mobile adhoc network every bit getting transmitted is costly in terms of power. In addition, real time multimedia transmission over the network poses serious challenges in terms of attainable throughput after considering the losses and the predominant issues of fading and synchronization.

Fading

Fading is a prime concern in QoS testing (Ericsson, 1999). Base-station coverage and range limitations become victims for fading. A building or a hill situated between the base station and the phone set can attenuate the signal, resulting in fading. These effects are predictable and mitigated by strategic base-station placement.

Wireless phone fading (Junshan Zhan et. Al, 2001) results when one or more reflected signals, delayed because their indirect path is longer, meet the directly-transmitted signal as it arrives at the receiver. Because of the delay, the reflected signals are slightly out of phase. The signals combine with the direct transmission additively one moment and subtractive the next moment, depending on the phase relationship. As a result, signal level

Table 2. Performance for different shifts with max buffer size=200 traffic=20ftps.running on RED

Sl. No.	Shift	Loss. probability	Peak delay	Delay variance
1	0	0.5	0.5989	0.0964
2	1	0.14	0.5920	0.0874
3	2	0.1065	0.5920	0.0821
4	4	0.1009	0.5920	0.0724
5	8	0.1009	0.5920	0.0672
6	12	0.1009	0.5920	0.0720

Table 3. Performance for different shifts with max buffer size=250 traffic=20ftps.running on RED

Sl. No.	Shift	Loss. probability	Peak delay	Delay variance
1	0	0.34	0.5989	0.0926
2	1	0.09796	0.5937	0.0856
3	2	0.08957	0.5937	0.0808
4	4	0.07792	0.5937	0.0739
5	8	0.07795	0.5920	0.0706
6	12	0.07795	0.5920	0.0827

fluctuates. The other outcome of fading is the origin of the long range dependency in the signal.

The task is to optimize both the quality of service and the system throughput. The solution scheme is based on the fast adaptive modulation and scheduling of the IP traffic that adapts to the short-term fading. I.e. during fading, the bitrates need to be controlled. This is realized through the predictions of the future channel quality with a neural network, in the form of loss rates involving all active mobile terminals.

Handling Fading Issue

There is much experimental evidence that the mobile adhoc network traffic processes exhibit ubiquitous properties of self-similarity (P. R. Morin, 1995) and long-range dependence LRD wherein the traffic is correlated over a wide range of time scales. It is not trivial to model such processes and their impact on the network and application performance.

Higher the order of the differential feedback in the DANN controller, more will be the dependency. It accurately models LRD as well as the implied self similarity. The signals taking multipath and faded channels suffer with self similarity and long range dependency where the shape of the autocorrelation remains invariant when observed over different time scales. This kind of dependency reduces the performance. The effective way of handling this issue is to predict the traffic and fading channel characteristics in advance and adjust the data rate so that the source does not further compound the fading effects. It is possible to control the impact of LRD by adjusting the prediction step in terms of the time units. The prediction has been carried out using a differentially fed artificial neural network

The prediction information, generally in terms of the packet loss probability, is provided to the data source at the appropriate intervals as an indication of the channel state. The sources then reduce the transmission rates or signal out busy mode or reduce the activities as applicable. The prediction makes it possible to adjust the rates well in advance and prevent the pumping of the packets over the faded channels at a higher rate. The effect of prediction step or shift on the performance is indicated in the simulation (Table 2 and Table 3)

Fading falls under two classes. It includes large-scale or long-term effects and small-scale or short-term effects. Large-scale fading lasts for a few seconds. The small-scale fading is of the order of milliseconds. Large-scale effects originate due to distance-related attenuation involving the terrain, buildings, and other obstacles between the transmitter and receiver. It may be seen as a relatively constant term when seen over a shorter time scale.

Small-scale effects originate due to the scattering or reflections of the transmitted signals with the surrounding objects. They impart rapid and large fluctuations to the signal strength. They are modeled as Gaussian distributed part (Peter Meinicke and Helge Ritter, 1999). A better estimation of these parameters is required to prevent rapid transmissions that results in more losses.

In general, the estimation over the multiple scales, each representing a particular communication scenario, would be more helpful. However, merging the information from these estimators meaningfully is a task.

Compensation for the multiple time scales fading typically requires the increase in transmission power. The time scales in which rate control and admission control decisions may be taken will be of importance. An ideal estimator happens to be the merger of these multiple time scale estimators and realizable using a DANN.

Synchronisation

The increasing quantity and diversity of the mobile communication traffic is creating a greater network loading (Li Zhang, 2003). The mobile network operators are installing micro and pico base stations as a means to open the network to a larger subscriber base. As a result, the cellular calls have to be handed-off more frequently and accurate timing of these hand-offs is essential to ensure satisfactory call completion and quality of service such as packet loss probability or throughput, delay etc.

The service providers will have differing approaches to the network synchronization for the range of issues from the periodical reconfiguration of facilities to the staggered hit in mobile services. The staggered hits result in frequency shifts well beyond the prescribed synchronization guidelines. They finally result in problems with voice and data transmissions.

A BTS needs synchronization to ensure the stable frequency for the on air wireless channels. If these channel frequencies drift, it results in co-channel interference. The Mobile switching centers and the base station controllers also require accurate time signals to assure a smooth handover when the user crosses packets. As seen by the end user, lack of synchronization can result in low voice quality, poor call set-up and even dropped calls. In other non-voice applications, it creates

serious QoS issues such as failed data downloads, jerky video etc.

Handling Synchronization Issues

With a prediction feedback in place, the throughput improves. It may be seen that, the QoS improves resulting in a better tolerance for the synchronization constraints. The prediction makes it possible to adjust the rates well in advance, providing sufficient time and fully utilize the underlying network. The mismatch in synchronization will be reflected as the variation in the prediction step. Hence its impact on the QoS can be limited by adjusting the prediction step. In the simulation result, reduction in the delay is shown in Figure 8 for a shift or prediction step of 8. 20 sources have been considered. The buffer size of the gateway is 200 packets. 120 sources are considered in the experiment. The simulation has been carried out with Simulink version 6 releases 12. The traces up to 70 ms are considered. Prediction is done with a DANN.

Figure 8. Delay versus time

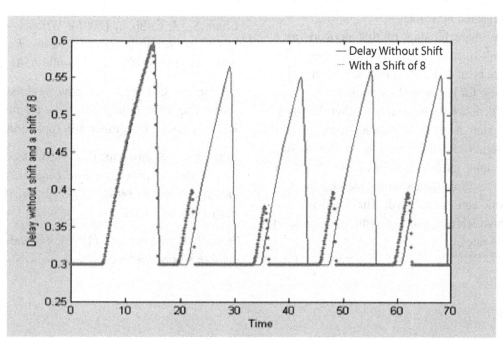

CONCLUSION

With differential feedback from the output to input of an ANN, it starts exhibiting interesting properties. These properties are correspondingly mapped on to the one observed in an adhoc mobile network. The missing characteristics of this network as a result of manifestation of these properties have been deduced providing an effective solution for the issues such as fading and synchronization. A feedback to the source to alter the transmission is to be provided based on the channel characteristics. In this work, it has been shown that by providing appropriate shifts to the feedback signal to the source, the long range dependency introduced by the multi channel fading path can be reduced. This will have improvement over the throughput and packet loss rates. In addition, the hazardous effects of the mismatch in the synchronization in the adhoc network can be minimized with the appropriate time shifts given to the feedback signal. The summary of what has been explained in the chapter is provided below. The usage of proposed model is stressed.

- Properties of DANN are mapped on to a congested network.
- The characteristics of this network as a result of manifestation of these properties have been deduced. It Provide effective solution for issues such as congestion
- A feedback to the source to alter the transmission is to be provided based on the channel characteristics. With this model, the long range dependency introduced by the multiple data sources loading the network can be reduced. The feedback improves throughput and reduces the packet loss rates.

REFERENCES

Aarts, E. H. L., & Korst, J. H. M. (1989). *Simulated annealing and Boltzmann machines*. Chichester, UK: Wiley.

Amari, S. (1982). Differential geometry of curved exponential families –Curvatures and information loss. *Annals of statistics*.

Amari, S. (1990). Mathematical foundations of neurocomputing. *Proceedings of the IEEE*, 1446–1463.

Amari, S. (1995). Information geometry of the EM and EM algorithms for neural networks. *Neural Networks*, 8(9), 1379–1408. doi:10.1016/0893-6080(95)00003-8

Amari, S. (1996). *Information geometry of neural networks-New Bayesian duality theory*.

Amari, S. (1998). Natural gradient works efficiently in learning. *Neural Computation*, 10, 251–276. doi:10.1162/089976698300017746

Amari, S., & Nagaoka, H. (2000). *Methods of information geometry*. AMS and Oxford university Press.

Chen, S., & Cobb, J. (2006). Wireless quality-of-service support. *Wireless Networks*, 12(4), 409–441. doi:10.1007/s11276-006-6541-2

Ericsson, N. C. (1999). Adaptive modulation and scheduling over fading channels. *Globecom99*, Rio de Janeiro, December 5-9, (pp. 2668-2672).

Frazier, M., & Jawerth, B. (1985). Decomposition of Besov spaces. *Indiana University Mathematics Journal*, 34(4), 777–779. doi:10.1512/iumj.1985.34.34041

Jawerth, B., & Peters, G. (1993). *Wavelets on non smooth sets of Rn*.

MacKay, D. J. C. (1992). A practical Bayesian framework for back propagation networks. *Neural Computation, 4*, 448–472. doi:10.1162/neco.1992.4.3.448

MacKay, D. J. C. (1992a). The evidence framework applied to classification networks. *Neural Computation, 4*, 720–736. doi:10.1162/neco.1992.4.5.720

Mallat, S., & Hwang, W. L. (1991). *Singularity detection and processing with wavelets. Preprint Courant Institute of Mathematical sciences*. New York University.

Manjunath, R., & Gurumurthy, K. S. (2002). Information geometry of differentially fed artificial neural networks. *TENCON, 3*, 1521–1525.

Manjunath, R., & Gurumurthy, K. S. (2002a). *System design using differentially fed artificial neural networks*. TENCON'02.

McKenzie, P., & Alder, M. (1994). Initializing the EM algorithm for use in Gaussian mixture modeling. In Gelsema, E. S., & Kanal, L. N. (Eds.), *Pattern Recognition in Practice IV* (pp. 91–105). Amsterdam, The Netherlands: Elsevier.

Meinicke, P., & Ritter, H. (1999). *Resolution based complexity control for Gaussian mixture models. Technical report*. Faculty of Technology, University of Bielefeld.

Morin, P. R. (1995). *The impact of self-similarity on network performance analysis*. Ph. D. dissertation, Carleton Univ., Dec.

Neal, R. (1996). *Bayesian learning in neural networks*. Springer Verlag.

Padhye, J., Firoiu, V., Towsley, D., & Kurose, J. (2000). Modeling TCP Reno performance: A simple model and its empirical validation. *IEEE/ACM Transactions on Networking, 8*(2), 133–145. doi:10.1109/90.842137

Rao, C. R. (1962). Efficient estimates and optimum inference procedures in large samples. *Journal of the Royal Statistical Society. Series B. Methodological, 24*, 46–72.

Soret, B., Torres, M. C. A., & Entrambasaguas, J. T. (2010). Analysis of the tradeoff between delay and source rate in multiuser wireless systems. *EURASIP Journal on Wireless Communications and Networking*, 2010.

Toral, H., Torres, D., & Estrada, L. (2009). Simulation and modeling of packet loss on VoIP traffic: A power-law model. *WSEAS Transactions on Communications, 8*(10).

Zhan, J. (2001). Unified spatial diversity combining and power allocation for CDMA systems in multiple time-scale fading channels. *IEEE Journal on Selected Areas in Communications, 19*(7).

Zhang, L. (2003). *Synchronisation techniques for high efficiency coded wireless systems*. PhD Thesis, Department of Electronics University of York July 2003.

Zhu, H., & Rohwer, R. (1995). *Bayesian invariant measurements of generalization for continuous distributions*. Technical Report NCRG/4352, Aston University.

KEY TERMS AND DEFINITIONS

ANN: Artificial neural network, a non linear system relating the output with the input and used for data prediction, generalization etc

DANN: Differentially fed artificial neural network where in a feed back is provided from output to input in an artificial neural network

QoS: Quality of service, a quantifier for the network traffic in terms of packet loss, delay and jitter

Network Congestion: A network is said to be in congested state when more data is pumped than it can handle

RED: Random early detection, an algorithm for computing the probability of packet drop in a network

Feedback Control: A mechanism that provides information on the status of the network to the data sources and thereby controls the traffic

Traffic Shaping: A mechanism to avoid congestion through rate control or otherwise

Chapter 9
Optimizing Path Reliability in IPTV Systems Using Genetic Algorithm

Mohammad Anbar
Tishreen University, Syria

Deo Prakash Vidyarthi
Jawaharlal Nehru University, India

ABSTRACT

IPTV system is meant to provide TV services through IP networks. IPTV is a next generation technology and is growing rapidly day by day across the globe. Providing TV services through IP networks reflects the audio-video service through the IP networks in IP format. TV packets are media and real-time packets in nature, therefore delivering these packets through the IP network is a big challenge. It needs to be done with utmost care and reliably for the timely delivery of these packets to ensure reliable packet transfer is a big issue in IPTV systems. Reliability, in such systems, depends on the failure rates of various components through which the packet passes. This chapter addresses the reliability issue in IPTV systems and suggests a possible solution to maximize it using Genetic Algorithms. The proposed model explores for the most reliable path among many available paths for the packet delivery. It helps in deciding the best available route passing through which reliability is maximized. Experimental results reveal the efficacy of the model.

DOI: 10.4018/978-1-4666-0203-8.ch009

INTRODUCTION

Services provided over the Internet, have increased in recent years with the evolution in networks technologies such as WiFi, WiMAX etc. Network devices that access these services have also increased. New forms of services for end users have been introduced in the interconnected communication infrastructure. Among such new services is IPTV, which provides TV services over IP-based networks. IPTV services are usually available as a combination of the three services consisting of video, audio and data (usually referred as triple play). The video component of IPTV triple play consists of Video on Demand (VoD) and broadcast TV, the audio component consists of Voice over IP (VoIP), and the data component consists of standard HTTP based applications. Triple play and Internet traffic are routed using uni-cast routing, while broadcast TV traffic is routed using multicast routing (Cha, Choudhury, Yates, Shaikh, & Moon, 2006). IPTV traffic, particularly VoD, constitutes a significant portion of the network traffic and has very stringent Quality of Service (QoS) and Quality of Experience (QoE) requirements.

Figure 1 shows the structure of IPTV system which consists mainly of IPTV head end, IP network (transport network), and Set Top Box (STB) users.

In IPTV system, IPTV head end is the video source where the signal is first encoded using some coding scheme, such as H.264 (Lee, Lee, Kim, & Shin) codec. By this encoding of the TV signal, the output bit rate of the source video signal is reduced. The compression performance of the H.264 is much higher than MPEG-2. Therefore, the encoder in the head end plays an important role in end to end video system. After coding, the output bit stream is encapsulated using Real-Time Protocol (RTP) which guarantees ordered delivery over an unreliable Internet Protocol (IP) network. The RTP data are generally encapsulated in User Datagram Protocol (UDP) and IP headers and then replicated in an IP network. The reliability of the data packet flow is decided by the reliability of the network routers and connecting links. The transport network is used to transmit the data coming from the head end based on the IP protocol. The role of transport network is to classify the packet and realize the queue-scheduling algorithm. The transport network delivers the data to the STBs of the subscribing consumers. The video receiver is used to decode the stream correctly from the transport network and then play it to the subscriber.

Reliability issue has been rarely addressed in IPTV systems, in general. (Kandavanam, Botvich, & Balasubramaniam, 2009) suggest a model for maximizing QoS assurance in IPTV has been proposed. The model combines the use of GAVNS algorithm (Genetic Algorithm with Variable Neighborhood Search) with the efficient

Figure 1. IPTV system structure

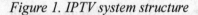
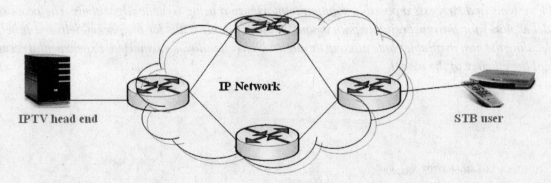

and accurate estimation of QoS requirements using empirical effective bandwidth estimations. (Obele, Seung, Jun, & Minho, 2009) have proposed IPTV business model in order to improve the service guarantee provided by the IPTV system. Their business model is based on the efficient packaging, advertising and delivery of IPTV contents and services to end-users. Their model however can be categorized under reliability models as it is concerned with improving the service guarantee.

Genetic Algorithm (GA) is an automated search technique which is based on the mechanism of natural genetics and natural selection. It is not good considering larger, potentially huge search space and navigating it for optimal solutions consuming huge amount of time. GA is a technique, applied in such cases, to produce near-optimal results in reasonable amount of time. GA is based on the principle of evolution and natural genetics. It combines the exploitation of past result with the exploration of the new areas of the search space by employing the survival of the fittest technique combined with a structured yet randomized information exchange. A GA-based model for reliability improvement in IPTV system has been proposed in this chapter. The proposed model considers reliability of both; routers and links in the transport network. It applies GA to search for the best route, in terms of reliability, in the transport network.

The chapter organization is as follows. The following section elaborates reliability issue in IPTV system and the parameters affecting the reliability. The optimization tool GA, used to solve the problem, has been briefed in the next section. The section after that elaborates the proposed model with the detailed explanation for reliability computation and its improvement using GA. The fifth section contains the experimental verification of the proposed model. In the final section, the observations of the results obtained about the performance of the model have been listed and discussed.

RELIABILITY IN IPTV SYSTEMS

Reliability is defined as the ability of a system to perform its stated functions under given conditions for a specified period of time. Any system, especially the communication systems, may consist of multiple components and reliability of such system is depicted by the reliabilities of these components integrally. As evident from Figure 1, IPTV system consists of IPTV head end, IP transport network and the STB. Further, the transport network consists of many routers and links that affect the reliability of the IPTV system. Multiple paths, offering different reliability support, might be available when trying to transport a flow of data packets from IPTV head end to the STB. Mostly, the routing decision is based on the shortest path. The obtained shortest path may not be reliable one. This is an important issue, which has been addressed here.

Path Reliability

Each component of the transport network has its own physical ability to perform its tasks. This ability is expressed by the failure rate of the component. Considering the failure rate of the router as α_i, the reliability of the router i for the duration T_i may be computed as

$$RR = e^{-\alpha_i . T_i} \tag{1}$$

Where T_i is the flow processing time at the router. It is computed as given by (Tanenbaum, 2004):

$$T_i = \frac{1}{\mu_i} \times \frac{1}{1 - \dfrac{\lambda_i}{\mu_i}} \tag{2}$$

Here λ_i and μ_i are packet arrival rate and packet processing rate for the router respectively.

Similarly, reliability of the link between the routers may be computed as:

$$RL_j = e^{-\beta_j . T_j} \tag{3}$$

Here, β_j is the failure rate of the link, and T_j is the time a flow takes to pass through the link j. This is computed using Equation 4.

$$T_j = \frac{1}{\eta_j} \times \frac{1}{1 - \dfrac{\psi_j}{\eta_j}} \tag{4}$$

ψ_j and η_j are the packet arrival rate and packet delivery rate for the link respectively. Delivery rate is an indication about how faster the packets are passed through the link. Note that the time a flow takes on a link is determined by the speed of the link as well as the current load.

The reliability of the router i and the link i together is computed as

$$R_i = RR_i \times RL_i \tag{5}$$

The total reliability (fitness function) of the path in the IPTV system is the product of the computed reliabilities of the routers and the associated links that appears in the path of the flow.

$$RT = \prod_{i=1}^{N} R_i \tag{6}$$

RT is the total reliability for the path, and R_i is the product obtained in Equation 5. N is the number of routers and associated links.

There might be many possible paths and the reliability may differ for each of these paths. It is because of the varying failure rates of the routers and communication links as well as differing load on the routers and the links.

GENETIC ALGORITHMS

Genetic Algorithm is a search procedure based on the Darwin's theory of the "survival of the fittest". Individuals, from the population of potential solutions, reproduce and the best solutions are opted over the number of generations. Genetic Algorithm (GA) is automated search and optimization algorithm based on the mechanics of natural genetics and natural selection. It is often applied on a potentially huge search space as navigating through a larger search space for optimal solutions may consume a great amount of time. GA, in such cases, is quite useful to produce sub-optimal results in reasonable amount of time. GA combines the exploitation of past result with the exploration of the new areas of the search space, by using the survival of the fittest technique combined with a structured yet randomized information exchange (Tripathi, Vidyarthi, & Mantri, 1996; Vidyarthi, & Tripathi, 2001; Vidyarthi, Tripathi, & Mantri, 1997; Mitchell, 1999; Goldberg, 2005; Moore, 2001).

GA has many good features such as broad applicability, ease of use, and global perspective; therefore have been applied to various search and optimization problems in the recent past. Because of their population based approach, GA has also been extended to solve other search and optimization problems such as multi-objective problems and scheduling problems (Ghribi, Masmoudi, & Derbel, 2008; Kotecha, & Popat, 2007; Watanabe, Hiroyasu, & Miki, 2002). Population in GA consists of number of individuals and each individual is considered as a solution for the problem in hand. The individual solution is also called chromosome which consists of many genes depending on the type of the problem being discussed. There are many ways to encode the candidate solutions. The pseudo-code of GA is as follows.

```
GA ()
{       Create a random population of a
given size;
        Evaluate the fitness function
for each individual in the popula-
tion;
        For number of generations
        {
                Select parents for re-
production;
                Perform crossover ();
                Perform mutation ();
                Evaluate population;
        }
}
```

THE PROBLEM

As discussed, IPTV system is an important system and the reliable delivery of the real-time packets is a big challenge in this. When a multicast stream of packets starts from the IPTV head end towards the STB, it passes through the transport network which is the IP based network in IPTV systems. At this point, the first home router decides the next hop for the flow of packets which further explores the next one and it continues until it reaches to the destination node. This is done according to their routing tables. Out of many path possibilities, to pass the flow through, shortest path is preferred if the objective is delivery time.

Main objective of this research is to ensure the reliable path as this is an important concern in IPTV system. Router searches for the route which is more reliable for the packet delivery. For a dense network, a good number of valid paths are possible to pass the flow varying between minimum and the maximum. The proposed model is a search procedure which considers many solutions in terms of path reliability and suggests the one with the optimal value.

Figure 2 shows routing through various paths (many nodes). Traditionally, in heterogeneous transport networks, the packets are forwarded from one node to another according to the routing tables and routing algorithms (the shortest path). The path to be selected from the node A to node D (Figure 2), is the one which passes through the node E. This is the shortest path but does not take into account that the selected node may not be reliable and may fail causing connection disturbance. The model, in this work, suggests the path which is most reliable. In other sense the path is having very less possibility of failure.

THE PROPOSED MODEL

The model considers a transport network with various routers connected by the transport links. Number of available routes among the routers varies between minimum (min) to maximum (max). Number of the packets in the considered flow of packets is n_pack which is an integer value and it varies depending on the network type being used for the transmission. As explained in section 3.1, each router has its physical failure rate, packet arrival rate and packet processing rate so does the link.

The proposed model uses GA to improve the reliability of the available paths and to select the best one. The model generates a population of a

Figure 2. Multi-path routing

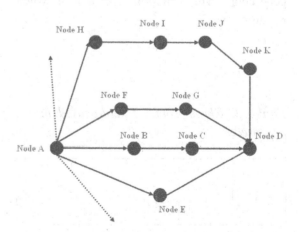

given size consisting of the individual (chromosome) depicted in Figure 3.

A population of individuals is generated. Each individual (chromosome) is represented by an array as depicted in Figure 3. The length of the generated chromosome varies depending on the number of routers in the path. For example (also evident from Figure 2), there are four paths from node A to node D with different intermediate routers. We may have four types of chromosomes of lengths: 3, 4, 4, 6. Four population of these size chromosomes are generated for the experiment as shown in Figure 3.

Here, $R_1 \ldots \ldots R_N$ are the reliabilities as computed in Equation 5.

Detailed explanation of the model is as follows. Considering an IPTV flow of packets consisting of n_pack packets, the model randomly generates an array of values representing the different number of routers on the available paths. Randomly generating the failure rates for both the links and the routers between 0 and 1, the model considers different ranges of values for the packet arrival and processing rate for the routers and the links. With all these available values, the model generates multiple initial population for each number of routers. GA is applied thereupon and the evolution process starts by crossing over all the initially generated individuals and evaluating the newly generated individuals. To avoid the local optima, the model uses mutation operation every five generations. The evolution process stops when results converge.

Figure 3. Chromosome structure used in the proposed model

R_1	R_2	....	R_N

EXPERIMENTAL RESULTS

To observe the performance of the proposed model, the experiments are designed as follows.

Wireless IP Transport Network

First set of experiment is for the wireless network. Obviously, in this various input values are in smaller range.

Experiment 1

This experiment is designed for 200 packets per flow. Other input parameters are as given below.

Number of routers in the path: min=10 routers, max=20 routers

Router parameters: λ = 1000 - 2000 packets/sec, μ = 2000 - 3000 packet/sec

Link parameters: ψ = 500 - 1000 packets/sec, η = 1000 - 1500 packets/sec

Multiple paths with different number of routers are generated. These are having varying reliability values. The notable observation from Figure 4 is that there are two paths with same number of routers (20 routers). Out of which, one has better reliability than the other. However the best path (with best reliability) to be selected is the one with 11 routers. Moreover, the model is performing well to improve the reliability for all the explored paths.

Experiment 2

This experiment is designed for 400 packets per flow. Other input parameters are as given below.

Number of routers in the path: min=20 routers, max=25 routers

Figure 4. 200 packets per flow

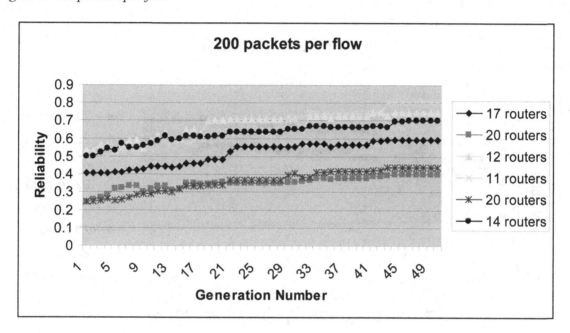

Router parameters: λ = 2000 - 4000 packets/sec, μ = 5000 - 10000 packet/sec

Link parameters: ψ = 1000 - 1500 packets/sec, η = 2000 - 4000 packets/sec

Eight paths are generated in this experiment. In order to increase the chances of having same number of routers in a path, minimum and maximum number of routers has been considered between 20 and 25. It's clear from Figure 5 that the recommended route is a route with 21 routers though there are some paths with 20 routers also. One of the routes with 23 routers has lesser reliability than the other routes while the other has better reliability than the routes with 20 and 22 routers. Again in the 23 router path the difference in the reliability values are quite observable.

Experiment 3

This experiment is designed for 800 packets per flow. Other input parameters are as given below.

Number of routers in the path: min=20 routers, max=25 routers

Router parameters: λ = 1000 - 2000 packets/sec, μ = 2000 - 3000 packet/sec

Link parameters: ψ = 500 - 1000 packets/sec, η = 1000 - 1500 packets/sec

The experiment 3 is done for large number of packets per flow and same range of number of routers as in experiment 2. It's shown in Figure 6 that there are two paths having 21 routers and two other having 23 routers. The observation here is that one of the paths with 21 routers has less reliability than other paths with 22 and 23 routers. In this case the path with higher reliability will be selected even so it has more number of routers. Number of packets per flow is bigger than the number of packets in experiments 1 and 2; therefore the values of reliabilities are less. Reliability improvement is also observed in this experiment.

Figure 5. 400 packets per flow

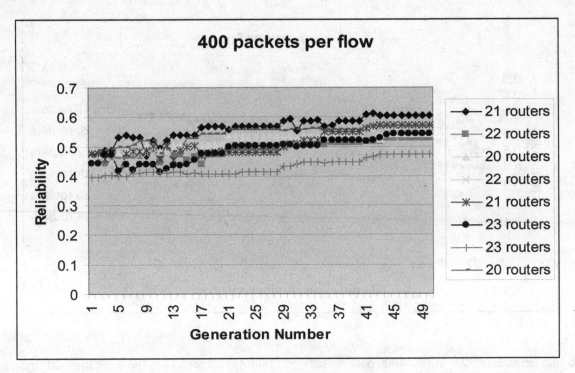

Figure 6. 800 packets per flow

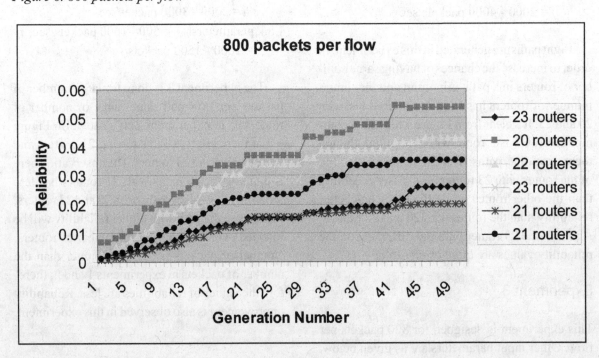

Experiment 4

Same set of parameters are used in this experiment and is repeated number of times. The purpose is to show the case in which a path with bigger number of routers and associated nodes having bigger value for reliability is recommended.

Seven populations for seven different paths are generated in this experiment in the range 20 till 25 routers. The only path with 22 routers is having better reliability than a path with 20 routers as clear from Figure 7. More important observation here is a path with 20 routers is not recommended here where a path of 21 routers is having better reliability than the one with 20 routers. In this experiment it has been proven that not always the path with less number of routers is having better reliability and it is justified as mentioned before due to the physical performances of the routers and the associated links of the path.

The previous experiments were conducted taking into account that the parameters such as the packet arrival rate and packet processing rate and number of packets per flow exist in a wireless IP network such as Cellular IP network. That was necessary to be shown because the IP transport network in IPTV system can be of any technology such as wired or wireless. To show the case of wired transport IP network this new experiment is conducted with the following parameters:

Wired IP Transport Network

Experiment 1

Generated values in this experiment suited to wired networks where number of packets per flow can be big such as 100,000 packets. Other input parameters are as given below.

Figure 7. 800 packets per flow

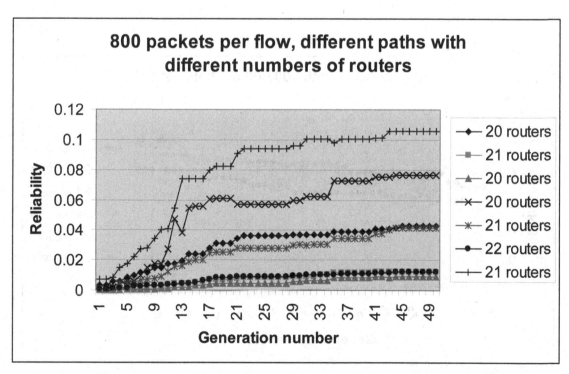

Number of routers in the path: min=20 routers, max=25 routers

Router parameters: λ =500,000-1000,000 packets/sec, μ = 1000,000 -150,000 packet/sec

Link parameters: ψ =300,000 – 500,000 packets/sec, η = 600,000 – 900,000 packets/sec

From Figure 8 and the previous figures it's clear that the route with less number of routers has the highest reliability. This can be justified by mentioning that the model based on the flow processing time at the router and the link as well. Therefore when the number of routers is less, the time taken to process the flow is less and as a result the reliability is less depending on Equations 1 and 3. This issue is always true in this way and the proposed model here can't change this reality, then what's the benefit of the proposed model if with less number of routers we get the highest reliability? The answer for this question can be shown from all figures but it is clearer in Figure 7. In Figure 7, there are several numbers of routers each with an improved reliability the

observation here is the highest reliability is for the route with 20 routers, this was clarified earlier, and the least reliability is for a route with 21 routers. This means that a route with 24 routers is better in sense of reliability than a route with 21 routers even it has shortest path. If the route with 20 routers was not an option among the others, the route with 24 routers will be the best to forward the flow and this is the importance of the proposed model.

Experiment 2

A path with bigger number of routers can be more reliable in the case of wired IP transport networks in IPTV. To prove this, same set of parameters were used again in this experiment and the experiment is repeated number of times, finally the results are shown in Figure 9.

The maximum number of routers randomly generated in this experiment is 25 routers. As clear from Figure 9, the path with 25 routers has higher reliability and therefore it is recommend-

Figure 8. Wired IP network

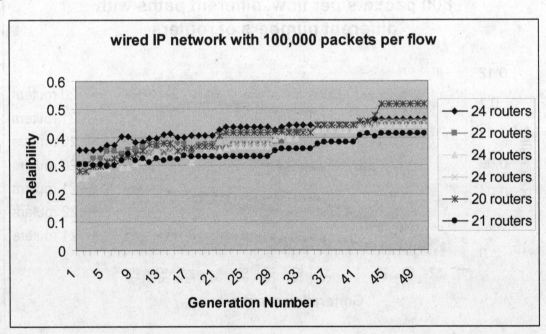

Figure 9. Path with bigger number of routers is more reliable

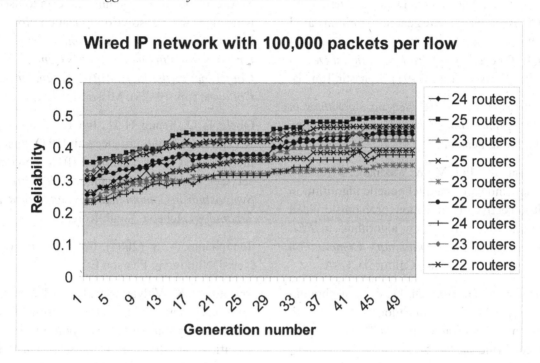

ed. The effect of GA is clear in improving the reliability of all the links is clear with the generations. The justification for this case is as mentioned before due to the different physical status of the routers and the associated links.

CONCLUSION

Due to the growing importance of IPTV systems, killing technology for the next generation of communication, this paper addresses an important issue of this system. Any IPTV system faces the problem of transferring real-time data packets and therefore, the reliable delivery becomes a key issue in this technology. The proposed work, in this chapter, is focused to be done in the transport IP network from the IPTH head end to the user STB. Usually many paths are available for forwarding a flow of IPTV packets through the IP network; the

objective is to choose the path with the maximum reliability. GA is used to improve the reliabilities of all the available routes and select the one with the best value of reliability. Experiments have been conducted with different numbers of packets per flow to be forwarded through different paths with different numbers of routers. The transport IP network can be wireless or wired; therefore both the cases have been shown through changing the experimental parameters. The proposed model depicts the efficacy for reliable path selection.

REFERENCES

Cha, M., Choudhury, G., Yates, J., Shaikh, A., & Moon, S. (2006). Case study: Resilient backbone design for IPTV services. In *Proceedings of Workshop on IPTV Services over World Wide Web*, Edinburgh, Scotland, United Kingdom.

Ghribi, S. F., Masmoudi, D. S., & Derbel, N. (2008). A multi objective genetic algorithm based optimization of wavelet transform implementation. In *Proceedings of 3rd International Design and Test Workshop*, (pp. 87–91). Monastir, Tunisia.

Goldberg, D. E. (2005). *Genetic algorithms in search, optimization, and machine learning*. New Delhi, India: Pearson.

Hiroyasu, T., Miki, M., & Watanabe, S. (2000). The new model of parallel genetic algorithm in multi-objective optimization problems-divided range multi-objective genetic algorithms. In *IEEE Proceedings of the Evolutionary Computation Congress*, (pp. 333-340). California, USA.

Kandavanam, G., Botvich, D., & Balasubramaniam, S. (2009). An optimization based approach to maximizing QoS assurance for IPTV triple play services on the Internet backbone. In *Proceedings of IEEE 34th Conference on Local Computer Networks*, (pp 406–413). Zurich, Switzerland.

Kotecha, K., & Popat, S. (2007). Multi objective genetic algorithm based adaptive QoS routing in MANET. In *Proceedings of IEEE Congress on Evolutionary Computation*, (pp. 1423–1428). Singapore.

Lee, Y., Lee, J., Kim, I., & Shin, H. (2008). Reducing IPTV channel switching time using H.264 scalable video coding. *IEEE Transactions on Consumer Electronics*, *54*(2), 912–919. doi:10.1109/TCE.2008.4560178

Mitchell, M. (1999). *An introduction to genetic algorithms*. London, UK: MIT Press.

Moore, M. (2001). Teaching students to use genetic algorithms to solve optimization problems. In *Proceedings of the Seventh Annual Consortium for Computing in Small Colleges Central Plains Conference on the Journal of Computing in Small Colleges*, (pp. 19–25). Missouri: USA.

Obele, B. O., Seung, H. H., Jun, K. C., & Minho, K. (2009). On building a successful IPTV business model based on personalized IPTV content & services. In *Proceedings of the 9th International Symposium on Communications and Information Technology*. Icheon, South Korea.

Tanenbaum, A. S. (2004). *Computer networks*. New Delhi, India: Pearson Education.

Tripathi, A. K., Vidyarthi, D. P., & Mantri, A. N. (1996). A genetic task allocation algorithm for distributed computing system incorporating problem specific knowledge. *International Journal of High Speed Computing*, *8*(4), 363–370. doi:10.1142/S0129053396000203

Vidyarthi, D. P., & Tripathi, A. K. (2001). Maximizing reliability of distributed computing system with task allocation using simple genetic algorithm. *Journal of Systems Architecture*, *47*(6), 549–554. doi:10.1016/S1383-7621(01)00013-3

Vidyarthi, D. P., Tripathi, A. K., & Mantri, A. N. (1997). Task partitioning using genetic algorithm. In *Proceedings of International Conference in Cognitive Systems*. New Delhi, India.

Watanabe, S., Hiroyasu, T., & Miki, M. (2002). Neighborhood cultivation genetic algorithm for multi-objective optimization problems. In *Proceedings of the 14th Asia-Pacific Conference on Simulated Evolution and Learning*, (pp. 198-202). Singapore.

Chapter 10
IP Connected Low Power Wireless Personal Area Networks in the Future Internet

Rune Hylsberg Jacobsen
Aarhus School of Engineering, Denmark

Thomas Skjødeberg Toftegaard
Aarhus School of Engineering, Denmark

Jens Kristian Kjærgaard
Tieto, Denmark

ABSTRACT

The Internet of Things is a key concept of the Future Internet. The Internet of Things potentially interconnects billions of small devices in a large ubiquitous infrastructure based on the Internet Protocol (IP). Typically, these devices will be limited in computational capacity, memory, and available energy and will suffer a high data loss rate when integrated into a network infrastructure. This poses significant challenges in the network design. This chapter describes the assumptions, technologies, and challenges for transmitting IPv6 over low power wireless personal area networks (LoWPANs). The authors address the key mechanisms from network aspects down to device design aspects and discuss how technologies interplay to make real application deployment practical for the Internet of Things.

INTRODUCTION

The Future Internet extends the current Internet from the communication between humans to the communication between humans and the surrounding devices such as small sensors. The Future Internet will use the Internet Protocol (IP)

as the foundation for communications. The IP protocols will serve as the common denominator from large systems to small devices by allowing interaction between networks build from different underlying transmission technologies – wired as well as wireless – and by reusing protocol layer implementations across different platforms. With IP as the unifying internetwork technology the number of communication translations reduces

DOI: 10.4018/978-1-4666-0203-8.ch010

from an *N-N* question to an *N*-1 question. There will still be a need for gateways in the Future Internet to cope with different network technologies and network characteristics, but by having IP as a common conceptual framework large economic savings will be provide in a global perspective.

Wireless sensor networks have evolved from the idea that small wireless devices distributed over large geographical areas can be used to collect information from the physical environment in many situations such as e.g. environmental and industrial monitoring. On the node-level, challenges result from the limited available resources. The handling of the unreliable networks and the large size of the networks becomes especially challenging when these sensors are interconnected.

Different wireless protocols have evolved for personal area networks and sensor networks as e.g. Z-wave, Bluetooth and Zigbee, and until recently the perception has been that a full-fledged IP stack was too large and complex to implement in small devices. However, based on the standardisation work in Internet Engineering Task Force (IETF) and Institute of Electrical and Electronics Engineer (IEEE) the foundation for realising IP in a small device domain has been made. Several research projects have shown that it is possible to realise sensor nodes with a fully functional IPv6 stack (Mazzer and Tourancheau, 2008).

In this chapter, we address the key concepts of low power wireless area personal network (LoWPAN) and demonstrate how efficient support for IPv6 over IEEE 802.15.4 links can be achieved. We explain the basis for IPv6 networking and we discuss how benefits of IP technology can be applied to limited, unreliable devices in the Future Internet. Throughout the chapter we discuss technologies and protocols in the context of sensor networks since these are the main applications of LoWPAN devices. Furthermore, we address the main building blocks for LoWPAN device designs, and we conclude the chapter by outlining future directions of work in the area.

BACKGROUND

During the past few years Future Internet has been on the research agenda on a European level (European X-ETP Group, 2010). Future Internet research has chosen a holistic perspective by taking into account all building blocks from users, services and applications down to the networks. Information and communication technology are becoming smarter, smaller and faster; and, at the same time, society is progressively becoming more densely connected. As a result, Internet supported services are entering a new phase of mass deployment which brings a large number of new opportunities; but also challenges in terms of scalability, capacity, throughput, mobility and security etc.

A main strategic challenge for the European Future Internet initiative is the concept of Internet of Things. At the network level, there is no global architecture for the Internet of Things, and there is still an ongoing debate on how much intelligence shall be distributed to the edge of the networks instead of a more centralised approach (Islam and Grégoire, 2010). Despite this ongoing debate several attempts to define the Internet of Things concept can be found in the literature. As an example Atzori, Iera, and Morabito (2010) describes Internet of Things as a world-wide network infrastructure of interconnected objects that are uniquely addressable and that communicate by using standard protocols.

To make the Internet of Things vision a reality, several key technologies must be developed and deployed. A number of leading radio device manufacturers have implemented wireless communication standards targeting a widespread use in embedded applications, such as control network, home automation and sensor networks. These applications generally require numerous low-cost nodes communicating over multiple hops to cover a larger geographical area. Furthermore, nodes must be able to operate unattended for years on modest batteries or even by means of energy harvesting from the environment. From a network perspective these application domains can be further enriched by the integration of a large number of heterogeneous objects into the Internet typically forming LoWPANs in the Future Internet architecture.

A LoWPAN is a communication network that allows wireless connectivity between devices with limited power targeting applications with relaxed throughput requirements. A LoWPAN typically connects the physical environment to real-world applications, e.g., wireless sensors. An appealing wireless standard for interconnecting wireless sensor networks is the IEEE 802.15.4 standard. In this particular case it seems that through a wise IP adaptation IEEE 802.15.4 devices can be incorporated into the IP architecture, and by using IPv6 the full deployment of the Internet of Things paradigm can be accomplished (Mayer and Fritsche, 2006; Mulligan, 2007; Hui and Culler 2010).

To meet with the vision of the Internet of Things the IETF has put effort into specifying protocols suitable for IP communications of limited devices. The IETF 6lowpan working group specifies protocols for delivering IPv6 datagrams over LoWPANs. Furthermore, the IETF roll working group brings about standards for routing over low power and lossy networks and a more recently formed IETF working group deals with constrained RESTful environments (CoRE) at the application protocol layer.

From a business perspective industrial associations like the IPSO Alliance complement the work of IETF and IEEE by supporting the introduction of products and services for Internet of Things into the market. The IPSO alliance specifies interoperability tests, conducts marketing activities and serves as an information repository for users seeking to understand the role of IP in networks of smart objects.

NETWORK ARCHITECTURE

The future global communication infrastructure will dominantly be based on IP technology and to a large extent use wireless technologies. The overall connectivity is based on the concept of having different network types connected directly or indirectly via some transit network. Each network type can support different application domains and functionalities and therefore it can be designed and implemented quite differently. However, significant operational advantages arise if a common way of interconnecting the different network types is used.

In Figure 1 the basic structure of the global network is shown with its three main constituents: the core, the access and the edge network. The core network, with its large routers and switches and high speed links, is typically connected via wired network links. The access network is partly wired and partly wireless with WiFi routers at private house-holds etc. The edge of the network, here referred to as the sensor edge network, is almost exclusively wirelessly connected. Additionally, the number of devices is increasing dramatically when we move from the centre towards the edge. A number of institutions have attempted to predict a realistic figure for the total number of edge devices as e.g. the World Wireless Research Forum (WWRF), who envisions "7 trillion wireless devices serving 7 billion people by 2017."

IP-based technologies already exist, are well-known and have large potential as an integrating communication technology (Nielsen and Jacobsen, 2005). It is a scalable technology that enables plug-and-play behaviour for most nodes. Software tools for diagnostics, management and commissioning of the networks are readily available. IP-based devices can be connected readily to other IP-based networks.

Systems must be built to handle different physical link layer technologies, yet with one common network layer i.e. IP. Fundamentally from the initial design of the IP protocols one

Figure 1. High-level structure and hierarchy of the global communication infrastructure and the way wireless technologies are used in the different levels

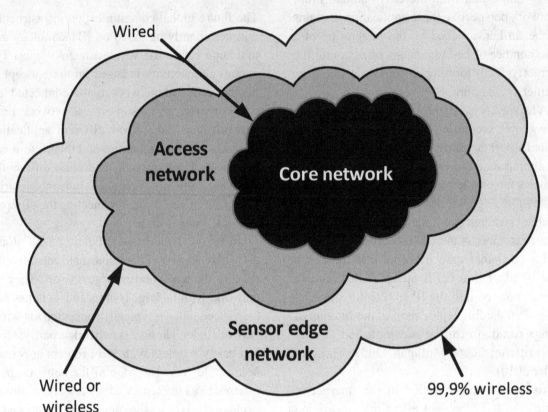

of the key design criteria was to build a system with one common network layer offering *IP-over-everything-and-everything-over-IP* illustrated by the so-called hourglass model (Deering, 1998). From an application point of view IP technology is the perfect choice of an underlying network infrastructure in very diverse domains e.g. for telecommunication, intelligent sustainable energy grids (smart grid), home automation, smart cities, connected healthcare, alarm systems, security installations etc.

We conclude that the Future Internet will be IP-based and wireless on the edge network. It will be composed of a large multitude of heterogeneous networks that interconnect billions of devices in a large connectionless network infrastructure.

Extending the Internet with LoWPANs

With the introduction of an IP-enabled LoWPANs connected to the Internet a number of radically different network characteristics come into play as compared to the current Internet. This is illustrated in Figure 3. First of all, the LoWPAN typically does not have a fixed network infrastructure. Given the size of the network this demands a self-configuring behaviour. Furthermore, the network must be able to handle nodes that join/leave the network unexpectedly and frequently. The nodes must be able to relay, switch or route packets received from neighbours in a multi-hop infrastructure.

When the Internet is extended with LoWPANs these islands of wireless embedded devices form

Figure 2. The hourglass design of the IP software stack. It is shown how the design can be interpreted as an hourglass with "IP over everything and everything over IP" (Adapted from Deering, 1998).

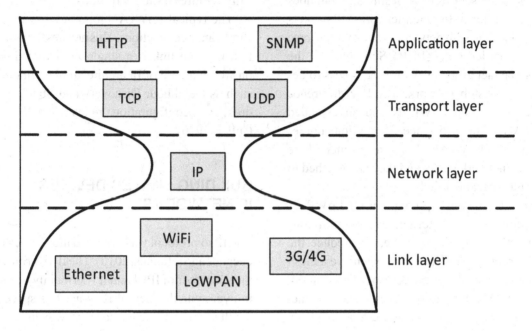

Figure 3. Extending the Internet with LoWPANs. Both the Router-over and Mesh-under network architecture are shown.

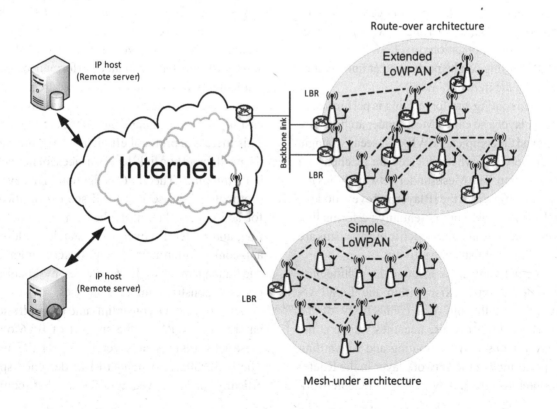

stub networks. A stub network is a network where IP packets are sent from or destined to, but does not act as a transit to other networks. IP packets destined for the stub networks have to transverse a (lossy) border router (LBR). Subsequently, the LBRs may act as gateways for the access to devices in the stub network. The key difference between a simple LoWPAN and an extended LoWPAN is the existence of multiple border routers in the LoWPAN. The border routers share the same network prefix and they are attached to a common backbone link.

Mesh topologies are common for LoWPAN extensions of the Internet. Mesh topologies extends the network coverage, and reduce the cost of infrastructure. In order to achieve a mesh topology, forwarding between nodes is required. In a LoWPAN this can be done in three distinct ways: by forming a link layer mesh, a LoWPAN mesh or by IP routing.

Defining the IP Link

An IP link hides the physical connectivity and the heterogeneity of the underling network infrastructure from the application. In a LoWPAN routing and forwarding can be performed at link layer as well as at the network layer.

When routing and forwarding is performed at the link layer a so called Mesh-under architecture exists and the complete LoWPAN is seen as a single IP sub-network, where devices are reached in a single IP hop. The Mesh-under network hides the radio specifics from the IP layer and every node in the LoWPAN network potentially performs link layer switching and link-specific mechanisms are needed to establish connectivity.

Alternatively, in a Route-over architecture multiple IP links exist within the LoWPAN network and the physical connectivity of the underlying infrastructure becomes visible at the IP layer. Consequently, routing and forwarding are performed at the network layer in the Route-over architecture and every node in the network

becomes a router. The access to end-devices typically requires multiple IP-hops.

The typical LoWPAN topology is a mesh of short-range connections. This negates the assumption that the link is a single broadcast domain on which a core of IP architectural components, such as Neighbour Discovery and Stateless Address Autoconfiguration, relies upon (Hui and Culler, 2010).

BUILDING LIMITED DEVICES IP NETWORKS

The IPv6 protocol was designed more or less two decades ago (Hughes, 2010). The IPv6 protocol is the successor of IPv4 and it was mainly designed to overcome the lack of IPv4 address space that resulted from the enormous growth in number of hosts connected to the Internet. A number of key differences between IPv4 and IPv6 are especially relevant for an efficient transport of IPv6 datagrams over LoWPANs. IPv6 requires the lowest value for the maximum transmission unit (MTU) to increase from 576 to 1280 bytes in the recognition of the growth in link bandwidth. To simplify routers and enhance performance, IPv6 implements fragmentation at the source, rather than in intermediate routers. IPv6 assumes multicast support as an integral part of the architecture. This increases protocol efficiency and eliminate the need for ad hoc link-level services for network bootstrapping. The IPv6 Neighbour Discovery protocol (ND), use link-local scoped multicast for address resolution, duplicate address detection, and router discovery. The stateless address autoconfiguration method simplifies configuration and management of IPv6 devices by enabling nodes to construct unique addresses.

Due to resource constraints and the multi-hop nature of LoWPANs, the support of IPv6 over these networks presents several design challenges. The IEEE 802.15.4 standard was designed specifically for long-lived applications that require the deployment of numerous low-cost nodes. The throughput is limited to 250 Kbps and the physical layer packet size length is limited to 127 bytes to ensure reasonably low packet error rates and to adapt to buffering capabilities of limited devices. The communication range is short (tens of meters) because the cost of transmission power decreases with the distance following an inverse square-law. Unlike most typical WPAN and WLAN installations, LoWPANs communicate over multiple hops. Due to these constraints and the multi-hop nature of LoWPANs, the support of IPv6 over LoWPAN networks presents several design challenges. Essentially, IPv6 datagrams are not a natural fit for LoWPANs. Low throughput, limited buffering capabilities, and small frame sizes make datagram fragmentation and compression a necessity for efficient operation. By introducing a protocol adaption layer between the networking and the link layer many design challenges can be circumvented.

- Single IP link vs. multiple IP links,
- IP link over PAN (mesh under)
- IP link over radio (route over)

6LoWPAN Adaptation

Basically, there are three main elements in the 6LoWPAN adaptation:

- Link layer forwarding. To support link layer forwarding of IPv6 datagrams, the adaptation layer may use link-level addresses for destination end-points of IP hops. Alternatively, the IP stack might realise intra-PAN routing via IP layer forwarding by constructing the IP address of the LoWPAN nodes, in which case each LoWPAN node becomes an IP hop.
- Fragmentation. IPv6 packets are fragmented into multiple link-level frames to accommodate the IPv6 minimum MTU requirement. The fragmentation and as-

sembly is performed in the 6LoWPAN adaptation layer and is transparent for the IP layer.
- Header compression. IPv6 header fields are compressed by making the usage of common values redundant. Header fields are omitted from a packet whenever the 6LoWPAN adaptation layer can derive these from assumptions of a shared context such as link-level information carried in the IEEE 802.15.4 frame. In the best case a UDP/IPv6 header can be compressed down to 7 bytes. However, it should be noted that 6LoWPAN does not efficiently compress when the communication is outside of the link-local scope or when multicasting is used.

The IETF RFC 4944 standard defines how the 6LoWPAN format for IPv6 communication is carried over IEEE 802.15.4 networks. The target for 6LoWPANs is applications that need wireless internet connectivity at low data rates. The mapping of IPv6 protocol to the IEEE 802.15.4 network introduces additional aspects that need to be addressed in the device and network design. Firstly, packet sizes must be adapted. IPv6 requires the MTU to be at least 1280 bytes whereas the IEEE 802.15.4 standard packet size is 127 bytes. A maximum frame overhead of 25 bytes leaves only 102 bytes of payload at the link layer. An optional, but highly recommended, security feature at the link layer adds additional overhead. For example, 21 bytes are consumed for AES-CCM-128 encryption leaving only 81 bytes for higher protocol layers, making the IPv6 (40 bytes), UDP (8 bytes), and TCP (20 bytes) headers seem exceedingly large. Secondly, IPv6 nodes are assigned 128-bit IP addresses in a hierarchical manner, through an arbitrary length network prefix. IEEE 802.15.4 devices may construct their unique IPv6 addresses by using either EUI-64 extended addresses or, after an association event, 16-bit addresses that are unique within a Personal Area

Network (PAN). In the latter case, a PAN ID for a group of physically collocated IEEE 802.15.4 devices is defined. Thirdly, IPv6 nodes are originally optimised for high speed links. Algorithms and protocols implemented at the higher protocol layers, e.g. TCP, are optimised to handle network problems such as congestion. In contrast, IEEE 802.15.4 devices focus on energy conservation and code size optimisation. Fourthly, an adaptation layer for interoperability and packet formats must be provided. The adaptation mechanism to allow interoperability between IPv6 domain and the IEEE 802.15.4 can best be viewed as a cross-layer problem. Fifthly, the mechanisms for handling of addressing must be taken into account. The management of addresses for devices that communicate across the two dissimilar domains of IPv6 and IEEE 802.15.4 is cumbersome.

To circumvent the problems of the unreliable wireless link of the LoWPAN robustness can be added to the communication by using acknowledgements and retransmissions at the link layer. Due to the end-to-end reliability requirement of most applications, it is crucial to design a network optimised in this sense. There are two well-known ways to achieve end-to-end reliability on multi-hop paths. The first approach utilises hop-by-hop retransmissions where each link layer hop retransmits lost frames when necessary. The second approach assumes that the link layer is unreliable and that retransmissions are performed end-to-end. However, the link layers perform retransmissions if necessary, but of course perfect reliability is only guaranteed through end-to-end mechanisms. An alternative is to adopt the unreliable link layer service and rely purely on multi-path routing. In this latter approach the proposed strategy involves fewer nodes and the overall traffic in the network is reduced. In general, specific optimisation depends on the application and network deployment scenario.

- Fragmentation and assembly,
- IPv6 header compression

6LoWPAN Header Format

The 6LoWPAN header format has been standardised in IETF RFC 4944. The 6LoWPAN standard uses header stacking to express specific capabilities in a self-contained sub-header i.e. mesh addressing, fragmentation and header compression. The header stack is simple to parse by the device, does not rely on dynamic state and allow the omission of headers when these are not needed. As an example the fragmentation header is omitted for small datagrams indicating that a single link layer frame carry the entire payload.

Figure 4 shows the header stacking for a 6LoWPAN device with details of the protocol fields in the relevant header. The two Frame Control (FC) bytes of the IEEE 802.15.4 header are used to identify the content of the link layer frame. The header contains a Sequence Number (SN). At the end of the IEEE 802.15.4 frame is the 2 bytes Frame Check Sequence (FCS) footer, which contains the cyclic redundancy check that the link layer uses to check for transmission errors. The addressing fields contain unique link layer addressing information for the source and destination. Addressing information is constructed from a EUI-64 identifier or a 16-bit short address established during bootstrapping.

The Mesh addressing header is defined by setting the first 2 bits to 10. The header contains IP layer addressing information. The fields V and F are used to define if the extended 64-bit address (EUI-64) or if the short 16-bit address is used for the originator address and the final destination address, respectively. Hop Left contains the number of IP hops left and is equivalent to the IPv6 Hop Limit. The Hop Left field is decremented by one for each forwarding node before sending the packet towards its next hop. Finally, the Source Address and the Destination Address are the link layer addresses for the originator and the final destination, respectively.

When a datagram needs to be fragmented the Fragment header of the 6LoWPAN encapsulation

Figure 4. 6LoWPAN header stacking (Adapted from the IEEE 802.15.4 and the IETF RFC 4944 standards)

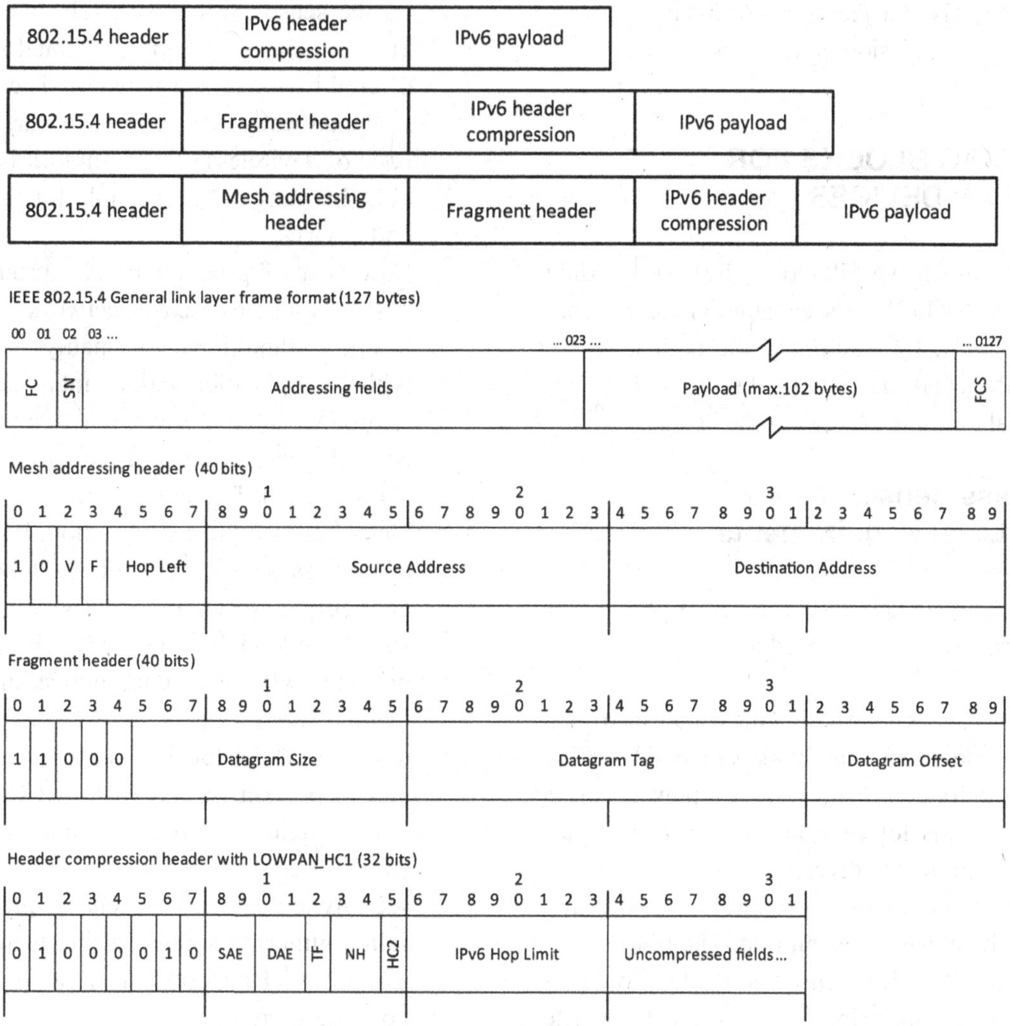

is used. It starts with the bit encoding 11000. The field Datagram Size defines the size of the entire IP packet before link layer fragmentation. The Datagram Tag is used to identify fragments from the same datagram. Except for the first fragment, a Datagram Offset is needed to specify the offset from the beginning of the payload datagram.

A header compression header HC1 is illustrated in Figure 4. The mechanism is identified by the 000010 bits (position 3-7) following the first 10 bit (position 1-2). The fields: source address encoding (SAE) and destination address encoding (DAE) defines the used compression for the source and destination address, respectively. The TF and the NH fields are one bit encodings to define if the IPv6 Traffic Class, Flow Label (TF bit) and IPv6 Next Header (NH) have been omitted. Finally, the HC2 bit defines if LOWPAN_HC2 compression follows. This allows the compression of transport layer protocols such as UDP.

Compared to other well-known compression mechanisms for IPv6 such as Robust Header Compression (ROHC), specified in IETF RFC 3095, the compression in a 6LoWPAN network integrate link layer with network layer compression. This is traditionally not done but it is highly desirable given the small packet sizes in the LoWPAN. Furthermore, 6LoWPAN uses a stateless compression mechanism.

BUILDING BLOCKS FOR LOWPAN DEVICES

In the following we will look at the basic building blocks of a 6LoWPAN capable wireless sensor node. Firstly, by examining the high level requirements and secondly by discussing the most essential building blocks for the design.

Wireless Sensor Network High Level Requirements

The high level requirements for a wireless sensor network can be summarised as:

- Wireless connected. The whole idea of a wireless sensor network is to avoid cabling both for communication and power. This is the basis for easy installation and for integration into diverse application domains such as outdoor environmental monitoring.
- Low power consumption. The power budget of wireless sensor networks should allow for operation based on a battery. The general quantification is that a wireless sensor network shall be able to run for at least 1 to 2 year out of an AA battery. This is a general rule setting some target on the power budget. In practice, the lifetime will be very dependent on the application of the sensor node. An obvious feature of battery powered sensors is to monitor the power level and request replacement or recharging before the power gets critically low.
- Evolutionary design. A wireless sensor network design should be able to adapt to different application and communication environments. The need for design changes during the lifetime of a sensor

node may arise due to new requirements on the sensor, but more likely due to request on changes in the combined service offered by the sensor network. The ability to dynamically add or replace part of the code of a wireless sensor network is desirable, but may not be feasible for the low-end devices.

- Low cost of production. The production cost of a wireless sensor network must be low and should be reasonably balanced with the application. It does not make sense to produce a radiator valve with a network control where the cost of the wireless sensor network is higher than the valve itself.
- No or very simple configuration. Basically a wireless sensor network shall be self-configuring. Installation of wireless sensor network shall be possible without any prior knowledge of communication. Any manual involvement during installation must be on the level of pushing a button and inspection of a red/green LED. The IPv6 stateless address autoconfiguration can be used, but attention must be paid to security and privacy aspects for providing self-configuring nodes. Pairing techniques as used by Bluetooth and Z-wave is one possible approach.

In the following we will look at the most significant building blocks for LoWPAN device designs that meet with the above mentioned requirements.

Microcontrollers

An essential building block of a wireless sensor network device is the microcontroller. Figure 5 shows a simple block diagram of a typical wireless sensor network device centred around the microcontroller unit.

The building blocks may be realised by one or more chips, but current chip technology allows embedding the logic into a single System-on-Chip

Figure 5. Wireless sensor network node blocks

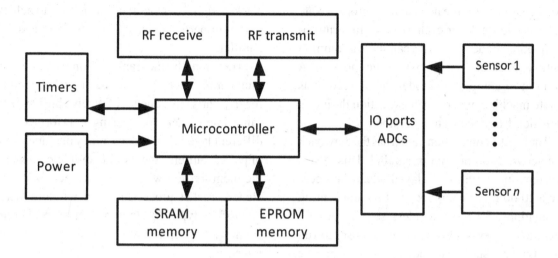

(SoC). Dividing functions on more chips may be more flexible and may allow more precisely matching of the wireless sensor network to the application, but chip internal communication is more power-efficient than driving signals across chip interconnects.

Table 1 lists the characteristics for some popular SoC microcontrollers for sensor network applications. Both 8-, 16- and 32-bits processor cores are used, but the CPU performance is not by itself that critical as a wireless sensor network is not expected to process large amount of data. Of course, the active periods of operation can be shorter with a more efficient CPU core.

Operating Systems

The task of an operating system is to manage low-level hardware features and provide an abstraction to application programs. The hardware constraints on a wireless sensor network node do not allow for an operating system in the traditional sense, and one might argue that an operating system is not needed at all.

Traditional operating systems implement some multiprocessing paradigm, where each process (thread) executes independently and is represented by a process state, a runtime stack and where a scheduler selects between active processes. On contrary, wireless sensor network

Table 1. SoC microcontrollers

Chip	CPU core	RAM	EPROM	RF	Link layer	Vendor
CC430f6137 (MSP430)	16-bit RISC	2K/4K	16K/32K	RF sub 1 GHz		Texas Instrument
ATMega128RFA1	8-bit RISC	16K	4K + 128K	Integrated 2.4 GHz RF	IEEE 802.15.4	Atmel
CC2530	8-bit 8051	8K	32K/64K/128K/256K	Integrated 2.4 GHz RF	IEEE 802.15.4 Zigbee	Texas Instrument
STM32W	32-bit ARM-M3	8K	128K	Integrated 2.4 GHz	IEEE 802.15.4	ST- Microelectronics
MC13224	32-bit ARM7	96K	128K	Integrated 2.4 GHz	IEEE 802.15.4	FreeScale

operating systems deploy a run-to-completion model. This avoids the need to have process state and runtime stack for each process. In a run-to-completion model processes can share a common runtime stack and in this way save memory. A pure run-to-completion model can be viewed as a state machine, where each execution defines a transition from one state to another.

The run-to-completion model has the drawback that activities do not run in parallel. This means that operations will be delayed when a process needs to do more complex and time consuming calculations. So most wireless sensor network operating systems adds some mechanism to run more time consuming processes in a pre-emptive manner.

Surprisingly, the support for different power management schemes in the popular wireless sensor network operating systems is limited and restricted to providing an application programming interface with access to power information and for control of sleep modes. It seems plausible to release the burden of power management from the applications and to integrate power management directly into the operating system scheduling and timer handling.

Table 2 list some common choices of operating systems for wireless sensor networks together with some key characteristics.

6LoWPAN Communication Stack

A 6LoWPAN protocol stack in a sensor node must be adapted to the constrained environment of the wireless sensor network. In a traditional IP stack design the general philosophy is to achieve optimum performance by processing packets in parallel.

Traditionally, the transmission part of a communication stack has a queue of packets and the receive parts have queues of receive buffers in the same time as packet processing is performed at the different layers. This concurrency demands pools of packet buffers, and would completely exhaust the memory of a wireless sensor network node. Hence, packet processing in a wireless sensor network is typically done packet by packet and even with reception and transmission running interleaved.

The uIPv6 stack is among the smallest open-source IPv6-ready protocol stacks (Durvy et al., 2008). The uIPv6 stack includes an implementation of the 6LoWPAN standard and it integrates into the Contiki operating system (Dunkels, Grönvall, and Voigt, 2004). The uIPv6 stack requires only 0,5 KB of SRAM for data structures, a minimum of 1,3 KB of SRAM for buffering, and 11,5 KB of flash RAM for the code. It has a single packet buffer for incoming and outgoing packets. The length of the buffer is the length of the link layer header plus 1280 bytes (i.e., the minimum link MTU for an IPv6 network). The main data structures in the stack are the interface address list and the neighbour cache, prefix list, and the default router.

Despite the limited constrained on memory both the uIPv6, as well as the commercial Arch Rock 6LoWPAN implementation, comply with

Table 2. Wireless sensor network operating system characteristics

Operating system	Execution model	Programming language	Program loading	Size (minimum)
Tiny OS	run-to-completion interruptable by events	nesC	static	3450 bytes
Contiki	run-to-completion with special pre-emptive threads	C	possibility to dynamically add modules	3875 bytes
FreeRTOS	microkernel with pre-emption	C	static	4400 bytes

the requirements set up by the IPv6 Ready Logo program (Hughes, 2010). The IPv6 Ready Logo program tests general IPv6 capability and is not tailored to wireless sensor network implementations in particular.

Power Management in Wireless Sensor Nodes

Sensor nodes must be able operate out a single battery for months or even years. Wireless sensor network nodes will typically be battery powered and the normative battery lifetime is 1 to 2 years. A standard AA battery can provide in the order of 1W-hour. The total power consumption with a running CPU and either the receive or transmit part active range from 52,8 to 119,8 mW. Hence, the wireless sensor network node will be able to run from 8,3 to 18,9 hours on an AA battery. Equivalently, the wireless sensor network can be running 0,09% to 0,21% of the time if the battery must last for one year. This also corresponds to running between 57 ms and 126 ms each minute. Table 3 compares the power consumption for a range of typically selected components.

The most power demanding part of a wireless sensor network are the RF blocks. Evolution in chip technology is not expected to allow for decreasing power consumption as fast for the RF blocks as for the other blocks. This is because the power consumption of the radio part is directly impacted by the signal strength that shall be produced. The needed signal strength is dependent on the distance between nodes, so more densely deployed networks will help and also some improvements in realisation of physical and link layers can be expected.

Laptops and mobile phones have introduced intelligent power management that reduces the clock frequency of processors when the requirement on processing is low or when the laptop is getting low on power. Such techniques can be adopted for wireless sensor network as well; however, this increases the complexity of the device. In general, for wireless sensor network it is considered more optimal to run a processor with shorter duty cycles than to lower the frequency overall.

The power consumption is reduced by switching between normal run-mode and sleep-mode. This can even be further refined by having different levels of sleep mode. In sleep-mode the microcontroller state must be stored before sleep and restored when revoked. One approach is to evoke the wireless sensor network node at a certain interval, operate for some time and then return to sleep mode. The interval must be set such that the wireless sensor network is alert to handle the requested events. On the other hand there is some overhead in power-up and power-down, which does not contribute to overall wireless sensor network processing.

Another approach is to have event driven power management, where the processor is awaked from sleep at either external events or scheduled timer events. Basically, in the event-driven approach the sensor device starts to do some task and returns to

Table 3. Power consumption comparison for SoCs

Chip	Deep sleep (uW)	Sleep w timer (uW)	CPU core	RF receive	RF transmit	CPU+max (RX,TX)
CC430f6137 (MSP430)	2,0	6,0	7,8	48,0	45,0	52,8
ATMega128RFA1	0,8		12,3	55,8	55,8	68,1
CC2530	1,2	3,0	19,5	74,4	90,0	109,5
STM32W	1,2	2,4	18,0	81,0	93,0	111,0
MC13224	1,3	29,9	24,1	72,6	95,7	119,8

sleep again. Before entering sleep-mode the device may calculate when it should be restarted. The difficulty in this approach is to respond efficiently to external events such as e.g. the reception of a packet. Having the RF receive part producing an event when packet reception is in progress only moves power management to the RF receive block. However, a decoupling of the power management and the RF receive control function is desired to allow the maximum flexibility of their respective design.

For the efficient operation of the wireless sensor network a time synchronisation mechanism is needed. Several different approaches and strategies for time synchronization in wireless sensor networks have been proposed (Elson and Estrin, 2001). However, a discussion on time synchronisation aspects is beyond the scope of this chapter.

A typical operation scenario for a wireless sensor network application is illustrated in Figure 6. A 6LoWPAN device that has lost its memory e.g. when it receives fresh batteries has to go through a bootstrapping sequence to get the sensor application up and running in continuous operation. After successful bootstrapping the device enters the state of continuous operation.

In addition to the application sending data, the figure shows protocol messages needed to maintain link state, neighbour relationships, routing topology and device configuration. Link state information and device configuration is sent by using trap messages over e.g. Simple Network Management Protocol (SNMP).

ROUTING IN UNRELIABLE NETWORKS

Routing is the process of selecting paths in a network along which to send network traffic. A routing protocol finds routes between nodes, over which data packets are forwarded towards the final destination, by discovering and exchanging network topology information. Routing protocols in wireless sensor networks are usually deployed at network layer in a Route-over network architecture. Routing protocols could be implemented at link layer as well, performing multi-hop routing at the link layer, adapted to the resource constrained environment. In this latter case, the link layer provides a Mesh-under network architecture linking all nodes together, i.e. connecting all IP nodes on

Figure 6. Device task sequence related to communication during bootstrapping and continuous operation. Note that the different signal sequences use different time scales.

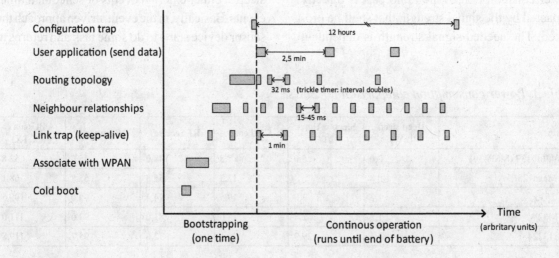

the link layer. However, the Route-over mechanism also lets IP routing protocols span different link technologies, enabling better integration into more capable networks. The following will consider routing in a Route-over approach in a homogeneous 6LoWPAN.

Wireless sensor network routing protocols must be adaptable to cope with the frequent changes in topology and in more radical cases, where the sensor nodes performs a cold boot, the protocols must be able to handle the establishment of network topology given that information of the topology prior sleep has been lost or is out-dated.

Nodes that participate in the routing process often transmit messages to determine their neighbours to establish awareness of their presence (neighbour discovery). By using the neighbouring relationships, routing protocols exchange network topology to generate routes or may exchange routes directly as part of a routing exchange.

Essentially, algorithm classes for routing can be categorised into a distance-vector class and a link-state class. Routers that use distance-vector protocols store local next hop information in its routing table. In a link-state protocol each node acquires complete information about the network, typically by flooding of the network. Each node calculates a shortest-path tree to each destination.

Link Reliability

The main causes of changes in network topology can be categorised as physical movement, radio channel changes, network performance, sleep schedules and node failure:

- Physical movement: The most evident reason for mobility is when nodes in a network physically move in relation to other nodes. This will change the wireless connectivity between pairs of nodes and may cause nodes to change their point of attachment to the network.

- Radio channel: Even under excellent channel conditions, various factors lead to heavy loss rates on wireless links (Ganesan et al., 2002). Changes in the environment cause changes in the characteristics of the radio transmission such as fading due to multipath propagation effects. These changes could require topology change even without physical movement of the nodes. Furthermore, packets errors can arise due to interference from nearby systems and interference effect can lead to the decision to change radio channel.

- Network performance: Packet loss and delay on wireless networks may be caused by poor signal strength, packet collisions, and lack of channel capacity or may lead to congestion at the nodes. A sustainable experience of a high packet loss could cause a node to change its point of attachment.

- Sleep schedules: Especially battery powered devices and devices depending on energy harvesting in wireless sensor networks use aggressive sleep schedules in order to save power. If a node finds itself attached to a sleeping router without a suitable duty cycle for the application, this may cause the node to move to a better point of attachment.

- Node failure: Wireless nodes tend to be prone to failure, for example due to battery depletion. The failure of a router causes a topology change for nodes using it as their default router.

When offering a complete IP solution all the way to the outer edge of the network the possibility of connecting end-to-end is directly offered.

Routing Topology

The dynamic topology of a wireless sensor network poses a real challenge in the design of a proper routing protocol and several routing protocols for wireless sensor networks have been proposed (Akkaya and Younis, 2005). Traditional distance-vector mobile ad hoc networks (MANET) protocols are also less suitable since they assume a high rate of mobility for all nodes in the network, whereas LoWPAN nodes are better characterised by more structured mobility within a set of stationary nodes. MANET protocols often use frequent floods to discover and maintain routes. This is a costly method in terms of power consumption for wireless sensor networks.

IPv6 Routing Protocol for Low Power and Lossy Networks

IP routing algorithms for mesh networking are developed in the IETF manet working group for generic ad hoc networks, and in the IETF roll working group specifically for wireless embedded applications. In particular, we will address one particular routing protocol proposed by roll working group below.

In the Routing Over Low power and Lossy networks (roll) working group of IETF has adopted standardisation work in the area of routing over low power and lossy networks. A solution called IPv6 Routing Protocol for Low power and Lossy Networks (RPL) protocol has been proposed by the working group. RPL is a reactive, distance-vector routing protocol designed for use in resource constrained networks. The aim of the protocol is to construct routing paths from sensors to a central "controller" acting as network sink. RPL constructs a destination oriented Directed Acyclic Graph (DAG) rooted at the sink. Downward routes support point-to-multipoint flows, from the DAG root towards the leaves. Downward routes also support point-to-point flows where point-to-point messages can flow towards a DAG root through an upward route, then away from the DAG root to a destination through a downward route. In the converged state, each router in the LoWPAN has identified a stable set of parents, on a path towards the root of the DAG, as well as a preferred parent.

A DAG allows the routing protocol to minimise resource requirements and the state complexity is small because nodes only need to maintain routes to upwards nodes e.g. its DAG parents.

Hence, the DAG is the central topology upon which routing is performed. The purpose of the DAG is to optimise routes from any node to the sink in the network according to an Objective Function (OF). The OF defines how nodes translate one or more metrics and constraints into a value called rank. The rank is basically the distance of the node from the backbone network. Furthermore, the OF also defines how nodes select parents. By using the construct of the OF the RPL protocol itself becomes agnostics to these metrics.

As a distance-vector protocol, RPL contains rules, restricting the ability for a node to change its rank. Specially, a node is allowed to assume a smaller rank than previously advertised (i.e. to logically move closer to the root) if it discovers a parent advertising a lower rank. It must then disregard all previous parents with higher ranks. The ability for a node to assume a greater rank (i.e. to logically move further away from the root) is restricted to avoid count-to-infinity problems in case all its former parents disappear.

Figure 7 illustrates the construction of a DAG with 20 sensor nodes. The arrows illustrate connections between nodes that can be mapped to some underlying physical infrastructure. From the figure it is seen that node 18 uses node 2 as its preferred parent since node 2 has better rank that node 14 or node 10. Hence, an IP packet destined for the Internet would travel the route $18 \rightarrow 2 \rightarrow LBR$.

RPL introduces a new ICMPv6 control message for signalling. A node broadcasts its DAG Information Option (DIO) messages using multicasting (which is broadcasting in practice for IEEE 802.15.4 networks). The DIO messages contain the information about the rank in the DAG, the OF and DAG it has joined in i.e. the DAG-ID. Any node that is connected to a non-RPL implementing node or a backbone network can act as

Figure 7. Routing in a wireless sensor network. The solid arrows show the established RPL attachments where the dashed lines illustrate some possible changes in topology.

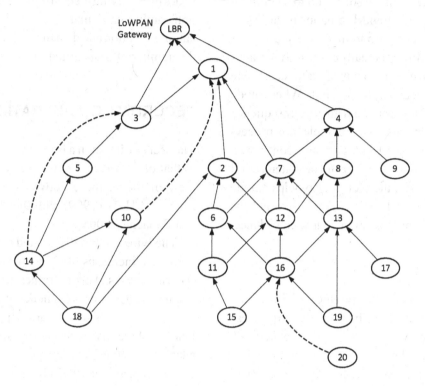

a root. DIOs are emitted periodically from each node, triggered by a timer (trickle timer) whose duration increases exponentially (doubled after each time it is sent). This way, DIOs propagate down to most distant nodes from root and help create a DAG in the network. Once a node receives a DIO, it calculates its rank based on the rank in the received DIO, and the cost of reaching the node from itself. RPL defines a number of rules for parent selection based on the quality of the links, the advertised OF, path cost, rank, etc. Any node that has lower rank than the node itself is considered to be a candidate parent. When a node joins the network, it may wait to receive a DIO or it may alternatively multicast a solicitation message called the DAG Information Solicitation (DIS), so that other nodes hearing the DIS starts sending DIOs, and the newly arrived node can join the DAG.

RPL constructs and maintains downward routes with Destination Advertisement Options (DAO) messages. Downward routes support point-to-multipoint flows, from the DAG roots toward the leaves. Downward routes also support point-to-point flows to any node in the DAG. Point-to-point messages can flow toward a DAG root through an upward route, then away from the DAG root to a destination through a downward route. A node multicast DAOs for one-hop reachability and unicast reachable prefix to their parents in the DAG to advertise their addresses and prefixes. The nodes that receive these DAOs, update their routing table. When no entry is available in the routing table, or for traffic to the root, a node will forward a packet up to its most preferred parent. Note that while sending packets up the DAG, a node must not forward it to a node with greater rank to prevent routing loops. In case no parent is available, the node can forward the data to a node with same rank. For point-to-point routing, the packet goes from the source up to a common ancestor of the source and destination in the DAG, and then it travels down to the destination.

The LBR will periodically emit DIO messages with new sequence number in order to recalculate the DAG and repair any broken link. When a node encounters a DIO message with greater sequence number, it again starts the parent selection process based on the updated link cost and confidence about the parents. Hence for the next iteration it has a better path to the root. It also helps a node find a parent in case their parent list is depleted due to unsuccessful probes or due to low confidence.

Scalability

The large and diverse measurement space of sensor nodes coupled with the typically large areas of deployment will yield very large network sizes. Current urban roll-outs are composed of sometimes more than one hundred nodes (Hui and Culler, 2010). Future roll-outs, however, may reach numbers in the tens of thousands to millions.

A good routing protocol has to be scalable and adaptive to the changes in the network topology. Thus protocols must perform well as the network grows larger or as the workload increases (Akkaya & Younis, 2005). A "flat" network hierarchy, e.g. single-tier network, can cause central nodes such as the border router to overload as the density of sensor nodes increases in the network. Such overload might cause latency in communication and the subsequent inadequate tracking of node events cause a degradation of the sensor network application.

To allow the network to cope with additional load and to be able to cover a large area of interest without degrading the service multiple gateways should be deployed. Furthermore, network clustering can be adopted to allow hierarchical routing schemes to be implemented. In addition, the clustering can be used to ensure an efficient

maintenance of the energy consumption of sensor nodes by involving them in multi-hop communication within a particular cluster and by performing data aggregation and data fusion in order to reduce the number of transmitted messages to the sink.

SECURITY CONSIDERATIONS

The security threat in a LoWPAN is much similar to that of ad hoc and sensor networks. An overview of the in these networks is provided by Zhou and Haas (1999) and Djenouri, Khelladi, and Badache, (2005).

The wireless and distributed nature of sensor networks increases the spectrum of potential security threats. This is further amplified by the resource constraints of the nodes, thereby preventing resource-intensive security approaches from being deployed. A viable security approach should adapt small code size, low power operation, low complexity, and small bandwidth across all nodes in the sensor network.

IPv6 over LoWPANs will require confidentiality and integrity protection. This can be provided at the application, transport, network, and at the link layer. A separate set of security considerations apply to bootstrapping a 6LoWPAN device into the network, as for example for initial key establishment. In the following, we will discuss the generalised threat model for LoWPAN devices as well as some of the proposed to circumvent the identified threats.

Threat Model for LoWPAN Devices

Basically, security threats arise from two different types of nodes. Failed nodes may perform operations incorrectly, introducing false and misleading information into the network. On the other hand, malicious nodes may deliberately disrupt the network using a variety of attacks.

The main threats to a wireless sensor network are as follows:

- ○ Availability. Forwarding and routing must be reliable to ensure the survivability of network services despite denial of service attacks.
- ○ Confidentiality ensures that certain information is protected from unauthorised entities. Beside the confidentiality of application data in the sensor network the routing and topology information itself should be kept private.
- ○ Integrity ensures that messages are transmitted unaltered over the network. The integrity of a network depends on all nodes in the network following correct networking procedures so that every node has correct behaviour with respect to communication. As an example threats to integrity might introduce incorrect routing information.
- ○ Authentication. Without authentication, a malicious node could masquerade as sensor node, thereby gaining unauthorised access to resources and sensitive information and interfering with the operation of the network.
- ○ Nonrepudiation ensures that the origin of a message cannot deny having sent the message. Nonrepudiation is useful for detection and isolation of compromised nodes.

The threat model used here distinguishes between external and internal attacks. External attacks are performed by unauthorised nodes or entities. These threats are likely to be more easily detected than threats from internal nodes. Internal attacks are posed by internal nodes, i.e. they are performed by authorised nodes within the wireless sensor network. These threats are likely to be more difficult to detect as they arise from trusted sources. Examples of possible attacks are: sleep deprivation attack where a malicious node causes other nodes to exhaust their resources by getting these nodes to do unnecessary processing. Eavesdropping compromises the confidentiality of information. The active interference attack, where malicious messages or signals interfere with the network operation, and the attack of replaying or reordering old messages can result in a denial of service situations.

It should be noted that the threat of having failed nodes is most serious if failed nodes are needed as part of the multi-hop routing and no alternative route can easily be established. By proper design of the network these threats can to some degree be circumvented. For instance, the proper sizing of the network allows multiple alternative routes to exist in the network.

Security Adaptations in 6LoWPAN

The 6LoWPAN adaptation can take advantage of the strong AES-128 link layer security mechanisms provided by IEEE 802.15.4 to secure message confidentiality. For network layer security, two models are applicable: end-to-end security for example using IPSec transport mode, or security that is limited to the wireless portion of the network, for example using a security gateway and IPSec tunnel mode. The disadvantage of adding security to the communication is the larger header size and complexity, which is significant at the LoWPAN packet frame. Currently, work is ongoing in the IETF 6lowpan working group to define the threat model and to adapt a light-weight security framework for limited, unreliable devices. One such promising approach is a light-weighted key management mechanism. However, while network layer security mechanisms such as IPsec and secure neighbour discovery are maturing, their feasibility for LoWPANs is still being questioned due to the resource constrains.

FUTURE DIRECTIONS

In sensor networks, energy consumption is of highest priority and the RF communication design blocks consume the most energy. Wireless sensor network designers strive to reduce the power consumption of the blocks in general. For the processor and memory parts it is likely that it will approximate the evolution expressed by Moore´s law, i.e. doubling of capacity each 18-24 months. The improvement for wireless sensor network is likely to be used to reduce size and power consumptions instead of increasing capacity and speed. The use of energy harvesting is an important aspect of LoWPAN devices. With a smart combination of energy efficient protocols and energy harvesting methods, the optimal solution for achieving autonomous and long-lasting LoWPANs can be reached.

Power management plays a significant role in prolonging node life time. The support of advanced power management schemes needs further research and it needs to be taken from a device-level to a network-level. The IEEE 802.15.4 standard defines only a limited set of power management mechanisms for devices. However, most commercial implementations and industrial standards built on IEEE 802.15.4 seem to forego the defined power management mechanisms.

Efficient protocol support is also needed for the IP based wireless sensor networks and the ongoing work of the IETF 6lowpan and IETF roll working groups is heading in this direction. This includes protocol optimisation for small devices such as neighbour discovery, compression mechanisms for TCP, light-weighted key management protocols as well as energy efficient routing protocols. In addition, a recently formed IETF CoRE working group is expected to bring significant contributions in this area.

Mobility based communication can potentially prolong the lifetime of wireless sensor networks and increase the connectivity of sensor nodes. Although movements can have severe impact on the received signal strength a global optimum for the network could still be achieved in some cases. Although some protocols already exist that take care of the link layer and networking, this area still has a lot of open research issues. More specific link layer protocols need to be developed that take into account the movement of the nodes, in addition to the development of low power features such as an adaptive duty cycle for lowering the idle listening and overhearing adapting to the dynamics of the network.

A security framework adapted to LoWPANs has to be sufficiently light-weighted to meet the constraints of the devices. On the other hand it also needs to be capable of providing the in-depth security required for the wireless sensor applications. Flexible security mechanisms must be developed and new generation of SoCs must offer basic security features as an embedded part of the chip.

Although a considerable number of studies on wireless sensor networks exist, most of them are based on simulations only. It will be most valuable for the community to have more experiments and field trials to substantiate the findings of simulation studies in wireless sensor networks research. A solid reality check of what can be achieved with the current state of the art is desirable.

CONCLUSION

Extending the Internet with LoWPANs is the next natural step towards a realisation of the Internet of Things in the Future Internet. In this chapter we have explained the essential protocols and technologies for IP-enabled LoWPANs connected to the Internet. We have described several required functions of such a system and we have discussed the most important aspects of device integration e.g. the design for energy efficiency and IP connectivity.

When used for internetworking, IP offers large advantages over dedicated network architectures bound to the underlying radio technology. The use of IP allows a reuse of architectures across technologies, and it makes communication between sensor nodes in a heterogeneous network highly feasible.

Technology and building blocks such as microcontroller, operating systems, and IP protocol stacks for interconnecting LoWPANs are available. Furthermore, their integration into diverse and constrained environments is supported by common methods and standards. In particular, we have discussed the recent work in the IETF 6lowpan and IETF roll working groups in the context of wireless sensor network as a dominant application domain of the Internet of Things. An obvious next step is the integration with commercial applications and services hereby bringing the benefits and applicability of IP technology to a broader community, including developers, manufactures and consumers.

To evolve technology further, research and development activities in areas such as the mobility, scalability and large-scale, high-density networks are needed alongside the continuous improvements and optimizations of protocols and technologies for IP-enabled LoWPANs.

REFERENCES

Akkaya, K., & Younis, M. (2005). A survey on routing protocols for wireless sensor networks. *Ad Hoc Networks*, *3*(3), 325–349. doi:10.1016/j. adhoc.2003.09.010

Atzori, L., Iera, A., & Morabito, G. (2010). The internet of things: A survey. *Computer Networks*, *54*(15), 2787–2805. doi:10.1016/j. comnet.2010.05.010

Deering, S. (1998). *Watching the waist of the protocol hour-glass*. 6th IEEE International Conference on Network Protocols.

Djenouri, D., Khelladi, L., & Badache, A. N. (2005). A survey of security issues in mobile ad hoc and sensor networks. *Communications Surveys & Tutorials, IEEE*, *7*(4), 2–28. doi:10.1109/COMST.2005.1593277

Dunkels, A., Grönvall, B., & Voigt, T. (2004). Contiki - A lightweight and flexible operating system for tiny networked sensors. *Annual IEEE Conference on Local Computer Networks*, (pp. 455-462).

Durvy, M., Abeillé, J., Wetterwald, P., O'Flynn, C., Leverett, B., Gnoske, E. et al. (2008). *Making sensor networks IPv6 ready* [Abstract].

Elson, J., & Estrin, D. (2001). Time synchronization for wireless sensor networks. *Proceedings of the 15th International Parallel & Distributed Processing Symposium*, (p. 186). Washington, DC, USA.

European X-ETP Group. (2010). *Future internet strategic research agenda*. Report No. FI-SRA V1.1. Brussels, Belgium: European Commission.

Ganesan, D., Krishnamachari, B., Woo, A., Culler, D., Estrin, D., & Wicker, S. (2002). *Complex behavior at scale: An experimental study of low-power wireless sensor networks*. No. Technical Report UCLA/CSD-TR 02-0013) UCLA Computer Science Department.

Hughes, L. E. (2010). *The second internet: Reinventing computer networking with IPv6*. InfoWeapons. Retrieved from www.infoweapons. com.

Hui, J. W., & Culler, D. E. (2010). IPv6 in low-power wireless networks. *Proceedings of the IEEE*, *98*(11), 1865–1878. doi:10.1109/JPROC.2010.2065791

Islam, S., & Grégoire, J. (2010). Network edge intelligence for the emerging next-generation internet. *Future Internet*, *2*(4), 603–623. doi:10.3390/fi2040603

Mayer, K., & Fritsche, W. (2006). IP-enabled wireless sensor networks and their integration into the internet. *Proceedings of the First International Conference on Integrated Internet Ad Hoc and Sensor Networks,* Nice, France. 5.

Mazzer, Y., & Tourancheau, B. (2009). Comparisons of 6LoWPAN implementations on wireless sensor networks. *International Conference on Sensor Technologies and Applications,* (pp. 689-692).

Mulligan, G. (2007). The 6LoWPAN architecture. *Proceedings of the 4th Workshop on Embedded Networked Sensors,* Cork, Ireland, (pp. 78-82).

Nielsen, T. T., & Jacobsen, R. H. (2005). Opportunities for IP in communications beyond 3G. *Wireless Personal Communications, 33*(3-4), 243–259. doi:10.1007/s11277-005-0570-5

Zhou, L., & Haas, Z. J. (1999). Securing ad hoc networks. *IEEE Network, 13*(6), 24. doi:10.1109/65.806983

ADDITIONAL READING

Alliance, I. P. S. O. IPSO alliance. http:// ipso-alliance.org

Bag, G., Shams, S. M. S., Akbar, A. H., & Raza, H. M. M. T. Ki-Hyung Kim, & Seung-Wha Yoo. (2009). Network assisted mobility support for 6LoWPAN. Consumer Communications and Networking Conference, 2009. CCNC 2009. 6th IEEE, 1-5.

Chen, X., Makki, K., Yen, K., & Pissinou, N. (2009). Sensor network security: A survey. *Communications Surveys & Tutorials, IEEE, 11*(2), 52–73. doi:10.1109/SURV.2009.090205

De Couto, D. S. J., Aguayo, D., Bicket, J., & Morris, R. (2005). A high-throughput path metric for multi-hop wireless routing. *Wireless Networks, 11*(4), 419–434. doi:10.1007/s11276-005-1766-z

Hong, X., Kong, J., & Gerla, M. (2006). Mobility changes anonymity: New passive threats in mobile ad hoc networks: Research articles. *Wirel. Commun. Mob. Comput., 6*(3), 281–293. doi:10.1002/wcm.395

Institute of Electrical and Electronics Engineers (IEEE). IEEE 802.15 WPAN task group 4 (TG4). http:// www.ieee802.org/ 15/ pub/ TG4.html

Internet Engineering Task Force (IETF). IPv6 over low power WPAN (6lowpan) working group. http:// www.ietf.org/ html.charters/ 6lowpan-charter.html

Internet Engineering Task Force (IETF). Routing over low power and lossy networks (roll) working group. http:// www.ietf.org/ html.charters/ roll-charter.html

Reddy, A. M. V., Kumar, A. V. U. P., Janakiram, D., & Kumar, G. A. (2009). Wireless sensor network operating systems: A survey. *Int. J. Sen. Netw., 5*(4), 236–255. doi:10.1504/IJSNET.2009.027631

Shelby, Z., & Bormann, C. (2010). *6LoWPAN: The wireless embedded internet*. Wiley.

Vasseur, J., & Dunkels, A. (2010). *Interconnecting smart objects with IP - the next internet*. Morgan Kaufmann.

Watteyne, T., Molinaro, A., Richichi, M., & Dohler, M. (2010). From MANET to IETF ROLL standardization: A paradigm shift in WSN routing protocols. Communications Surveys & Tutorials, IEEE, PP(99), 1-20.

Yick, J., Mukherjee, B., & Ghosal, D. (2008). Wireless sensor network survey. *Computer Networks, 52*(12), 2292–2330. doi:10.1016/j.comnet.2008.04.002

Zhao, J., & Govindan, R. (2003). Understanding packet delivery performance in dense wireless sensor networks. Proceedings of the 1st International Conference on Embedded Networked Sensor Systems, Los Angeles, California, USA. 1-13.

KEY TERMS AND DEFINITIONS

6LoWPAN: An IPv6-enabled LoWPAN that is prepared for a potential large scale network.

Internet of Things: A world-wide network infrastructure that interconnects uniquely addressable physical and virtual objects by means of standardised communication protocols.

IP version 6 (IPv6): Internet protocols version 6 (IPv6) is the successor of the Internet protocol version 4 (IPv4).

LoWPAN: A Low power Wireless Personal Area Network (LoWPAN) is a network of short-range wireless links resulting from interconnecting low power communication devices.

Mesh-Under Architecture: Hides the network link specifics from the IP layer. Every node in the Mesh-under LoWPAN network becomes a switching node and link-specific mechanisms are needed to establish connectivity.

Power Management: A feature of some electrical appliances, especially copiers, computers and computer peripherals such as monitors and printers that turns off the power or switches the system to a low-power state when inactive.

Route-Over Architecture: Offers a network of multiple IP hops. It lets IP routing protocols span different link technologies, enabling better integration into more capable networks.

Wireless Sensor Network: Consists of geographically distributed autonomous sensor devices that cooperatively monitor physical or environmental conditions, such as temperature, sound, vibration, pressure, motion etc.

Chapter 11
Token Based Mutual Exclusion in Peer-to-Peer Systems

Mayank Singh
ABV-Indian Institute of Information Technology and Management, India

Shashikala Tapaswi
ABV-Indian Institute of Information Technology and Management, India

ABSTRACT

Mutual exclusion is one of the well-studied fundamental primitives in distributed systems, and a number of vital solutions have been proposed to achieve the same. However, the emerging Peer to Peer systems bring forward several challenges to protect consistent and concurrent access to shared resources, as classical peer-to-peer systems, like Napster, Gnutella, et cetera, have been mainly used for sharing files with read only permission. In this chapter, the authors propose a quorum based mutual exclusion algorithm that can be used over any Peer to Peer Distributed Hash Table (DHT). The proposed approach can be seen as extension to traditional Sigma protocol for mutual exclusion in Peer to Peer systems. The basic idea is to reduce message overhead with use of smart nodes present in each quorum set and message passing between the current owners of resource with next resource requester nodes.

INTRODUCTION

Over the past several years, peer-to-peer systems have generated many headlines across several application domains. The increased popularity of these systems has led researchers to study their overall performance and their impact on the underlying Internet. The unanticipated growth in popularity of peer-to-peer (P2P) systems has raised a number of significant problems. Mutual Exclusion is one of such problems which has not been yet been thoroughly studied in the P2P domain. It is crucial for design of P2P systems. Many problems involving replicated data, computational resources etc. require mutual exclusion.

The problem of mutual exclusion can be described as a collection of asynchronous processes, each alternately executing a critical and a

DOI: 10.4018/978-1-4666-0203-8.ch011

non-critical section that must be synchronized so that no two processes ever execute their critical sections concurrently. It was first described and solved by Dijkstra in (Dijkstra, 1965). Distributed mutual exclusion introduces some new requirements which can be summarized as follows:

- **Safety:** At most one process may execute in critical section at any time.
- **Liveness:** Every request for a critical section is eventually granted.

Even though mutual exclusion is a classical, well studied problem in distributed systems and several viable solutions have been proposed, it yet remains to be completely explored in the P2P domain. Directly adapting the mutual exclusion algorithms from distributed computing literature is not possible due to the differences in the underlying system models, one of which is the absence of any centralized index server to keep track of membership and to ensure consistency. Classical decentralized algorithms use several rounds of all-to-all communication which is unscalable. Mutual exclusion algorithms that currently exist do not have scalability and efficiency, which makes their applicability limited. This gives rise to new challenges that need to be tackled in order for this field to become successful in the future.

Today P2P and the Grid are in the same developmental stage, as traditional distributed systems were about a decade ago. Concepts like scalability and fault-tolerance need to be reworked for this new generation of distributed environment. One of the fundamental obstacles to overcome is to provide a mechanism to share resources transparently and efficiently across a large number of independent hosts. Resources can be either computational resources or data, and access to them should be controlled in a completely decentralized manner, even in the presence of high churn.

Since each resource can have multiple replicas, the problem in question becomes even more challenging. Access to that resource is controlled by a set of replicas. In order to access it, majority of the replicas must reach a consensus. The concept of a quorum set is defined to be a group of nodes such that the intersection of any two quorum sets must not be empty. A token ring approach to mutual exclusion is one where all the nodes are arranged in a ring formation and a token is constantly circulated. When a node acquires the token from its neighbor it checks to see if it is attempting to enter a critical region. If so, it enters the region, does all the work it needs to and leaves the region. Token is then passed to the next node in the ring.

The main contribution of this study is the design and discussion of a proposed protocol for achieving mutual exclusion in dynamic P2P systems. This goal is accomplished while maintaining a low message overhead and reducing the burden on the replicas of controlling access to the critical section, by distributing the load evenly among the quorum set nodes. Another important contribution is its ability to be incorporated with any generic P2P DHT (Stoica, 2001), (Ratnasamy, Francis, Handley, Karp, & Shenker, 2001), depending on the application requirements.

A mutual exclusion algorithm must satisfy the following requirements (Velazquez, 1993):

- At most one process can execute its critical section at a given time.
- If no process is in its critical section, any process requesting to enter its critical section must be allowed to do so in finite time.
- When competing processes concurrently request to enter their respective critical sections, the selection cannot be postponed indefinitely.
- A requesting process cannot be prevented by another one to enter its critical section within a finite delay.

Even though over the last decade mutual exclusion in distributed systems have attracted a great deal of attention, it is not possible to directly use the proposed solutions into the P2P domain. The non – acceptance of these solutions lies in the differences of the underlying system models. In the P2P scenario, each resource can have multiple replicas, which makes mutual exclusion even more challenging as access to that resource is controlled by its set of replicas.

We propose a theoretical token based mutual exclusion model to achieve mutual exclusion in P2P domain. The basic idea is quite simple: utilizing the fact that intermediate nodes of each quorum set has the replica list of resource id which falls in that particular quorum set if upon receiving the request for resource access, they found the resource id of intended resource, it immediately stop forwarding the request and directly send the request to the owner currently accessing the resource in the context. These intermediate nodes are referred as smart nodes. When the owner of that resource completes its critical section, it sends the token of the same to the next resource requester.

PEER TO PEER SYSTEMS

A quick look at the literature reveals a considerable number of different definitions of "peer-to-peer", mainly distinguished by the "broadness" they attach to the term. The strictest definitions of "pure" peer-to-peer refer to totally distributed systems, in which all nodes are completely equivalent in terms of functionality and tasks they perform. These definitions fail to encompass, for example, systems that employ the notion of "supernodes" (nodes that function as dynamically assigned localized mini-servers) such as Kazaa, which are, however, widely accepted as peer-to-peer, or systems that rely on some centralized server infrastructure for a subset of non core tasks (e.g. bootstrapping, maintaining reputation ratings, etc).

According to a broader and widely accepted definition, "peer-to-peer is a class of applications that take advantage of resources—storage, cycles, content, human presence—available at the edges of the internet". This definition, however, encompasses systems that completely rely upon centralized servers for their operation (such as the notorious Napster), as well as various applications from the field of Grid computing. Overall, it is fair to say that there is no general agreement about what "is" and what "is not" peer-to-peer.

This lack of agreement on a definition—or rather the acceptance of various different definitions—is, to a large extent, due to the fact that systems or applications are labeled "peer-to-peer" not because of their internal operation or architecture, but rather as a result of how they are perceived "externally", that is, whether they give the impression of providing direct interaction between computers. As a result, different definitions of "peer-to-peer" are applied to accommodate the various different cases of such systems or applications.

From above perspective, the two defining characteristics of peer-to-peer architectures are the following:

- The sharing of computer resources by direct exchange, rather than requiring the intermediation of a centralized server. Centralized servers can sometimes be used for specific tasks (system bootstrapping, adding new nodes to the network, obtain global keys for data encryption), however, systems that rely on one or more global centralized servers for their basic operation (e.g. for maintaining a global index and searching through it—Napster, Publius) are clearly stretching the definition of peer-to-peer. As the nodes of a peer-to-peer network cannot rely on a central server coordinating the exchange of content and the operation of the entire network, they are required to actively participate by independently and unilaterally performing tasks such as searching for other nodes, locating or caching content, routing information and messages, connecting to or disconnecting from other neighboring nodes, encrypting, introducing, retrieving, decrypting and verifying content, as well as others.

- Their ability to treat instability and variable connectivity as the norm, automatically adapting to failures in both network connections and computers, as well as to a transient population of nodes. This fault-tolerant, self-organizing capacity suggests the need for an adaptive network topology that will change as nodes enter or leave and network connections fail or recover, in order to maintain its connectivity and performance.

Therefore the following definition can be proposed:

Peer-to-peer systems are distributed systems consisting of interconnected nodes able to self organize into network topologies with the purpose of sharing resources such as content, CPU cycles, storage and bandwidth, capable of adapting to failures and accommodating transient populations of nodes while maintaining acceptable connectivity and performance, without requiring the intermediation or support of a global centralized server or authority.

P2P vs. Client-Server

There is no clear border between a client-server and a P2P model. Both models can be built on a spectrum of levels of characteristics (e.g., manageability, configurability), functionality (e.g., lookup versus discovery), organizations (e.g., hierarchy versus mesh), components (e.g., DNS), and protocols (e.g., IP), etc. Furthermore, one

Figure 1. High level view of P2P

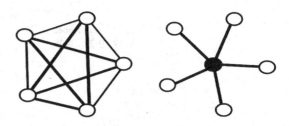

model can be built on top of the other or parts of the components can be realized in one or the other model. Finally, both models can execute on different types of platforms (Internet, intranet, etc.) and both can serve as an underlying base for traditional and new applications.

Components of a P2P System

P2P applications are composed of a generic architecture, which consists of the following parts:

- *Communication:* P2P model covers a wide spectrum of communication paradigms. At one end of the spectrum are desktop machines mostly connected via stable, high-speed links over the Internet, at the other end of the spectrum, are small wireless devices such as PDAs or even sensor-based devices that are connected in an ad-hoc manner via a wireless medium.

The fundamental challenge of communication in a P2P system is overcoming the problems associated with the dynamic nature of peers. Either intentionally (e.g., because a user turns off her computer) or unintentionally (e.g., due to a, possibly dial-up, network link failing) peer groups frequently change. Maintaining application-level connectivity in such an environment is one of the biggest challenges for P2P systems.

Figure 2. Comparison between P2P and client server trade-off

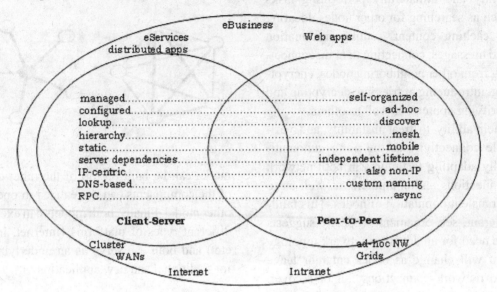

- **Group Management:** Peer group management includes discovery of other peers in the community and location and routing between those peers. Discovery of peers can be highly centralized such as in Napster, highly distributed such as in Gnutella, or hybrid.
- **Robustness:** There are three main components that are essential to maintaining robust P2P systems:
  - Security
  - Resource aggregation
  - Reliability.

Security is one of the biggest challenges for P2P infrastructures. A benefit of P2P is that it allows nodes to function as both a client and a server. However, transforming a standard client device into a server poses a number of risks to the system. Only trusted or authenticated sources should have access to information and services provided by a given node. Unfortunately, the security requirement either requires potentially cumbersome intervention from the user, or interaction with a trusted third party. Centralizing

the task of security is often the only solution even though it avoids the P2P benefit of a distributed infrastructure.

- **Class-Specific:** above components are applicable to any P2P architecture, application-specific components abstract functionality from each class of P2P application
  - Scheduling applies to parallelizable or compute-intensive applications
  - Compute-intensive tasks are broken into pieces that must be scheduled across the peer community
  - Metadata applies to content and file management applications. Metadata describes the content stored across nodes of the peer community and may be consulted to determine the location of desired information.
  - Messaging applies to collaborative applications. Messages sent between peers enable communication.
  - Management supports managing the underlying P2P infrastructure.

BASIC CONCEPTS

The resources such as data, files, etc., can be replicated in distributed systems to enhance availability as well as response time. However, a protocol must be used to maintain data consistency. Theoretically, quorum agreements should be used to maintain replicated data because its minimality and completeness. They have long been used (e.g.,(Gifford,1979), (Thomas,1979),(Garcia-Molina,&Barbara,1985), (Herlihy,1986) to solve the problem of replica consistency. A quorum, q, is a set of nodes in the network, and a quorum system is a set of quorums, Q, such that every two quorums in Q share at least one node. That is, given two quorums, q, q', Q, there exists some node i q q'; the intersection of these two quorums is non-empty.

In order to ensure the consistency of the data, when a node chooses to modify the data, it notifies some quorum, say, q Q, of the modification; when a node wants to access the data, it contacts some quorum, say, q' Q. Since the two quorums, q and q', intersect at some node, we can be sure that the read operation that accesses the data learns about the earlier modification.

Figure 3. Sample quorum setup

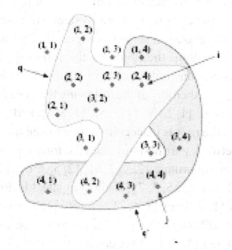

RELATED WORK

Distributed mutual exclusion protocols can be categorized in two categories (Velazquez,1993),(Raynal,1991). These are quorum based protocols (Ricart, &Agrawala,1981), (Maekawa,1985) and token based protocols (Raymond,1989). Our approach proposes a combination of these two types of protocols.

Previous research has been conducted in efficient routing messages to the nodes holding a particular resource like the Chord(Stoica,2001) and the Pastry (Rowstron, &.Druschel, 2001) protocols, which are examples of structured P2P DHTs and choose their neighbors intelligently to lower the latency and message cost of routing to O(log n).

Sigma(Lin, Lian, Chen, &Zhang,2004) is the current existing protocol for providing mutual exclusion in P2P systems, which would fall into the "permission-based" category (Lamport,1978). It is implemented inside a DHT and adopts queuing and cooperation between clients and replicas, to enforce a quorum consensus scheme.

Quorum Based Algorithms

Different types of algorithms are designed to achieve ME, each having their own pros and cons, but each algorithm tries to minimize the number of messages, improve robustness etc. There is always a tradeoff between number of messages required, robustness and distributed nature of the algorithm. The motivation for introducing quorum based algorithms is to balance this trade off, optimize the number of messages and provide resilience.

Garcia-Molina and Barbara (Garcia-Molina,&Barbara,1985) have proposed the notion of a **coterie** which generalizes the notion of **quorums** and this can be used for many solutions such as Mutual Exclusion, replica control etc.

We now formalize the notion of Coterie [6]:

Coterie: Let U be the set of nodes that compose the system. *A* set of groups S is a coterie under U if

1. $G \in S \Rightarrow G \subseteq U \wedge G \neq \theta$
2. (**Intersection property**) $\vee G, H \in S : G \cap H \neq \theta$, i.e. they must have a non-empty intersection.
3. (**Minimality property**) $\vee G, H \in S : G \not\subset H$, i.e. there are no two quorum sets G and H in S such that G is super set of H.

The minimality property is not necessary for correctness but is useful for efficiency. We can see this intuitively, for example if the cardinality of all quorums is constant, then the algorithm will be more distributive and symmetric (i.e. for any node to enter its CS, it need to do same amount of work in a similar fashion as others will).

Coteries can be used to develop protocols that guarantee ME. For example, to enter its CS, a process at site i is required to receive permission from some quorum of sites, S_i in the network. If all sites in S_i grant permission the process is allowed to enter its CS, because it guarantees that no other site can take permission from any other quorum S_j. Note, however, that this simple protocol can't provide a safe ME solution. Additional mechanisms are needed to tackle with deadlocks, site crashes, network partitions etc. Using this basic idea many algorithms are designed with varying costs, complexity, robustness etc.

Following describes some of these ideas:

Using Trees and Quorums

One more idea is to mix trees with quorums as proposed by *Divyakant Agrawal and Abbadi* by (Agrawal, & El Abbadi, 1991). In that paper they claim that the algorithm is the first distributed ME protocol to tolerate both site failures and network partitions while in the best case incur-

ring logerthmic costs in the size of the network. Note that in this discussion, failure implies node crashes as well as network partitions. In *Maekawa's* algorithm (Maekawa, 1985) only one set S_i is associated with any site i (Note that even though a site i is a member of d quorums, only one quorum S_i is the home set of i). This makes the protocol vulnerable to failures since the failure of any site i S_i prevents other site j S_j to enter their CS. This scheme ensures fault tolerance by providing several alternatives to a site requesting ME.

In this algorithm ([Agrawal, & El Abbadi, 1991) the network is logically organized as a binary tree, and a site i is not associated with a specific quorum S_i instead it can choose any available quorum. The algorithm tries to construct a quorum by selecting any path starting at root and ending with any of the leaves. If successful, this set of sites forms the quorum. If it fails to find a path as a result of failure (or inaccessibility due to network partition) of a site, say j, the algorithm must substitute for that site with two paths, both of which start with the children of j and terminate with leaves. Note that each path must terminate with a leaf (this condition is necessary to make the algorithm resilient to crashes and network partitions). So if the leaf in a path is inaccessible, a quorum can not be formed and algorithm terminates with error (but it never malfunctions). We can observe that all possible quorums have a non null intersection, even in case of failures.

Consider a distributed system with seven sites organized as shown in Figure 4. Following the algorithm, the union of the following tree quorums constitutes a coterie. If no failures have occurred, then any of the following four sets form a quorum: {1, 2, 4}, {1, 2, 5}, {1, 3, 6}, and {1, 3, 7}. If the root is inaccessible (due to site failures or network partitioning), then the following four sets are quorums: {2, 4, 3, 6}, {2, 5, 3, 6}, {2, 4, 3, 7}, and {2, 5, 3, 7}. If site 2 or site 3 is down, then {1, 4, 5} or {1, 6, 7} respectively form quorums. If both sites 1 and 2 are down, then {4, 5, 3, 6} and {4, 5, 3, 7} are candidates for quorums.

Similarly, if sites 1 and 3 are inaccessible, the sets {2, 4, 6, 7} and {2, 5, 6, 7} are quorums. Finally, if sites 1, 2, and 3 are inaccessible, then the only possible quorum is {4, 5, 6, 7}.

From the construction of the quorum, we can see in case of no failures $|S_i| = \log N$. The paper (Agrawal, El Abbadi,1991) shows that the best and worst case requires $O(\log N)$ and $O((N+1)/2_\daleth)$ messages respectively for a site to enter its CS.

Heuristically Aided Algorithms

Previous ME algorithms share a common property that they are deterministic in the sense that they do not use state information of the system which can be obtained by exchanging messages or by implicit means to guide their actions. In heuristically aided algorithms the sites maintain some state information of the system which can be used in selecting heuristics to guide it.

One such algorithm by *Mukesh Singhal* (Singhal,1989) is based on the token based algorithm (Suzuki, &Kasami,1985). In this algorithm whenever a site intends to invoke ME, it uses a heuristic to guess from its available state information what sites of the system are probably holding or are likely to have the token and sends REQUEST messages to only those sites rather than to all the sites. Consequently, the proposed algorithm requires fewer messages per ME as compared to (Suzuki, &Kasami,1985). Also a performance

Figure 4. A sample hierarchy of 7 site network

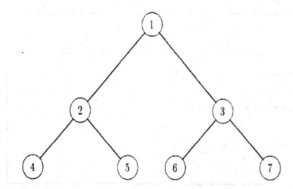

study to illustrate the improvement is given in the algorithm.

One can easily note that such heuristics is key to such algorithms. The heuristic should be such that given locally available state information of the system; a site should be able to guess a set of sites which are likely to have the token. There are several such heuristics which immediately come to mind. For example, in one obvious heuristic, a site sends a token REQUEST message only to the site to which it forwarded the token last. However, it can be easily visualized that in this heuristic a token REQUEST message may end up in an endless chase of token, and user response time will be poor due to serial propagation of the REQUEST. A better heuristic proposed by the algorithm (Singhal,1989) is to send the REQUEST to those sites which are already in the request queue for the token. Note, however, that the success of a heuristic depends upon the correctness/credibility of the state information it is operating on. The algorithm shows that it is robust to failures and node partitions.

SYSTEM MODEL

Formally speaking, our system model is as follows:

- ∘ The basic entities in the system are called nodes (or peers).
- ∘ The intermediate nodes in each quorum set which knows the owner currently accessing the resource in the context are called smart nodes.
- ∘ Nodes are interconnected over P2P DHT that allows routing of messages between any other nodes.
- ∘ Each resource e.g., a file or a computational resource corresponds to a set of replicas, that are responsible for granting access to that resource.
- ∘ The replicas are always available, but their internal states may be randomly reset. This is also termed as the fail-

ure-recovery models in (Ricart, & Agrawala,1981).The nodes rejoin the network with the same node Id.

○ Clients and replicas communicate via messages across unreliable channels. Messages can be replicated, lost, but never forged.

○ The number of clients is unpredictable and can be very large with high churn in the system – may enter and leave the system anytime.

○ Peers are not malicious and will not fail.

In the context of this paper, both clients and replicas are peers in the DHT (in practice, however, it's only the replicas that have to be DHT members).

PROPOSED PROTOCOL

In order to achieve less message overheading and better load-balancing characteristics, the proposed protocol maintains the queue of requests for access of the resource at the peer that is currently in the critical section as contrast with at the replica as is the case in the Sigma protocol.

The step wise step description of proposed protocol along with pseudo code of the steps is as follows in Box 1 and Box 2:

State Variables

• When a node wants access to a particular resource, it sends requests with timestamp to all the governing replicas of that resource, using the P2P DHT routing mechanism. We have used Lamport's

Box 1.

```
peer_id                       // the identity of the client
resource_id                   // intended resource id (requested by    the
peer)
response [ ]                  // responses from replica
replica_owner                 // replica's winner
owner                         // current resource owner
queue                         // request queue maintained by current resource
owner
replica_list[ ]               //list of replicas contained by intermediate
nodes
replica_owner_timestamp       // timestamp of replica's winner
```

Box 2.

```
Request(CS)  //request for critical section
{
   timestamp:= GetLogicalClock();  //lamport's clock
         for each R[i] node
     sendRequest(R[i], peer_id, timestamp, resource_id);
}
```

logical clock (Raymond, 1989) to generate timestamp.

- Intermediate nodes who receive the request check their replica list for the intended resource id. If succeed, the REQUEST message is stopped being forwarded and in place of that an ENQUEUE message is sent directly to the node currently accessing the resource in context. If failed, it forwards the REQUEST message to other peers.

- Upon receiving the REQUEST message at the target node, that replica will check if it has voted already or not. If the replica has not voted before, it will vote for the current requester. A RESPONSE message is send directly to the original requester of the REQUEST message. This RESPONSE message consists of the peer id and timestamp of the replica's owner (i.e., the node this replica has voted for). If the replica has voted before for some other peer, this information would be that of the other peer (Box 3).

- Whenever a requesting node receives a RESPONSE message, it computes if it has received a majority of replica votes. If so, it sends a WIN message to all the replicas, declaring itself as the new owner of the resource. The replica list entry is updated as this message is routed to all the replicas. If nobody has recieved enough votes, the requesters send out a YIELD message to each of the replicas that has voted for it (Box 4).

Box 3.

```
onRequest(R[i], peer_id, timestamp, resource_id);
{
if (relpica_list[ ].Contains (resource_id))
                    {
                                    sendEnqueue(peer_id, timestamp) to owner;
                        }
                else
{
                                    forward sendRequest to its neighbours;
                        }
    if (replica_owner = nil)
                        {
                                    replica_owner:= peer_id;
                                    replica_owner_timestamp:= timestamp;
                        }
    else
                        {
                                    \\ replica's winner is some other peer
}
            sendResponse(R[i],
    replica_owner, replica_owner_timestamp);
        }
```

- When an ENQUEUE message reaches the owner of the resource that is being requested, the owner adds the requester's id to its queue as shown in Box 5.
- In order to release a resource, a RELEASE message is sent beginning at the current owner of the resource and is targeted to all the governing replicas for that resource. Clean-up has been done as this message is being sent to the replicas. Once the message reaches its target replica, owner information of that replica is updated.

- When the owner of the resource has executed critical section using that resource, it leaves the critical section and sends a TOKEN message to the node next in line. The TOKEN message that is sent consists of the updated request queue (Box 6).

Box 4.

```
onResponse(R[i], replica_owner, replica_owner_timestamp)
{
    response[i].replica_owner:= replica_owner;
    response[i].timestamp:= replica_owner_timestamp;
  if (enough responses received)
    {
        winner:= ComputeWinner();
        if (winner = self)        // case 1
              {
                send Win(winner) message to all the replicas;
               }
            else if (winner = nil)
            { // case 2
                for each response[i].owner is self
                      {
                            sendYield(R[i], id);
                            Clear(response[i]); // reset the state
                      }
            }
                wait(); // case 3: some one else wins, just wait
      }
    }
          onWin(winner)
{
    each replica updates its part of the replica list entry (Next and Previ-
ous node pointers);
 }
```

Box 5.

```
onEnqueue(peer_id, timestamp)
{
        queue.Insert(peer_id, timestamp);
}
```

Box 6.

```
Release (CS)
    {
        for all R[i] of CS            //for all replicas of resource i
        sendRelease(R[i], self);
        queue.start:= queue.next;
        Send Token message to the queue.start;
        sendToken(queue);
    }

    onRelease(R[i], self)
      {
            all the intermediate nodes update their replica list;
            reset the owner information of the replica;
      }
```

FAILURE HANDLING

The proposed protocol works fine if the working environment is free from failures. Though the types of failures that can occur include:

- Failure of intermediate nodes of the quorum set.
- Failure of replica/s.
- Failure of node currently present in the critical section and maintaining the queue of requests.

Failure of the node that is currently in the critical section and is who is holding the token and also maintaining the queue of requests can have the worse effect on the entire system. A scheme inspired from traditional router advertising mechanism has been proposed to handle this failure. The idea is to replicate the waiting queue maintained by current resource owner to all the other requesters. These n+1 nodes which include the n waiting nodes and current owner as well, can use a periodic advertisement message among themselves, to propagate the updates or to know if a particular node has failed. Whenever the request queue is updated, this change is propagated to the other n nodes of this waiting queue. These updates are ordered by sequence numbers so that, in case of failure, we can use the most recent copy of the request queue. "Ping" messages are sent periodically from n waiting nodes to the node holding the token, at a low frequency to detect the node failure. When the node holding the token fails, among the waiting nodes, the node with the highest sequence number will have the most updated copy of the queue. This node routes a message to all the replicas declaring itself as the owner of the resource.

Figure 5. A state of the protocol, where Request1 is presently in the critical section and Request2 which is supposed to use the same resource has been inserted in the requester queue with timestamp at current resource owner

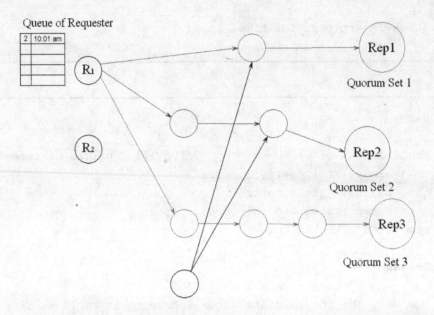

Figure 6. A state of the protocol, where Request1 is presently in the critical section and Request2 and Request3 which is supposed to use the same resource has been inserted in the requester queue with timestamp at current resource owner. When Request4 sends out its request for the same resource, its request is intercepted by quorum set smart nodes before reaching the replica, and therefore ENQUEUE messages are sent to Request1 and it inserts Request4 to its requester queue.

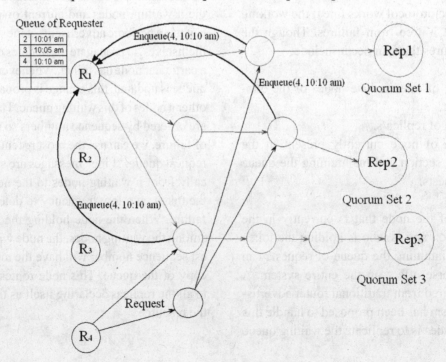

Failure of intermediate nodes within a quorum set is detected by using the *Next* and *Previous* pointers maintained by each node, as part of its replica list entry.

In case of other failures, only probabilistic correctness can be guaranteed by the proposed protocol which is discussed in detail in next section.

CORRECTNESS

As seen with mutual exclusion, correctness is an elusive concept involving considerations such as: – Deadlock/Livelock, Starvation and Fairness. Correctness of P2P mutual exclusion algorithms can be ensured if the safety properties (nothing bad will ever happen) and liveness properties (something good will eventually happen) of distributed mutual exclusion are upheld.

Without replica failures the protocol satisfies mutual exclusion since no two nodes can ever be in a critical section at the same time. Assuming that two nodes are simultaneously in the critical section for a resource then both nodes must have received a majority of the votes from the set of replicas that control the resource, which is not possible with the proposed protocol similar to sigma protocol.

In case of a replica failing and randomly resetting its state, it may happen that subsequent requests reach the replica resulting in a grant. Considering a resource with N replicas needed for mutual exclusion, the probability of such a series of events breaking mutual exclusion is given by: $P = 1 - (1 - P_r)^N$ where P_r is the probability of a single replica failing and randomly resetting its state.

Deadlock is impossible as timestamps have been used along with introducing release timeouts for nodes. Starvation is also not possible as ordering of requests has been done on First-In-First-Out (FIFO) basis with timestamp as the parameter for the ordering. Fairness is maintained as requests to access a particular resource are granted in FIFO ordering.

CONCLUSION

In this work, the proposed protocol is independent of underlying DHT implementation, thus providing a generalized solution to the addressed problem. The purpose behind proposing the protocol is load balancing and fault-tolerance improvement. The proposed protocol, through their hybrid (quorum and token-based) schemes, is able to keep the load on the replicas relatively low.

FUTURE SCOPE

The concept of logical replica can be further extended (Zhang, 2004). The next step can be to simulate this theoretical model under the real life environment. An important future direction of this research would be to port some existing P2P applications to use various protocols for handling their mutual exclusion needs. A general set of APIs for the mutual exclusion protocols can be developed so that future applications can make use of the proposed algorithm in a modular fashion, without worrying about the low level mutual exclusion details and DHT implementation.

REFERENCES

Agrawal, D., & El Abbadi, A. (1991). An efficient and fault tolerant solution for distributed mutual exclusion. *ACM Transactions on Computer Systems, n.d.*, 9.

Dijkstra, E. W. (1965). Solution of a problem in concurrent programming control. *Communications of the ACM, 8*, 569. doi:10.1145/365559.365617

Garcia-Molina, H., & Barbara, D. (1985). How to assign votes in a distributed system. *Journal of the ACM, 32*(4), 841–860. doi:10.1145/4221.4223

Gifford, D. K. (1979). Weighted voting for replicated data. In *Proceedings of the Seventh Symposium on Operating Systems Principles*, (pp. 150–162).

Herlihy, M. (1986). A quorum-consensus replication method for abstract data types. *ACM Transactions on Computer Systems, 4*(1), 32–53. doi:10.1145/6306.6308

Lamport, L. (1978). Time, clocks and the ordering of events in a distributed system. *Communications of the ACM, 21*, 558–565. doi:10.1145/359545.359563

Lin, S., Lian, Q., Chen, M., & Zhang, Z. (2004). *A practical distributed mutual exclusion protocol in dynamic peer-to-peer systems*. International Workshop on P2P Systems (IPTPS).

Maekawa, M. (1985). A √n algorithm for mutual exclusion in decentralized systems. [TOCS]. *ACM Transactions on Computer Systems, 3*(2). doi:10.1145/214438.214445

Ratnasamy, S., Francis, P., Handley, M., Karp, R., & Shenker, S. (2001). A scalable content-addressable network. In *Proceedings of ACM SIGCOMM*.

Raymond, K. (1989). *A tree-based algorithm for distributed mutual exclusion*. TOCS.

Raynal, M. (1991). A simple taxonomy for distributed mutual exclusion algorithms. *ACM SIGOPS Operating Systems Review, 25*(2).

Ricart, G., & Agrawala, A. K. (1981). An optimal algorithm for mutual exclusion in computer networks. *Communications of the ACM, 24*(1). doi:10.1145/358527.358537

Rowstron, A., & Druschel, P. (2001). *Pastry: Scalable, distributed object location and routing for large-scale peer-to-peer systems, middleware*.

Singhal, M. (1989). A heuristically-aided algorithm for mutual exclusion in distributed systems. *IEEE Transactions on Computers, 38*(5), 61–77. doi:10.1109/12.24268

Stoica, I. (2001). A scalable peer-to-peer lookup service for Internet applications. In *Proceedings of ACM SIGCOMM*, San Deigo, CA.

Suzuki, I., & Kasami, T. (1985). A distributed mutual exclusion algorithm. *ACM Transactions on Computer Systems, 3*, 344–349. doi:10.1145/6110.214406

Thomas, R. H. (1979). A majority consensus approach to concurrency control for multiple copy databases. *Transactions on Database Systems, 4*(2), 180–209. doi:10.1145/320071.320076

Velazquez, M. G. (1993). *A survey of distributed mutual exclusion algorithms*. Technical Report CS-93-116, Colorado State University.

Zhang, Z. (2004). *The power of DHT as a logical space*. To appear in FTDCS'04.

KEY TERMS AND DEFINITIONS

Distributed Hash Table: Distributed hash table (DHT) to support fast data locating and system scalability.

Mutual Exclusion: Mutual exclusion is used to avoid the simultaneous use of a common resource.

Peer to Peer Systems: Peer to Peer Systems are computers or networks used in a distributed application architecture that partitions tasks or workloads between peers. Peers are equally privileged, equipotent participants in the application. They are said to form a peer-to-peer network of nodes.

Quorum Sets: A quorum is a set of nodes such that any two quorums have at least one common node.

Chapter 12
Random Early Discard (RED) Queue Evaluation for Congestion Control

Md. Shohidul Islam
Dhaka University of Engineering & Technology, Bangladesh

Md. Niaz Morshed
Dhaka University of Engineering & Technology, Bangladesh

Sk. Shariful Islam
Dhaka University of Engineering & Technology, Bangladesh

Md. Mejbahul Azam
Dhaka University of Engineering & Technology, Bangladesh

ABSTRACT

Congestion is an un-avoiding issue of networking, and many attempts and mechanisms have been devised to avoid and control congestion in diverse ways. Random Early Discard (RED) is one of such type of algorithm that applies the techniques of Active Queue Management (AQM) to prevent and control congestion and to provide a range of Internet performance facilities. In this chapter, performance of RED algorithm has been measured from different point of views. RED works with Transmission Control Protocol (TCP), and since TCP has several variants, the authors investigated which versions of TCP behave well with RED in terms of few network parameters. Also, performance of RED has been compared with its counterpart Drop Tail algorithm. These statistics are immensely necessary to select the best protocol for Internet performance optimization.

DOI: 10.4018/978-1-4666-0203-8.ch012

INTRODUCTION

AQM is receiving wide attention as a promising technique to prevent and avoid congestion collapse in packet-switched networks. It is a form of router queue management based on a proactive approach. By providing advanced warning of incipient congestion, end nodes can respond to congestion before router buffer overflows and hence ensure improved performance (Jain, 1990). In this chapter, we represent a comprehensive performance analysis of Random Early Detection (RED) algorithm. We show that RED provides fair sharing of the bottleneck link capacity and avoids phenomena such as lock-out inherent in Tail Drop. The RED algorithm tends to drop packets from each connection in proportion to the transmission rate the flow has on the output link. Moreover, it can serve incoming traffic guaranteeing stable results as the data load and arrival conditions vary. We investigate how high priority User Datagram Protocol (UDP) traffic affects the performance of lower priority Transmission Control Protocol (TCP) traffic when they share the same bottleneck link with one or two classes of service. The RED algorithm does not minimize the number of dropped packets as expected, but it manages to achieve improved performance when compared to the Tail Drop. Moreover, we found out that even though the arrival of competing UDP traffic generally hurts the performance of the TCP connection running, Tail Drop provides better results to the TCP connection when the UDP flow starts simultaneously with the TCP traffic. Indeed, it prevents the Slow Start phase from being excessively aggressive thus avoiding phenomena such as Slow Start overshoot and severe congestion states. Our results confirm most of the theoretical properties of the RED algorithm. It is substantiated that RED will be useful to provide fair sharing of resources and improved performance in a wide range of environments, including a variable number of connections with different data loads and throughputs.

LITERATURE REVIEW

Active queue management has been recommended by the Internet Engineering Task force (IETF) as a way of mitigating the above stated performance limitations of TCP over drop tail networks. Random Early Detection (RED) is the first active queue management algorithm proposed for deployment in TCP/IP networks (Floyd, Jacobson, 1999). The basic idea behind an active queue management algorithm is to convey congestion notification early to the TCP endpoints so that they can reduce their transmission rates before queue overflow and sustained packet loss occur. It is now widely accepted that RED controlled queue performs better than a drop-tail queue. However, RED has some parameter tuning issues that need to be carefully addressed for it to give good performance under different network scenarios. Random early detection (RED), also known as Random Early Discard or Random Early Drop is an active queue management algorithm (Floyd, Jacobson, 1993). It is also a congestion avoidance algorithm. In the traditional tail drop algorithm, a router or other network component buffers as many packets as it can, and simply drops the ones it cannot buffer. If buffers are constantly full, the network is congested.

Tail drop distributes buffer space unfairly among traffic flows. Tail drop can also lead to TCP global synchronization as all TCP connections "hold back" simultaneously, and then step forward simultaneously. Networks become underutilized and flooded by turns. RED addresses these issues. It monitors the average queue size and drops (or marks when used in conjunction with ECN) packets based on statistical probabilities. If the buffer is almost empty, all incoming packets reaccepted. As the queue grows, the probability for dropping an incoming packet grows too. When the buffer is full, the probability has reached 1 and all incoming packets are dropped. RED is more fair than tail drop, in the sense that it does not possess a bias against bursts traffic that uses only a small portion of the bandwidth. The more a host transmits, the more likely it is that its packets are dropped. Early detection helps avoid global synchronization. The most common technique of queue management is a tail drop. In this method packets are accepted as long as there is space in the buffer. When it becomes full, incoming packets are dropped. This kind of approach results in dropping large number of packets in the time of congestion. This can result in lower throughput and TCP synchronization (Floyd, 1997).

Congestion Control

An important issue in packet-switched network is congestion. Congestion in a network may occur if the load on the network—the number of packets sent to the network—is greater than the capacity of the network— the number of packets a network can handle. Congestion control refers to the mechanisms and techniques to control the congestion and keep the load below the capacity.

In general we can divide congestion control mechanisms into two broad categories:
- ○ Open-loop congestion control (prevention)
- ○ Closed-loop congestion control (removal).

Open-Loop Congestion Control (Prevention)

In open-loop congestion control, policies are applied to prevent congestion before if happens. In these mechanisms, congestion control is handled by either the source or the destination. We give a brief list of policies that can prevent congestion.

- Retransmission Policy
- Window Policy
- Acknowledgement Policy
- Discarding Policy
- Admission Policy

Closed-Loop Congestion Control (Removal)

In Closed-loop congestion control mechanisms try to alleviate congestion after it happens. Several mechanisms have been used by different protocols. We describe a few of them here.

- Back Pressure.
- Choke Point.
- Implicit Signaling.
- Explicit Signaling.
- Backward Signaling.
- Forward Signaling.

Full Queues

Studies of Internet traffic shows that the packet arrival process is bursty (Leland, Taqqu, Willinger, & Wilson, 1994). This means that routers need to be designed for handling bursty traffic by actively avoiding congestion and delays of packets. The bursty traffic causes the full queues problem which affects the performance with tail-drop queue management (Jae Chung, Mark Claypool). Tail drop has no method for limiting the amount of buffer space being used in the queue. Therefore, it is possible for the mechanism to maintain a full (or, almost full) status for long periods of time. If the queue is full or almost full, an arriving burst will cause multiple packets to be dropped.

Multiple packet drops can cause underutilization of the network because multiple drops may cause many hosts to reduce their transmission rates simultaneously. Also, dropping multiple packets may punish bursty flows harder then other flows and thus breaking goal of fairness among flows. Another effect of the full queues problem is that by allowing the queue to grow large, the average queue size increases, which again causes an additional delay of packets traversing the router (Jae Chung, Mark Claypool). If the queue management mechanism can control the amount of buffer space used, without increasing the total number of packet drops, then the mechanism reduces the overall propagation delay of packets traveling through the router. Thus, the queuing mechanism will provide lower delays which are important for interactive services like the Web.

MOTIVATION

RED was originally described by Floyd and Jacobson (1992, September) and was later recommended for deployment on Internet routers (Braden, Clark, Crowcroft, Davie, Deering) with expectations that it would benefit the overall performance or at least not have any negative effects on performance.

All available empirical evidence shows that the deployment of active queue management mechanisms in the Internet would have substantial performance benefits. There are seemingly no disadvantages to using the RED algorithm, and numerous advantages. Consequently, we believe that the RED active queue management algorithm should be widely deployed. We should note that there are some extreme scenarios for which RED will not be a cure, although it won't hurt and may still help. An example of such a scenario would be a very large number of owns, each so tiny that its fair share would be less than a single packet per round trip time. (Braden, Clark, Crowcroft, Davie, Deering... Zhang).

The primary motivation for developing RED is to provide a router based mechanism for congestion avoidance. Congestion control of Internet traffic is implemented by TCP implementations on the hosts on the edge of the network. However, the hosts have very limited information regarding the general state of the network and therefore have limited information for choosing an appropriate sending rate. The router on the other hand, has Very precise knowledge about its state. By developing active queue mechanisms it may be possible to propagate this knowledge to the hosts by dropping packets early. Essentially this may improve the general ability to choose a suitable sending rate

and thus avoid congestion (Himanshu, Agarwal, Velmurugan). The idea was originally proposed by Van Jacobson in 1989, and more recently it has gained momentum resulting in the RED manifesto which recommends wide spread deployment of RED on Internet routers. Additional motivation for developing RED was the problems observed with tail-drop queue management. These include:

- Full Queues,
- Global synchronization, and
- Bias against bursty traffic.

BACKGROUND

Random Early Detection (RED), also known as random early discard or random early drop is an active queue management algorithm. It is also a congestion avoidance algorithm. In the traditional tail drop algorithm, a router or other network component buffers as many packets as it can, and simply drops the ones it cannot buffer. If buffers are constantly full, the network is congested. Tail drop distributes buffer space unfairly among traffic flows. Tail drop can also lead to TCP global synchronization as all TCP connections "hold back" simultaneously, and then step forward simultaneously. Networks become under- utilized and flooded by turns. RED addresses these issues. It monitors the average queue size and drops (or marks when used in conjunction with ECN) packets based on statistical probabilities. If the buffer is almost empty, all incoming packets are accepted. As the queue grows, the probability for dropping an incoming packet grows too. When the buffer is full, the probability has reached 1 and all incoming packets are dropped. RED is more fair than tail drop, in the sense that it does not possess a bias against bursty traffic that uses only a small portion of the bandwidth. The more a host transmits, the more likely it is that its packets are early detection helps avoid global synchronization.

Goals of RED Queue

The basic idea is that one should not wait till the buffer is full in order detect detection(drop packets), but start detecting congestion before the buffer overflows. Congestion signals could still be through packet dropping, but could now also be through marking of packets without the need to actually drop them.

Some of the goals of the RED buffer management are:

- Accommodate short bursts that might be delay sensitive, but not to allow the average queue size increase too much. Using some low past filtering of the queue size, the aim is to detect congestion that lasts long enough (Mikkel Christiansen, 2001).
- Drop tail and random drop gateways have a bias against bursty traffic. Indeed in such buffers, the more traffic of a connection is bursty, the more likely it is that the queue will overflow during the arrival time of packets of that connection.
- Avoid synchronization; in drop tail buffer, many connections may receive a congestion signal at the same time leading to undesirable oscillations in the throughputs. Such oscillations signals are chosen using randomization (Agata KREMPA).
- Control the average queue size. Note that this also means controlling the average queuing delay.

RED ALGORITHM

Random Early Detection (RED) is an active queue management algorithm that complements congestion avoidance mechanism and helps to improve performance of congested nodes. The operating of

RED algorithm consists of measuring the average queue size and dropping arriving packets probabilistically when queue size exceeds specified threshold (Jacobson, Karels, 1988). Minimum threshold is an average queue size below which no packets are dropped. Maximum threshold state the average queue size above which all of the incoming packets are dropped.

For the average queue size that enclose between minimum and maximum threshold, probability of dropping packets varies linearly from 0 to max_p (typically 0,1). Characteristic of probability of dropping packets is shown in Figure1. This kind of approach results in dropping packets though the buffer is not full. Dropping packets early can be very useful as the dropped packets indicate the state of congestion in congestion control mechanism. It can prevent buffer from overflowing as senders reduce their transmission speed in response to the early congestion notification. The RED algorithm consists of two main parts. The first part estimates the burstiness of the traffic by maintaining a weighted average queue size. The second part takes the packet drop decision based on the weighted average queue size and the number of packets processed since the previous drop (Floyd, Jacobson, 1993, August).

Calculation of the weighted average queue size (*avg*) is done using a low-pass filter which

Figure 1. RED drop probability dependence on parameters

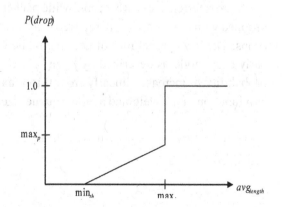

is an exponential moving average (EWMA). This essentially means that *avg* only changes when changes in the queue size have certain duration

$$avg \leftarrow (1 - w_q)avg + w_q \times q; \quad where \; 0 < w_q \leq 1 \tag{1}$$

where q is the instantaneous queue size, and w_q is the weight. If $w_q = 1$, then *avg* corresponds to the instantaneous queue size. Periods may occur where the router is idle, i.e. the queue is empty. When a packet arrives to an empty queue, the idle period is taken into account. This is done by estimating the number of packets (m) that might have been transmitted since the queue became empty, and using that estimate for estimating the average queue size.

$$m \leftarrow (time - q_{time})/s \tag{2}$$

$$avg \leftarrow (1 - w_q)^m \times avg \tag{3}$$

Where time is the current time, and q_{time} is start of the queue idle time. S is a typical transmission time for a small packet. RED operates in three different packet drop modes depending on the value of the weighted average queue size compared to the threshold values min_{th} and max_{th}. If the weighted average queue size lies below min_{th} no packets are dropped. If *avg* lies above max_{th} then all arriving packets are dropped. When *avg* lies between the two thresholds, RED drops packets probabilistically. The packets dropped while in this mode are referred to as early drops, while packets dropped while *avg* > max_{th} are referred to as force drops. The drop probability of packets, while in early drop mode, is described by p_b and p_a. The probability p_b increases linearly from 0 to max_p as a function of the weighted average queue size:

$$p_b \leftarrow max_p(avg - min_{th})/(max_{th} - min_{th}) \tag{4}$$

Where max_p describes the maximum drop probability and $(min_{th} \leq avg \leq max_{th})$. The drop probability p_a increases as a function of p_b and the number count of packets that has arrived since the previous drop.

$$p_a \leftarrow p_b/(1 - count \times p_b) \tag{5}$$

Where, $count < (1/p_b)$. Inclusion of count in the drop probability calculation ensures that packet drops are close to a uniform distribution. In early drop mode, flows are expected to experience packet drops roughly proportional to the share of the bandwidth being used at the router, simply because sending a higher number of packets through the router increases the chance of experiencing a packet drop due to the uniform distribution of drops. Furthermore, evenly distributing the packet drops may help avoid global synchronization effects where many senders reduce their windows simultaneously, thus increasing the burstiness of the traffic. It is expected that RED removes the bias against flows that send traffic in Bursts. A traditional tail-drop queuing mechanism may overflow when a burst of traffic arrives, resulting in a large percentage of the packets in the burst being dropped (Hoeffding, W). RED, on the other hand, will try to absorb the burst, and avoid dropping sequence of packets. However, these advances are removed if the mechanism is pushed into force drop mode too often. To complete the description of the RED algorithm we have included a detailed Description of the algorithm.

RED Algorithm

Saved Variables

avg: Average queue size
q_{time}: Start of the queue idle time
count: Packets since last dropped packet

Fixed Parameters

w_q: Queue weight
max_{th}: Minimum threshold
min_{th}: Maximum threshold
max_p: Maximum drop probability
s: is a typical transmission time for a small packet

Other

q: Current queue size
time: Current time

Initialization

1. $avg \leftarrow 0$
2. $count \leftarrow 1$
3.   for each packet arrival, Calculate the new weighted average queue size *avg*:
4.   If the queue is nonempty then
     $avg \leftarrow (1 - w_q)avg + w_q \times q$
5.   else $m \leftarrow (time - q_{time})/s$
     $avg \leftarrow (1 - w_q)^m \times avg$
6.   if $(min_{th} \leq avg \leq max_{th})$ then Increment *count*

Calculate packet drop probability p_a:

$$p_b \leftarrow max_p(avg - min_{th})/(max_{th} - min_{th})$$

$$p_a \leftarrow p_b/(1 - count \times p_b)$$

with probability p_a: Drop the arriving packet

$count \leftarrow 0$

else if $(max_{th} \leq avg)$ then Drop the arriving packet

$count \leftarrow 0$

else

$count \leftarrow -1$

When queue becomes empty

$q_{time} \leftarrow time$

Evaluating the effect of using a queuing mechanism is difficult due to the dynamic and complex environment under which it operates. There are two issues to this: First, the evaluation models describe an environment well enough to provide sufficiently accurate results. Second, is the described a relevant environment. In the following sections we look closer at how queue management mechanisms have been evaluated, describing the approach used, and emphasizing interesting Results regarding RED, and particularly RED parameter settings. The original RED (Floyd, Jacobson, 1993, August) demonstrates that RED operates as intended through four simulations. Each simulation addresses some particular aspect of the functionality that the authors want to examine. In the following we describe these Simulations. This is mainly interesting because the method used for the experiments has been one of the main sources of inspiration when designing tests of other queuing mechanisms.

Network Simulator (NS-2) is currently the most widely used simulator for testing and experimenting with networks. Each simulation runs for 1-10 seconds, under which the queue size on the router is measured along with packet statistics such as transmission, drop and retransmission times. In total we present ample number of the simulations which can be summarized as follows:

- Show that RED is able to control the average queue size in response to a dynamically changing load.
- Demonstrate that RED has superior performance over tail-drop queuing when two identical flows are competing for bandwidth.

- Study the effect of using RED in an environment with heavy congestion.
- Study how RED treats bursty traffic sources compared to tail-drop queuing.

The goal with the first simulation is to show that RED is able to control the average queue size at the router in response to a dynamically changing load. This is done by simulating four FTP flows with different bandwidth-delay products sending traffic, to a sink placed on a shared bottleneck link, through a RED router. Flows are started sequentially with fixed interval of 0.2s; resulting in a simulation that displays the behavior of RED as the load increases on the router. As expected, the results show that RED is successful in controlling the average queue size on the bottleneck router in response to the dynamically increasing load. A second simulation demonstrates that RED has superior performance over tail drop queuing when two identical flows are competing for bandwidth.

BACKGROUND OF NS-2

NS-2 is an object-oriented simulator, with an OTcl interpreter as the frontend. The simulator supports a class hierarchy in C++ (also called the compiled hierarchy),and a similar hierarchy within the OTcl interpreter (also called the interpreted hierarchy) (ns Tutorial, *The ns Manual*, 2003).The two hierarchies are closely related to each other, from the user's perspective, there is a one-to-one correspondence between a class in the Tcl Object. Users create new simulator objects through the interpreter, these object are instantiated within the interpreter, and are closely mirrored by a corresponding object in the compiled hierarchy (Mikkel Christiansen, 2001).

Setting RED Parameter in NS-2

The parameters of RED in NS-2 are provided in the following objects

- **Bytes_:** Takes either the value"true" if we work in the "byte mode" or "false" in the packet mode. I n the "byte mode", the size of an arriving packet affects the likelihood of marking it.
- **Queue-in-bytes_:** The average queue size will be measured in bytes if it is set to "true" in that case, also thresh and maxthresh_ are scaled by the estimated average packet size parameter mean_pktsize_. It is "false" by default.
- **Thres_:** Is the minimum queue size threshold min_{th}.
- **Maxthres_:** Is the minimum queue size threshold max_{th}.
- **Mean_pktsize_:** Is the estimate of the average packet size in bytes. The default value is 500.
- **Q_weight:** The weight factor w_q in computing the average queue length.
- **Wait_:** This is a parameter that allows maintaining an interval between packets when set to true.
- **Linterm_:** This is the reciprocal of max_p. Its default value 10.
- **Setbit_:** Is "false" in the case that RED is used to actually drop packets and is "true" if RED marks the packet with a congestion bits, instead.
- **Drop-tail:** This is a parameter that allows when setting its value to true, to use the drop tail policy when queue overflows or when the average queue size exceeds $max_{th.}$

TCL and OTCL Programming

TCL(Tool command language) is used for millions of people in the world. It is a language with a very easy integration with other languages. TCL was created by Jhon Outerhout. The characteristics of these languages are:

- It allows a fast development
- It provide a graphics interface

- It is compatible with many plat forms
- It is flexible for integration
- It is easy to use
- It is free

Simulation Initialization and Termination

An ns simulator starts with the command '**set ns [new Simulator]**'. This line declares new variable *ns* using the **set** command. In general people declares it as ns because it is an instance of the **Simulator** class, so an object. The code [**new Simulator**] is indeed the instantiation of the class **Simulator** using the reserved word **new** [21]. In order to have output files with data on the simulation (trace files) or files used for visualization (name files), we need to create the files using the "**open**" command

```
#Open the Trace file
set tracefile1 [open out.tr w]
$ns trace-all $tracefile1
#Open the NAM trace file
set namfile [open out.nam w]
$ns namtrace-all $namfile
```

The above creates a data trace file called "out.tr" and a nam visualization trace file (for the NAM tool) called "Out.nam". Within the tcl script these files are not called explicitly by their names, but instead by pointers that are declared above and called "tracefile1" and "namfile" respectively. The first and fourth lines in the example are only comments, they are not simulation commands. Remark that they begin with a # symbol. The second line open the file "out.tr" to be used for writing, declared with the letter "w". The third line uses a simulator method called trace-all that have as parameter the name of the file where the traces will go. The last line tells the simulator to record all simulation traces in NAM input format. It also gives the file name that the trace will be written to later by the command $ns flush-trace.

The termination of the program is done using a "finish" procedure.

```
#Define a 'finish' procedure
proc finish{} {
global ns  tracefile1 namfile
$ns flush-trace
close $tracefile1
close $namfile1
exec nam out.nam &
exec grep "a" red-queue.tr > ave.tr
exec grep "Q" red-queue.tr > cur.tr
exit 0
}
```

The word *proc* declares a procedure in this case called **finish** and without arguments. The word **global** is used to tell that we are using variables declared outside the procedure. The simulator method "**flush-trace**" will dump the traces on the respective files. The tcl command "**close**" closes the trace files defined before and **exec** executes the nam program for visualization. Remark that we pass the real name of the file of traces to nam and not the pointer namfile it is unexternal command. The command **exit** will ends the application and return the number 0 as status to the system. Zero is the default for a clean exit. At the end of the ns program we should call the procedure "**finish**" and specify at what time the termination should occur.

Simulation Topology

In real world, number of senders and receivers as well as their relative position, internal communication can be various in patterns. Different types of protocols can also be used in the same network. Such type of network has been considered for our experiment. TCP and UDP protocols have been taken here under consideration. Duplex channel is necessary due to the presence of TCP sender because acknowledgement of each received packet must be propagated through this channel in reverse order from destination to source.

Figure 2. Simulation topology

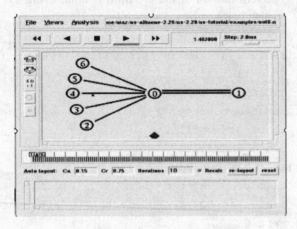

Running the Simulation Program

In the OTcl script, the program *first.tcl* was written to implement the network for simulation. To run it, command line *ns first.tcl* is enough in the shell. FTP sessions had been created between a TCP source and a TCP sink. Data transfer between source and sink will be performed via a base station, source is connected to base station through full duplex wired link and sink is connected to base station via wireless link. The TCP throughput at sink will be calculated. This TCP throughput is the performance parameter. TCP Throughput for various TCP Source and Sinks for various throughput vs. time, congestion window vs. time and for throughput vs. various delay of the wired link are mentioned here.

Structure of Trace File

Trace file consist of all the information of simulation. To analyze the simulation, trace file information is extracted from it using a program. The information is easily distinguishable because they maintain an order among them. Each column (from left to right) of trace file contains data about the following parameters.

Functions with their brief description have been provided as below:

- ○ The first field is the event type. It is given by four possible symbols r, +, −, d which corresponds respectively to receive, en-queued, de-queued and dropped.
- ○ The second field indicates the time of event occurs.
- ○ Gives the input node of the link at which the event occurs.
- ○ Gives the output node of the link at which the event occurs.
- ○ Gives the packet type. It may be TCP, CBR, and ACK so on. It depends on the applications.
- ○ Gives the packet size.
- ○ Some flags.

- This is the flow id(fid) of IPv6 that the user can set for each flow at the input OTcl script. This field can be used for further analysis. This field is used to specify the color of the NAM display.
- It is the source address given in the form 'node.port'.
- It is the destination address given in the same form of source address.
- This is the network layer protocol's packet sequence number. Even through UDP

Figure 3. Fields appearing in a trace file

Event	Time	From node	To Node	Pkt type	Pkt size	Flags	Fid	Src addr	Dst addr	Seq num	Pkt Id

Table 1. Trace file data explanation

Field position	Function of the field
1	Operation performed in the simulation
2	Simulation time of event occurrence
3	Node 1 of what is being traced
4	Node 2 of what is being traced
5	Packet type
6	Packet size
7	Flags
8	IP flow identifier
9	Packet source node address
10	Packet destination node address
11	Sequence number
12	Unique packet identifier

Figure 4. Segment of trace file showing TCP connection establishment

```
+  1  0  2  tcp  40  -------  1 0.0  4.0  0  2
-  1  0  2  tcp  40  -------  1 0.0  4.0  0  2
r  1.01004  0  2  tcp  40  -------  1 0.0  4.0
+  1.01004  2  3  tcp  40  -------  1 0.0  4.0
-  1.01004  2  3  tcp  40  -------  1 0.0  4.0
r  1.02036  2  3  tcp  40  -------  1 0.0  4.0
+  1.02036  3  4  tcp  40  -------  1 0.0  4.0
-  1.02036  3  4  tcp  40  -------  1 0.0  4.0
r  1.050424  3  4  tcp  40  -------  1 0.0  4.0
+  1.150424  4  3  ack  40  -------  1 4.0  0.0
-  1.150424  4  3  ack  40  -------  1 4.0  0.0
r  1.180488  4  3  ack  40  -------  1 4.0  0.0
+  1.180488  3  2  ack  40  -------  1 4.0  0.0
-  1.180488  3  2  ack  40  -------  1 4.0  0.0
r  1.190808  3  2  ack  40  -------  1 4.0  0.0
+  1.190808  2  0  ack  40  -------  1 4.0  0.0
-  1.190808  2  0  ack  40  -------  1 4.0  0.0
r  1.200848  2  0  ack  40  -------  1 4.0  0.0
```

implementations in a real network do not use sequence number, NS keeps track of UDP packet sequence number for analysis purposes.

- The last field shows the unique id of the packet.

At the starting, by transmitting the packets named SYNC and ACK (of 40 bytes each) between source and destination, TCP connection establishment is accomplished as shown in Figure 4. After that, Figure 5 and Figure 6 represent the fragment of trace files for TCP and UDP transmission respectively.

EXPERIMENTAL RESULT

A lot of effort has been done for making theoretical background for RED queue and evaluating its performances with existing TCP versions in NS-2. TCP includes eleven variants (Tahoe, FullTcp, TCP/Asym, Reno, Reno/Asym, Newreno, Newreno/Asym, Sack1, Fack, Vegas and VegasRBP) as source and five (TCPSink, TCPSink/Asym, Sack1, DelAck and Sack1/DelAck) as destination, implemented in NS-2 (*The ns*

Manual, 2003). We use five TCP variants like as Reno, Newreno, Sack1, Fack, Vegas. The reason behind the variations of TCP is that each type possesses some special criteria Simulation results show some positive effect of using RED queue in the TCP protocol in a simple mixed network. The performance has been evaluated under various network and load situations.

Figure 5. Segment of trace file for TCP packet transmission

```
File   Edit   Search   Preferences   Shell   Macro   Windows
+  181.630472  5  0  tcp  592  -------  0 5.0  1.3  4838  53990
-  181.630472  5  0  tcp  592  -------  0 5.0  1.3  4838  53990
+  181.630472  5  0  tcp  592  -------  0 5.0  1.3  4839  53991
-  181.630946  5  0  tcp  592  -------  0 5.0  1.3  4839  53991
r  181.631946  5  0  tcp  592  -------  0 5.0  1.3  4838  53990
+  181.631946  0  1  tcp  592  -------  0 5.0  1.3  4838  53990
r  181.632419  5  0  tcp  592  -------  0 5.0  1.3  4839  53991
+  181.632419  0  1  tcp  592  -------  0 5.0  1.3  4839  53991
d  181.632419  0  1  tcp  592  -------  0 5.0  1.3  4839  53991
r  181.636046  0  1  tcp  592  -------  0 5.0  1.3  4821  53788
+  181.636046  1  0  ack  40  -------  0 1.3  5.0  4821  53992
-  181.636046  1  0  ack  40  -------  0 1.3  5.0  4821  53992
r  181.636206  1  0  ack  40  -------  0 1.3  5.0  4818  53985
+  181.636206  0  5  ack  40  -------  0 1.3  5.0  4818  53985
-  181.636206  0  5  ack  40  -------  0 1.3  5.0  4818  53985
-  181.636343  0  1  tcp  592  -------  0 5.0  1.3  4825  53796
r  181.637238  0  5  ack  40  -------  0 1.3  5.0  4818  53985
+  181.637238  5  0  tcp  592  -------  0 5.0  1.3  4840  53993
-  181.637238  5  0  tcp  592  -------  0 5.0  1.3  4840  53993
r  181.638711  5  0  tcp  592  -------  0 5.0  1.3  4840  53993
+  181.638711  0  1  tcp  592  -------  0 5.0  1.3  4840  53993
r  181.642812  0  1  tcp  592  -------  0 5.0  1.3  4822  53790
+  181.642812  1  0  ack  40  -------  0 1.3  5.0  4822  53994
-  181.642812  1  0  ack  40  -------  0 1.3  5.0  4822  53994
r  181.642972  1  0  ack  40  -------  0 1.3  5.0  4819  53987
+  181.642972  0  5  ack  40  -------  0 1.3  5.0  4819  53987
-  181.642972  0  5  ack  40  -------  0 1.3  5.0  4819  53987
-  181.643109  0  1  tcp  592  -------  0 4.0  1.2  5389  53794
r  181.644004  0  5  ack  40  -------  0 1.3  5.0  4819  53987
+  181.644004  5  0  tcp  592  -------  0 5.0  1.3  4841  53995
-  181.644004  5  0  tcp  592  -------  0 5.0  1.3  4841  53995
```

Figure 6. Segment of trace file for UDP packet transmission

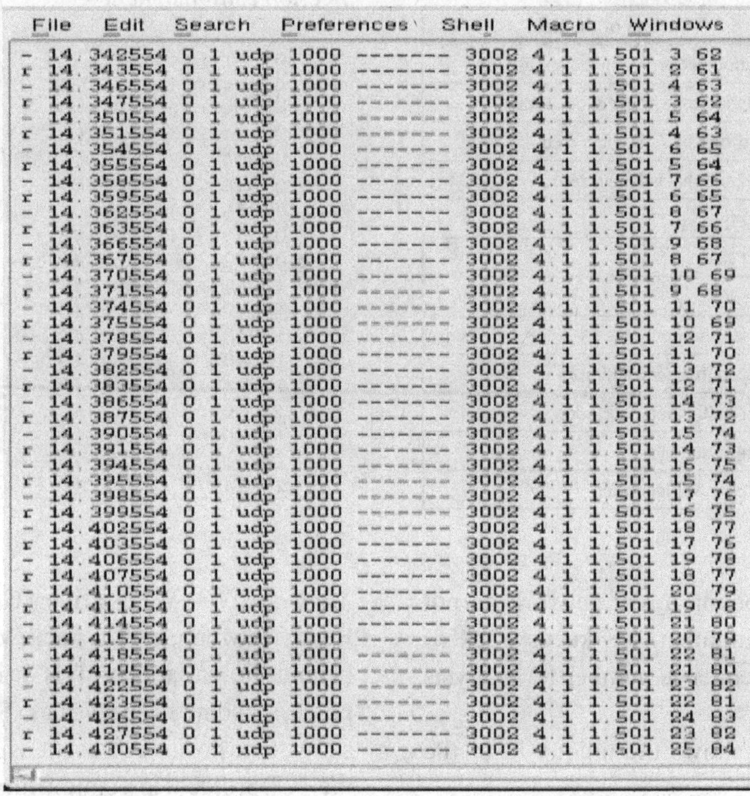

In the following subsequent sections, performance analysis of RED model, comparison of RED performance with TCP and UDP, comparison of RED Algorithm with Drop Tail and Average and Current Queue size evolution have been depicted.

Performance Analysis of RED Model

We started our simulation with minimum threshold 15 and maximum threshold 35. Average queue size lies between min and max threshold. We varied the minimum threshold (min_{th}) each time and the number of packets were counted at destination node in case of several TCP variants during entire

Table 2. Packet received for simulation time 70s

TCP Variants	Threshold				
	15	20	25	30	35
Reno	863	1192	845	701	729
Newreno	702	773	782	784	751
Vegas	851	778	691	685	615
Fack	809	731	723	624	764
Sack1	864	877	789	827	785

Figure 7. Graph of received packet for simulation time 70s

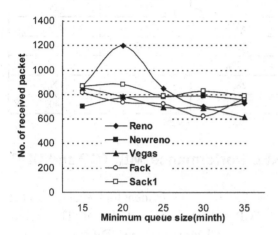

Figure 8. Graph of received packet for simulation time 140s

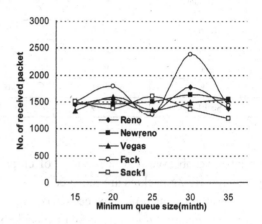

Table 3. Packet received for simulation time 140s

TCP Variants	Minimum Threshold				
	15	20	25	30	35
Reno	1448	1540	1311	1772	1377
Newreno	1452	1454	1493	1622	1541
Vegas	1335	1582	1350	1480	1541
Fack	1499	1786	1253	2381	1429
Sack1	1503	1379	1602	1365	1182

Table 4. Packet received for simulation time 210s

TCP Variants	Minimum Threshold				
	15	20	25	30	35
Reno	2686	2638	2375	1949	2300
Newreno	2697	2545	2013	2173	2303
Vegas	2249	2275	2294	2428	2197
Fack	2792	2463	2908	2127	2369
Sack1	2274	2406	2192	2546	2068

Figure 9. Graph of received packet for simulation time 210s

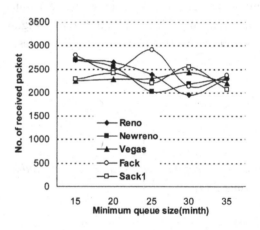

simulation period; from trace file whose amount has been shown in Table 2 through Table 5.

From Figure 7, it is observed that RED queue is very important for controlling the congestion. It can handle the congestion if user can tune the min_{th} and max_{th} perfectly. RED queue has been monitored very carefully and it is founds that if

we increase the min_{th} then the packet drop decreases as shown in Table 2. We also apply the RED queue against various TCP versions- Reno, Newreno, Fack,Vegas and Sack1.In Newreno, when we increase the min_{th} then the number of packets successfully received increased except for Vegas and Fack that show a little bit falling trend.

Finally, we observe for entire simulation duration when threshold is increased then variation occurs in received packet among various TCP

Table 5. Packet received for simulation time 280s

TCP Variants	Minimum Threshold				
	15	20	25	30	35
Reno	3140	3403	3311	3321	2900
Newreno	3384	3227	3205	3263	2926
Vegas	2628	2743	2778	2539	2791
Fack	3541	3083	2852	2682	4292
Sack1	3889	3214	3053	3236	3402

variants. We observe that at the time of empty queue all arriving packets are received.

When average queue size exceeds max threshold or less than minimum threshold then packets are dropped which is shown in above all tables and corresponding figures. We have found that Newreno TCP variant is the best because mean number of received packet is high and mean number of dropped packet is low depending Figure 7 through Figure 10 and corresponding tables.

RED Performance with TCP and UDP

From Figure 11, it is evident that received packet for TCP is greater than that of UDP. The performance of TCP is greater than UDP. By using RED model it was observed that congestion control in TCP is much more than UDP. So decision came to light that RED model control the congestion accurately.

To compare the performance it is found that TCP behaves better with RED than UDP because packet received is higher in it with respect to UDP. That is why packet loss is lower in TCP. For packet drop, it is clear that packet drop is higher

Figure 10. Graph of received packet for simulation time 280s

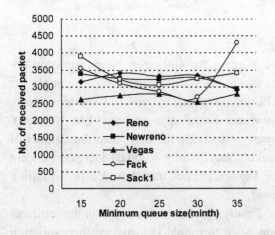

Figure 11. RED performance with TCP and UDP in terms of packet receiving

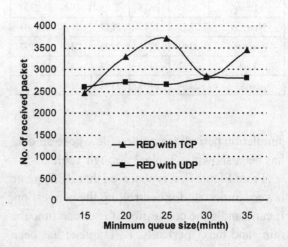

Table 6. Performance of RED with UDP and TCP in terms of packet receiving

Time	Packet Received for UDP at min_{th}				
	15	20	25	30	35
70s	672	794	757	792	746
140s	1299	1228	1181	1487	1339
210s	1998	1800	2129	2088	1961
280s	2586	2698	2633	2793	2785
Time	Packet Received for TCP at min_{th}				
	15	20	25	30	35
70s	569	663	636	541	834
140s	1354	1606	1437	1659	1612
210s	2726	2374	2421	2247	2414
280s	2451	3282	3694	2830	3435

Figure 12. RED performance with TCP and UDP in terms of packet dropping

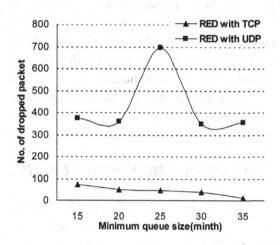

in UDP than TCP and also occurs more congestion in it. It is possible to control congestion in TCP using RED model.

Comparison of RED Algorithm with Drop Tail

In scenario with RED algorithm, slightly more packets were sent through the network. What is more interesting the proportion between number of received TCP packets and number of received UDP packets was a little shifted.

When RED algorithm was used less UDP packets and at the same time, more TCP packets were received (1. 7% more TCP packets sent). This feature slightly lessens the unfairness in allocation of bandwidth among responsive and non-responsive flows. Greater end-to-end delay in scenario with Tail Drop algorithm is a result of heavy load that UDP traffic creates. Queue is maintained in almost full state and cause buffer delay to increase. The use of RED results in keeping the average queue length small and reduces the overall delay as buffer delay is smaller. The only disadvantage of using RED queue manage-

Table 7. Performance of RED with UDP and TCP in terms of packet dropping

Time	Packet Dropped for UDP at min_{th}				
	15	20	25	30	35
70s	25	67	24	131	30
140s	122	106	58	118	32
210s	242	112	429	161	432
280s	372	359	696	349	354
Time	Packet Dropped for TCP at min_{th}				
	15	20	25	30	35
70s	0	0	0	0	0
140s	24	13	8	7	5
210s	36	32	31	25	17
280s	71	48	47	36	12

Table 8. Performance of RED with drop tail buffer

Packet type	Packet Received for	
	Drop Tail	RED
TCP Packets	1310	1332
UDP Packets	1120	1110

ment algorithm in case of mixed TCP and UDP traffic is greater number of dropped packets. With only TCP flows present, number of dropped packets is smaller when active queue management is used. Presence of UDP flow causes a state of heavy load in the network. As UDP flows do not respond to congestion indication, more packets have to be dropped to keep the average queue length small.

CONCLUSION AND FURTHER WORK

Random Early Detection gateways are an effective mechanism for congestion avoidance at the gateway level. The objective of this chapter is to test the performance of RED algorithm when it is used with different TCP variants and hence finding better-responding variants under several network parameters. After that, a comparative analysis has been drawn whether UDP or TCP works fairly with RED and then performance of Drop Tail algorithm has been measured and compared with its contemporary RED algorithm. To test the efficiency of using active queue management in such scenario, test was performed in NS-2 simulator. The simulation results show that even when non-responsive flows are present, RED algorithm is useful. It helps increase throughput and reduce delay. The lock out phenomenon is also reduced. The most interesting part is that active queue management helps slightly lessen the unfairness in allocation of bandwidth among Various TCP variants. There are many areas for further research on RED gateways. One area for further research concerns traffic dynamics with a mix of Drop Tail and RED gateways, as would result from partial deployment of RED gateways in the current internet. Besides, RED performance can be evaluated and compared with eXplicit Congestion control Protocol (XCP).

REFERENCES

Balakrishnan, H., Venkata, N., Padmanabhan, S. S., & Katz, R. H. (1997). A comparison of mechanisms for improving TCP performance over wireless links. *IEEE Transactions on Networking, 5*(6).

Behrouz, A., & Forouzan, S. C. (2004). *Data communication and networking* (3rd ed.). New Delhi.

Braden, B., Clark, D., Crowcroft, J., Davie, B., Deering, S., Estrin, D., ... Zhang, L. (1998). *RFC 2309: Recommendations on queue management and congestion avoidance in the Internet.* RFC.

Chandra, H., Agarwal, A., & Velmurugan, T. (2010). Analysis of active queue management algorithms & their implementation for TCP/IP networks using OPNET simulation tool. *International Journal of Computers and Applications, 6*(11).

Christiansen, M. (2001, October). *The performance of HTTP traffic under random early detection queue management.* Department of Computer Science, Aalborg University, Denmark.

Chung, J., & Claypool, M. (n.d.). *NS by example.* Retrieved from http:// perform.wpi.edu/ NS/

Floyd, S. (1992, March). Issues in flexible resource management for datagram networks. *Proceedings of the 3rd Workshop on Very High Speed Networks.*

Floyd, S. (1997). *RED: Discussions of setting parameters.* Retrieved from http:// www.aciri. org/ floyd/ REDparameters.txt

Floyd, S., & Jacobson, V. (1992, September). On traffic phase effects in packet-switched gateways. *Internetworking Research and Experience, 3*(3), 115–156.

Floyd, S., & Jacobson, V. (1993). *The synchronization of periodic routing messages.* SIGCOMM93.

Floyd, S., & Jacobson, V. (1993, August). Random early detection gateways for congestion avoidance. *IEEE/ACM Transactions on Networking, 1*(4), 397. doi:10.1109/90.251892

Floyd, S., & Jacobson, V. (1994, April). The synchronization of periodic routing messages. *IEEE/ACM Transactions on Networking, 2*(2), 122. doi:10.1109/90.298431

Floyd, S., & Jacobson, V. (1998, April). *Recommendations on queue management and congestion avoidance in the Internet.* RFC 2309.

Floyd, S., & Jacobson, V. (1999). Random early detection gateways for congestion avoidance. *ACM Transactions on Networking, 1*(4).

Hashem, E. (1989). *Analysis of random drop for gateway congestion control,* (p. 103). Report LCS TR-465, Laboratory for Computer Science, MIT, Cambridge, MA.

Hoeffding, W. (1963). Probability inequalities for sums of bounded random variables. *Journal of the American Statistical Association, 58*(301). doi:10.2307/2282952

Jacobson, V. (1988, August). Congestion avoidance and control. *Computer Communication Review, 18*(4), 314–329. Retrieved from ftp://ftp.ee.lbl.gov/papers/conga-void.ps.Zdoi:10.1145/52325.52356

Jacobson, V., & Karels, M. (1988, November). Congestion avoidance and control. *Proceedings of SIGCOMM'88.*

Jain, R. (1990, May). Congestion control in computer networks: Issues and trends. *IEEE Network,* 24–30. doi:10.1109/65.56532

KREMPA. (n.d.). Analysis of RED algorithm with responsive and non responsive flows. *Poznan University of Technology Academic Journals.*

Leland, W. E., Taqqu, M. S., Willinger, W., & Wilson, D. V. (1994, February). On the self similar nature of Ethernet traffic (extended version). *IEEE/ACM Transactions on Networking, 2*(1). doi:10.1109/90.282603

Miyoshi, M., Sugano, M., & Murata, M. (2001). Performance evaluation of TCP throughput on wireless cellular networks. *IEEE Vehicular Technology Conference (VTC),* (vol. 3, pp. 2177 –2181).

NS. (2003, December). *The NS manual.* The VINT Project: A Collaboration between researchers at UC Berkeley, LBL, USC/ISI, and Xerox PARC.

NS. (2003, December). *NS simulator for beginners.* Lecture notes, 2003-2004, Univ. de Los Andes, Merida, Venezuela and ESSI, Sophia-Antipolis, France.

NS Tutorial. (n.d.). Retrieved from http://www.isi.edu/nsnam/ns/tutorial/nsindex.html

Riva, O. (2003). *Analysis of Internet transport service performance with active queue management in a QoS enabled network.* University of Helsinki, Department of Computer Science.

Tannenbaum, A. S. (1996). *Computer networks* (3rd ed.). Prentice Hall.

KEY TERMS AND DEFINITIONS

Buffer: Buffer is the memory associated with the sender, receiver and other intermediate nodes of the network to temporarily hold the packet bits until their processing is completed.

Congestion: The overcrowding state of network when huge number of packets beyond the link's capacity clogged with the aim of transporting.

Network Topology: Topology refers to the geometrical orientation of nodes and links of the network that shows how the nodes are interconnected. For instance, star, bus, ring and mesh are the typical examples of network topology.

TCP Variants: The categories of TCP/IP protocols that share the major TCP/IP features but vary under certain criteria among themselves. Examples of TCP variants are Tahoe, Reno, Newreno, Vegas, Fack, Sack1 e.t.c.

Throughput: Throughput is the amount of packets in byte received per unit time at destination node of the network.

Chapter 13

A Comparative Study of Evolutionary Algorithms for Maximizing Reliability of a Flow in Cellular IP Network

Mohammad Anbar
Tishreen University, Syria

Deo Prakash Vidyarthi
Jawaharlal Nehru University, India

ABSTRACT

The rapid development in technology, witnessed in daily communication, especially in wireless communication, is a good motivation for performance improvement in this field. Cellular IP access network is a suitable environment where a micro mobility of mobile users is implemented and managed. The reliability of Cellular IP network during the communication is an important characteristic measure and must be considered while designing a new model. Evolutionary Algorithms are powerful tools for optimization and problem solving, which require extracting the best solution from a big search space. This chapter explores the reliability issue in Cellular IP of a flow of packets passing through the route from a source to a destination. The main aim of the chapter is to maximize the reliability of the flow passing through a route having number of routers. Two Evolutionary Algorithms (EAs), Genetic Algorithm (GA) and Particle Swarm Optimization (PSO), have been used for this purpose, and a comparative study between the two is performed. Experimental studies of the proposed work have also been performed.

DOI: 10.4018/978-1-4666-0203-8.ch013

INTRODUCTION

Different operations such as handoff, paging and routing are performed by the Mobile Hosts (MHs) in Cellular IP network, which consists of many cells controlled by the base stations (BSs). Routing, in Cellular IP network, is done on hop-by-hop basis. The structure of Cellular IP network, depicted in Figure 1, explains the reason for hop-by-hop routing. Each base station in the network is configured with a downlink and an uplink and when a packet destined to a MH encounters a BS it simply forwards it to the next hop as per the routing information available in the routing cache (RC) with each BS (Campbell, & Gomez, 2000). Routing is an important operation as a good deal of processing time is involved here that desires the components to be available during this period to make the routing reliable.

Technically, base stations in Cellular IP networks serve as routers for a flow of packets intended to be sent to a MH under the control of BS till it reaches the final destination. During the routing operation, each BS checks it's RC to find the route through which the flow is to be directed. Working as a router, BS's CPU is involved in packet processing operation. Some amount of time is involved to process a packet at CPU router. This time period is important for a flow as the routers should not fail during this period for reliable transmission. Router CPU is a scarce resource (Tanenbaum, 2004) and the reliability of the flow should be maximized in Cellular IP network.

It is important in Cellular IP networks how the data packets are transmitted and processed through a route. Doing so is an important job to be done in this type of wireless networks, which manage the micro mobility of the users and the time is an important parameter in it. Reliability is the probability that the network, consisting of various components, performs its intended function for a given time period when operated under normal (or stated) environmental conditions. The

Figure 1. Structure of cellular IP network

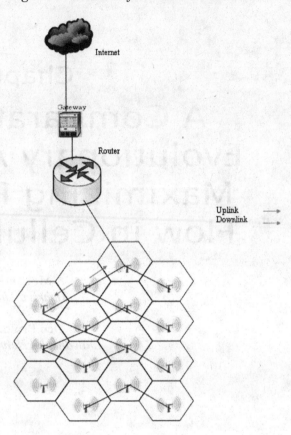

unreliability of a connection is the probability that the experienced outage probability for the connection is larger than a predefined maximum tolerable value. The connection reliability is related to the traffic parameters (Zhao, Shen, & Mark, 2006). Base stations in a wireless cellular IP network environment are prone to failure (Prakash, Shivaratri, & Singhal, 1999). Due to the failure of a base station, all the connections in the failed cell area get terminated and all the services are interrupted until the failed base station is restored. Base station failure significantly degrades the performance and bandwidth utilization of the Cellular IP networks. Specifically, services for high priority ongoing calls such as real-time traffic could be interrupted, which is usually not acceptable.

Some of the models that address the other reliability issues in cellular networks have been briefed here. Three cost functions associated with the retransmission-based partially reliable transport service were introduced in (Marasli, Amer,& Conrad, 1996). An algorithm for computing low-latency recovery strategy in a reliable network was proposed in (Zhang, Ray, Kannan, & Iyengar, 2003). An optimal forward link power allocation model for data transmission was proposed by the authors in (Sun, Krzymien, Jalai, 1998). A soft handoff/power distribution scheme for cellular CDMA downlinks and its effect on connection reliability had been studied by (Zhao, Shen, & Mark, 2006). A neural-network-based multicast routing algorithm was explained in (Kumar, & Venkataram,2000) for constructing a reliable multicast tree that connects the participants of a multicast group. A protocol called Reliable Mobile Multicast Protocol (RMMP) was introduced and analyzed by (Liao, Ke, & Lai, 2000) to provide reliable multicast services for mobile IP networks. The mobility agent in mobile IP was extended to assist reliable multicasting for mobile devices.

In recent past the applications of EAs, useful search procedures, have attracted attention of researches of diverse fields as a problem solving tool. Many algorithms are classified under the category of evolutionary algorithms such as Genetic Algorithm and Particle Swarm Optimization. These two algorithms have been applied widely and successfully for solving optimization problems. Researchers of mobile computing have used EAs for bandwidth reservation (Anbar,& Vidyarthi, 2009). Other applications used EA for resource reservation in Cellular IP networks (Anbar,& Vidyarthi, 2009). EAs start with an initial population which normally is the potential solution to the problem. The population consists of individuals, called chromosomes, at the implementation level. A new set of chromosomes is created, in every generation, using information from the individuals of the previous generations. Generating the initial populations in GA and PSO

is usually done randomly. Evolution reflects the possibility of generating new offspring which is likely to be better than the parents in some features.

The rest of this paper is organized as follows. In the following section, reliability of a flow in Cellular IP networks has been explained. After that is a section on the proposed models for reliability maximization using both GA and PSO have been analyzed and explained. A comparative study between both the models using the experiments has been shown in the section following that. The final section contains the conclusions derived from the study.

RELIABILITY OF A FLOW IN CELLULAR IP NETWORK

During the communication between a node and a MH from another network, a flow of packets passes through a path consisting of number of routers before it reaches the final destination (MH). Processing and delivering the flow to the MH should be made reliable.

Routing

It is important to discuss the routing operation in Cellular IP network because the reliability issue, the main objective of this work, is discussed for the routing operation.

Two types of routing are often used in communication systems; end-to-end routing and hop-by-hop routing. In general, hop-by-hop routing is used in mobile communications (Heimlicher,& Karaliopoulos,2007) especially in Cellular IP(Campbell, & Gomez, 2000). Hop-by-hop routing may help in reducing energy consumption and packet processing time(Sobrinho, 2002). The main principle of hop-by-hop routing is that the packets are forwarded (routed) according to an independent decision taken by the router (base station in case of Cellular IP networks) based on the destination addresses for the incoming flow. Each base station, in Cellular IP network, maintains a routing cache. Two types of information are stored in the routing cache; the source IP address and the previous neighbor through which the packet reached the current base station. In hop-by-hop routing, one packet carrying the path to the destination information is enough as entry to the routing table and there is no need for carrying the full header to the destination by the packets to be followed (Heimlicher,& Karaliopoulos,2007). Definitely, the route information must be updated through the data packets being sent. As long as the mobile host is sending packets through this route regularly, the routing cache will keep valid routing information. It is to be noted that route in Cellular IP network stays valid for a specific period of time known as route-time-out (Jayaram, Sen, Kakani, & Das, 2000).

Each router in the Cellular IP network has a packet processing capacity and a policy to accept or reject a flow if the load exceeds its capacity. A router may not accept a flow if it is preloaded by the maximum allowable limit as per its policy (capacity) (Jayaram, Sen, Kakani, & Das, 2000). According to the queuing theory, a flow must reserve enough router CPU cycles in order to avoid a long queue delay. Real-time flows, as delay sensitive flows, must be given the required CPU cycles to ensure that they are processed reliably in minimum time at the router.

Data Packet Flow

Packet flow in Cellular IP network can be defined as a sequence of packets sent from a correspondent host (CH) residing in another network to a MH in this Cellular IP network. This flow is routed from its source to the final destination passing through the Gateway of the network and processed at each router (base station) in the route. Data traffic can be classified into two categories i.e. real-time and non-real-time traffic and both types of packet flows are involved in Cellular IP network. Since each base station in the network has its own capacity to

process a number of packets at a time as mentioned earlier, the queues at the base station will be built up over the time. A packet scheduling algorithm is required to manage the traffic at the router (base station). This work is not concerned about a packet scheduling algorithm; rather it focuses on the reliability of the flow until delivery. I.e. the proposed model in this work considers that the CPU cycle is reserved for processing real-time data packet flows and therefore; when the queue is built up at the router, it contains real-time packets only. Thus, the scheduling algorithm is not required at this time. After considering the real-time flow in the route, the next step in this work is how to deliver this flow reliably to its final destination. This goal is achieved by reducing the flow processing time when passing through the base stations in the route which in turn increases the reliability.

Reliability

Reliability is an important issue for any system of utmost utility. It reflects the ability of a system to perform its tasks and functions in proper manner without failure. Reliability is a general term and is ambiguous unless the associated aspect is specified. In some systems, the reliability might be associated with the quality of production; in others it may be associated with the validity of the system. In wireless communication, it is associated with many aspects such as Quality of Service, Connection Completion, Packet Loss, etc. For example, a wireless system is reliable in terms of connection completion if it is able to preserve an important connection during a communication. Any designed model for improving the performance of a communication system should be reliable depending on the purpose for which the model has been developed. In Cellular IP network, many models have been developed such as the one developed by (Anbar, & Vidyarthi, 2009) in which bandwidth management has been proposed. This model is reliable in terms of Connection Dropping Probability that it reduces.

Another model proposed by (Anbar, &Vidyarthi, 2009), reduces the processing time at the router for a flow consisting of number of packets. Therefore, reliability is associated with the model being designed. Reliability is a rational issue, i.e. there is no specific value of reliability to decide a particular model to be reliable. The important issue is that the reliability should improve. Thus, if the reliability through a model improves even it has a smaller value is acceptable depending on the circumstances and the parameters used in the model. Reliability of a system depends on various components of the system. The paper considers a Cellular IP system with the concerned resource as router CPU time. Reliability of the system depends on the reliabilities of its base stations. Since each base station, in a route from the source to the destination, is different from the other in physical properties, load, etc., each base station has its own failure rate and therefore its attribution towards the system's reliability. So, the reliability of the flow is decided according to the reliabilities of the base stations, present in the route, being passed through during the routing operation.

EVOLUTIONARY ALGORITHMS FOR RELIABILITY MAXIMIZATION

The proposed models in this paper maximize reliability based on the flow processing time minimization (Anbar, &Vidyarthi, 2010) in Cellular IP network. The models use two famous EAs algorithms; GA and PSO. Detailed explanation about both the models using PSO and GA is as follow.

Using PSO

The proposed work considers availability of router CPU time to process the flow based on the failures of the base stations. Failure of the base station means the failure of its CPU in processing the packets passing through in the given time period. This proposed model is derived from the model to process the flow as discussed in (Anbar, &Vidyarthi, 2010).

The reliability of the flow depends on the services of the base stations (its availability) that appear in the route. The availability of these services is measured from the failure rates of the devices (base station). The failure of the base station is determined by various factors such as the transmission power, heat, signal to noise ratio between the terminal equipment and the base station etc. In this model, the reliability parameter is chosen to be represented by the exponential distribution during the processing of a flow of packets. This means that this entity (BS) which has been in use for some time (any number of hours) is as good as a new entity in regard to the amount of time remaining until the entities fail (Khanbary, &Vidyarthi, 2009). Thus the reliability of the base station (router) over the time period T_i is

$$R_i = e^{-\alpha_i T_i} \tag{1}$$

Where, α is the failure rate of the base station (Figure 2) and T is the time taken by the base

Figure 2. Different base stations with their failure rates

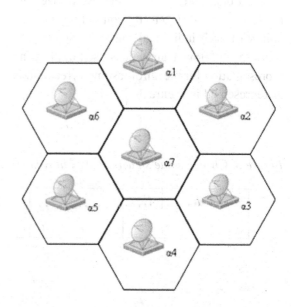

station (router) to process the flow of packets in the router.

The model is designed so as to maximize the reliability of the system. The simulation study is conducted using router CPU time management strategy developed by(Anbar, & Vidyarthi, 2010). To observe the effect of number of routers and number of packets per flow on the reliability of the designed network system, experiments have been conducted for different number of routers and different number of packets per flow.

As the data packet flow passes through the route consisting of m number of routers, the total reliability of the system is computed as

$$R = \prod_{i=1}^{m} e^{-a_i T_i} \tag{2}$$

To obtain the best reliability for the designed network system, the reliability R in Equation (2) is to be maximized which has been considered as the fitness function used in POS based model.

Using GA

The GA based model uses the same objective as used in PSO based model i.e. the function specified in Equation (2). The model maximizes the reliability of the system by computing the reliability of each individual router in the specific route for the flow. Data values used in the gene representation for the chromosome is real and is as represented in Figure 3.

Here R_i, as mentioned before, is the reliability of a flow at each router in the route. Fitness function used to evaluate the solutions in this model is R, as specified in Equation (2).

COMPARATIVE STUDY

Experiments are conducted on randomly generated values of packet processing rates and packet arrival rates in the given range with the objective of maximizing the reliability of the processed flow consisting of a given number of packets in a specific route.

Packet arrival rate is in the range 500 – 1000 packets/sec, packet processing rate is in the range 1000-1500 packets/sec. In all the experiments X-axis shows two values: the iteration number for PSO based model with a step of 10 and the number of generations with a step of 1 for GA based model. Y-axis indicates the reliability of the flow.

Experiment 1

Input values:

  λ= 500 – 1000 packets/sec, μ= 1000 – 1500 packets/sec.
  Number of packets per flow is 200.
  Number of routers: 8.
  0 < failure rate of routers $\leq$ 1

Experiment 2

Input values:

Figure 3. Chromosome structure used in router CPU time management

R_1	R_2	R_3	. . . .	. . . .	. . . .	R_M

Table 1. End results reliability for 400 packets per flow

Number of packets	Number of routers	Reliability	
		GA	PSO
400 packets	8	0.676215	0.728261
	12	0.601767	0.687972
	16	0.456049	0.590513
	20	0.346404	0.509523

Table 2. End results reliability for 600 packets per flow

Number of packets	Number of routers	Reliability	
		GA	PSO
600 packets	8	0.47029	0.57218
	12	0.418435	0.526582
	16	0.173058	0.276008
	20	0.284007	0.315575

$\lambda= 500 - 1000$ packets/sec, $\mu= 1000 - 1500$ packets/sec.
Number of packets per flow is 200.
Number of routers: 12.

Experiment 3

Input values:
$\lambda= 500 - 1000$ packets/sec, $\mu= 1000 - 1500$ packets/sec.
Number of packets per flow is 200.
Number of routers: 16.

Experiment 4

Input values:
$\lambda= 500 - 1000$ packets/sec, $\mu= 1000 - 1500$ packets/sec.
Number of packets per flow is 200.
Number of routers: 20.

Experiment 5

Input values:
$\lambda= 500 - 1000$ packets/sec, $\mu= 1000 - 1500$ packets/sec.
Number of packets per flow is 400.

The end results for different number of packets and 400 packets per flow are shown in Table 1.

Experiment 6

Input values:

$\lambda= 500 - 1000$ packets/sec, $\mu= 1000 - 1500$ packets/sec.
Number of packets per flow is 600.

The end results for different number of packets and 600 packets per flow are shown in Table 2.

Experiment 7

Input values:
$\lambda= 500 - 1000$ packets/sec, $\mu= 1000 - 1500$ packets/sec.
Number of packets per flow is 800.

The end results for different number of packets and 600 packets per flow are shown in Table 3.

Table 3. End results reliability for 800 packets per flow

Number of packets	Number of routers	Reliability	
		GA	PSO
800 packets	8	0.430419	0.509921
	12	0.471204	0.485224
	16	0.313263	0.353407
	20	0.102407	0.165995

Figure 4. Reliability for 8 routers and 200 packets per flow

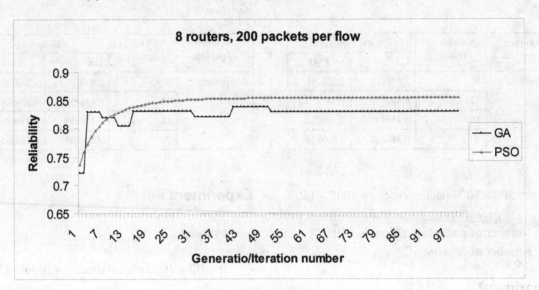

Figure 5. Reliability for 12 routers and 200 packets per flow

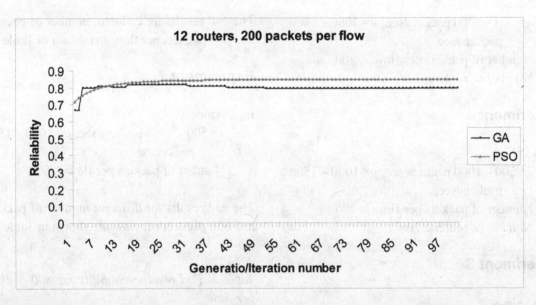

Observations

The following observations are noticeable for the model verified through the experiments.

- The reliability of flow is increased in both GA based model and PSO based model, as derived from all the graphs and tables.

- It's observed that reliability in PSO based model is increasing in an exponential manner. The values are not fluctuating from high value to low value and vise-versa; the values are rather increasing smoothly as noticed from Figures 4, 5, 6 and 7.

- In GA based model the reliability vales are fluctuating. The reason may be the cross-

Figure 6. Reliability for 16 routers and 200 packets per flow

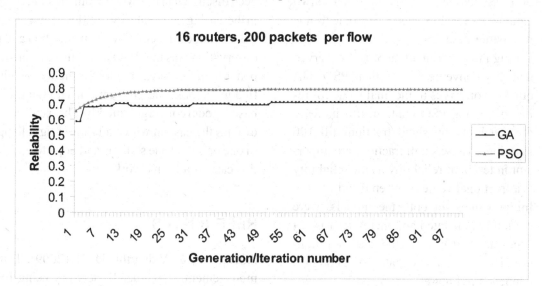

Figure 7. Reliability for 20 routers and 200 packets per flow

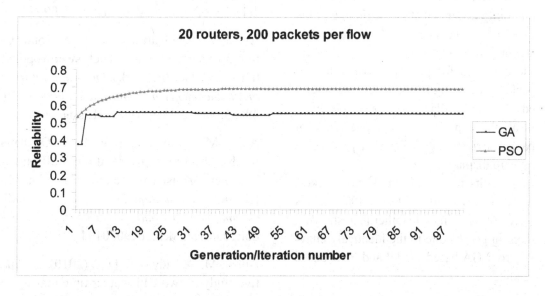

over and the mutation operations taking place in GA based model, where the new generated populations might be better or sometime worse than the previous one.

• For both the GA based model and the PSO based model it is observed that when the number of routers and number of packets per flow increase the reliability value decreases. This justifies the computation as

more packets and more routers in the route will add more failure possibility.

• PSO based model, as indicated by all the figures and tables, performs better than GA based model. The reason could be stated as the PSO based model deals directly with the main controlling parameters i.e. packet arrival rate and packet processing rate and thus ultimately derives better reliability. In turn, PSO based model modifies these two parameters for flow processing time to furnish better reliability.

- During the experimentation, it is observed that GA converges faster than PSO. GA quickly converges to the final value for reliability while PSO continues to increase the reliability by small fractions till 100 iterations. These small fractions are important in terms of reliability as the reliability is a fractional value between 0 and 1.
- Initial values, in both the models, were randomly generated and therefore it is not necessary that PSO should start at a higher value of reliability than GA. Though it happened in Figures 4, 5, 6 and 7.
- Failure rates are the physical properties of the base stations so these values were randomly generated at the beginning of the experiment and kept fixed for each base station.
- More ranges for packet arrival rate and packet processing rate can be experimented. As the similar behavior is observed in all the experiments only one range of packet arrival rate and packet processing rate are displayed.
- End results for bigger number of packets per flow e.g. 400, 600 and 800 packets were arranged in table rather than showing them in graphs due to the identical behavior from GA based model and PSO based model.

CONCLUSION

The proposed work introduces the concept of reliability for flow processing in Cellular IP network and analyzes it. Two models; GA based model and PSO based model for enhancing the reliability of a flow in Cellular IP networks have been discussed in this work. Both the models help in increasing the reliability of a flow. Experiments were conducted using GA and using PSO and the observation was that PSO based model performs better than GA based model for the reason clarified in the observations section. Though the GA based model converges quickly. The paper did not discuss the case in which a failure might happen in one or more base stations and hope to consider this case as a future work.

REFERENCES

Anbar, M., & Vidyarthi, D. P. (2009). Buffer management in cellular IP network using PSO. [IJMCMC]. *International Journal of Mobile Computing and Multimedia Communications, 1*(1), 78–93. doi:10.4018/jmcmc.2009070106

Anbar, M., & Vidyarthi, D. P. (2009). Router CPU time management using particle swarm optimization in cellular IP networks. *International Journal of Advancements in Computing Technology, 1*(2), 48–55. doi:10.4156/ijact.vol1.issue2.6

Anbar, M., & Vidyarthi, D. P. (2009). On demand bandwidth reservation for real-time traffic in cellular IP network using particle swarm optimization. [IJBDCN]. *International Journal of Business Data Communications and Networking, 5*(3), 53–66. doi:10.4018/jbdcn.2009070104

Anbar, M., & Vidyarthi, D. P. (2010). Comparative study of two CPU router time management algorithms in cellular IP networks. *International Journal of Network Management, 21*(2), 120–129.

Campbell, A. T., Gomez, J., Kim, S., Valko, A. G., Chieh-Yih, W., & Turanyi, Z. R. (2000). Design, implementation, and evaluation of cellular IP. *IEEE Personal Communications, 7*(4), 42–49. doi:10.1109/98.863995

Heimlicher, S., & Karaliopoulos, M. (2007). End-to-end vs. hop-by-hop transport under intermittent connectivity. In *Proceedings of the first International Conference on Autonomic Computing and Communication Systems*, Article No. 20, Rome, Italy.

Jayaram, R., Sen, S. K., Kakani, N. K., & Das, S. K. (2000). Call admission and control for quality-of-service (QoS) provisioning in next generation wireless networks. *ACM Wireless Networks Journal*, *6*(1), 17–30. doi:10.1023/A:1019160708424

Khanbary, L. M. O., & Vidyarthi, D. P. (2009). Reliability based channel allocation using genetic algorithm in mobile computing. *IEEE Transactions on Vehicular Technology*, *58*(8), 4248–4256. doi:10.1109/TVT.2009.2019666

Kumar, B. P. V., & Venkataram, P. (2000). Reliable multicast routing in mobile networks: A neural-network approach. In *Proceedings of IEE in Communications*, *2003*, 377–384.

Liao, W., Ke, C.-A., & Lai, J.-R. (2000). Reliable multicast with host mobility. In *Proceedings of IEEE Global Telecommunications Conference*, (pp. 1692–1696). San Francisco, USA.

Marasli, R., Amer, P. D., & Conrad, P. T. (1996). Retransmission-based partially reliable transport service: An analytic model. In *Proceedings of the 15th Annual Joint Conference of the IEEE Computer Societies: Networking the Next Generation*, (pp. 24-28).

Prakash, R., Shivaratri, N. G., & Singhal, M. (1999). Distributed dynamic fault-tolerant channel allocation for cellular networks. *IEEE Transactions on Vehicular Technology*, *48*(6), 1874–1888. doi:10.1109/25.806780

Sobrinho, J. L. (2002). Algebra and algorithms for QoS path computation and hop-by-hop routing in the internet. [TON]. *IEEE/ACM Transactions on Networking*, *10*(4), 541–550. doi:10.1109/TNET.2002.801397

Sun, S., Krzymien, W. A., & Jalai, A. (1998). Optimal forward link power allocation for data transmission in CDMA systems. In *Proceedings of Ninth IEEE International Symposium on Personal, Indoor and Mobile Radio Communications*, (pp. 848-852). Boston, MA.

Tanenbaum, A. S. (2004). *Computer networks*. New Delhi, India: Pearson Education.

Zhang, D., Ray, S., Kannan, R., & Iyengar, S. S. (2003). A recovery algorithm for reliable multicasting in reliable networks. In *Proceedings of IEEE 32nd International Conference on Parallel Processing*, (pp. 493-500). Kaohsiung, China.

Zhao, D., Shen, X., & Mark, J. W. (2006). Soft handoff and connection reliability in cellular CDMA downlinks. *IEEE Transactions on Wireless Communications*, *5*(2), 354–365. doi:10.1109/TWC.2006.1611059

Chapter 14
Blending Augmented Reality with Real World Scenarios Using Mobile Devices

Alexiei Dingli
University of Malta, Malta

Dylan Seychell
University of Malta, Malta

ABSTRACT

In this work, the authors present methods that add value to the current Web by connecting administrators of a space such as a city with its visitors. The mobile device has nowadays become an important tool in the hands of visitors of cities and the authors present it as a gateway for the administrators to their visitors. The authors present a method that processes various environmental factors during a visit and uses these factors as a context for presenting the recommendations. In this work, the authors also propose a method that can measure queues in a city, and by knowing the overall picture of the situation, it provides individual recommendations of separate mobile devices accordingly. This chapter shows, therefore, the three main steps in the process of recommendation systems: collecting information, processing the recommendations, and presenting them in an attractive way. In this case the authors focus on presenting recommendations through augmented reality in order to provide an attractive tool for end users, which would, at the end of the day, connect them further to the city over the Internet.

DOI: 10.4018/978-1-4666-0203-8.ch014

INTRODUCTION

Recent development in mobile wireless networks allowed for a more effective and easy way for users to connect to the internet from their mobile device from practically everywhere. In this chapter we are presenting a technique which takes advantage of this internet development in order to a connect end users on a mobile device with the administration of the place they are visiting. This adds value to the internet because makes use of all the advantages of using a mobile device (localisation, Augmented Reality and so on) and utilises the same device to act as a portal for quality information provided in that space. Besides this, the proposed technique allows the users to additionally connect to the web in order to acquire further information.

Mobile applications are always becoming more diverse, particularly with the improvement in development environments and the respective distribution of these development tools. Nevertheless, there is still the need for carefully built applications which carefully study the needs of the users. In this chapter we will explore a system which can be adopted as a mobile application which assists a visitor in any city hosting this system.

The first section of this chapter will study the problem faced by tourists when visiting a city. This will follow towards the study of these problems and what tourists normally do to overcome these problems. Subsequently a brief technical overview of Augmented Reality will be explored in the context of using this technology on a mobile device. The second section would then bring the problems to a lower level of abstraction and explores solutions while proposing a high level design of such a hybrid system. After the design is presented, different applications of augmented reality in this context together with details about the queue solution technique are given.

The aim of this chapter is to present an overview of the problems and how they are tackled by different solutions, starting at an abstract level towards the design of the system and employment of mobile technology to tackle these problems.

By making use of such a technique, it is believed that more value is added to the current web. Such a technique takes advantage of the openings provided by the emergence of the Web 2.0 by allowing the end users to be co-producers of information. This technique allows the users to contribute to the information source through their mobile device by making use of the context provided by this application.

Background

This section studies the need of an end user in a space. This study is important because it gives a deeper understanding of what users need and subconsciously expect out of an information source which in the case of this application is the internet connecting them to the web and to the source provided by administration.

Going around a City

This section will explore how tourists navigate around a city. Brown and Chalmers explain that while a tourist goes around a city he/she faces some 'problems'. However, they emphasise that one should not tackle these problems in a negative way since they claim that in tourism "getting there is half the fun" (Brown & Chalmers, 2003). Several solutions are subsequently presented, answering the former 'problems'.

Tourist Problems

Brown and Chalmers identified the following problems which tourists face while on holiday:

- **What to do:** This problem tends to seem a clear one. Brown and Chalmers explain that unlike work, there is not a particular or strict goal which must be reached by the end of the holiday. The tourists face a much "open-ended" since tourism entails a choice from various activities such as commercial activities, social activities and so on. Brown and Chalmers also say that some tourists may be visiting a different place because of business but sometimes the difference between leisure and business is not a clear-cut. (Brown & Chalmers, 2003)

- **How:** The second problem which tourists find is the way in which how they are going to do the said attractions. Brown and Chalmers say that an issue in this case is the cultural norms possible minor clashes when the difference of the culture of the tourist and that of the place being visited clash. The tourist needs to be equipped with knowledge about how to get something in the place in which is being visited to avoid exploitation. (Brown & Chalmers, 2003)

- **When:** This problem is related to time management of the tourist and the importance of optimising their visit so that they visit as much sites of interest as possible. Brown and Chalmers explain that tourists are constrained with time since their visit in the destination is limited since they need to go back home. (Brown & Chalmers, 2003)

- **Where:** The final and also natural problem for tourists is that of finding where things are. This is the final part of the puzzle which links the other problems. There are different attractions which tourists can visit and they are also restricted with the time at hand to go around the attractions. Brown and Chalmers emphasise that tourists "need to avoid spending too much time travelling between places" (Brown & Chalmers, 2003).

Tourist Solutions

While the 'problems' described above are no the be taken as something negative, one has to understand that "travelling and finding out where to go is part of the very enjoyment of tourism" (Brown & Chalmers, 2003). This also means that while on holiday, tourists are not essentially looking for the optimised path for going around. Tourists should be given some abstract guidance and given space to work through the 'problem' (Brown & Chalmers, 2003).

In their study, Brown and Chalmers dedicate substantial time in investigating the solution which tourists find to the above problems.

- **Sharing the visit:** Since tourism is in itself a social activity, tourists seek collaboration to solve their problems. Brown and Chalmers presented a "video-blog" of tourists collaborating at a station and explain how tasks are divided in order to solve the problem. The division of the task took the form of one tourist checking the map while the other checked the environment around. While tourists discuss issues about their trip in a very highly mobile manner, they also meet the desire of visiting different attractions (Brown & Chalmers, 2003). Tourists seem to depend on the "word of mouth" advice and exchange of information since they are after all establishing "social bonds or enjoying the company of new people" (Brown & Chalmers, 2003).

- **Guidebooks:** The guidebook is one of the tools in the hands of tourists. In their study, Brown and Chalmers explored the advantages of paper publications and they claim that it is important to know since it helps when creating the digital equivalent. There are different forms of guide books but they all essentially present information for tourists in a structured way. Guidebooks also include recommendations for the tourists and thus help tourists reducing their uncertainty (Brown & Chalmers, 2003). Guidebooks nonetheless sometime provide limited information when describing how to find a location of interest since it might not always be clear or tourist might confuse what they are seeing with what is written on the guide book. Brown and Chalmers present a conversation of two tourists using a guidebook in finding their way to a location and conclude that the best solution is GPS assistance. (Brown & Chalmers, 2003)

- **Maps:** Maps are also an essential tool which tourists use in conjunction with a guidebook (maybe) in order to navigate around a city. Brown and Chalmers claim that maps are the second popular tourist publication after the guidebook since in their study numerous tourists were observed making use of a map. Maps allow the tourists to explore the location and sometimes they end up meeting attractions along the way which are different from those originally planned (Brown & Chalmers, 2003). Nonetheless, when using a printed map, tourists might not be essentially going in the correct direction. Brown and Chalmers say that a second feature of a map is the "combination with guidebooks". As explained above, guidebooks provide the tourists with context and can help the tourists if also assisted by a map to put the geography presented on the map in the context provided by the guidebook. Brown and Chalmers mentioned in their study a particular case of tourist who spent over twenty minutes at a train station in Glasgow reading a mountain map which would help him in planning his walk (Brown & Chalmers, 2003). It is interesting since he was not using the map to find his way but to learn about what would help him.

- **Pre- and Post-visiting:** Brown and Chalmers proposed the last solution to be pre-visiting and post-visiting places in order to manage their holiday. Pre-visiting is about planning the holiday before or while being at the destination. Post-visiting is about extending the enjoyment of the holiday personally or with other once the holiday is over. Brown and Chalmers stress that the combination of "talk and interaction" helps tourist do the most of their holiday in both activities (Brown & Chalmers, 2003).

  ○ **Pre-Visiting:** One does a pre-visit of a place whenever he/she looks for information about the destination before actually going there, thus planning beforehand. Brown and Chalmers claim that besides being practical, pre-visiting is also enjoyable for tourists since it "extends the excitement of the holiday and builds anticipation" (Brown & Chalmers, 2003). Pre-visiting does not only happen before visiting the destination but also during the holiday as Brown and Chalmers explain that planning of the holiday actually goes on even during the holiday.

  ○ **Post-Visiting:** As the name implies, post-visiting is about "reminiscing and sharing" the experience which the tourist had during his holiday (Brown & Chalmers, 2003). The tourist would organise the photographs or media gathered during his holiday and share the experience with other people who may or may have not been at the holiday.

- **Queuing:** An underlying problem continuously faced by tourists is the time at hand when visiting a particular city. Normally tourists are bound by a limited time in a city and have to tackle the problems mentioned by Browns and Chalmers in that restricted time frame. Queues add to this problem since they are the major "time-wasters" when a tourist is visiting a city. Similarly, this is a problem for the city administration as well. Most tourists tend to visit a particular attraction simply because it might be more promoted than other attractions. It is the intention of every city administration to have tourists approximately equally distributed around the attractions offered in the city.

Mobile Technology in Tourism

Mobile technology is deemed highly adequate in the area of tourism. Brown and Chalmers go a step further and claim that *"tourism is one obvious application area"* of mobile technology (Brown & Chalmers, 2003). Throughout their paper they stress the mobile nature of tourists and thus imply that mobile devices might be a potential tool. Schmidt-Belz et al also dictate the same philosophy in their study named *"Location-based mobile tourists services"* and explain that the vision is that of offering a wide range of services for tourists on mobile devices (Schmidt-Belz, Laamanen, Poslad, & Zipf, 2003). In a more recent paper, Cutrí et al confirm the ever improving computational power of mobile devices and this helps for more mobile applications to be developed to better the experience of tourists (Cutrí, Naccarato, & Pantano, 2008).

Motivation

There are various efforts which strive to introduce and integrate the application of mobile technology in the area of tourism. The Finnish institute for Management Systems Research (IAMSR)[1] in the University of Åbo Akademi is engaged into various projects which work on this motivation. In their paper, Tétard and Patokorpi present a conceptual framework to relate technology with tourism and

cultural heritage in their field of research (Tétard & Patokorpi, 2004).

The model in figure 1 shows the merging of these three main areas. The work of IAMSR lies in the middle most overlap of the three regions. The Technology region represents the technological developments taking place which are opening doors of opportunities for other sectors to use the mobile technology and also the ICT companies and institutes which drive this development of technology. Similarly, the Tourism region includes in it the tourism expertise and the tourist agencies driving the industry. The city, which in the case of IAMSR is the City of Turku, also lies in the tourism region. Finally, in the region of Cultural Heritage, one finds the notion of cultural heritage and the cultural institutions safeguarding the notion and protecting the interest. In their paper justifying this project, Tétard and Patokorpi (Tétard & Patokorpi, 2004) stress that the stakeholders of this process are not just individual users but also five stakeholders which are brought together:

Figure 1. A framework for research on cultural heritage tourism and mobile ICT (Source: (Tétard & Patokorpi, 2004))

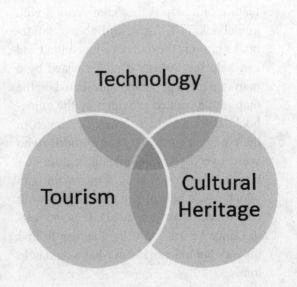

- Individual Users
- Curators
- Researchers
- Community
- Entrepreneurs

Tétard and Patokorpi explain that technology helps the researchers and curators distribute resources and research findings. They also underline that entrepreneurs also play a major role and should "take advantage of the cultural artefacts" thus create a supply to satisfy the demand of tourists and the community in the process of appreciating the heritage in question (Tétard & Patokorpi, 2004).

Augmented Reality

This section is intended to provide the reader with background about the field of augmented reality. It will explore the theory behind augmented reality, different applications of augmented reality and the techniques which deliver augmented reality to these applications. Augmented reality is in itself a relatively modern area which users find it attractive and useful due to the way it presents information extracted from the web.

Context

In each survey of augmented reality, Azuma (Azuma, Baillot, Behringer, Feiner, Julier, & MacIntyre, 2001) always presented and quoted the wider the picture of the *reality-virtuality continuum* which was originally presented by Milgram et al in 1994 (Milgram, Takemura, Utsumi, & Kishino, 1994).

The reality-virtuality continuum presented by Milgram et al is a spectrum of mixed reality having the real environment at one end and the virtual environment at the other end as illustrated in Figure 2. As a matter of fact, the aim of their paper was to "*classify the relationships between augmented reality and the larger class of technologies which are referred to as 'Mixed Reality'*" (Milgram, Takemura, Utsumi, & Kishino, 1994).

The diagram presented in figure 2 allows us to put augmented reality into a context. The far left of the diagram is the class of all objects which are totally real. Conversely, the class in the far right represents an environment which is totally virtual. Nokia describes the plane presented by Milgram et al (Milgram, Takemura, Utsumi, & Kishino, 1994) as a "*spectrum*" of ways in which "*people can interact with other people or with information*" (Nokia Research Center (NCR), 2009). Nokia go deeper by giving examples of the extremes in order to help us acquaint ourselves with the domain. For the Real Environment, they give an example of a face to face conversation while for the Virtual Environment they present us with an example of a single video game (Nokia Research Center (NCR), 2009).

Augmented reality is thus the addition of virtual elements to the real world and is a variation of Virtual Environments (Azuma R. T., 1997) in the sense that unlike virtual reality the user can still see elements of the real world while using an AR system. Other authors have also expressed augmented reality as an integration of the virtual and the real world.

In his survey of augmented reality (Azuma R. T., 1997), Ronald Azuma summarised from his findings that the characteristics of an augmented reality system are:

- Combination of real and virtual environments

Figure 2. Milgram et al concept of RV-Continuum (Adapted from: (Milgram, Takemura, Utsumi, & Kishino, 1994))

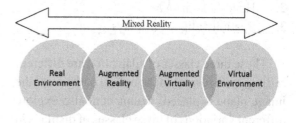

- Interaction within the environments in real time
- A 3-Dimensional representation of both environments for the alignment of virtual and real objects

At a later stage in this chapter, different applications of augmented reality will be explored. This definition gives room for different variations of augmented reality systems and thus robust enough to survive over twelve years of technical development in this field. These characteristics were in fact reassured in 2001 in the second survey which Azuma was leading (Azuma, Baillot, Behringer, Feiner, Julier, & MacIntyre, 2001).

On a more technical level, in their book "*Spatial Augmented Reality*", Bimber and Raskar describe augmented reality systems as:

...image-forming systems that use a set of optical, electronic and mechanical components to generate images somewhere on the optical path in between the observer's eyes and the physical object to be augmented.(Bimber & Raskar, 2005)

Displays

A display is placed along the optical path since it is effectively the only place along which a display device may be located. The optical path domain is divided by different classes of possible adaptations of augmented reality systems, namely (Bimber & Raskar, 2005):

1. Head-mounted/attached displays
2. Hand-held displays
3. Spatially aligned displays

These three classes of adaptation are different settings with respect to the optical path where the image plane is placed. Azuma et al also explore different variations of these classes of displays in

their survey published in 2001 (Azuma, Baillot, Behringer, Feiner, Julier, & MacIntyre, 2001).

The diagram in figure 3 shows the placement of the different classes of displays in the real world as they are naturally laid in the optical path. Nonetheless, Milgram et al also introduce another dimension to displays (Milgram, Takemura, Utsumi, & Kishino, 1994). They categorise the displays into two key categories:

1. "See-through" AR displays
2. Monitor based or Video based AR displays

Each of the classes proposed by Bimber (Bimber & Raskar, 2005) can be of any type of the two described by Milgram *et al* (Milgram, Takemura, Utsumi, & Kishino, 1994). The combination of the two gives us a better degree of freedom when exploring the different displays at hand and where to apply them. Nonetheless, each display to be effectively used in augmented reality must be properly calibrated and thus the imposed objects must be "*accurately positioned relative to each other*" for such a system to be effective (McGarrity & Tuceryan, 1999).

"Monitor/Video-Based" AR Displays

A monitor based display would provide the user with a "*window on the world*" and thus the user

Figure 3. Displays along the line of sight (Adapted from: (Bimber & Raskar, 2005))

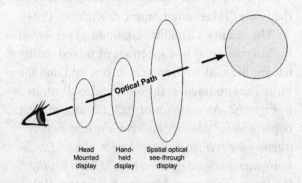

Head Mounted display   Hand-held display   Spatial optical see-through display

Figure 4. The relation of different types of displays (Source: Seychell & Dingli, 2010)

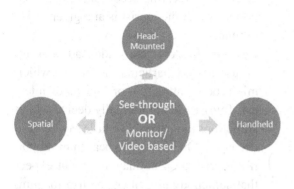

will not be totally immersed since one is not necessarily in the real place were the events are situated (Milgram, Takemura, Utsumi, & Kishino, 1994). Piekarski refers to this technique as "*video combined displays*" (Piekarski, 2004). In practice, this technique uses cameras to which feeds the real image in the computer simultaneously with the graphical image to be imposed (Piekarski, 2004).

Piekarski describes how this display involves an computational effort of image processing when combining the virtual with the real world before presenting it on a display as an "*entire image*" (Piekarski, 2004). He also explains that in such a technique, the quality tends to be superior since the computer has control and "*access to both incoming and outgoing images*" (Piekarski, 2004).

Variations of this concept exist with different devices substituting the camera. For example, the technique described by Nakamoto *et al* uses ultrasound to extract details from the real world and capturing real features (Nakamoto, *et al*., 2002).

Hand-Held Displays

This class of displays refers to those displays which one finds in the middle of the optical path shown on figure 3 above. In their 2001 survey, Azuma et al describe this class as a "*flat panel LCD that use an unattached camera to provide video see-through-based augmentations*" and also

serve as a "*window which shows the real object with an AR overlay*" (Azuma, Baillot, Behringer, Feiner, Julier, & MacIntyre, 2001).

Nonetheless, when Azuma et al did the survey in 2001, mobile phones were still at their early stages in their product life cycle and multimedia capabilities were not a mainstream on mobile devices. Due to this reason, they did not explore this area into depth. In 2009, Nokia claimed that they were engaged in numerous research projects in the field of mixed reality where they also said that mobile phones "*can be used to connect the physical world with the vast amounts of online information*" (Nokia Research Center (NCR), 2009).

Yet, limitations exist in this type of display as well. Bimber and Raskar outline an obvious limitation which is often put aside. When using a hand held device, the user is in the first place restricted from performing in a hands-free working environment (Bimber & Raskar, 2005). They also state that most of the hardware in a hand held device is usually "*targeted for other applications*" implying that might not be the most efficient when using within AR applications (Bimber & Raskar, 2005).

Finding all Answers on the Mobile Device

When developing this application we always kept in mind the context of a tourist visiting the city in question accompanied by a human guide. Throughout such a setting one assumes that the guide:

- knows the way towards a particular event[3]
- decides to which places tourists are taken
- can give details when the tourist arrives at a location
- can put a series of visits in context of a given interest

On the other hand, here follows a brief list of what a human guide may find difficult to provide the tourist with:

- Multimedia
  - showing how the location appears during different times of the year
  - exhibiting different uses of a location
  - expressing any other artistic concept which is location bound
- Knowledge of the number of people waiting to enter an event at that point in time
- Capability of rating an event or a location

One therefore concludes that a virtual guide in a mobile application must at least provide the tourist with the support which is expected out of a human guide. Nonetheless, a virtual mobile city guide can exploit technological advantages to add value to the user experience when visiting the city. These may be employed to provide the user with capabilities mentioned above which a human guide may not be able to provide in normal[4] circumstances. A key advantage is the connection of the mobile device to the internet in order to provide quality information which is timely and in context.

What is Expected by Such Systems?

Certain shortcomings of a human guide may be solved by using technological features. Nonetheless, one must ensure that the replacement of the assumed support of the human guide is adequately translated and performed by the mobile application.

- **Navigation:** When touring a city accompanied by a human guide, a tourist feels secure when navigating through the city. The application must provide the user with trustworthy navigational assistance throughout the tour. This support needs to be coupled with an up to date illustration of events, appearing according to the location at which the tourist is at a given point in time.

- **Leadership:** A human guide leads a group of tourists to particular locations which might be an attraction or a place of interest. Tourists do not normally decide which attractions to visit or have little say in these decisions. One must also bear in mind that if a tourist is on holiday, he might expect that somebody else plans the trip for him, without having the tourist making extra effort to visit a location. The application should therefore be capable of recommending relevant events and locations and constantly prompt the tourist with suggestions. Suggestions may be based on location or on the type of attractions which tourists like.

Solutions and Recommendations

We propose a paradigm based on three fundamental steps with the metaphor of preparing a plate and serving it. The first step is that of collecting information from sources around the user which would make the application more relevant and in touch with the reality that the user is experiencing. After collecting these ingredients, the next natural step is processing them in a recipe which would make all aspects blend together. Finally, the plate must be served in a neat and attractive way to be attractive for the visitors to consume. It is important that information collected and processed is presented to the end user in a clean fashion and attractive enough to use. This is one of the key reasons why we suggest the use of augmented reality.

In the block diagram presented in figure 5, one can see the main components of such a system. It is initially organised in a backend region and a front end region. The back-end contains the modules collecting the information and processing it

Figure 5. Block diagram of the system (Source: Seychell and Dingli)

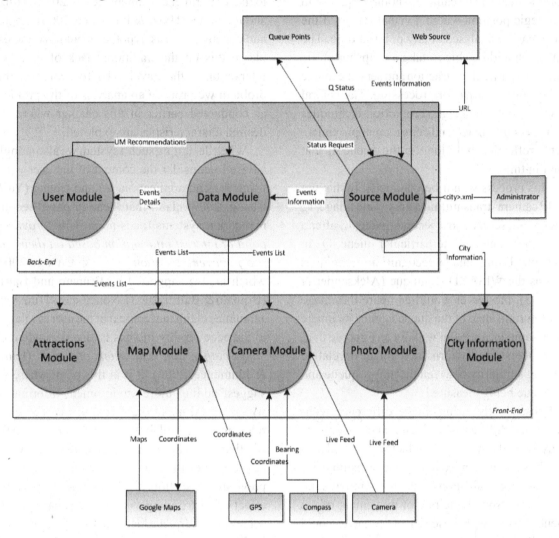

(Step 1 and Step 2). The Source Module shown in the diagram entails the processes of collecting information about the city from the administrator. The module subsequently deals with information sources, in this case the Queue stations and the web source, to collect the dynamic information and it is then responsible of handing it to the Data Module for effective storage and retrieval. Recommendations are then specifically generated in the User Module which would hold statistical information about the user and would then present recommendations accordingly. On the side of the front end, one can find all the modules which

are responsible for the presentation of information to the user. The Map module would for instance present information on the map in relation to the current position of the user. The Augmented Reality presentation is then processed and presented through the Camera Module.

Step 1: Collecting Information – Collecting Information about Queues

One of the information sources around such a system would be cameras distributed along different sites of interests, designed specifically to monitor queues. The cameras should be placed in a strategic position where a visual image of the queue can be analysed at any point in time. The camera should be able to take a snapshot of the queue of a particular attraction and send the image to the central server for processing. The central server would use image recognition techniques to process the image and return an approximate factor reflecting how long is the queue at that point in time.

This process would be conducted by having the IP camera[5] transmitting a grey scale image, I_1, to the main server and a second image, I_2, after a given time factor of the particular queue, Q_i, in question. Using image recognition techniques such as the WISARD technique (Aleksander *et al*, 1993), the server would compare the image of the current state of the queue against an image of the same location but without any people in it. The process would return a percentage or relative value of similarity between the empty queue and the queue being measured.

Subsequently, using image difference techniques, the difference between I_1 and I_2 would be analysed and a waiting time factor is also identified. It is recommended to take more readings for more precise evaluation of the queue movement. In the background, the rate of movement of the queue together with the length of the queue would be evaluated with other metrics and weighted accordingly for the recommendation algorithm to distribute tourists around the different attractions feeding the main server with these images and thus reporting queue statuses.

Step 2: Putting the Ingredients Together - Recommendation Engine

The backbone of such system is the recommendation engine driving the application. The back-end would be harvesting information from the pre-set data sources and processing it together with other environmental feeds. Recommender systems are designed to provide the users with advice similar to that of a travel consultant (Ricci, 2002). Hinze and Junmanee (Hinze & Junmanee, 2006) support and concur with this hypothesis but nevertheless blame this on the traditional lack of focus on interaction in the travel aids. To overcome this problem we propose an analysis of the problem as conducted earlier in this chapter where the desired characteristics are explored.

When designing such a system we also stongly advise to consider the context of the user while using the end application. Yu and Chang (Yu & Chang, 2009) claim that location based recommendation systems focus mainly on *"providing point of interest information based on their (the user) current location"* (Yu & Chang, 2009) which is also supported by Brunato and Battiti (Brunato & Battiti, 2003). Nonetheless Hinze and Junmanee claim that context of the user in relation to the accessibility of sites is also dependent on *"the weather, time and means of travel"* (Hinze & Junmanee, 2006). It is at this point where we suggest adding more environment information which would make the recommendations more relevant and useful for the user. Together with the weather and other parameters, the system would also consider the queue factor discussed in the previous subsection in order to get the desired effect of distributing visitors. This can only be achieved if the queue factor is strongly considered in the recommendation algorithm.

Step 3: Presenting the Final Product - Augmented Reality

Augmented Reality is an innovative and practical way to display information while providing a real time support capable enough to set the user in the right orientation. As explored in earlier parts of this chapter, augmented reality superimposes a computer generated graphic on the real environment being captured by the camera of the mobile device.

Figure 6. Making use of geo-information (Source: Seychell & Dingli, 2010)

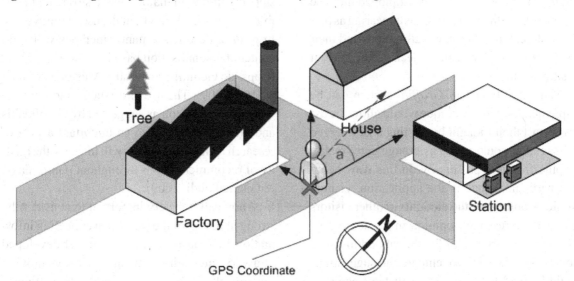

By making use of geographical readings from the device, augmented reality can be given more relevance as explained in the figure below.

Figure 6 shows how augmented employs geographical information and a bearing to present the user with augmented reality and thus guide the user to the destination. In the general design of the recommendation system, this module should be an independent module which receives information from the data modules and generates the respective video-based augmented reality with the acquired information.

Figure 7 shows a photograph which was taken while a user was using the Virtual Mobile City Guide (VMCG) within Valletta, the capital city of Malta (Seychell & Dingli, 2010). The image shows the flags grouped in line since the device was looking at the grouped attractions from a distance. One can observe that in this case study, the user is presented with a compass in the bottom right corner which indicates the attractions as orange dots. In the main area, live stream from the camera is displayed on the screen and flags marking the respective attractions are superimposed accordingly. This system used the Wikitude[6] API which was developed by Mobilizy which is

a company which is engaged in the innovative field of augmented reality and developed this API which provides developers with a very innovative concept to employ in their applications.

'*Virtual Signage*' can also be implemented using augmented reality. A similar technique to the one displayed above in the VMCG (Seychell & Dingli, 2010), can be employed to create virtual signs in the roads of the city, showing the places of interest which are relevant to the user.

Figure 7. The VMCG being used in Valletta (Source: Seychell & Dingli, 2010)

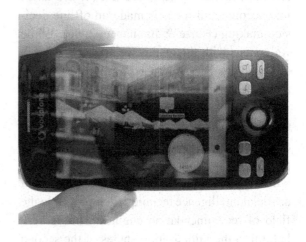

Intelligent algorithms can be employed and use augmented reality to create signs appearing as part of the street but with filtered attractions and their respective direction with respects to the current position of the user.

Similarly, a '*Virtual Graffiti*' system can be implemented. This technique would allow the users to post their thought by posting a geo-tagged message and would appear as an augmented reality graphic for other passers-by. In this way, being in a particular mode in the application, visitors would be able to see the thoughts of other visitors and also express their opinion in the same way. This can be very useful for the city administration as well since improvements and suggestions could be read with further relevance since they are specifically placed in a location which the visitor visited.

FUTURE RESEARCH DIRECTIONS

While during this chapter we focused on the process leading to an effective recommendation system by making use of technologies such as augmented reality and mobile technology, we propose more concentration and future advancement in more detail in any of the three key steps.

Hinze and Junmanee (Hinze & Junmanee, 2006) claim that the characteristics of mobile recommendation systems are not always taken into account and focus is made on offline decision making (Hinze & Junmanee, 2006). While we concur with this claim we suggest research efforts in involving the user during recommendation process.

In their paper, Tang and McCalla (Tang & McCalla, 2004) discussed the importance of having artificial learners to help overcome the Cold-Start problem in recommendation systems. Research will also be made in the employment of different artificial intelligence techniques employed in the field of recommendation engines. This is very helpful in the initialisation stages of the second

step together with maintaining a strong and flexible user profile throughout the use of the system. Lops *et al* describe semantic methods which do content personalisation based on the user profile (Lops, de Gemmis, Semeraro, Musto, Narducci, & Bux, 2009). The use of ontologies to improve web personalisation as suggested by Garofalakis and Giannakoudi is also an important aspect of research in this field since it will improve the quality of recommendations throughout (Garofalakis & Giannakoudi, 2009).

Above all it is very important to consider the strong potential of the web when collecting information. In the last two decades, the web developed in a very interesting way and is always moving towards the direction of being a very diverse source of information. The recent emergence of Social Networks is very important to note since it is a mine of precious information which could help such recommendation systems provide the user with most relevant information after studying patterns in these networks. This has to be coupled with the emergence of the Semantic Web and current explorations in the field of linked data (Bizer et al, 2008).

CONCLUSION

This chapter explored the theoretical background related to the problem faced by tourists when visiting a city and how to support them by making use of the internet. This adds value to the internet because it allows end users to be co contributors by giving feedback while receiving quality information from administrators. The background explored how tourists behave when they are faced by these problems and what solutions are normally sought. Background research was also presented for the field of augmented reality with particular focus given to augmented reality techniques when employed on a mobile device.

After this exploration of literature we presented a problem definition of how to handle these problems and solutions and translate them to feasible software addressing the needs of the users. Subsequently, a system was proposed matching the cooking metaphor. This addressed the key stages of a recommendation system: collecting information, processing recommendations and presenting them to the user in an attractive manner. After proposing this system, we re-visited it in more detail and explained future developments to improve such systems. New emerging areas which will surely add value to recommendation systems were explored and more literature which will strengthen this lie of thought can be found in the final sections of this chapter.

REFERENCES

Aleksander, I., Thomas, W. V., & Bowden, P. A. (1993). WISARD: A radical step forward in image recognition. *Sensor Review*, *4*(3), 120–124. doi:10.1108/eb007637

Azuma, R., Baillot, Y., Behringer, R., Feiner, S., Julier, S., & MacIntyre, B. (2001). *Recent advances in augmented reality*. Malibu, CA: IEEE.

Azuma, R., Hoff, B., Neely, H. III, & Sarfaty, R. (1999). *A motion-stabilized outdoor augmented reality system*. *IEEE Virtual Reality '99* (p. 8). Houston, TX: IEEE.

Azuma, R. T. (1997). *A survey of augmented reality*. Malibu, HI: Hughes Research Laboratories.

Bimber, O., & Raskar, R. (2005). *Spatial augmented reality - Merging real and virtual worlds*. Wellesley, MA: A K Peters, Ltd.

Bizer, C., Heath, T., Idehen, K., & Berners-Lee, T. (2008). Linked data on the Web (LDOW2008). In *Proceeding of the 17th International Conference on World Wide Web, WWW '08*, (pp. 1265–1266). New York, NY: ACM.

Brown, B., & Chalmers, M. (2003). Tourism and mobile technology. *Eighth European Conference on Computer Supported Cooperative Work* (p. 20). Helsinki, Finland: Kluwer Academic Press.

Brunato, M., & Battiti, R. (2003). *A location-dependent recommender system for the Web*. Budapest, Hungary: MobEA Workshop.

Castellano, G., & Torsello, M. A. (2009). How to derive fuzzy user categories for Web personalization. In Castellano, G., & Fanelli, A. M. (Eds.), *Web personalities in intelligent environments*. Berlin, Germany: Springer-Verlag. doi:10.1007/978-3-642-02794-9_4

Cutrí, G., Naccarato, G., & Pantano, E. (2008). *Mobile cultural heritage: The case study of Locri. Edutainment 2008, LNCS 5093* (pp. 410–420). Berlin, Germany: Springer-Verlag.

Garofalakis, J., & Giannakoudi, T. (2009). Explointing ontologies for Web search personalization. In Castellano, G., & Fanelli, A. M. (Eds.), *Web personalities in intelligent environments*. Berlin, Germany: Springer-Verlag. doi:10.1007/978-3-642-02794-9_3

Hinze, A., & Junmanee, S. (2006). Advanced recommendation models for mobile tourist information. *14th International Conference on Cooperative Information Systems* (pp. 643-660). Montpellier, VT: Springer Verlag.

Lops, P., de Gemmis, M., Semeraro, G., Musto, C., Narducci, F., & Bux, M. (2009). A semantic content-based recommender system integrating folksonomies for personalized data. In Castellano, G., & Fanelli, A. M. (Eds.), *Web personalities in intelligent environments*. Berlin, Germany: Springer-Verlag. doi:10.1007/978-3-642-02794-9_2

McGarrity, E., & Tuceryan, M. (1999). A method for calibrating see-through head-mounted displays for AR. *IEEE 2nd International Workshop on Augmented Reality (IWAR 99)* (p. 10). San Francisco, CA: IEEE.

Milgram, P., Takemura, H., Utsumi, A., & Kishino, F. (1994). Augmented reality: A class of displays on the reality-virtuality continuum. In Das, H. (Ed.), *Telemanipular and Telepresence Technologies*.

Nakamoto, M., Sato, Y., Miyamoto, M., Nakamjima, Y., Konishi, K., Shimada, M., et al. (2002). *3D ultrasound system using a magneto-optic hybrid tracker for augmented reality visualization in laparoscopic liver surgery*.

Nokia Research Center (NCR). (2009). Mobile mixed reality. *Nokia Technology Insights Series*, 4.

Piekarski, W. (2004). *Interactive 3D modelling in outdoor augmented reality worlds*. Adelaide, Australia: University of South Australia.

Ricci, F. (2002). *Travel recommender systems*. IEEE Intelligent Systems.

Schmidt-Belz, B., Laamanen, H., Poslad, S., & Zipf, A. (2003). Location-based mobile tourist services - First user experiences. *Information and communication technologies in tourism International Conference* (p. 10). Helsinki, Finland: Springer-Verlag Wein.

Seychell, D., & Dingli, A. (2010). *Virtual mobile city guide*. University of Malta.

Tang, T., & McCalla, G. (2004). *Utilizing artificial learners to help overcome the cold-start problem in a pedagogically-oriented paper recommendation system. AH 2004* (pp. 245–254). Berlin, Germany: Springer-Verlag.

Tétard, F., & Patokorpi, E. (2004). Cutural heritage tourism and mobile ICT. *IADIS International Conference e-Society 2004*, (pp. 868-871). Avila, Spain.

Yu, C.-C., & Chang, H.-P. (2009). *Personalized location-based recommendation services for tour planning in mobile tourism. EC-Web 2009* (pp. 38–49). Berlin, Germany: Springer-Verlag.

ADDITIONAL READING

Bae, J., Lee, J. Y., Kim, B. C., & Ryu, S. (2006). *Next Generation Mobile Service Environment and Evolution of Context Aware Services. EUC 2006*. International Federation for Information Processing.

Berners-Lee, T., Cailliau, R., & Groff, J.-F. (1992). The world-wide web. *Computer Networks and ISDN Systems*, *25*(4-5), 454–459. doi:10.1016/0169-7552(92)90039-S

Berners-Lee, T., & Fischetti, M. (1999). *Weaving the Web: The Original Design and Ultimate Destiny of the World Wide Web by its Inventor*. Harper San Francisco.

Bono, E. d. (1998). *Simplicity*. London: Penguin.

Bush, V. (1945). As we may think. *Atlantic Monthly*, *176*(1), 101–108.

Chevest, K., Davies, N., Mitchell, K., & Friday, A. (1999). The Role of Connectivity in Supporting Context-Sensitive Applications. *1st International symposium on Handheld and Ubiquitous Computing* (pp. 193-207). Karlsruhe, Germany: Springer-Verlag London.

Corby, O., Dieng-Kuntz, R., Gandon, F., & Faron-Zucker, C. (2006). Searching the semantic web: approximate query processing based on ontologies. *Intelligent Systems, IEEE*, *21*(1), 20–27. doi:10.1109/MIS.2006.16

Haralambos Marmanis, D. B. (2009). *Algorithms of the Intelligent Web*. Manning Publications Co.

Huang, W., & Webster, D. (2004). Enabling context-aware agents to understand semantic resources on the wwwand the semantic web. In *Proceedings of the 2004 IEEE/WIC/ACM International Conference on Web Intelligence*, WI '04, pages 138–144, Washington, DC, USA. IEEE Computer Society.

Meier, R. (2010). *Professional Android 2 Application Development*. Indiana: Wiley Publishing Inc.

Mencar, C., Castiello, C., Del'Agnello, D., & Fanelli, A. M. (2009). A System for Fuzzy Items Recommendation. *Web Person*. In *Intel. Environ.* Springer-Verlag Berlin.

Negnevitsky, M. (2005). *Artificial Intelligence - A Guide to Intelligent Systems*. Essex: Pearson Education Limited.

Singhal, A. (2001). Modern Information Retrieval: A Brief Overview. *Bulletin of the IEEE Computer Society Technical Committee on Data Engineering, 24*(4), 35–42.

van Wamelen, J., & de Kool, D. (2008). Web 2.0: a basis for the second society? In *Proceedings of the 2nd International Conference on Theory and Practice of Electronic Governance*, ICEGOV '08, pages 349–354, New York, NY, USA. ACM.

KEY TERMS AND DEFINITIONS

Augmented Reality: The process of superimposing a computer generated graphic over a view of the real environment.

Geo-Tagging: Referencing or tagging a particular object, e.g. an image, by making use of geographical information such as GPS coordinates

Localisation: A classification of techniques which provide location context in relation to a particular location by making use of different techniques which could be outdoor (GPS, Galileo etc.) and indoor (RF-ID etc.).

Recommendation Systems: Systems which provide the user with advice about a particular domain after processing

Semantic: Web: A web in which information handlers (such as machines) would understand the information being handled. This is a field of study which goes hand in hand with research about knowledge representation.

Social Web: A by-product of the advancement of the web resulting in websites enabling end-users to be co-producers of information and in this case interacting with other user of the web by sharing personal information.

WISARD: A recognition system developed by scientists at the Brunei University which uses statistical pattern classification to recognise changes between images and thus returning a similarity measure.

ENDNOTES

[1] www.iamsr.abo.fi

[2] All existing systems are separate from the human body. There are no implanted systems in the human body thus to date, the space domain where to implement an augmented reality system is in the optical path.

[3] An event may be a one off event such as a show or a recurrent event such as a museum which is daily open for visitors.

[4] Physically, there might be circumstances where guides in a city are equipped with communication devices to solve some of the problems mentioned in the second list.

[5] A camera connected to the internet and transmitting the live feed over internet protocol

[6] http://www.wikitude.org

Chapter 15
Pervasive Internet via Wireless Infrastructure– Based Mesh Networks

Nabanita Das
Indian Statistical Institute, India

ABSTRACT

With the arrival of Wi-Fi, WiMax, Zigbee, and other wireless network standards, the penetration of Internet in daily life has surged significantly. While the usage of Internet access in urban areas is steadily increasing in recent years, rural people are still suffering from the effect of the digital divide, mainly due to the poor coverage by Internet service providers in remote areas. This chapter aims to provide a cost-effective reliable broadband Internet access solution for rural people in the form of Wireless Mesh Network (WMN) whose coverage can be easily extended in a multi-hop fashion. Starting from a general description of the WMN architecture and protocol developments, this chapter focuses on the primary design issues and challenges for making Internet pervasive through WMN's that demand innovations in protocols at different layers and perfect integration. The brief discussion on the research works and related experimental testbeds shows that WMN with its unique features seems to be a promising solution to provide next generation Internet access to areas that are too remote to receive it via cable or DSL, or where upgrading the landlines to broadband is highly cost-prohibitive. Finally, this chapter concludes introducing various open issues and research challenges still to be addressed and resolved in coming days to make this solution commercially viable.

INTRODUCTION

The rapid evolution of communication technology along with the tremendous growth in information technology has opened the possibility of making Internet pervasive (Poslad, 2009; Ishmael et al.,

DOI: 10.4018/978-1-4666-0203-8.ch015

2008; Maza et al., 2005) so that it can be accessed by people at all levels and at every corner of the world. Today there is no doubt that the Internet can make a significant contribution to improve the quality of life in developing nations. For urban users, email, search engines, on-line purchase, chatting, video streaming etc. have become an indispensable part of our daily life. However, in most developing countries, for example, in India and China, where roughly 40 percent of the global population lives in, the progress of Internet is rather slow. Recent studies revealed the fact that the Internet is comparatively more pervasive in China mainly in the form of research and education networks, where they account for more than half a million users. However, these countries have large rural populations and should be motivated to make the Internet pervasive, and to invent new applications of it to address the requirements of people living in villages and remote places. High levels of pervasiveness will require service to the lower urban classes and villages, which raises issues of public access, attractive value-added services in villages, education and information in regional languages etc.. With recent advances in wireless Internet technology, high speed wireless connections are now readily available on laptops, cell phones, and other mobile computing devices. The biggest misconception about wireless Internet access is that it is assumed to be omnipresent. That simply isn't the case. Wireless Internet service providers (WISPs) will have to operate a series of towers that transmit their Internet signals in a fashion similar to the cell phone base stations. This is a costly endeavor and hence is not feasible in areas with low population or low demand. In present scenario, it seems that it will take many years before PCs become affordable to the bulk of urban residents. Moreover it requires the establishment and facilitation of public access points, and it suggests that Internet access might be provided by upgrading the privately run public telephone offices already existing. However reliable, affordable and easy access to telecommunication services is still not available to the people of rural areas in most under-developed countries. Hence self-provisioning and community ownership of low cost, distributed infrastructure is becoming a viable alternative to increase the penetration of telecommunication services in rural world. The recent emergence of wireless mesh network (WMN) technology (Akyildiz, Wang, & Wang,

2005; Bruno, Conti, & Gregori, 2005) can help significantly to improve the coverage of telecommunication services and Internet in these regions.

Compared to the current broadband Internet access paradigm, which relies on cable and DSL systems that are centrally managed, mesh networking is organic where everyone in the neighborhood cooperates and contributes network resources (Microsoft, n.d.). When enough neighbors cooperate and forward each others packets, they do not need to install an Internet gateway individually but instead can share faster, cost-effective Internet access via gateways that are distributed in their neighborhood.

The objective of this chapter is to present a comprehensive study of the WMN network architectures and protocols proposed so far for various application areas with special emphasis on expanding the Internet access facilities to remote areas. Besides describing the previous works on WMN system architectures, this chapter also attempts to identify the fundamental problem of ensuring cooperation among ad hoc nodes in a competitive scenario that is the basic assumption in any ad hoc network.

WIRELESS MESH NETWORKS: AN OVERVIEW

In recent years, the tremendous growth in the demand for high-speed Internet access for multimedia services has caused the innovation of new broadband technologies using wireless infrastructure. So far, the mobile ad hoc networks (MANETs) have been studied extensively for its ease of deployment and self-organizing capability that can function without the support of any backbone (Bellfiore et al., 2003; Johnson, Maltz, & Hu, 2004; Huang & Lai, 2002). However, the responsibility of forwarding data packets on each and every node of MANET, makes the design complicated and not suitable for applications like Internet access. Whereas infrastructure-based wireless networks offer better option in spite of their higher cost for the backbone set up. As a consequence, a new approach, namely the wireless mesh network (WMN) that combines the infrastructure based wireless networking with MANET has evolved that provides a low-cost and fast-deployment solution to meet the user demand for faster Internet access (Akyildiz, Wang, & Wang, 2005; Bruno, Conti, & Gregori, 2005). In fact, WMN is a promising wireless technology for numerous applications like broadband home networking, building automation, community networking, strategic battlefield and anti-terror communications and finally an emerging class of uses still to be explored for sensor networks (Akyildiz et al., 2002). To make Internet pervasive, WMN may play an important role to offer this facility beyond the areas under existing telecommunication coverage.

Architectural Features

A typical WMN is comprised of two types of nodes, mesh routers and mesh clients (Akyildiz, Wang, & Wang, 2005). Mesh routers are usually built on dedicated embedded systems or general purpose computers equipped with multiple wireless interfaces, in general, having the added functionalities of gateway / repeaters. Also, any conventional node like PC's, laptops, PDA's, palmtops or phones, IP phones, or many other devices, just equipped with wireless network interface cards (NIC) can act as mesh nodes, i.e., routers or clients. Each node operates not only as a host but as a router to forward others packets as well, forming a self-organized and self-configured network with low cost, easy maintenance and reliable service. The mesh routers with gateway/ bridge functionalities can integrate a WMN with other existing wireless networks, like cellular, sensor, Wi-Fi, WiMAX, WiMedia and Zig-Bee networks as shown in Figure 1. Thus, WMNs can be seen

Figure 1. Hybrid wireless mesh network: solid (dash) lines indicate wired (wireless) links (Akyildiz, Wang, & Wang, 2005)

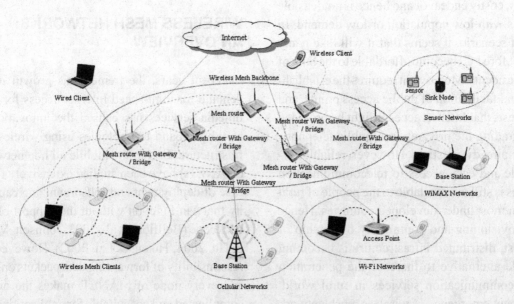

as an excellent way to keep users connected with existing backbones using minimal upfront costs in the following three categories:

In Backbone WMNs, the mesh routers form a backbone network, and any client can directly communicate with a mesh router only. The IEEE 802.16 technologies are mostly used, and the mesh routers with gateway capability can connect the WMN with other existing networks, like the Internet, cellular or sensor networks. Community networks can be built using backbone WMN's, where routers may be placed on rooftops acting as access points to the clients in its neighborhood using short-range radios. For communication within the backbone, the routers use long range communication techniques. In Client WMN's, in absence of any mesh routers, the client nodes may take the responsibility of routing and self-configuration. However, in absence of any gateway/bridge functionalities, they can't integrate with any other existing networks. It can act as a stand alone community network for local communications only. In Hybrid WMN's, mesh clients can communicate directly with the mesh routers, as well as with other mesh clients. However, only mesh routers are capable of interconnecting the WMN with outer networks. This is the most versatile configuration. With the routing capability of client nodes the coverage and connectivity of the networks are improved.

Comparison with MANET

It is a debatable question whether WMN is a subclass of Mobile Ad hoc Networks, or vice versa. MANET represents the class of self-organizing networks where all nodes are mobile and are capable of point to point communication. In case of WMN, the hybrid type, in general, the routers are typically static and constitute a wireless backbone to be used by the mobile end users, i.e., the mesh clients. Therefore, from architectural viewpoint, MANET's are more general and WMN's may be considered as a special class of MANET. On

the contrary, regarding functional capabilities, WMN's with all ad hoc networking capabilities necessitates more complex mesh routers with gateway / bridge functionalities to integrate it with various existing networks, like cellular, Wi-Fi, the Internet and the sensor networks. Hence, WMN's have more diversified capabilities compared to MANET's (Akyildiz, Wang, & Wang, 2005).The *presence of a backbone* in WMN's makes the routing and self-configuration easier in WMN compared to that in MANET. The end users in WMN are free from the responsibilities of routing and self-organization whereas in MANET it is not the case. Therefore, the load and hence energy consumption in mobile end users in WMN are much less. Also the presence of *multiple radios* in mesh routers enable simultaneous communication within backbone, for routing and self-configuration through one radio, and communication with the end users via another radio. But in MANETs, all communications take place through the same radio in individual nodes. This feature obviously improves the capacity of WMN's significantly. Since in ad hoc networks, the end user nodes may be mobile, and they perform the routing and self-organization for the network, the complexity of the devices is higher compared to that in WMN's. Also, to cope up with the node mobility they need sophisticated algorithms consuming more energy and computation power in end nodes and at the same time sacrifices robustness and reliability due to frequent topology changes caused by mobility of users.Therefore it is evident that though the WMN's are essentially ad hoc networks, the presence of the backbone network consisting of the static routers with no severe energy constraints makes the network more robust and reliable, capable of executing complex multihop routing and self-configuration algorithms on the routers keeping the mobile end users free of these responsibilities reducing their cost, computation and communication load and hence facilitating longer life. Hence, the MAC or the routing protocols optimized for mesh routers may not be suitable for the mesh clients, as the optimization criteria may be different for the two nodes- for routers it may be the QoS, whereas for clients it may be the power efficiency. Moreover to offer the connectivity to other existing networks, such as cellular, or Wi-Fi, or sensor networks, the routers must resolve the issues related to compatibility and interoperability, which are not relevant in MANET's.

Protocols and Standards: New Developments

Diverse WMN architectures have been proposed so far for different usage scenarios which explore various challenges for designing and realizing a WMN. Acknowledging the potential of this technology, industries have already prepared standards and marketed networking products.

With the already developed protocol stack for ad hoc networks, an evident question that surfaced as a point of contention is, whether to implement the additional mesh functionalities at the media-access level (Layer 2) or network level (Layer 3). As for example, Intel proposes to implement it at the media-access control (MAC) layer to avoid difficulties assigning Internet Protocol (IP) addresses to devices that cannot be directly seen at the network layer (Intel, n.d.).

Recently, Microsoft has implemented ad-hoc routing and link quality measurement in a loadable MS Windows module in Layer 2.5, called the Mesh Connectivity Layer (MCL) (Microsoft, n.d.). It implements a virtual network adapter, so that to the rest of the system the ad-hoc network appears just as an additional (virtual) network link. MCL implements a modified version of DSR (Dynamic Source Routing: an IETF protocol) that is called Link Quality Source Routing (LQSR) to support link quality metrics. To higher layer software, MCL appears to be just another Ethernet link, albeit a virtual link. To lower layer software, MCL appears to be just another protocol running over the physical link. This design has several signifi-

cant advantages. First, higher layer software runs unmodified over the ad-hoc network. On testbeds, both IPv4 and IPv6 run over the ad-hoc network. The current implementation supports Ethernet-like physical link layers (e.g. 802.11 and 802.3) but the architecture accommodates link layers with arbitrary addressing and framing conventions. The virtual MCL network adapter can multiplex several physical network adapters, so the ad-hoc network can extend across heterogeneous physical links. Third, the design can support other ad-hoc routing protocols as well.

Another distinguishing feature in WMN's is the use of multiple radios and multiple channels (Blostein & Lieb, 2003; Gupta & Kumar, 2000; Ghosh, Sinha, & Das, 2003; Raniwala, Hopalan, & Chiueh, 2004; Ko et al., 2007; Draves, Padhye, & Zill, 2004) in mesh routers that requires additional complexity in the MAC layer for efficient management. Radios are becoming low-priced, and good scheduling algorithms have been already developed. It predicts the use of multiple radios in each router with the support of multi-radio MAC. Another challenge is to decide on the number of channels available to each radio. In multi-channel multi-radio MAC, a radio may include multiple parallel RF front-end chips under a single MAC layer. A node has multiple radios each with its own MAC and physical layers. Hence to coordinate communications over all channels of a node a virtual MAC, namely the multi-radio unification protocol (MUP) (Adya et al., 2004) is required on top of it. Microsoft has already developed a technique called slotted seeded channel hopping (Bahl, Chandra, & Dunagan, 2004), which boosts the spectrum efficiency of single-radio meshes using fast switching among three 20-MHz channels. However, the NICs (network interface cards) with the capacity of switching channels fast, is yet to be developed. With present technology, it takes several milliseconds. But with new technologies if channel switching can be done faster, we can use the spectrum much more effectively using single-radio mesh at a much lower cost and with much simpler protocols.

Due to the poor scalability in the MAC layer, protocols for IEEE 802.11 (Zhu et al., 2004; Cali, Conti, & Gregori, 2000; Walker et al., 2010) ad hoc mode are not suitable for multihop mesh networks. Recently, a standard 802.11s has been proposed that will require a single-radio mode but will also support multiple-radio options. To improve the scalability, 802.11s uses cellular wireless LAN access points to relay information in multihop fashion. As access points and users are added, the capacity increases, as in the Internet. Several task groups are formed to resolve the issues regarding architectural specifications, QoS, routing and MAC protocols, and security.

PERVASIVE INTERNET VIA WMN

In the last decade, the market of Internet has expanded tremendously, major commercial access providers are extending the range of service offerings and the number of users served. From *Internet Usage and World Population Statistics, June 30, 2010*, the global Internet penetration is 28.7% only showing a growth rate of 444.8% in the last decade (2000-2010). However, rural and low-income people are in general under-served and are likely to remain so in the foreseeable future. The reasons are that the customers are scattered with low density, and therefore expensive to reach, and often they cannot afford high-priced services, and hence are neglected by the commercial service providers. It is obvious that the access to Internet as a means of communication and information resources offers an excellent opportunity to the rural people to find education, jobs, health services and a lot more.

According to a survey conducted jointly by *IMRB International* and *Internet and Mobile Association of India (IAMAI)*, the number of active Internet users (those who have used Internet at least once in the last one month) in rural India

increased by 27% to 4.2 million in 2009 from 3.3 million in 2008 and is expected to further grow by 28% to 5.4 million by the end of 2010. The survey reveals that 85% of Internet users in rural India used emails in 2009, while 67% of the rural users accessed music and video over the Internet. About 48% of the people claimed to have used the Internet for educational research and 42% claimed to have used it for general information search. It shows that people in rural areas are also becoming aware of the uses of Internet and can utilize it for their benefits. However, in rural areas there are not many options for high speed and good quality Internet. A lot of people who live in villages don't have access to DSL or cable which are mostly used in urban areas. In that case the common practices for Internet access are:

- **Satellite Internet:** if the area is covered by communication satellite; even then the cost of the receiver and the service plan charge may be high depending on the quality of service (QoS) requirements.
- **Long-range Wi-Fi:** having an access point within the range of the antenna that is connected with a backbone network via Ethernet connection: each terminal should remain within the range of the access point limiting the coverage.
- **Wireless broadband card:** can operate within the range of a cellular network base station only- which may not be available in remote areas.

All the above mentioned modes of operation demand the existence of some backbone network (eHow, n.d.) within the range of the user transceiver which may not be available for rural areas in developing underdeveloped countries in general.

With high data rate, large network coverage, strong quality of service (QoS) capabilities and cheap network deployment and maintenance costs, wireless mesh networks can be a prospective solution for pervasive Internet access in a flexible and cost-effective way. The wireless mesh clients in the form of laptops or desktops, or PDAS or mobile phones may serve as the user terminals. Data from these terminals through WMN routers placed on rooftops may gather to a gateway in a local utility center, say a local school / college/ community library or an Internet kiosk. This gateway in turn connects the WMN with an existing wireless network like cellular/ Wi-Fi / Wi-Max etc. enabling the users to access Internet. The three important key features: the use of wireless transmission, the multi-hop communication between any pair of nodes, and the existence of multiple paths in WMNs make it appealing for providing Internet access where no other options can be applied due to the lack of infrastructure. Wireless transmission offers ubiquitous coverage for both mobile and stationary users whereas multi-hop communication reduces the maintenance cost and multi-path facility offers better reliability of wireless access to Internet. However, this concept of Internet access is still in a very nascent stage and is to be studied extensively with experimental set ups before it can culminate some practical and commercial implementations. Lot of design issues for WMN itself are yet to be resolved in a feasible way and especially its effectiveness in serving rural areas with the access of Internet involves a lot of challenges.

DESIGN ISSUES AND CHALLENGES

As it has been mentioned earlier, the nodes of a WMN may be of two types: mesh clients and mesh routers. Various user terminals such as desktops, laptops, PDA's, mobile phones equipped with wireless network interface cards can communicate directly with mesh routers. No communication backbone network is needed for that. Mesh routers with gateway / bridge functionalities can integrate the WMN with various other wireless networks in its vicinity like the cellular, Wi-Fi and WiMax networks. In rural areas where communication

infrastructure exists only at some remote places, it is possible to install mesh routers in some places like schools, health centers, libraries, local post offices, local police stations etc. to cover the region so that users can access Internet facilities using elementary and inexpensive user terminals like mobile phones or PDA's etc. as mesh clients. Finally some mesh routers which have access to any infrastructure based wireless networks, like cellular, or WiFi or WiMax networks can act as gateways and route the Internet traffic for the rest of the mesh network.

Deployment of WMNs can be done easily and incrementally incurring very little upfront cost. However, there are lots of crucial issues to be resolved before a WMN can serve our purpose of bringing Internet access to every corner of the world. The major concerns are: WMN lacks scalability. As the number of hops increases the throughput drops appreciably. In fact in all layers starting from physical up to the application layer, unresolved issues are there which should be addressed appropriately. Some of the important issues are highlighted below.

- **Radio Propagation:** Our objective is to extend the coverage of existing wireless networks without sacrificing the channel capacity and reliability. To increase the capacity (Gupta & Kumar, 2000) and efficiency of wireless networks, many advanced radio technologies (Bellfiore et al., 2002; Blostein & Lieb, 2003; Ramanathan et al., 2004) have been proposed so far such as directional and smart antennae, MIMO, reconfigurable radios, cognitive/ agile radios (Lane, 2003; McHenry, 2003) etc. to provide non-line-of-sight links between terminals, less interference and long range. It is obvious that some of these recent developments are still in their infancy. However, their implementations require associated changes in the MAC layer also. So, it definitely requires cross-layer redesign. Moreover, the physical layer transmission rate of a node in WMNs is much higher than that in any cellular networks. Depending on the density of mesh routers, the distances in each hop, the nature of media, the traffic pattern and the cost of user terminals, the suitable radio technology is to be adopted that can support the Internet access for heterogeneous terminals and networks.

- **Channel Allocation:** In most of the works on ad hoc networks, so far, a single channel communication is studied extensively. Since, multiple channels are usually available in the frequency band of a wireless transceiver, multiple channel usage may increase the capacity of the network (Gupta & Kumar, 2000; Ghosh, Sinha, & Das, 2003; Ghosh, Sinha, & Das, 2006). It is a well-known fact that the channel bandwidth is the most precious and the most contentious resource for wireless networks. However, FCC finds that about 70% of the allocated spectrum remains under utilized. Since in WMNs the users may be mobile in nature, it is difficult to estimate the traffic load and hence conventional static channel planning will not be suitable. On the contrary, the newly proposed viable frequency planning, namely the cognitive radio, or software defined radio (Lane, 2003; McHenry, 2003) may offer convenient paradigms for WMN. However, simultaneous communication via multiple transceivers using multiple channels may be of theoretical interest for enhancing the throughput of the system. But for Internet access applications, due to increased cost and complexity at the terminals it may not offer practical solutions unless inexpensive technologies come up.

- **Media Access:** For any other wireless networks, media access control is an important area of research for WMNs as well. Since,

WMNs are multi-hop networks without any central control, the media access control should be distributed in nature. Hence TDMA and CDMA are difficult to implement due to the requirement of synchronization in time (TDMA) or code (CDMA) which are hard to achieve in a large multihop distributed network. On the other hand the conventional distributed multiple access schemes like CSMA/CA has the demerits of low frequency reuse efficiency which in turn reduces the throughput of the network appreciably. For example, the widely used versions of IEEE 802.11 MAC protocol fail to achieve satisfactory throughput when the number of hops is just greater than or equal to 4 only (Zhu et al., 2004; Cali, Conti, & Gregori, 2000; eHow, n.d.). Therefore, for the Internet access via WMN, since our objective is to increase the network coverage through multihop paths, it is a great challenge to design appropriate MAC protocol that may overcome this serious limitation on number of hops in WMNs.

- **Routing:** Since WMNs are essentially ad hoc networks, the routing protocols developed for ad hoc networks (Johnson, Maltz, & Hu, 2004; Raniwala, Hopalan, & Chiueh, 2004; Draves, Padhye & Zill, 2004; Royer & Perkins, 2000) can be applied to it. However, since the mesh routers are in general less mobile and hence are devoid of power constraints simpler routing protocols can be adopted for mesh routers with more emphasis on the throughput and QoS. Another important concern is that in multihop routing the basic assumption is the cooperation among the nodes. The challenge is that in a commercial WMN for the Internet access how the pricing and billing are to be implemented. Also, in a wide public network how we can ensure cooperation without any fail (Santi, 2005).

- **Compatibility:** To make Internet accessible to remote areas the proposed solutions require that the WMNs should be integrated with various existing wireless networks such as IEEE 802.11, 802.16, 802.15 etc. It is obvious that the features of these networks may vary significantly. In this heterogeneous paradigm, integration is a challenging issue to maintain the performance of the overall system. Adaptive protocols are to be developed for various layers, the MAC layer, network layer and transport layer, to resolve the problem efficiently. For real-time delivery, in case of Internet services, no existing solution for ad hoc networks (Walker et al., 2010; Maltz, Broch, & Johnson, 2001; Lundgren et al., 2006) can be adopted and tailored due to the hybrid ad hoc and infrastructure based architecture of WMN. In fact no protocols in the lower layers can provide perfect support for the application layer. Therefore, to make existing Internet applications work efficiently under the architecture of proposed WMNs, it is a great challenge to develop efficient adaptive algorithms.

- **Scalability:** As it has been mentioned earlier, scalability is a vital issue for WMNs in general. As the size of the network in terms of number of hops increases, MAC protocols may result significant drop in throughput, routing protocols may fail to find routing paths and transport protocol may suffer frequent connection breaks. Moreover for Internet broadband services, besides the end-to-end delay various additional QoS requirements are to be fulfilled. Hence the protocols at different layers should take into consideration the performance metrics such as delay jitter, packet loss ratios, fault-tolerance, load balancing (Ganjali & Keshavarzian, 2004; Chatterjee & Das, in

press) etc. as well. Therefore, it is a great challenge to develop efficient algorithms for the application layers to satisfy the QoS requirements of real-time Internet applications on WMN.

RECENT ACTIVITIES

Since all the required components for WMN are readily available in the market in the form of IEEE 802.11 MAC protocol developed for ad hoc networks, in general, many testbeds (Walker et al., 2010; Sombrutzki et al., 2006; Aguayo et al., n.d.; BWN Lab, n.d.; Bucciol et al., 2007; ADHOCSYS, n.d.) have been established in educational research labs and industries. However, the testbeds are really very limited in size and the performance study on those hardly can be extrapolated to the real scenarios as is shown in Figure 2.

- **MIT's Roofnet:** To connect the Ethernet networks with Internet gateways using 50 wireless nodes in apartments in Cambridge, MA, the experimental set up Roofnet (Aguayo et al., n.d.) was developed. It required no configuration but that leads to long routing paths. Moreover, the radio links were often of poor quality. IEEE 802.11 b protocol shows that both average throughput and latency worsens drastically with the increase in the number of hops again proving the poor scalability of WMN.

- **BWN Mesh:** Georgia Institute of Technology designed the testbed based on IEEE 802.11b/g (BWN Lab, n.d.). It consists of 15 routers, many of them are connected to the next generation Internet testbed, wireless sensor network testbeds, Wi-fi and Wi-Max networks. The nodes were laptops and desktops situated in dif-

Figure 2. The gap between experimental facilities and implementation of future Internet

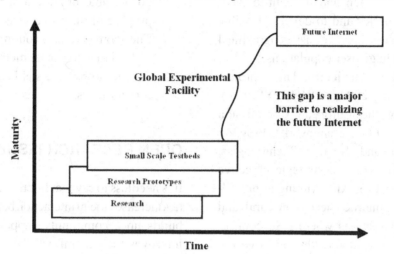

ferent rooms of the same floor. New adaptive protocols are developed and tested on this integrated network for routing, MAC layer and transport layer respectively.

- **MobiMESH Project:** This project started by ANTLab, Politecnico di Milano in 2004 to create an experimental platform for testing innovative solutions for routing and mobility management coupled with the goal of designing advanced mesh networking solutions and products for the market (MobiMesh, n.d.). It developed a complete Wireless Mesh platform with automatic node configuration, fast adaptive routing, multi-radio multi- frequency operation, and frequency aware and quality-aware route selection. It offered broadband and excellent VoIP services. The designed testbed can be extended to offer the ability to develop new features and tailor the product to customer needs in short time.

- **CICNet:** With the initial mission to provide information services to the major research universities in eight midwestern states of USA, CICNet has evolved to serve the information and connectivity needs of the entire region (Hankins, 1994).

With a large rural population in this area CICNet acts as a regional service provider with the assistance from Local Information Utility (LIU) centers, a means of access for every member of the community to local and community information resources and to the Internet. LIUs are built on existing local resources such as a district school, community center or a public library. Local institutions may initiate collaborative partnerships with local business groups, community coalitions, or even a local Internet Service Provider such as a telephone or cable television operator. With experience the LIUs will broaden their applications to integrate educational, business, cultural and governmental information resources. These local organizations, in turn, deals with regional service providers like CICNet providing low-cost access to information resources statewide. To achieve this goal, CICNet and other service providers should develop technical, human and capital resources to plan and implement the LIUs realistically. Through its Rural Datafication project CICNet attempts to strengthen the state networks to deliver Internet services in difficult-to-reach and difficult-to-serve user communities and to develop feasible solutions that scales to vast geographical regions and huge user populations.

- **ADHOCSYS Project:** This project (Bucciol et al., 2007; ADHOCSYS, n.d.), financed by the European Commission under the 6th Framework Program Information and Society Technologies, was initiated with the strategic objective of 'Broadband for All'. Aiming at providing reliable Internet access in rural and mountainous regions where DSL connections are not available due to coverage limit, the ADHOCSYS network provides a cost-effective solution based on multi-hop wireless mesh network technologies. In a typical ADHOCSYS architecture, the first tier backbone network is a standard multi-hop wireless network consisting of several long wireless links following IEEE 802.11 protocols, directional antennas and fine tuning. The second tier nodes act as access points for the end-users. It is basically a mesh access network which takes care of the physical (PHY) and Medium Access Control (MAC) layer issues in 802.11 wireless networks. The OLSR (Optimized Link State Routing) protocol is adopted with several enhancements implemented by the ADHOCSYS project. In order to validate the developed broadband access solution, a real-life operational wireless mesh network has been deployed in a mountainous region in Northern Italy. The performance of the developed solution has been evaluated based on the deployed real-life network. From the real-life network experiment it becomes evident that link stability is of critical importance for the proper functioning of a WMN and that traditional hop-count based routing would

not be able provide a stable path for the purpose of Internet access (Li et al., 2010). The conventional routing must be enhanced to incorporate metric-based routing in order to provide stable and reliable path for end-users.

OPEN RESEARCH ISSUES

It is needless to say that Internet use in communities increases social interaction between neighbors, builds up a community support structure, and improves the general well being of community residents. For extensive penetration into rural areas Wireless Mesh Networks can be disruptive to the current residential broadband Internet access paradigm, which relies solely on cable and DSL being deployed in individual homes. However, in the age of multiple competing wireless technologies, and naturally occurring environmental fluctuations, wireless multihop mesh networks continue to be the second option to wired networks in terms of robustness and capacity. In spite of that, in areas beyond the coverage of WISP's, wireless mesh networks may offer a low-cost solution for wireless Internet access. However, enough commercial applications and value are to be added to attract neighborhood communities to universally adopt such networks in a wide-scale. Over and above this, some fundamental issues are yet to be resolved before WMN's for the Internet access can be made commercially viable.

In WMN's, like any other ad hoc networks, a basic assumption is that all nodes cooperate unconditionally to forward others packets whenever necessary. However, it is well known from economy that in a competitive environment, humans tend to act selfishly in order to protect their individual interests.

Let us consider a typical scenario where a single access point (AP) exists to offer wireless

Internet access to the users via multihop WMN. For successful implementation, it is assumed that whenever a new user intends to join the network (not within the range of the AP), users already accessing the service must cooperate to forward its packets to and from the AP. However, the connected nodes, in principle, will be interested to drop its packets since a new user joining the network will consume the network resources like energy, bandwidth etc. causing a drop in the QoS of the existing users. This selfish node behavior can have a dramatic impact on the network performance unless adequate measures are taken at the design stage.

It is quite challenging to develop techniques to stimulate and ensure cooperation among the competitive nodes of the network. The most natural way for this is to give incentives for data forwarding, either in the form of *reputation* (Buchegger & LeBoude, 2002; Michiardi & Molva, 2002), or *money transfer* (Buttyán & Hubaux, 2003). In the former case, each node will be monitored by its neighboring nodes, and the selfish nodes will be excluded. So, a rational node, in general, prefers to forward packets to avoid the risk of being excluded. By the second approach, a node willing to send a packet via some intermediate node must pay money to the relay nodes for their service. However, robust protocols are to be developed, especially for the Internet access WMN's where it is really hard to ensure cooperation due to the most unpredictable and variable nature of users.

Also, to build up a commercial system for Internet access via WMN's, *truthfulness* of the system (Santi, 2005) is to be guaranteed to the users. In this system, when a new customer subscribes to the service, the provider will give a 'users kit' which implements the routing protocol used for establishing the connection along with many more service options. The subscriber has to pay, say a fixed monthly fee, along with a variable per connection cost, also a customer can earn money when it forwards others packets. A selfish user might be tempted to manipulate his user's kit to maximize his profit. The protocol must be such that it is in the interest of the service provider, to give the customer every details of the payment scheme and to convince the users that cheating is in no way profitable.

In the literature, game theory based models are developed to resolve the problem of routing and data forwarding or any other network wide operations assuming that the nodes are rational and truthful. However, in a real network application scenario, like the Internet, it is quite challenging to develop appropriate model where the assumptions are hardly true.

CONCLUSION

The self-organized and self-configured WMN seems to offer a feasible solution for expanding the Internet access facility in rural areas beyond the coverage of backbone infrastructure. With Internet as the starting point, we can promote a large number of enterprises which can enable the rural micro enterprise flourish in rural areas to improve their quality of life. Some academic research labs and industries have already developed and tested experimental set ups. However the field results reveal the fact that still the performance are far below the satisfactory level. From the experience of CICNet or ADHOCSYS projects it is clear that many open research issues are still there that demand innovations in protocols at different layers and perfect integration. The research works and related experimental or testbed results infer that WMN with its unique features seems to be a promising solution to provide next generation Internet access to areas that are too remote to receive it via cable or DSL, or where upgrading the landlines to broadband is highly cost-prohibitive. But to make a successful implementation of it a lot of challenges related to radio link instability, link-metric based routing, QoS provisioning, self-configuration, self-healing, security, energy source, reliability prediction, guaranteed cooperation and truthfulness of the system etc. are still to be addressed and resolved in coming days.

REFERENCES

ADHOCSYS. (n.d.). *Website*. Retrieved from http://www.adhocsys.org

Adya, A., Bahl, P., Padhye, J., Wolman, A., & Zhou, L. (2004). *A multiradio unification protocol for IEEE 802.11 wireless networks*. IEEE BroadNets 2004.

Aguayo, D., Bicket, J., Biswas, S., De Couto, D. S. J., & Morris, R. (n.d.). *MIT roofnet implementation*. Retrieved from http:// pdos.lcs.mit.edu/ roofnet/ design/

Akyildiz, F., Su, W., Sankarasubramaniam, Y., & Cayirci, E. (2002). Wireless sensor networks: A survey. *Computer Networks*, *38*(4), 393–422. doi:10.1016/S1389-1286(01)00302-4

Akyildiz, I. F., Wang, X., & Wang, W. (2005). Wireless mesh networks: A survey. *Computer Networks*, *47*(4), 445–487. doi:10.1016/j.comnet.2004.12.001

Bahl, P., Chandra, R., & Dunagan, J. (2004). SSCH: Slotted seeded channel hopping for capacity improvement in IEEE 802.11 ad hoc wireless networks. *ACM Annual International Conference on Mobile Computing and Networking* (MOBICOM), 2004, (pp. 216-230).

Bellfiore, S., Foutz, Y., Govindaradjula, R., Bahceci, I., Balanis, C. A., & Spanias, A. S., Duman, T. M. (2002). Smart antenna system analysis, integration and performance for mobile ad hoc networks (MANETs). *IEEE Transactions on Antennas and Propagation*, *50*(5), 571–581. doi:10.1109/TAP.2002.1011222

Blostein, S. D., & Lieb, H. (2003). Multiple antenna systems: Their role and impact in future wireless access. *IEEE Communications Magazine*, *2003*, 94–101. doi:10.1109/MCOM.2003.1215645

Bruno, R., Conti, M., & Gregori, E. (2005). Mesh networks: Commodity multihop ad hoc networks. *IEEE Communications Magazine*, *43*(3), 123–131. doi:10.1109/MCOM.2005.1404606

Bucciol, P., De Martin, J. C., Vandoni, L., Zicca, G., Giani, G. M., & Giulini, M. (2007). S*pecifi. cation of algorithms for static reconfiguration of ad-hoc network, and multimedia services,* final version ADHOCSY.S project. *Deliverable, D14,* IST-2004–IST-026548.

Buchegger, S., & LeBoude, J. (2002). Performance analysis of the confidant protocol: Cooperation of nodes- Fairness in dynamic ad hoc networks. *Proceedings of ACM Mobihoc*, 2002, (pp. 9-19).

Buttyán, L., & Hubaux, J. (2003). Stimulating cooperation in self-organizing mobile ad hoc networks. *Mobile Networks and Applications*, *8*(5), 579–592. doi:10.1023/A:1025146013151

Cali, F., Conti, M., & Gregori, E. (2000). Dynamic tuning of the IEEE 802.11 protocol to achieve a theoretical throughput limit. *IEEE/ ACM Transactions on Networking*, *8*(6), 785–799. doi:10.1109/90.893874

Chatterjee, P., & Das, N. (in press). On load-balanced data gathering techniques for lifetime maximization in wireless sensor networks. To appear, *Wireless Sensor Networks*. Nova Science Publishers. *Inc.*

Draves, R., Padhye, J., & Zill, B. (2004). *Routing in multi-radio multi-hop wireless mesh networks*. ACM MobiCom, Philadelphia, PA, September 2004. eHow. (n.d.). *How to get high speed Internet access in rural areas*. Retrieved from http:// www. ehow.com/ how_4792750_speed-internet- access-rural-areas.html

Ganjali, Y., & Keshavarzian, A. (2004). Load balancing in ad hoc networks: Single path routing vs. multipath routing. INFOCOM, March 2004, (pp. 1120-1125).

Ghosh, S. C., Sinha, B. P., & Das, N. (2003). Channel assignment using genetic algorithm based on geometric symmetry. *IEEE Transactions on Vehicular Technology*, *52*(4), 860–875. doi:10.1109/TVT.2003.808806

Ghosh, S. C., Sinha, B. P., & Das, N. (2006). Coalesced CAP: An improved technique for frequency assignment in cellular networks. *IEEE Transactions on Vehicular Technology*, *55*(2), 640–653. doi:10.1109/TVT.2005.863351

Gupta, P., & Kumar, P. R. (2000). The capacity of wireless networks. *IEEE Transactions on Information Theory*, *46*(2), 388–404. doi:10.1109/18.825799

Hankins, J. L. (1994). The CICNet rural datafication project: Extending network access and services. *Internet Research*, *4*(1), 71–74. doi:10.1108/10662249410798858

Huang, L., & Lai, T. (2002). On the scalability of IEEE 802.11 ad hoc networks. *ACM International Symposium on Mobile Ad Hoc Networking and Computing* (MOBIHOC), 2002, (pp. 173-182).

Intel. (n.d.). Mesh networks demonstrations. Retrieved from http:// www.intel.com/ idf/ us/ fall2003/ presentations/ F03USWNTS116_OS.pdf

Ishmael, J., Bury, S., Pezaros, D., & Race, N. (2008). Deploying rural community wireless mesh networks. *IEEE Internet Computing*, *12*(4), 22–29. doi:10.1109/MIC.2008.76

Johnson, D. B., Maltz, D. A., Hu, Y.-C. (2004). *The dynamic source routing protocol for mobile ad hoc networks (DSR)*. IETF Internet-Draft: work in progress, July 2004.

Ko, B.-J., Misra, V., Padhye, J., & Rubenstein, D. (2007). *Distributed channel assignment in multi-radio 802.11 mesh networks*. IEEE WCNC 2007, Hong Kong, China, March 2007.

Lab, B. W. N. (n.d.). *Wireless mesh networks research project*. Retrieved from http:// www.ece. gatech.edu/ research/ labs/ bwn/ mesh/

Lane, B. (2003). *Cognitive radio technologies in the commercial arena*. In FCC Workshop on Cognitive Radios, May 2003.

Li, F. Y., Bucciol, P., Vandoni, L., Fragoulis, N., Zanoli, S., Leschiutta, L., & Lázaro, O. (2010). *Broadband Internet access via multi-hop wireless mesh networks: Design, protocol and experiments*. Wireless Personal Communication, January, Springer.

Lundgren, H. (2006). Experiences from the design, deployment and usage of the UCSB testbed. *IEEE Wireless Communications*, *13*(2), 18–29. doi:10.1109/MWC.2006.1632477

Maltz, D. A., Broch, J., & Johnson, D. B. (2001). Lessons from a fullscale multihop wireless ad hoc network testbed. *IEEE Personal Communication*, *8*(1), 8–15.

Maza, S., Lazaro, O., Cunha, N., Vandoni, L., & Li, F. Y. (2005). *Broadband access via ad hoc networks: A solution for rural and mountain regions*. Broadband Europe Conference, Bordeaux, France, Dec. 2005.

McHenry, M. (2003). *Frequency agile spectrum access technologies*. In FCC Workshop on Cognitive Radios, May 2003.

Michiardi, P., & Molva, R. (2002). Core: A collaborative repudiation mechanism to enforce node cooperation in mobile ad hoc networks. *Proceedings of IFIP Conference on Security, Communications and Multimedia*, 2002, Washington, DC.

Microsoft. (n.d.). Mesh networks. Retrieved from http://research.microsoft.com/ mesh/

MobiMesh. (n.d.). *MS Thesis on MobiMesh.* Retrieved from www.mobimesh.eu/ index. php?option= com_content&task

Poslad, S. (2009). *Ubiquitous computing: Smart devices, environments and interactions.* Wiley.

Ramanathan, R., Redi, J., Santivanez, C., Wiggins, D., & Polit, S. (2004). Ad hoc networking with directional antennas: A complete system solution. In *IEEE Wireless Communications and Networking Conference* (WCNC), 2004, (pp. 375–380).

Raniwala, A., Hopalan, K., & Chiueh, T. (2004). Centralized channel assignment and routing algorithms for multi-channel wireless mesh networks. *ACM Mobile Computing and Communications Review, 8*(2), 50–65. doi:10.1145/997122.997130

Royer, E., & Perkins, C. E. (2000). An implementation study of the AODV routing protocol. *Proceedings Wireless Communication and Networking Conference,* (pp. 1003–1008). IEEE Press.

Santi, P. (2005). *Topology control in wireless ad hoc and sensor networks.* John Wiley & Sons Ltd. doi:10.1002/0470094559

Sombrutzki, R., et al. (2006). Self-organization in community mesh networks: The Berlin roofnet. *Proceedings of the 1st Workshop on Operator-Assisted (Wireless Mesh) Community Networks,* (pp. 1–11). IEEE Press.

Walker, B., Seastrom, J., Lee, G., & Lin, K. (2010). Addressing scalability in a laboratory-based multihop wireless testbed. *Journal Mobile Networks and Applications, 15*(3).

Zhu, H. (2004). A survey of quality of service in IEEE 802.11 networks. *IEEE Wireless Communications, 11*(4), 4–14.

Chapter 16

Smart Rooms:
A Framework for Inferencing Using Semantic Web Technology in Ambient Intelligent Network

Biplab K. Sarker
University of New Brunswick, Canada

Julian Descottes
University of New Brunswick, Canada

Mohsin Sohail
University of New Brunswick, Canada

Rama Krishna Kosaraju
University of New Brunswick, Canada

ABSTRACT

In this chapter, the authors present a framework to provide useful and accurate information to users based on data collected from rooms in a building comprised of wireless sensor networks. The authors call a room "smart room" when a room is considered suitable for a particular purpose. For instance, a dark room for a conference, a bright room for a party, et cetera, which can be determined according to the data available from various positions of sensors located in each room and a sensor network of a building. The authors undertook the task of designing a semantic inferencing framework for a smart room. This led to automatic extraction of information from the central repository or even when the data is in a transient state (dynamic) in the network. The chapter discusses a practical way of building a query system using semantic Web technology and tools. Similar systems are becoming more feasible nowadays, and industrial leaders are moving forward to build them from commercial view point. The chapter is concluded with some future directions of the system.

DOI: 10.4018/978-1-4666-0203-8.ch016

INTRODUCTION

Semantic web technologies are getting more attractions due to the large number of open sourced tools available nowadays. Big vendors like Google, Microsoft, Yahoo have started to consider using this technology in their products to better produce query results for end users. Semantic web technology has huge applicability in information retrieval systems, decision support systems and recommender systems. The main advantages of using the technology is to make the software agents to understand the problem/domain space based on some facts from semi-structured/structured data and thus extract some new facts with the power of inferencing. Thus, it helps to reduce work load of human being which is practically very time consuming or sometimes impossible.

Wireless Sensor Networks (WSN) have become more prevalent in both the industrial and commercial market. The reason for this prevalence is due to various factors which include miniaturization of electronic components, better transport layer protocols and low energy access protocols. A lot of the success is also contributed towards the open source Operating System, called TinyOS (Satyanarayanan, 2002), that sensors have installed on them. Such networks are used for remote environment monitoring, surveillance, industrial automation, civil and structural analysis (Remagnino & Forest, 2005). These networks are designed to be integrated in the human surroundings in such a way that they are un-noticeable. Additionally, the number of sensors present in a target environment can exceed 1000 sensors easily as they can be placed anywhere and hence, give the overall environment the characteristic of any-where-any-time information. The data from all these sensors is received by a central gateway and then processed for information on the basis of which reactions might occur. For example, the temperature of a room can be constantly monitored through temperature sensors throughout the room and on the basis of this data decisions

can be made in how to control the HVAC system for the room. It can be seen that WSN inherently generate a large amount of data which has to be stored at a central repository. In order to make efficient and quick use of this data, Semantic Web techniques can be used to enable machines/computers to "understand" the data. This can lead to the automatic extraction of information from the central repository or even when the data is in a transient state in the network.

This chapter describes a framework for Semantic Inferencing that we proposed. It also gives an overview of the various tools that we have used to automate the process of the creation of our framework. The next section of the chapter describes the steps involved in this process. The section following that describes the 'sensor network ontology' which is considered as the backbone of this framework. The data mapping mechanism (i.e. data that are collected from sensor networks) for the ontology to create a knowledge base is presented in the fourth section. The section after that describes the transformation of fact and rules in RuleML and the inferencing process with some sample queries. Finally, we discussed on some of our future works.

SMART ROOM FRAMEWORK

The steps to create a framework and tools used are given below (see also Figure 1).

1. The very first part of the framework is the creation of Ontology. In this part the concepts used in our application are defined and arranged in a conceptual hierarchy. The Ontology creation was done by a tool from Altova called *SemanticWorks*.
2. This second part was the instance document creation. In other words, ontology has to be populated with data which are called here as instances. So, once the Ontology is available, the next step is to create an instance

Figure 1. The Smart Room framework and tools used

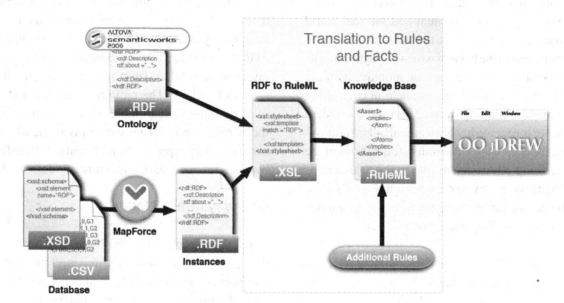

document based on it. Most of the data in an ambient intelligent environment is quiet dynamic and usually occupied a large database. Hence, it is required to create a system which could automatically extract data from such databases and map it onto the ontology classes. In order to achieve this goal in an automated and efficient manner another Altova tool called *MapForce* is used.

3. The third part of the framework is to create a knowledge base based on a pool of rules and facts, from the instance document. This required the conversion of the document into a format that could be understood by the inference engine easily. In order to achieve this goal and to use RuleML as the language for creation of the knowledge base, an XSLT is created to perform the conversion from the instance document to RuleML facts and rules.

4. Finally, OOjDrew was used as the inference engine. This section would take queries in a *Prolog* fashion and respond with answers based on the knowledge base created in the previous step.

THE SMART ROOM ONTOLOGY

In order to better understand the ontology of the Semantic smart room domain in a ambient intelligent environment, the background in Wireless Sensor Networks (WSN) is necessary. It is not possible to create a complete Ontology with a complete understanding of the domain at hand. Hence, the first part of this section discussed a brief background on wireless sensor networks which play an integral role in the ontology.

Background

WSN have played an integral role in the realization of Mark Wiser's vision of ubiquitous computing (Weiser, 1995). His envisioned the seamless integration of the computing worlds into the "fabric of reality" so that their presence could not be detected and their role would no longer be obtrusive. The nature of such a computing environment also needed to be proactive and not reactive. For all these to occur many building blocks are needed one of which is WSN.

Such networks act as the connection between the computing environment and the real world (Figure 2). They provide the facilities of sensing parameters on the basis of which pro-active events can occur for e.g. the constant monitoring of the temperature of the room can help in controlling the air-conditioning system in a more efficient manner in order to lower electrical bills. Additionally, these networks also translate decisions of the computing environment into real world actions (actuators). It can be clearly seen that WSN are integral for the implementation of a ubiquitous environment (Satyanarayanan, 2002).

WSN are based on three basic building blocks:
1. Radio modules
2. Gateways/Base Nodes
3. Sensor Nodes

Radio Modules

Radio modules form the basic building block of a WSN (Figure 3). They are small computing devices that have limited processing, storage and wireless transmission capabilities. The radio modules

Figure 2. Typical topological view of a WSN (Crossbow Manuals (Crossbow, n.d.))

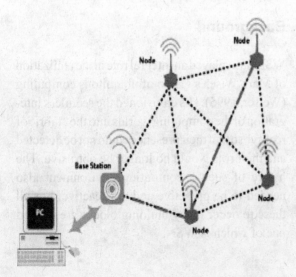

are disturbed throughout the area that has to be monitored or analyzed. These modules then autonomously create a topology amongst themselves so that messages/packets can be transferred from one point to another. This topology is essentially a Mesh topology. The radio modules are a part of every other node of the WSN as they provide the Wireless transmission capability to the whole network. They support bi-directional data transfer between the base station and other nodes.

Gateways/Base Nodes

A WSN gateway is a Radio Node attached to a device that is capable of transferring/translating the packets from the WSN to another network/protocol (Figure 3). An example would be to receive data from a particular node and then translating it from the Sensor network protocol to the TCP/IP protocol so it can be transferred over the Internet. These gateways are connected to networks that are not as resource constrained as the sensor network. One of the criteria's for an efficient sensor network is a multi-year battery life. In order to achieve this, the computationally intensive tasks can be transferred over from the WSN through the base station into a more computationally powerful network where energy consumption is not a constraint.

Sensor Nodes

A WSN Sensor node is a Radio Node attached to a device that is capable of sensing various parameters in the target environment (Figure 3). The sensor nodes are responsible for the monitoring of physical parameters such as temperature, humidity, pressure etc. and then converting them into a format (analog-to-digital) that can transferred over the WSN over multiple-hops towards the base station. Without the sensor nodes there would be no information for the network to work on and hence, the sensor nodes are an important part of the WSN.

One of the key features of WSN is the ability to self-configure them into a network without any human intervention. Additionally, they are also capable of self-healing themselves if one of the radio modules goes down due to a malfunction. Such networks self-configure them in such a way that packets can be routed to other nodes or base stations through the shortest path.

Figure 3. (Top) MIB 520 ethernet gateway, (Middle) MPR2400 Radio Module, (Bottom) MTS420 sensor module. (All figures have been taken from Crossbow's website (Crossbow, n.d.))

Ontology Building Process

As it has been stated before the sensor is an integral part an ambient intelligent network and from the previous background we clearly understand what a sensor can be composed of. So with this knowledge we can create the conceptual design of a sensor and it's parts. In Figure 4, it can be seen that every sensor is made of a gateway, data acquisition modules or a radio module. Furthermore the sensor Node itself is a subclass of Sensor family which would have a particular vendor, ID and model name.

Furthermore each of the Sensor types are explained in detail as well. Notice that the concepts(also known as classes) keep going into depth and will eventually end up with atomic data types such as strings or integers. In this case, the data acquisition modules have a parameter associated to them that they measure and the parameter has a value as well as a standard unit associated with it as well.

Now all the above mentioned concepts/classes make up the Sensor network. However, there is a particular condition that needs to be satisfied if a sensor network needs to work properly. We realized that every node in a wireless network has to have a radio module otherwise it will have no way of being a part for the sensor network. In other words a sensor network cannot have a node that does not have a radio module associated with it. This restriction was quite interesting and was difficult to develop in the ontology. Eventually, we were able to make this restriction work successfully.

The ontology that we have created is composed of two distinct parts: the room artifacts and the sensor network. Now that we have explained the desired concepts of the sensor network we move to the room artifacts. In order to keep the overall ontology simple, we did not make the objects too complicated. We just dealt with two types of objects (Chairs and Lights) in this case.

Figure 4. Ontological view of sensor nodes

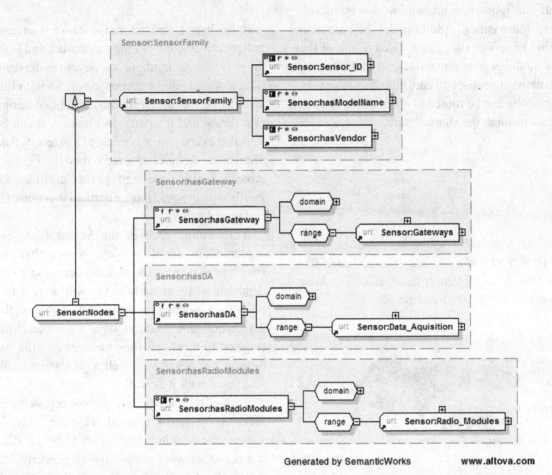

Generated by SemanticWorks   www.altova.com

It can be noticed that every object is also associated with a sensor node. This senor node is responsible for keeping a note of the context of the object so that the database can be populated with the information about it. Finally, we present the overall Ontology (in the form of various instances) in which we show a particular room with various objects and a sensor network (Figure 5).

INSTANCE DOCUMENT GENERATION

In order to have a practical system, we have to look at the problem from the data source perspective as well. A sensor network generates tremendous amount of data, and in order to keep this data we can use large Relational Database Management Systems (RDBMS). To create a practical semantic application, this data has to be integrated in a way that is suitable for easy extraction. Now we have the ontology, we have to create an instance document by mapping the elements in the ontology with the corresponding elements in the database. In order to do so a mapping mechanism is needed between the ontology concepts and the database. On the basis of this mapping an instance document can be generated which is populated with the fields from the database. These instances along with RDF will be used in making Rules and Facts. To generate the instance document we have decided to use a tool called Altova MapForce.

Figure 5. Ontological view of a Smart Room

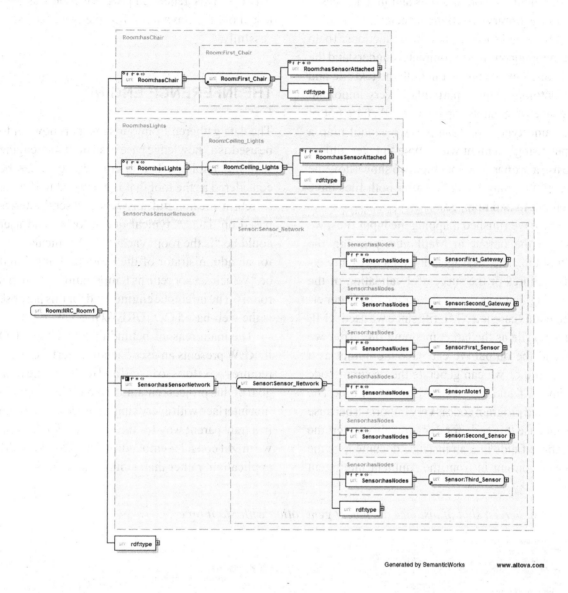

Generated by SemanticWorks   www.altova.com

MapForce

MapForce is a powerful visual tool for building web services and integrating the most prevalent data formats like XML, database and flat files. MapForce maps the contents of one component with the contents of another component. An XML, or text document, a database, or EDI file, can be mapped to a different target XML document, CSV text document, EDI file, or database. Databases as well as EDI documents can also be used as data sources, and map data to multiple XML Schemas, EDI documents, or other databases.

In order to achieve the desired mapping two sources are needed, namely, the database and the Schema File. In our project, to make things simple as possible we created a CSV file as our database for the sensors with mock up data. This CSV file acts as the first source of data in MapForce. Then we insert the XML Schema file. This is the target file. After we insert both the input files in the MapForce we start mapping the corresponding elements in both the files and in many cases by using library functions, special component/structures and some user defined functions. To do the mapping one has to completely understand the type of elements present in both the text file and the ontology. This is particularly very important because we cannot map elements that are not of the same type. For example, we cannot map a type 'string' element with a type 'integer' unless we use a proper function. Figure 6 shows how the overall mapping looks like after both files have been put in and mapped.

Once we finished mapping the input files, we viewed the output in MapForce. pressing the output tab. The message pane tells us of any errors, failures or the successful validation of the mapping that was done. The output that is generated in this case is a XML file since we used XML Schema file as the target mapping file. After we viewed the output we can save the output as a XML file or we can generate the program code in Java, C# and C++ from Altova MapForce The generated program code is very important because we can use this code for dynamically convert the database fields into an instance document as the data is coming in from the Ambient intelligent

network. This generated program code was then tested out in a Java platform like NetBeans successfully.

THE INFERENCE ENGINE

The data gathered from our sensors is now set to be used as a knowledge base in an inference engine with the ontology. The inference engine can be considered as the tool that is supposed to be able to return meaningful answers to users' queries based on data. A typical query for an end-user could be "Is the room vacant ?". A typical query for an administrator of the room/building could be "Which sensor returns temperature data in this room". The inference engine used for this purpose is the web-based OO jDREW(jDREW, n.d.).

The main reasons behind the choice that OO jDREW presents an user friendly interface and it requires no efforts to install and to run it. The final goal of this project remains to have a full application interface with every single part described here in a transparent way for the end user. So, later on we might consider embedding OO jDREW in the application, rather than simply using it.

Figure 6. Screen shot of instance document generation with MapForce

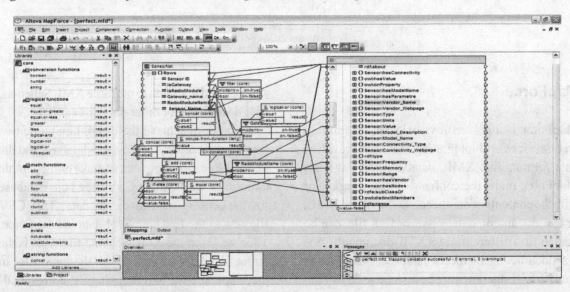

Interfacing the Altova Tools and OOjDREW

The previous sections showed how we managed to use Altova tools to create RDF instances (RDF file) describing the data coming from the sensors, as well as the ontology of the sensor network and the room. However the inference engine, OOjDREW can not directly read from RDF files in order to populate it's knowledgebase. Thus, a translation step is necessary, from the RDF files to rules and facts in an OOjDr\eW supported language.. OOjDREW allows to use either POSL (POsitional SLotted language) or RuleML to describe a knowledge base. The rule language chosen for this project is RuleML. Below are two simple examples of the kind of transformation required in this regard.

The 'facts' extracted from an RDF file is created by Altova's Mapforce. The 'rules' extracted from the ontology is created by Altova's Semantic Works. The content of the ontology is supposed to be static to a certain extent, so the translation of the ontology to RuleML could be done manually. However, that can not be done with the files coming from Mapforce, since they're supposed to be generated dynamically. Since automated translation was necessary for one part of the RDF files, it was decided to translate all the files automatically. The tool chosen for this conversion is XSLT. It is particularly useful to the task described here: turn one XML format into another XML format. Plus, XSLT is easy to interface in java, so it will integrate well in a full application.

Figure 7. Inside the rdf:RDF element

From RDF to RuleML using XSLT

In order to understand how this XSLT program works, it is necessary to understand how the RDF files are structured. Both topics are going to be detailed in parallel. Our RDF document can be considered as a collection of rdf:Description elements encapsulated in a rdf:RDF element. Thus the first thing that is done by the program is to reach that rdf:RDF element (Figure 7). That is done in Box 1.

Inside the RDF: RDF Element

The main element of an RDF file is the rdf:RDF element. It has a collection of rdf:Description as children. Once the "rdf:RDF" element has been

Box 1.

```
<xsl:template match="rdf:RDF">
        <Assert>
                <And mapClosure="universal">
                        <xsl:call-template name="t_descr"/>
                </And>
        </Assert>
</xsl:template>
```

detected, we have to go through every "rdf:Description" child. That part is done using "<xsl:for-each select="rdf:Description">" as demonstrated in Box 2:This "for-each" calls a template named "get_type" for each Description element. At that time we already extract the name of the object this rdf:Description is about. It can either be the name of an instance, of a class. It is stored in the ItemName parameter and it is going to be passed to every template used after this point. From now on the XSLT templates are quite large and won't be inserted here for readability.

A child of the "rdf:RDF" element is a Description element which is either about an instance or a class. The job of the template "get_type" is to figure out whether the Description element is about an instance or a class. Since instances are using a different namespace (such as "Sensor" in "Sensor:Sensor_ID"), if the element has a child with a name starting with something different from "rdf" or "rdfs", then it has to be an instance. Then the element is forwarded to the template managing instances. Otherwise, it's a class.

Inside the Description of a Class

Since the only class rule we are generating for the time being is the one coming from "subClassOf" relations, we simply extract the "rdfs:subClassOf" element from the children of the node if it exists. Then it's forwarded to the template managing "subClassOf" rules.

The last template simply has to extract the name of the class contained in the "rdf:Description" child of the "rdfs:subClassOf" element. See Box 3.

The "Data_Aquisition" name has been passed as a parameter to the template (Figure 8). So this template is now able to build an output (Box 4).

Inside the Description of an Instance

On the other hand, if it is an instance we're dealing with, it means that the content of the node is a set of facts describing the instance (Figure 9). See Box 5 for instance.

Even though it is describing an instance, there is still a little processing to do. Every child cor-

---

Box 2.

```
<xsl:template name="t_descr">
        <xsl:for-each select="rdf:Description">
                <xsl:call-template name="get_type">
                        <xsl:with-param name='ItemName'
                                         select="substring-after(@
rdf:about,$fpath)"/>
                </xsl:call-template>
        </xsl:for-each>
</xsl:template>
```

Box 3.

```
<rdf:Description rdf:about="Data_Aquisition">
        <rdfs:subClassOf>
                <rdf:Description rdf:about="SensorFamily"/>
        </rdfs:subClassOf>
</rdf:Description>
```

```
Box 4.

<Implies>
        <Atom>
                <Rel>Data_Aquisition</Rel>
                <Var>X</Var>
        </Atom>
     <Atom>
                <Rel>SensorFamily</Rel>
                <Var>X</Var>
        </Atom>
</Implies>
```

responds to a fact that is going to have a RuleML output. First of all, the "rdf:type" child corresponds to the class of the instance. This element will have the output shown in Box 6.

All the other facts are turned into binary facts as seen in Box 7.

Using XSLT with Java

As said before, this XSLT can easily be used in Java. Below is a simple Java program which uses the library "javax.xml.transform". It simply translates the file "SensorNet.rdf" to "SensorNet.ruleml" using "rdfToRuleML.xsl".

```
public class transformed {
    public static void main(String[] args)  throws TransformerException,
    TransformerConfigurationException, FileNotFoundException, IOException
    {
        String inputFile = "SensorNet.rdf";
        String xslFile = "rdfToRuleML.xsl";
        String outputFile = "SensorNet.ruleml";
    TransformerFactory tFactory = TransformerFactory.newInstance();
        Transformer transformer =
                    tFactory.newTransformer(new StreamSource(xslFile));
        transformer.transform(new StreamSource(inputFile),
                    new StreamResult(new FileOutputStream(outputFile)));
    }
}
```

Querying the Sensor Network

The file obtained after the execution of the java program is ready to be parsed by OOjDREW. Without going through an useless tutorial of OOjDREW, below are simply the steps required before querying OOjDREW.

- Copy/Paste the RuleML file in the Knowledge Base field of OOjDREW.
- Check that the "RuleML 0.88" checkbox is checked.
- Click "Parse Knowledge Base"

After that, queries can be executed on the knowledge base. For the time being, we mainly used it to check the coherence of the sensor network. Below is a set of queries about the nature of the sensor network available. All the queries are written in POSL.

Sample Query #1

Sensor_Networks(?x).

This query asks which sensor networks are available. Our current test environment contains one sensor network, called "Sensor_Network".

Answer for Query #1

```
$top():-Sensor_Networks(Sensor_Network).
    Sensor_Networks(Sensor_Network).
```

Figure 8. Inside the description of a class

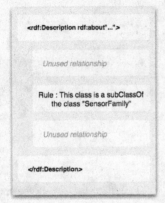

Figure 9. Inside the description of an instance

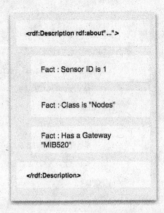

Box 5.

```
<rdf:Description rdf:about="Third_Sensor">
        <Sensor:hasDA>
                <rdf:Description rdf:about="MTS310_Sensor2"/>
        </Sensor:hasDA>
        <rdf:type>
                <rdf:Description rdf:about="Nodes"/>
        </rdf:type>
        <Sensor:Sensor_ID>4</Sensor:Sensor_ID>
        <Sensor:hasRadioModules>
                <rdf:Description rdf:about="MICAz"/>
        </Sensor:hasRadioModules>
</rdf:Description>
```

Box 6.

```
<Atom>
        <Rel>Nodes</Rel>
        <Ind>Third_Sensor</Ind>
</Atom>
```

Box 7.

```
<Atom>
        <Rel>Sensor_ID</Rel>
        <Ind>Third_Sensor</Ind>
        <Ind>4</Ind>
</Atom>
```

Sample Query #2

Sensor_Networks(?x), hasNodes(?x,?y).

This query also asks for the sensor networks available, but also wants the nodes contained in this sensor network.

Answer for Query #2

The sensor network contains five nodes for the time being and the query returns five answers of the same form as below such as First_Gateway... Fifth_Gateway

```
$top():-Sensor_Networks(Sensor_Network),hasNodes(Sensor_Network, First_Gateway).
    Sensor_Networks(Sensor_Network).
    hasNodes(Sensor_Network, First_Gateway).
$top():-Sensor_Networks(Sensor_Network),hasNodes(Sensor_Network, Fifth_Gateway).
    Sensor_Networks(Sensor_Network).
        hasNodes(Sensor_Network, Fifth_Gateway).
```

Sample Query #3

```
Sensor_Networks(?x), hasNodes(?x,?y),
    hasGateway(?y,?z), Sensor_ID(?y,?w).
```

This time the query is more precise. We are only querying about the nodes that have a gateway. And for such nodes, we want to display the ID.

Answer for Query #3

The sensor network contains 2 nodes which have a Gateway: First Gateway with ID 0 (Figure 10) and Second Gateway with ID 2 (Figure 11).

```
$top():-Sensor_Networks(Sensor_Network),hasNodes(Sensor_Network,
    First_Gateway),hasGateway(First_Gateway,
    MIB520_Gateway),Sensor_ID(First_Gateway, 0).
```
- Sensor_Networks(Sensor_Network).
- hasNodes(Sensor_Network, First_Gateway).
- hasGateway(First_Gateway, MIB520_Gateway).
- Sensor_ID(First_Gateway, 0).

```
$top():-Sensor_Networks(Sensor_Network),hasNodes(Sensor_Network,
    Second_Gateway),hasGateway(Second_Gateway,
    MIB600_Gateway),Sensor_ID(Second_Gateway, 0).
```
- Sensor_Networks(Sensor_Network).
- hasNodes(Sensor_Network, Second_Gateway).
- hasGateway(Second_Gateway, MIB600_Gateway).
- Sensor_ID(Second_Gateway, 0).

Sample Query #4 (Box 8)

For example the Sensor #0, has connectivity problems with it's gateway. One can simply check the webpage of the connection used by the gateway through this query. The only input from the user is the ID of the sensor. Then the relationships established in the ontology are sufficient to go through all the facts of the knowledge base and to find the URL, the user is interested in.

Answer for Query #4

```
$top():-Sensor_ID(First_Gateway, 0),hasGateway(First_Gateway, MIB520_Gateway),
    hasConnectivity(MIB520_Gateway,USB),Connectivity_Webpage(USB,www.usb.com).
    Sensor_ID(First_Gateway, 0).
    hasGateway(First_Gateway, MIB520_Gateway).
    hasConnectivity(MIB520_Gateway, USB).
        Connectivity_Webpage(USB, www.usb.com).
```

CONCLUSION AND FUTURE WORK

Our main objective in this project was to build a semantic inferencing framework that can give us meaningful results of the query as much precious/accurate as possible. Our results showed that we achieved them to some extent and got useful answers. However, in our system, the queries have to be typed in a certain way or in a specific format. So, the queries and the results may not be very useful to an end user or a user must be trained in advance for the purpose. To overcome this constraint is one of our main future goal. We also plan to check the suitability of new inferencing/reasoning engine such as 'Pellet' and 'RacerPro' and' Sparql' query language for the purpose

We also built a fully automated process between a data file and an inferencing engine, using semantic web tools and techniques. To make our system better, we will concentrate further on creation of new rules in the system. We will start to define them manually and eventually will introduce a way to semi-automate/automate the process. Another way to make our system more

Figure 10. Screenshot for sample query #3 first gateway

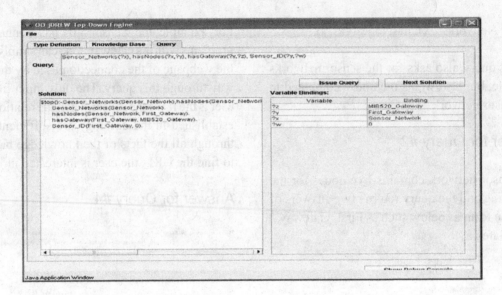

Figure 11. Screenshot for sample query #3 second gateway

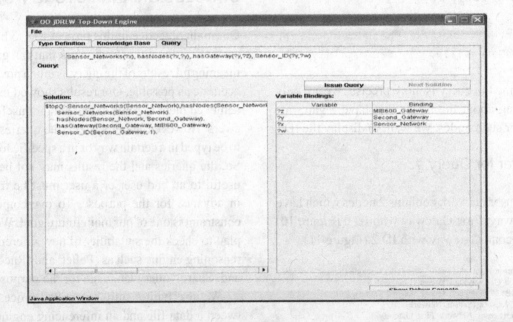

Box 8.

```
SensorID(?sensor, 0), hasGateway(?sensor,?gateway),
        hasConnectivity(?gateway,?conn), Connectivity_Webpage(?conn,?URL).
```

useful is by extending the ontology for 'conditions' and 'actions' and/or introducing 'reaction' rules in the system so that based on the answers, the system can act as more like a decision support system or recommender system.

ACKNOWLEDGMENT

The work was done when the authors were affiliated with the Faculty of Computer Science, UNB.

REFERENCES

Crossbow. (n.d.). *Crossbow Technology®, Inc.* Retrieved from http://www.xbow.com

Daconta, M. C., Obrst, L. J., & Smith, K. T. (2003). *The Semantic Web: A guide to the future of XML, Web services and knowledge management*. Wiley Publishing. jDREW. (n.d.). Object Oriented jDREW. Retrieved from http://www.jdrew.org/oojdrew/

Remagnino, P., & Forest, G. L. (2005). Ambient intelligence: A new multidisciplinary paradigm. *IEEE Transactions on Systems. Man & Cybernetics: Part A, 35*, 1–6. doi:10.1109/TSMCA.2004.838456

Satyanarayanan, M. (2002). A catalyst for mobile and ubiquitous computing. [IEEE.]. *Pervasive Computing, 1*, 2–5. doi:10.1109/MPRV.2002.993138

Weiser, M. (1995). The computer for the 21st century. *Scientific American, Special Issue: The Computer in the 21st Century.*

ADDITIONAL READING

Altova Products http://www.altova.com/products.html

Grigoris Antoniou and Frank van Harmelen. (2008). *A Semantic Web Primer* (2nd ed.). MIT Press.

Johan Hjelm. (2001). *Creating the Semantic Web with RDF: Professional Developer's Guide*. John Wiley & Sons, Ltd.

Compilation of References

Aarts, E. H. L., & Korst, J. H. M. (1989). *Simulated annealing and Boltzmann machines*. Chichester, UK: Wiley.

Abdel-Aal, R. E. (2005). Improved classification of medical data using abductive network committees trained on different feature subsets. *Computer Methods and Programs in Biomedicine, 80*(2), 141–153. PubMed doi:10.1016/j.cmpb.2005.08.001

Ackerman, E., Gatewood, L. C., Rosevear, J. W., & Molnar, G. D. (1965). Model studies of blood-glucose regulation. *The Bulletin of Mathematical Biophysics, 27*, 21–37. PubMed doi:10.1007/BF02477259

Adan, I., Bekkers, J., Dellaert, N., Vissers, J., & Yu, X. (2009). Patient mix optimization and stochastic resource requirements: A case study in cardiothoracic surgery planning. *Health Care Management Science, 12*, 2. doi:doi:10.1007/s10729-008-9080-9

ADHOCSYS. (n.d.). *Website*. Retrieved from http://www.adhocsys.org

Adya, A., Bahl, P., Padhye, J., Wolman, A., & Zhou, L. (2004). *A multiradio unification protocol for IEEE 802.11 wireless networks*. IEEE BroadNets 2004.

Agrawal, D., & El Abbadi, A. (1991). An efficient and fault tolerant solution for distributed mutual exclusion. *ACM Transactions on Computer Systems, n.d.*, 9.

Agrawal, G. P. (2002). *Fiber-optic communications systems*. John Wiley & Sons. doi:10.1002/0471221147

Aguayo, D., Bicket, J., Biswas, S., De Couto, D. S. J., & Morris, R. (n.d.). *MIT roofnet implementation*. Retrieved from http:// pdos.lcs.mit.edu/ roofnet/ design/

Akkaya, K., & Younis, M. (2005). A survey on routing protocols for wireless sensor networks. *Ad Hoc Networks, 3*(3), 325–349. doi:10.1016/j.adhoc.2003.09.010

Aktin, T., & Ozdemir, R. G. (2009). An integrated approach to the one-dimensional cutting stock problem in coronary stent manufacturing. *European Journal of Operational Research, 196*, 737–743. doi:doi:10.1016/j.ejor.2008.04.005

Akyildiz, F., Su, W., Sankarasubramaniam, Y., & Cayirci, E. (2002). Wireless sensor networks: A survey. *Computer Networks, 38*(4), 393–422. doi:10.1016/S1389-1286(01)00302-4

Akyildiz, I. F., Wang, X., & Wang, W. (2005). Wireless mesh networks: A survey. *Computer Networks, 47*(4), 445–487. doi:10.1016/j.comnet.2004.12.001

Aleksander, I., Thomas, W. V., & Bowden, P. A. (1993). WISARD: A radical step forward in image recognition. *Sensor Review, 4*(3), 120–124. doi:10.1108/eb007637

Amari, S. (1982). Differential geometry of curved exponential families –Curvatures and information loss. *Annals of statistics*.

Amari, S. (1990). Mathematical foundations of neurocomputing. *Proceedings of the IEEE*, 1446–1463.

Amari, S. (1996). *Information geometry of neural networks-New Bayesian duality theory*.

Amari, S., & Nagaoka, H. (2000). *Methods of information geometry*. AMS and Oxford university Press.

Amari, S. (1995). Information geometry of the EM and EM algorithms for neural networks. *Neural Networks, 8*(9), 1379–1408. doi:doi:10.1016/0893-6080(95)00003-8

Amari, S. (1998). Natural gradient works efficiently in learning. *Neural Computation, 10*, 251–276. doi:doi:10.1162/089976698300017746

Anbar, M., & Vidyarthi, D. P. (2009). Buffer management in cellular IP network using PSO. [IJMCMC]. *International Journal of Mobile Computing and Multimedia Communications, 1*(1), 78–93. doi:10.4018/jmcmc.2009070106

Anbar, M., & Vidyarthi, D. P. (2009). On demand bandwidth reservation for real-time traffic in cellular IP network using particle swarm optimization. [IJBDCN]. *International Journal of Business Data Communications and Networking, 5*(3), 53–66. doi:10.4018/jbdcn.2009070104

Anbar, M., & Vidyarthi, D. P. (2009). Router CPU time management using particle swarm optimization in cellular IP networks. *International Journal of Advancements in Computing Technology, 1*(2), 48–55. doi:10.4156/ijact.vol1.issue2.6

Anbar, M., & Vidyarthi, D. P. (2010). Comparative study of two CPU router time management algorithms in cellular IP networks. *International Journal of Network Management, 21*(2), 120–129.

Ankolenkar, A., Burstein, M., Hobbs, J., Lassila, O., Martin, D., & McIlraith, S. … Zeng, H. (2001). DAML-S: A semantic markup language for Web services. In *Proceedings of SWWS '01* (pp. 411-430). Stanford, USA.

Anzböck, R., & Dustdar, S. (2003). Interorganizational workflow in the medical imaging domain. In *Proceedings of the 5th International Conference on Enterprise Information Systems (ICEIS)*. Angers, France: Kluwer Academic Publishers.

Anzböck, R., & Dustdar, S. (2003a). *Medical Web services workflows with BPEL4WS*. Retrieved from http:// www.infosys.tuwien.ac.at/ Staff/ sd/ papers/ MedicalServices WorkflowsWith BPEL4WS.pdf

Anzböck, R., & Dustdar, S. (2004). Modeling medical Web services. *BPM 2004, Conference on Business Process Management, LNCS 3080*, (pp. 49–65). Springer.

Anzböck, R., & Dustdar, S. (2005). Modeling and implementing medical Web services. *Data & Knowledge Engineering, 55*(2), 203–236. doi:doi:10.1016/j.datak.2005.03.009

Atzori, L., Iera, A., & Morabito, G. (2010). The internet of things: A survey. *Computer Networks, 54*(15), 2787–2805. doi:10.1016/j.comnet.2010.05.010

Azuma, R. T. (1997). *A survey of augmented reality*. Malibu, HI: Hughes Research Laboratories.

Azuma, R., Baillot, Y., Behringer, R., Feiner, S., Julier, S., & MacIntyre, B. (2001). *Recent advances in augmented reality*. Malibu, CA: IEEE.

Azuma, R., Hoff, B., Neely, H. III, & Sarfaty, R. (1999). *A motion-stabilized outdoor augmented reality system. IEEE Virtual Reality '99* (p. 8). Houston, TX: IEEE.

Bahl, P., Chandra, R., & Dunagan, J. (2004). SSCH: Slotted seeded channel hopping for capacity improvement in IEEE 802.11 ad hoc wireless networks. *ACM Annual International Conference on Mobile Computing and Networking* (MOBICOM), 2004, (pp. 216-230).

Balakrishnan, H., Venkata, N., Padmanabhan, S. S., & Katz, R. H. (1997). A comparison of mechanisms for improving TCP performance over wireless links. *IEEE Transactions on Networking, 5*(6).

Balakrishnan, S., Narayanasamy, R., & Savarimuthu, N. (2009). Feature subset selection using Nomogram in Type II Diabetes databases. *Indian Journal of Medical Informatics, 4*(1), 5-5. ISSN 0973-9254

Baransel, C., Dobosiz, W., & Gewicburzynski, P. (1995). Routing in multi-hop packet switching networks: G-b/s Challenge. *IEEE Network Magazine, 9*(3), 38–61. doi:10.1109/65.386051

Basu, K. (2010). *QoS mapping of IP flows over ATM cell streams: Models for mapping variable length IP packets over fixed length ATM cells* (pp. 54–63). Saarbrücken, Germany: Lambert.

Becvar, Z., & Zelenka, J. (2006). Handovers in mobile WiMAX. *Research in Telecommunication Technology, 1*, 147–150.

Beech, A. J. (2001). Market-based demand forecasting promotes informed strategic financial planning. [PubMed]. *Healthcare Financial Management, 55*(11), 46–56.

Behrouz, A., & Forouzan, S. C. (2004). *Data communication and networking* (3rd ed.). New Delhi.

Belghith, A., & Nuaymi, L. (2008). Comparison of WiMAX scheduling algorithms and proposals for the rtPS QoS class. In *14th European Wireless Conference, 2008* (EW 2008) (pp. 1-6). Prague.

Belghith, A., Nuaymi, L., & Maille, P. (2008, September). *Pricing of real-time applications in WiMAX systems.* IEEE 68th Vehicular Technology Conference (VTC2008), Calgary, Canada.

Bellfiore, S., Foutz, Y., Govindaradjula, R., Bahceci, I., Balanis, C. A., & Spanias, A. S., Duman, T. M. (2002). Smart antenna system analysis, integration and performance for mobile ad hoc networks (MANETs). *IEEE Transactions on Antennas and Propagation, 50*(5), 571–581. doi:10.1109/TAP.2002.1011222

Benatallah, B., Sheng, Q. Z., Ngu, A. H. H., & Dumas, M. (2002). *Declarative composition and peer-to-peer provisioning of dynamic Web services* (pp. 297–308). ICDE.

Bergman, R. N., Phillips, L. S., & Cobelli, C. (1981). Physiologic evaluation of factors controlling glucose tolerance in man: measurement of insulin sensitivity and beta-cell glucose sensitivity from the response to intravenous glucose. *The Journal of Clinical Investigation, 68*(6), 1456–1467. PubMed doi:10.1172/JCI110398

Berners-Lee, T., & Fischetti, M. (1999). *Weaving the Web: The original design and ultimate destiny of the World Wide Web by its inventor.* San Francisco, CA: Harper.

Berry, R., & Modiano, E. (October 2004). The role of switching in reducing the number of electronic ports in WDM networks. *IEEE Journal of Selected Areas in Communication, 22*(8).

Berry, R., & Modiano, E. (2005, August). Optimal transceiver scheduling in WDM/TDM networks. *IEEE Journal on Selected Areas in Communications, 23*(8). doi:10.1109/JSAC.2005.852240

Bestetti, A., Giambene, G., & Hadzic, S. (2008). WiMAX: MAC layer performance assessments. *3rd International Symposium on Wireless Pervasive Computing (ISWPC 2008),* (pp. 490-494).

Bimber, O., & Raskar, R. (2005). *Spatial augmented reality - Merging real and virtual worlds.* Wellesley, MA: A K Peters, Ltd.

Bizer, C., Heath, T., Idehen, K., & Berners-Lee, T. (2008). Linked data on the Web (LDOW2008). In *Proceeding of the 17th International Conference on World Wide Web, WWW '08,* (pp. 1265–1266). New York, NY: ACM.

Blostein, S. D., & Lieb, H. (2003). Multiple antenna systems: Their role and impact in future wireless access. *IEEE Communications Magazine, 2003,* 94–101. doi:10.1109/MCOM.2003.1215645

Bolle, R., Connell, J., Pankanti, S., & Ratha, N. (2003). *Guide to biometrics.* New York, NY: Springer.

Bortfeld, T., Chan, T. C. Y., Trofimov, A., & Tsitsiklis, J. N. (2008). Robust management of motion uncertainty in intensity-modulated radiation therapy. *Operations Research, 56*(6), 1461–1473. doi:doi:10.1287/opre.1070.0484

Braden, B., Clark, D., Crowcroft, J., Davie, B., Deering, S., Estrin, D., …. Zhang, L. (1998). *RFC 2309: Recommendations on queue management and congestion avoidance in the Internet.* RFC.

Breu, R., Hafner, M., Weber, B., Alam, M., & Breu, M. (2004). *Towards model driven security of inter-organizational workflows. Institut for Informatics.* University of Innsbruck.

Bromba, M. (n.d.). *Bio-identification frequently asked questions.* Retrieved from http://www.bromba.com/ faq/ biofaqe.htm

Brown, B., & Chalmers, M. (2003). Tourism and mobile technology. *Eighth European Conference on Computer Supported Cooperative Work* (p. 20). Helsinki, Finland: Kluwer Academic Press.

Brunato, M., & Battiti, R. (2003). *A location-dependent recommender system for the Web.* Budapest, Hungary: MobEA Workshop.

Bruni, M., Conforti, D., Sicilia, N., & Trotta, S. (2006). A new organ transplantation location-allocation policy: A case study of Italy. *Health Care Management Science, 9*(2), 125–142. PubMed doi:10.1007/s10729-006-7661-z

Bruno, R., Conti, M., & Gregori, E. (2005). Mesh networks: Commodity multihop ad hoc networks. *IEEE Communications Magazine, 43*(3), 123–131. doi:10.1109/MCOM.2005.1404606

Brzezinski, A., & Modiano, E. (2005, November). Dynamic reconfiguration and routing algorithms for IP-over-WDM networks with stochastic traffic. *Journal of Lightwave Technology, 23*(10). doi:10.1109/JLT.2005.855691

Bucciol, P., De Martin, J. C., Vandoni, L., Zicca, G., Giani, G. M., & Giulini, M. (2007). *Specification of algorithms for static reconfiguration of ad-hoc network, and multimedia services,* final version ADHOCSY.S project. *Deliverable, D14,* IST-2004–IST-026548.

Buchegger, S., & LeBoude, J. (2002). Performance analysis of the confidant protocol: Cooperation of nodes- Fairness in dynamic ad hoc networks. *Proceedings of ACM Mobihoc,* 2002, (pp. 9-19).

Buttyán, L., & Hubaux, J. (2003). Stimulating cooperation in self-organizing mobile ad hoc networks. *Mobile Networks and Applications, 8*(5), 579–592. doi:10.1023/A:1025146013151

Calhoun, G. M. (2003). Third generation wireless systems: *Vol. 1. Post Shannon signal architecture.* Boston, MA: Artech House.

Cali, F., Conti, M., & Gregori, E. (2000). Dynamic tuning of the IEEE 802.11 protocol to achieve a theoretical throughput limit. *IEEE/ACM Transactions on Networking, 8*(6), 785–799. doi:10.1109/90.893874

Campbell, A. T., Gomez, J., Kim, S., Valko, A. G., Chieh-Yih, W., & Turanyi, Z. R. (2000). Design, implementation, and evaluation of cellular IP. *IEEE Personal Communications, 7*(4), 42–49. doi:10.1109/98.863995

Carlson, A. B. (2010). *Communication systems* (5th ed.). Singapore: McGraw Hill International.

Carvalho, L., et al. (2010). Synchronizing Web browsing data with browserver. In *Symposium on Computers and Communications* (pp.738-743). IEEE.

Castellano, G., & Torsello, M. A. (2009). How to derive fuzzy user categories for Web personalization. In Castellano, G., & Fanelli, A. M. (Eds.), *Web personalities in intelligent environments.* Berlin, Germany: Springer-Verlag. doi:10.1007/978-3-642-02794-9_4

Cha, M., Choudhury, G., Yates, J., Shaikh, A., & Moon, S. (2006). Case study: Resilient backbone design for IPTV services. In *Proceedings of Workshop on IPTV Services over World Wide Web,* Edinburgh, Scotland, United Kingdom.

Chadwick, K., Good, J., Kerr, G., McGee, F., & O'Mahaonv, F. (2001). *Biometric authentication for network access and network application.*

Chammakhi Msadaa, I., Câmara, D., & Filali, F. (2010). Mobility management in WiMAX networks. In Tang, S.-Y., Müller, P., & Sharif, H. R. (Eds.), *WiMAX security and quality of service: An end-to-end perspective* (pp. 179–210). Chichester, UK: John Wiley & Sons, Ltd. doi:10.1002/9780470665749.ch7

Chandra, H., Agarwal, A., & Velmurugan, T. (2010). Analysis of active queue management algorithms & their implementation for TCP/IP networks using OPNET simulation tool. *International Journal of Computers and Applications, 6*(11).

Chant, C., Wilson, G., & Friedrich, J. O. (2005). Validation of an insulin infusion nomogram for intensive glucose control in critically ill patients. *Pharmacotherapy, 25*(3), 352–359. PubMed doi:10.1592/phco.25.3.352.61594

Chan, V., Hall, K., Modiano, E., & Rauschenbach, K. (1998, December). Architectures and technologies for high-speed optical data networks. *Journal of Lightwave Technology, 16*(12). doi:10.1109/50.736582

Chatterjee, P., & Das, N. (in press). On load-balanced data gathering techniques for lifetime maximization in wireless sensor networks. To appear, *Wireless Sensor Networks.* Nova Science Publishers. *Inc.*

Chen, J., Jiao, W., & Guo, Q. (2005). An integrated QoS control architecture for IEEE 802.16 broadband wireless access systems. In *Global Telecommunications Conference, 2005 (IEEE GLOBECOM),* vol. 6 (pp. 3335-3340). St. Louis, MO.

Chen, L., Modiano, E., & Saengudomlert, P. (January 2006). Wave band switching in optical networks. *Computer Networks (Special Issue on Optical Networks).*

Chen, L., & Modiano, E. (2004, December). Dynamic routing and wavelength assignment with optical bypass using ring embeddings. *Optical Switching and Networking (Elsevier)*, *2004*, 34–42.

Chen, S., & Cobb, J. (2006). Wireless quality-of-service support. *Wireless Networks*, *12*(4), 409–441. doi:doi:10.1007/s11276-006-6541-2

Cho, B. H., Yu, H., Lee, J., Chee, Y. J., Kim, I. Y., & Kim, S. I. (2008). Nonlinear support vector machine visualization for risk factor analysis using nomograms and localized radial basis function kernels. *IEEE Transactions on Information Technology in Biomedicine*, *12*(2). PubMed

Christiansen, M. (2001, October). *The performance of HTTP traffic under random early detection queue management*. Department of Computer Science, Aalborg University, Denmark.

Chung, J., & Claypool, M. (n.d.). *NS by example*. Retrieved from http:// perform.wpi.edu/ NS/

Cimino, J. J., Hayamizu, T. F., Bodenreider, O., Davis, B., Stafford, G. A., & Ringwald, M. (2009). The caBIG terminology review process. *Journal of Biomedical Informatics*, *42*(3), 571–580. PubMed doi:10.1016/j.jbi.2008.12.003

Claro, D. B., Albers, P., & Hao, J. K. (2005). *Selecting Web services for optimal composition*. In ICWS: International Workshop on Semantic and Dynamic Web Processes.

Clemson, B., Tang, Y., Pyne, J., & Unal, R. (1995). Efficient methods for sensitivity analysis. *System Dynamics Review*, *11*, 31–49. doi:doi:10.1002/sdr.4260110104

Clinton, W. J. (1997, 18 May). *Commencement Address at Morgan State University, 1997*.

Conforti, D., & Guido, R. (2005). Kernel-based support vector machine classifiers for early detection of myocardial infarction. *Optimization Methods and Software*, *20*(2-3), 401–413. doi:doi:10.1080/10556780512331318164

Constantinescu, I., Faltings, B., & Binder, W. (2004). Type based service composition. In *WWW Conference Alternate Track Papers & Posters*, (pp. 268-269).

Cote, M. J., & Tucker, S. L. (2001). Four methodologies to improve healthcare demand forecasting. [PubMed]. *Healthcare Financial Management*, *55*(5), 54–58.

Crossbow. (n.d.). *Crossbow Technology®, Inc*. Retrieved from http://www.xbow.com

Cukic, B., & Bartlow, N. (2005). Biometric system threats and countermeasures: A risk based approach. In *Proceedings of the Biometric Consortium Conference* (BCC 05), Crystal City, VA, USA, Sept. 2005.

Cutrí, G., Naccarato, G., & Pantano, E. (2008). *Mobile cultural heritage: The case study of Locri. Edutainment 2008, LNCS 5093* (pp. 410–420). Berlin, Germany: Springer-Verlag.

Daconta, M. C., Obrst, L. J., & Smith, K. T. (2003). *The Semantic Web: A guide to the future of XML, Web services and knowledge management*. Wiley Publishing. jDREW. (n.d.). Object Oriented jDREW. Retrieved from http://www.jdrew.org/ oojdrew/

Daugman, J. (1999). Recognizing persons by their iris patterns. In Jain, A. K., Bolle, R., & Pankanti, S. (Eds.), *Biometrics: Personal identification in a networked society*. Norwell, MA: Kluwer.

Deci, E. L., & Ryan, R. M. (1991). A motivational approach to self: Integration in personality. In R. Dienstbier (Ed.), *Nebraska Symposium on Motivation, vol. 38: Perspectives on motivation* (pp. 237-288). Lincoln, NE: University of Nebraska Press.

Deering, S. (1998). *Watching the waist of the protocol hour-glass*. 6th IEEE International Conference on Network Protocols.

Dermott, D. M. (1997). *PDDL - The planning domain definition language*.

Desper, R., Khan, J., & Schäffer, A. A. (2004). Tumor classification using phylogenetic methods on expression data. *Journal of Theoretical Biology*, *228*(4), 477–496. PubMed doi:10.1016/j.jtbi.2004.02.021

Dijkstra, E. W. (1965). Solution of a problem in concurrent programming control. *Communications of the ACM*, *8*, 569. doi:10.1145/365559.365617

Djenouri, D., Khelladi, L., & Badache, A. N. (2005). A survey of security issues in mobile ad hoc and sensor networks. *Communications Surveys & Tutorials, IEEE*, *7*(4), 2–28. doi:10.1109/COMST.2005.1593277

Dong, S., Insley, J., Karonis, N. T., Papka, M. E., Binns, J., & Karniadakis, G. (2006). Simulating and visualizing the human arterial system on the teragrid. *Future Generation Computer Systems*, *22*(8), 1011–1017. doi:doi:10.1016/j.future.2006.03.019

Dougherty, H. (2010). Facebook reaches top ranking in US. *Hitwise Intelligence*. Retrieved November 30, 2010, from http://weblogs.hitwise.com/ heather-dougherty/ 2010/03/ facebook_reaches_ top_ranking_i.html

Draves, R., Padhye, J., & Zill, B. (2004). *Routing in multi-radio multi-hop wireless mesh networks*. ACM MobiCom, Philadelphia, PA, September 2004. eHow. (n.d.). *How to get high speed Internet access in rural areas*. Retrieved from http:// www.ehow.com/ how_4792750_speed-internet- access-rural-areas.html

Dunkels, A., Grönvall, B., & Voigt, T. (2004). Contiki - A lightweight and flexible operating system for tiny networked sensors. *Annual IEEE Conference on Local Computer Networks*, (pp. 455-462).

Durvy, M., Abeillé, J., Wetterwald, P., O'Flynn, C., Leverett, B., Gnoske, E. et al. (2008). *Making sensor networks IPv6 ready* [Abstract].

Eichelberg, M., Aden, T., Riesmeier, J., Dogac, A., & Laleci, G. (2005). A survey and analysis of electronic healthcare record standards. *ACM Computing Surveys*, *37*(4). doi:doi:10.1145/1118890.1118891

Elson, J., & Estrin, D. (2001). Time synchronization for wireless sensor networks. *Proceedings of the 15th International Parallel & Distributed Processing Symposium*, (p. 186). Washington, DC, USA.

Ericsson, N. C. (1999). Adaptive modulation and scheduling over fading channels. *Globecom99*, Rio de Janeiro, December 5-9, (pp. 2668-2672).

Eschelbeck, G. (2000). Active security: A proactive approach for computer security systems. *Network and Computer Application*, *23*, 109–130. doi:doi:10.1006/jnca.2000.0103

European X-ETP Group. (2010). *Future internet strategic research agenda*. Report No. FI-SRA V1.1. Brussels, Belgium: European Commission.

Finarelli, H. J. Jr, & Johnson, T. (2004). Effective demand forecasting in 9 steps. [PubMed]. *Healthcare Financial Management*, *58*(11), 52–58.

Flessa, S. (2003). Priorities and allocation of health care resources in developing countries: A case-study from the Mtwara region, Tanzania. *European Journal of Operational Research*, *150*(1), 67–80. doi:doi:10.1016/S0377-2217(02)00786-5

Floyd, S. (1992, March). Issues in flexible resource management for datagram networks. *Proceedings of the 3rd Workshop on Very High Speed Networks*.

Floyd, S. (1997). *RED: Discussions of setting parameters*. Retrieved from http:// www.aciri.org/ floyd/ REDparameters.txt

Floyd, S., & Jacobson, V. (1993). *The synchronization of periodic routing messages*. SIGCOMM93.

Floyd, S., & Jacobson, V. (1998, April). *Recommendations on queue management and congestion avoidance in the Internet*. RFC 2309.

Floyd, S., & Jacobson, V. (1999). Random early detection gateways for congestion avoidance. *ACM Transactions on Networking, 1*(4).

Floyd, S., & Jacobson, V. (1992, September). On traffic phase effects in packet-switched gateways. *Internetworking Research and Experience*, *3*(3), 115–156.

Foster, I., von Laszewski, G., Thiruvathukal, G. K., & Toonen, B. (1998). A computational framework for telemedicine. *Future Generation Computer Systems*, *14*(1–2), 109–123. doi:doi:10.1016/S0167-739X(98)00013-2

Fowler, M., & Scott, K. (1998). *UML distilled: Applying the standard object modeling language (M. Fowler with K. Scott* (Addison, W. L. O. T. S., Ed.).

Fraternali, P., Rossi, G., & Sánchez-Figueroa, F. (2010). Rich Internet applications. [IEEE.]. *IEEE Computing*, *14*(3), 9–12.

Frazier, M., & Jawerth, B. (1985). Decomposition of Besov spaces. *Indiana University Mathematics Journal*, *34*(4), 777–779. doi:doi:10.1512/iumj.1985.34.34041

Freddy, L., & Alain, L. (2006). *A formal model for semantic web service composition* (pp. 385–398). ISWC.

Ganesan, D., Krishnamachari, B., Woo, A., Culler, D., Estrin, D., & Wicker, S. (2002). *Complex behavior at scale: An experimental study of low-power wireless sensor networks.* No. Technical Report UCLA/CSD-TR 02-0013) UCLA Computer Science Department.

Ganjali, Y., & Keshavarzian, A. (2004). Load balancing in ad hoc networks: Single path routing vs. multipath routing. INFOCOM, March 2004, (pp. 1120-1125).

Garcia-Molina, H., & Barbara, D. (1985). How to assign votes in a distributed system. *Journal of the ACM, 32*(4), 841–860. doi:10.1145/4221.4223

Garofalakis, J., & Giannakoudi, T. (2009). Explointing ontologies for Web search personalization. In Castellano, G., & Fanelli, A. M. (Eds.), *Web personalities in intelligent environments*. Berlin, Germany: Springer-Verlag. doi:10.1007/978-3-642-02794-9_3

Gerstel, O., & Ramaswami, R. (2000, October). Optical layer survivability - An implementation perspective. *IEEE Journal on Selected Areas in Communications, 18,* 1885–1899. doi:10.1109/49.887910

Ghiani, G., Laporte, G., & Musmanno, R. (2004). *Introduction to logistics systems planning and control*. Wiley.

Ghosh, S. C., Sinha, B. P., & Das, N. (2003). Channel assignment using genetic algorithm based on geometric symmetry. *IEEE Transactions on Vehicular Technology, 52*(4), 860–875. doi:10.1109/TVT.2003.808806

Ghosh, S. C., Sinha, B. P., & Das, N. (2006). Coalesced CAP: An improved technique for frequency assignment in cellular networks. *IEEE Transactions on Vehicular Technology, 55*(2), 640–653. doi:10.1109/TVT.2005.863351

Ghribi, S. F., Masmoudi, D. S., & Derbel, N. (2008). A multi objective genetic algorithm based optimization of wavelet transform implementation. In *Proceedings of 3rd International Design and Test Workshop*, (pp. 87–91). Monastir, Tunisia.

Giannakis, G. B. (2001). *Signal processing in wireless and mobile communications* (*Vol. 1*). Prentice Hall.

Gifford, D. K. (1979). Weighted voting for replicated data. In *Proceedings of the Seventh Symposium on Operating Systems Principles*, (pp. 150–162).

Gilbert, H. (1998). *Deploying optical networking components.* McGraw-Hill. Manchester, J., Anderson, J., Doshi, B., & Dravida, S. (May 1998). IP over SONET. *IEEE Communications Magazine, 36*(5), 136–142.

Gillies, J., & Cailliau, R. (2000). *How the Web was born: The story of the World Wide Web*. Oxford, UK: Oxford University Press.

Glisic, S. G. (2007). *Advanced wireless communications* (2nd ed.). UK: Wiley.

Goldberg, D. E. (2005). *Genetic algorithms in search, optimization, and machine learning*. New Delhi, India: Pearson.

Grandinetti, L., & Pisacane, O. (2008). Web services for optimal clinical support systems. In *Proceedings of the 2008 International Conference on Semantic Web and Web Services*, Las Vegas, Nevada, USA.

Grandinetti, L., Conforti, D., & De Luca, L. (1998). CAMD and TeleEEG: Software tools for telemedicine applications. In Sloot, P., Bubank, M., & Hertzberger, B. (Eds.), *High Performance Computing and Networking* (*Vol. 1401*, pp. 64–73). Lecture Notes in Computer Science Berlin, Germany: Springer–Verlag.

Grandinetti, L., & Pisacane, O. (2011). Web based prediction for diabetes treatment. *Future Generation Computer Systems, 27*(2), 139–147. doi:doi:10.1016/j.future.2010.08.001

Grobman, W. A., & Stamilio, D. M. (2006). Methods of clinical prediction. *American Journal of Obstetrics and Gynecology, 194*(3), 888–894. PubMed doi:10.1016/j.ajog.2005.09.002

Gruber, T. (1993). A translation approach to portable ontology specifications. *Knowledge Acquisition, 5,* 199–220. doi:doi:10.1006/knac.1993.1008

Gupta, P., & Kumar, P. R. (2000). The capacity of wireless networks. *IEEE Transactions on Information Theory, 46*(2), 388–404. doi:10.1109/18.825799

Gu, Q. (2008). *RF system design of transceivers for wireless communications*. New Delhi, India: Springer.

Guzick, D. S., Overstreet, J. W., Factor-Litvak, P., Brazil, C. K., Nakajima, S. T., Coutifaris, C., et al. (2001). Sperm morphology, motility, and concentration in fertile and infertile men. *The New England Journal of Medicine, 345*, 1388–1393. PubMed doi:10.1056/NEJMoa003005

Hamby, D. M. (1994). A review of techniques for parameter sensitivity analysis of environmental models. *Environmental Monitoring and Assessment, 32*, 135–154. doi:doi:10.1007/BF00547132

Hankins, J. L. (1994). The CICNet rural datafication project: Extending network access and services. *Internet Research, 4*(1), 71–74. doi:10.1108/10662249410798858

Harrell, F. E. (2001). *Regression modeling strategies: With applications to linear models, logistic regression, and survival analysis*. New York, NY: Springer.

Hashem, E. (1989). *Analysis of random drop for gateway congestion control,* (p. 103). Report LCS TR-465, Laboratory for Computer Science, MIT, Cambridge, MA.

Hashmi, N., Myung, D., Gaynor, M., & Moulton, S. (2005). A sensor-based, Web service-enabled, emergency medical response system. In *Proceedings of the Mobisys 2005 Workshop on End-to-End Sense and Respond Systems.*

Haux, R. (1989). Knowledge-based decision support for diagnosis and therapy: On the multiple usability of patient data. [PubMed]. *Methods of Information in Medicine, 28*(2), 69–77.

Hazael-Massieux, D. (2009). *Report on the W3C Workshop on the Future of Social Networking.* Retrieved November 30, 2010, from http:// www.w3.org/ 2008/09/ msnws/ report.pdf

Heimlicher, S., & Karaliopoulos, M. (2007). End-to-end vs. hop-by-hop transport under intermittent connectivity. In *Proceedings of the first International Conference on Autonomic Computing and Communication Systems,* Article No. 20, Rome, Italy.

Herlihy, M. (1986). A quorum-consensus replication method for abstract data types. *ACM Transactions on Computer Systems, 4*(1), 32–53. doi:10.1145/6306.6308

Herman, A. (2000). *The World Wide Web and contemporary cultural theory: Magic, metaphor, power* (1st ed.). Routledge.

Hickson, I. (Ed.). (2010). *The WebSocket API.* W3C Working Draft. Retrieved November 30, 2010, from http://dev. w3.org/ html5/ websockets/

Hinze, A., & Junmanee, S. (2006). Advanced recommendation models for mobile tourist information. *14th International Conference on Cooperative Information Systems* (pp. 643-660). Montpellier, VT: Springer Verlag.

Hiroyasu, T., Miki, M., & Watanabe, S. (2000). The new model of parallel genetic algorithm in multi-objective optimization problems-divided range multi-objective genetic algorithms. In *IEEE Proceedings of the Evolutionary Computation Congress,* (pp. 333-340). California, USA.

HL7 Organization. *Health Level 7.* (2000). Retrieved from http:// www.hl7.org

Hludov, S., Meinel, C., Noelle, G., & Warda, F. (2000). *PACS for teleradiology.* Retrieved from medicineonline. de.

Hoeffding, W. (1963). Probability inequalities for sums of bounded random variables. *Journal of the American Statistical Association, 58*(301). doi:10.2307/2282952

Huang, L., & Lai, T. (2002). On the scalability of IEEE 802.11 ad hoc networks. *ACM International Symposium on Mobile Ad Hoc Networking and Computing* (MOBI-HOC), 2002, (pp. 173-182).

Hübner, U. (2008). The supply chain model of ebusiness in healthcare. In *eBusiness in Healthcare, Health Informatics, Part IV,* (pp. 299-318). DOI: 10.1007/978-1-84628-879-1_14

Hughes, L. E. (2010). *The second internet: Reinventing computer networking with IPv6.* InfoWeapons. Retrieved from www.infoweapons.com.

Hui, J. W., & Culler, D. E. (2010). IPv6 in low-power wireless networks. *Proceedings of the IEEE, 98*(11), 1865–1878. doi:10.1109/JPROC.2010.2065791

IEEE802.16. (2004). IEEE standard for local and metropolitan area networks-Part 16: Air interface for fixed broadband wireless access systems.

IEEE802.16e. (2005). IEEE standard for local and metropolitan area networks-Part 16: Air interface for fixed and mobile broadband wireless access systems.

Intel. (n.d.). Mesh networks demonstrations. Retrieved from http:// www.intel.com/ idf/ us/ fall2003/ presentations/ F03USWNTS116_ OS.pdf

Ishmael, J., Bury, S., Pezaros, D., & Race, N. (2008). Deploying rural community wireless mesh networks. *IEEE Internet Computing, 12*(4), 22–29. doi:10.1109/MIC.2008.76

Islam, S., & Grégoire, J. (2010). Network edge intelligence for the emerging next-generation internet. *Future Internet, 2*(4), 603–623. doi:10.3390/fi2040603

Jacobson, V., & Karels, M. (1988, November). Congestion avoidance and control. *Proceedings of SIGCOMM'88.*

Jain, A. K., & Ross, A. (2001). *Learning user-specific parameters in a multibiometric system*. Retrieved from http:// www.rossarun.jain. cse.msu.edu

Jain, A. K., Flynn, P., & Ross, A. A. (2008). *Handbook of biometrics*. New York, NY: Springer.

Jain, A. K., Nandakumar, K., & Nagar, A. (2008). Biometric template security. *EURASIP Journal on Advances in Signal Processing, 8*(2), 1–17. doi:doi:10.1155/2008/579416

Jain, A. K., Ross, A., & Pankanti, S. (2006). Biometrics: A tool for information security. *IEEE Transactions on Information Forensics and Security, 1*(2), 125–143. doi:doi:10.1109/TIFS.2006.873653

Jain, R. (1990, May). Congestion control in computer networks: Issues and trends. *IEEE Network*, 24–30. doi:10.1109/65.56532

Jaques, P. A., & Viccari, R. M. (2006). Considering students' emotions in computer-mediated learning environments. In Ma, Z. (Ed.), *Web-based intelligent e-learning systems: Technologies and applications* (pp. 122–138). Hershey, PA: Information Science Publishing.

Jawerth, B., & Peters, G. (1993). *Wavelets on non smooth sets of Rn.*

Jayaram, R., Sen, S. K., Kakani, N. K., & Das, S. K. (2000). Call admission and control for quality-of- service (QoS) provisioning in next generation wireless networks. *ACM Wireless Networks Journal, 6*(1), 17–30. doi:10.1023/A:1019160708424

Johnson, D. B., Maltz, D. A., Hu, Y.-C. (2004). *The dynamic source routing protocol for mobile ad hoc networks (DSR)*. IETF Internet-Draft: work in progress, July 2004.

Johnston, D., & Yaghoobi, H. (2004). *Peering into the WiMAX spec: Part 1 & 2*. Intel Corp. Retrieved October 22, 2010, from http:// www.eetimes.com/ design/ communications-design/ 4009277/ Peering-Into-the-WiMAX-Spec-Part-1

Jones, S. S., Thomas, A., Evans, R. S., Welch, S. J., Haug, P. J., & Snow, G. L. (2008). Forecasting daily patient volumes in the emergency department. *Academic Emergency Medicine, 15*(2), 159–170. PubMed doi:10.1111/j.1553-2712.2007.00032.x

Kandavanam, G., Botvich, D., & Balasubramaniam, S. (2009). An optimization based approach to maximizing QoS assurance for IPTV triple play services on the Internet backbone. In *Proceedings of IEEE 34th Conference on Local Computer Networks*, (pp 406–413). Zurich, Switzerland.

Kartalopoulos, S. V. (2008). Network security. *Conference on Next Generation Intelligent Optical Networks*, (pp. 191–251).

Kattan, M. W., Eastham, J. A., Stapleton, A. M., Wheeler, T. M., & Scardino, P. T. (1998). A preoperative nomogram for disease recurrence following radical prostatectomy for prostate cancer. *Journal of the National Cancer Institute, 90*, 766–771. PubMed doi:10.1093/jnci/90.10.766

Kattan, M. W., Zelefsky, M. J., Kupelian, P. A., Cho, D., Scardino, P. T., & Fuks, Z. (2003). Pretreatment nomogram that predicts 5-year probability of metastasis following three-dimensional conformal radiation therapy for localized prostate cancer. *Journal of Clinical Oncology, 21*, 4568–4571. PubMed doi:10.1200/JCO.2003.05.046

Kershaw, T. S., Lewis, J., Westdahl, C., Wang, Y. F., Rising, S. S., Massey, Z., & Ickovics, J. (2007). Using clinical classification trees to identify individuals at risk of STDs during pregnancy. *Perspectives on Sexual and Reproductive Health, 39*, 141–148. PubMed doi:10.1363/3914107

Khanbary, L. M. O., & Vidyarthi, D. P. (2009). Reliability based channel allocation using genetic algorithm in mobile computing. *IEEE Transactions on Vehicular Technology, 58*(8), 4248–4256. doi:10.1109/TVT.2009.2019666

Ko, B.-J., Misra, V., Padhye, J., & Rubenstein, D. (2007). *Distributed channel assignment in multi-radio 802.11 mesh networks.* IEEE WCNC 2007, Hong Kong, China, March 2007.

Kooper, R., Shirk, A., Lee, S. C., Lin, A., Folberg, R., & Bajcsy, P. (2008). 3D medical volume reconstruction using Web services. *Computers in Biology and Medicine, 38*(4), 490–500. PubMed doi:10.1016/j.compbiomed.2008.01.015

Kotecha, K., & Popat, S. (2007). Multi objective genetic algorithm based adaptive QoS routing in MANET. In *Proceedings of IEEE Congress on Evolutionary Computation*, (pp. 1423–1428). Singapore.

Koulouzis, S., Zudilova-Seinstra, E., & Belloum, A. (2010). Data transport between visualization web services for medical image analysis. *Procedia Computer Science, 1*(1), 1721–1730. doi:doi:10.1016/j.procs.2010.04.194

Kraus, J. D. (2007). *Antennas for all applications* (3rd ed.). New Delhi, India: Tata McGraw Hill.

KREMPA. (n.d.). Analysis of RED algorithm with responsive and non responsive flows. *Poznan University of Technology Academic Journals.*

Kumar, B. P. V., & Venkataram, P. (2000). Reliable multicast routing in mobile networks: A neural-network approach. In *Proceedings of IEE in Communications, 2003,* 377–384.

Kuran, M. S., & Yilmaz, B. (2006). Quality of service in mesh mode IEEE 802.16 networks. *International Conference on Software, Telecommunications and Computer Networks (SoftCOM)* (pp. 107-111). Split, Croatia.

Lab, B. W. N. (n.d.). *Wireless mesh networks research project.* Retrieved from http:// www.ece.gatech.edu/ research/ labs/ bwn/ mesh/

Lamport, L. (1978). Time, clocks and the ordering of events in a distributed system. *Communications of the ACM, 21,* 558–565. doi:10.1145/359545.359563

Lane, B. (2003). *Cognitive radio technologies in the commercial arena.* In FCC Workshop on Cognitive Radios, May 2003.

Lau, V. K. N., & Wok, Y. K. R. K. (2006). *Channel adaptive technologies and cross layer designs for wireless systems with multiple antennas.* Wiley.

Lee, W. C. Y. (1998). *Mobile communications engineering* (2nd ed.). Singapore: McGraw Hill.

Lee, Y., Lee, J., Kim, I., & Shin, H. (2008). Reducing IPTV channel switching time using H.264 scalable video coding. *IEEE Transactions on Consumer Electronics, 54*(2), 912–919. doi:10.1109/TCE.2008.4560178

Lehne, P. H., & Pettersen, M. (1999). An overview of smart antenna technology for mobile communications systems. *IEEE Communications Surveys, 2*(4).

Leland, W. E., Taqqu, M. S., Willinger, W., & Wilson, D. V. (1994, February). On the self similar nature of Ethernet traffic (extended version). *IEEE/ACM Transactions on Networking, 2*(1). doi:10.1109/90.282603

Lemon, S. C., Roy, J., Clark, M. A., Friedmann, P. D., & Rakowski, W. (2003). Classification and regression tree analysis in public health: Methodological review and comparison with logistic regression. *Annals of Behavioral Medicine, 26,* 172–181. PubMed doi:10.1207/S15324796ABM2603_02

Li, F. Y., Bucciol, P., Vandoni, L., Fragoulis, N., Zanoli, S., Leschiutta, L., & Lázaro, O. (2010). *Broadband Internet access via multi-hop wireless mesh networks: Design, protocol and experiments.* Wireless Personal Communication, January, Springer.

Liao, W., Ke, C.-A., & Lai, J.-R. (2000). Reliable multicast with host mobility. In *Proceedings of IEEE Global Telecommunications Conference*, (pp. 1692–1696). San Francisco, USA.

Lin, S., Lian, Q., Chen, M., & Zhang, Z. (2004). *A practical distributed mutual exclusion protocol in dynamic peer-to-peer systems.* International Workshop on P2P Systems (IPTPS).

Lipsman, A. (2010). U.S. online display advertising market delivers 22 percent increase in impressions vs. year ago. *ComScore.* Retrieved November 30, 2010, from http:// www.comscore.com/ Press_Events/Press_Releases/ 2010/11/ U.S._Online_ Display_ Advertising_ Market_ Delivers_ 22_ Percent_ Increase_ in_ Impressions

Liu, Y. (2001). *E-commerce agents, marketplace solutions, security issues, and supply and demand.* Springer.

Lizcano, D., Soriano, J., Reyes, M., & Hierro, J. (2009). A user-centric approach for developing and deploying service front-ends in the future internet of services. [Inderscience Publishers, Switzerland.]. *International Journal of Web and Grid Services, 5*(2), 155–191. doi:10.1504/IJWGS.2009.027572

Lomas, K. J., & Eppel, H. (1992). Sensitivity analysis techniques for building thermal simulation programs. *Energy and Building, 19*, 21–44. doi:doi:10.1016/0378-7788(92)90033-D

Lops, P., de Gemmis, M., Semeraro, G., Musto, C., Narducci, F., & Bux, M. (2009). A semantic content-based recommender system integrating folksonomies for personalized data. In Castellano, G., & Fanelli, A. M. (Eds.), *Web personalities in intelligent environments.* Berlin, Germany: Springer-Verlag. doi:10.1007/978-3-642-02794-9_2

Lubsen, J., Pool, J., & Van der Does, E. (1978). A practical device for the application of a diagnostic or prognostic function. [PubMed]. *Methods of Information in Medicine, 17*, 127–129.

Lundberg, N. (2000). *Impacts of PACS on radiological work.* Department of Informatics, University of Gothenburg.

Lundgren, H. (2006). Experiences from the design, deployment and usage of the UCSB testbed. *IEEE Wireless Communications, 13*(2), 18–29. doi:10.1109/MWC.2006.1632477

Lu, W. W. (2002). *Broadband wireless mobile.* UK: Wiley.

Lu, Y., & Han, J. (2003). Cancer classification using gene expression data. *Information Systems, 28*(4), 243–268. doi:doi:10.1016/S0306-4379(02)00072-8

MacKay, D. J. C. (1992). A practical Bayesian framework for back propagation networks. *Neural Computation, 4*, 448–472. doi:doi:10.1162/neco.1992.4.3.448

MacKay, D. J. C. (1992a). The evidence framework applied to classification networks. *Neural Computation, 4*, 720–736. doi:doi:10.1162/neco.1992.4.5.720

Maekawa, M. (1985). A √n algorithm for mutual exclusion in decentralized systems. [TOCS]. *ACM Transactions on Computer Systems, 3*(2). doi:10.1145/214438.214445

Mah, P. (2010). Facebook unveils new messaging system to rule them all. *FierceCIO.* Retrieved November 30, 2010, from http:// www.fiercecio.com/ techwatch/ story/ facebook-unveils-new- messaging-system- rule-them-all/ 2010-11-16

Mallat, S., & Hwang, W. L. (1991). *Singularity detection and processing with wavelets. Preprint Courant Institute of Mathematical sciences.* New York University.

Maltoni, D., Maio, D., Jain, A. K., & Prabhakar, S. (2009). *Handbook of fingerprint recognition.* New York, NY: Springer.

Maltz, D. A., Broch, J., & Johnson, D. B. (2001). Lessons from a fullscale multihop wireless ad hoc network testbed. *IEEE Personal Communication, 8*(1), 8–15.

Manjunath, R., & Gurumurthy, K. S. (2002a). *System design using differentially fed artificial neural networks.* TENCON'02.

Manjunath, R., & Gurumurthy, K. S. (2002). Information geometry of differentially fed artificial neural networks. *TENCON, 3*, 1521–1525.

Mansfield, A. J., & Wayman, J. L. (2002). *Best practices in testing and reporting performance of biometric devices,* (version 2.01, p. 11). Middlesex, UK: Centre of Mathematics and Scientific Computing National Physical Laboratory.

Mao, Z. M., Randy, H., Katz, E., & Brewer, A. (2001). *Fault-tolerant, scalable, wide-area Internet service composition.*

Marasli, R., Amer, P. D., & Conrad, P. T. (1996). Retransmission-based partially reliable transport service: An analytic model. In *Proceedings of the 15th Annual Joint Conference of the IEEE Computer Societies: Networking the Next Generation,* (pp. 24-28).

Marginian, D., & Walker, J. (2009). *Direct Web remoting - Easy Ajax for Java.* Retrieved November 30, 2010, from http:// directwebremoting.org

Marović, B., & Jovanović, Z. (2006). Web-based grid-enabled interaction with 3D medical data. *Future Generation Computer Systems, 22*(4), 385–392. doi:doi:10.1016/j.future.2005.10.002

Marsh, A., Simistirab, F., & Robb, R. (1998). VR in medicine: Virtual colonoscopy. *Future Generation Computer Systems, 14*(3-4), 253–264. doi:doi:10.1016/S0167-739X(98)80025-3

Martin, J. (2001). Web services: The next big thing. *XML-Journal, 2.* Retrieved from http://www.sys-con.com/xml/

Matsubara, D., & Miki, K. (2004). *Method and apparatus for peer-to-peer access.* Patent US 2004/0148434 A1, July 2004.

Mayer, K., & Fritsche, W. (2006). IP-enabled wireless sensor networks and their integration into the internet. *Proceedings of the First International Conference on Integrated Internet Ad Hoc and Sensor Networks,* Nice, France. 5.

Mayumi, H., & Masakazu, O. (2005). Applying XML Web services into health care management. In *Proceedings of the 38th Annual Hawaii International Conference on System Sciences (HICSS'05): Vol. 06.* Washington, DC: IEEE Computer Society.

Maza, S., Lazaro, O., Cunha, N., Vandoni, L., & Li, F. Y. (2005). *Broadband access via ad hoc networks: A solution for rural and mountain regions.* Broadband Europe Conference, Bordeaux, France, Dec. 2005.

Mazzer, Y., & Tourancheau, B. (2009). Comparisons of 6LoWPAN implementations on wireless sensor networks. *International Conference on Sensor Technologies and Applications,* (pp. 689-692).

McGarrity, E., & Tuceryan, M. (1999). A method for calibrating see-through head-mounted displays for AR. *IEEE 2nd International Workshop on Augmented Reality (IWAR 99)* (p. 10). San Francisco, CA: IEEE.

McHenry, M. (2003). *Frequency agile spectrum access technologies.* In FCC Workshop on Cognitive Radios, May 2003.

McKenzie, P., & Alder, M. (1994). Initializing the EM algorithm for use in Gaussian mixture modeling. In Gelsema, E. S., & Kanal, L. N. (Eds.), *Pattern Recognition in Practice IV* (pp. 91–105). Amsterdam, The Netherlands: Elsevier.

Meinicke, P., & Ritter, H. (1999). *Resolution based complexity control for Gaussian mixture models. Technical report.* Faculty of Technology, University of Bielefeld.

Michiardi, P., & Molva, R. (2002). Core: A collaborative repudiation mechanism to enforce node cooperation in mobile ad hoc networks. *Proceedings of IFIP Conference on Security, Communications and Multimedia,* 2002, Washington, DC.

Microsoft. (n.d.). Mesh networks. Retrieved from http://research.microsoft.com/mesh/

Milgram, P., Takemura, H., Utsumi, A., & Kishino, F. (1994). Augmented reality: A class of displays on the reality-virtuality continuum. In Das, H. (Ed.), *Telemanipular and Telepresence Technologies.*

Mitchell, M. (1999). *An introduction to genetic algorithms.* London, UK: MIT Press.

Miyoshi, M., Sugano, M., & Murata, M. (2001). Performance evaluation of TCP throughput on wireless cellular networks. *IEEE Vehicular Technology Conference (VTC),* (vol. 3, pp. 2177 –2181).

MobiMesh. (n.d.). *MS Thesis on MobiMesh.* Retrieved from www.mobimesh.eu/index.php?option=com_content&task

Modiano, E., & Narula Tam, A. (May 2002). Survivable lightpath routing: A new approach to the design of WDM-based networks. *IEEE Journal of Selected Areas in Communication, 20*(4).

Modiano, E. (1999, March). WDM based packet networks. *IEEE Communications Magazine,* (March): 130–135. doi:10.1109/35.751510

Modiano, E., & Barry, R. (1999, February). Architectural considerations in the design of WDM-based optical access networks. *Computer Networks,* 1999.

Molisch, A. F. (2003). *Wideband wireless digital communications.* New Delhi, India: PE.

Moore, M. (2001). Teaching students to use genetic algorithms to solve optimization problems. In *Proceedings of the Seventh Annual Consortium for Computing in Small Colleges Central Plains Conference on the Journal of Computing in Small Colleges*, (pp. 19–25). Missouri: USA.

Moralis, A., Pouli, V., Papavassiliou, S., & Maglaris, V. (2009). A Kerberos security architecture for Web services based instrumentation grids. *Future Generation Computer Systems, 25*(7), 804–818. doi:doi:10.1016/j.future.2008.11.004

Morin, P. R. (1995). *The impact of self-similarity on network performance analysis*. Ph. D. dissertation, Carleton Univ., Dec.

Mukherjee, B., Banerjee, D., Ramamurthy, S., & Mukherjee, A. (1996, October). Some principles for designing a wide area WDM optical network. *IEEE Journal on Selected Areas in Communications, 4*(5), 684–696.

Mulligan, G. (2007). The 6LoWPAN architecture. *Proceedings of the 4th Workshop on Embedded Networked Sensors*, Cork, Ireland, (pp. 78-82).

Myers, C., & Green, T. (2004). Forecasting demand and capacity requirements. [PubMed]. *Healthcare Financial Management, 58*(8), 34–37.

Nakamoto, M., Sato, Y., Miyamoto, M., Nakamjima, Y., Konishi, K., Shimada, M., et al. (2002). *3D ultrasound system using a magneto-optic hybrid tracker for augmented reality visualization in laparoscopic liver surgery*.

Narayanan, S., & McIlraith, S. (2002). *Simulation, verification and automated composition of Web services*. In: Eleventh International World Wide Web Conference. NEMA and Global Engineering Group. (1998). *DICOM 3 standard*. Retrieved from http:// www.nema.org

Narula, A., Modiano, E., & Brzezinski, A. (October 2004). Physical topology design for survivable routing of logical rings in WDM based networks. *IEEE Journal of Selected Areas in Communication, 22*(8).

Neal, R. (1996). *Bayesian learning in neural networks*. Springer Verlag.

Neely, M., & Modiano, E. (2007, June). Logarithmic delay for N x N packet switches under crossbar constraints. *IEEE/ACM Transactions on Networking, 15*.

Nielsen, T. T., & Jacobsen, R. H. (2005). Opportunities for IP in communications beyond 3G. *Wireless Personal Communications, 33*(3-4), 243–259. doi:10.1007/s11277-005-0570-5

Nigmatulina, K. R., & Larson, R. C. (2009). Living with influenza: Impacts of government imposed and voluntarily selected interventions. *European Journal of Operational Research, 195*(3), 613–627. doi:doi:10.1016/j.ejor.2008.02.016

Nokia Research Center (NCR). (2009). Mobile mixed reality. *Nokia Technology Insights Series*, 4.

North, A. (2010). Wave open source next steps: "Wave in a box". Retrieved November 30, 2010, from http:// googlewavedev.blogspot.com/ 2010/ 09/ wave-open-source-next- steps-wave- in-box.html

NS Tutorial. (n.d.). Retrieved from http:// www.isi.edu/ nsnam/ns/ tutorial/ nsindex.html

NS. (2003, December). *NS simulator for beginners.* Lecture notes, 2003-2004, Univ. de Los Andes, Merida, Venezuela and ESSI, Sophia-Antipolis, France.

NS. (2003, December). *The NS manual*. The VINT Project: A Collaboration between researchers at UC Berkeley, LBL, USC/ISI, and Xerox PARC.

Nuaymi, L. (2007). *WiMAX: Technology for broadband wireless access*. Wiley. doi:10.1002/9780470319055

O'Gorman, L. (2003). Comparing passwords, tokens, and biometrics for user authentication. *Proceedings of the IEEE, 91*(12), 2019–2040. doi:doi:10.1109/JPROC.2003.819605

Obele, B. O., Seung, H. H., Jun, K. C., & Minho, K. (2009). On building a successful IPTV business model based on personalized IPTV content & services. In *Proceedings of the 9th International Symposium on Communications and Information Technology*. Icheon, South Korea.

Oestges, C., & Clerckx, B. (2007). *MIMO wireless communications*. UK: Elsevier.

Oosterwijk, H. (2005). *DICOM basics*. OTech Inc/Cap Gemini Ernst and Young.

Opera. (2010). Opera Unite user guide. *Opera Software.* Retrieved November 30, 2010, from http:// unite.opera. com/

Oppliger, R. (2002). *Internet and Intranet security* (2nd ed.). Artech House Publishers. FIPS Pub. (1994, September 28). *FIPS Pub 190: Guideline for the use of advanced authentication technology alternatives.* FIPS Pub. (1994, February 9). *FIPS Pub 185: Escrowed encryption standard.* FIPS Pub. (1997, February). *FIPS Pub 196: Entity authentication using public key cryptography.* FIPS Pub. (2002, March). FIPS Pub 198: The keyed-hash message authentication code (HMAC).

Ostrow, A. (2010). It's official: Facebook passes 500 million users. *Mashable.* Retrieved November 30, 2010, from http:// mashable.com/ 2010/07/ 21/ facebook-500-million-2/

Padhye, J., Firoiu, V., Towsley, D., & Kurose, J. (2000). Modeling TCP Reno performance: A simple model and its empirical validation. *IEEE/ACM Transactions on Networking, 8*(2), 133–145. doi:doi:10.1109/90.842137

Pannell, D. J. (1997). Sensitivity analysis of normative economic models: Theoretical framework and practical strategies. *Agricultural Economics, 16,* 139–152. doi:doi:10.1016/S0169-5150(96)01217-0

Pato, M. V., & Moz, M. (2008). Solving a bi-objective nurse rerostering problem by using a utopic pareto genetic heuristic. *Journal of Heuristics, 14*(4), 359–374. doi:doi:10.1007/s10732-007-9040-4

Paulraj, A. (2006). *Introduction to space time wireless communications.* Cambridge, UK.

PC Magazine. (1999, March). *The future of Internet security.*

Peleg, M., & Tu, S. (2006). Decision support, knowledge representation and management in medicine. IMIA Yearbook of Medical Informatics 2006. *Methods of Information in Medicine, 45*(1), 72–80.

Perminov, V. V., Perepelitsina, E. Y., Antsiperov, V. E., & Nikitov, D. S. (2008). Remote medical consultations over the Internet: An implementation based on Web-service technologies. *Journal of Communications Technology and Electronics, 53*(1), 104–112. doi:doi:10.1134/S1064226908010130

Perreault, L., & Metzger, J. (1999). A pragmatic framework for understanding clinical decision support. *Journal of Healthcare Information Management, 13*(2), 5–21.

Persson, M., & Persson, J. A. (2009). Health economic modeling to support surgery management at a Swedish hospital. *Omega, 37,* 853–863. doi:doi:10.1016/j.omega.2008.05.007

Piclin, N., Pintore, M., Wechman, C., & Chrétien, J. R. (2004). Classification of a large anticancer data set by adaptive fuzzy partition. *Journal of Computer-Aided Molecular Design, 18*(7), 577–586. PubMed doi:10.1007/s10822-004-4076-0

Piekarski, W. (2004). *Interactive 3D modelling in outdoor augmented reality worlds.* Adelaide, Australia: University of South Australia.

Polemi, D. (1998). Trusted third party services for health care in Europe. *Future Generation Computer Systems, 14*(1–2), 51–59. doi:doi:10.1016/S0167-739X(98)00008-9

Poslad, S. (2009). *Ubiquitous computing: Smart devices, environments and interactions.* Wiley.

Power, D. J., Politou, E. A., Slaymaker, M. A., & Simpson, A. C. (2006). Securing Web services for deployment in health grids. *Future Generation Computer Systems, 22*(5), 547–570. doi:doi:10.1016/j.future.2005.09.003

Prakash, R., Shivaratri, N. G., & Singhal, M. (1999). Distributed dynamic fault-tolerant channel allocation for cellular networks. *IEEE Transactions on Vehicular Technology, 48*(6), 1874–1888. doi:10.1109/25.806780

Proakis, J. G. (2001). *Digital Communications* (4th ed.). Singapore: McGraw Hill.

Raghuwanshi, S. K., & Srinivas, T. (2009). *Numerical study of propagation in optical waveguides and devices.* International VDM Publisher Germany.

Rajasekarana, M. P., Radhakrishnana, S., & Subbarajb, P. (2010). Sensor grid applications in patient monitoring. *Future Generation Computer Systems, 26*(4), 569–575. doi:doi:10.1016/j.future.2009.11.001

Ramanathan, R., Redi, J., Santivanez, C., Wiggins, D., & Polit, S. (2004). Ad hoc networking with directional antennas: A complete system solution. In *IEEE Wireless Communications and Networking Conference* (WCNC), 2004, (pp. 375–380).

Ramaswami, R., & Sivarajan, K. (2002). *Optical networks: A practical perspective* (2nd ed.). Morgan Kaufmann.

Raniwala, A., Hopalan, K., & Chiueh, T. (2004). Centralized channel assignment and routing algorithms for multi-channel wireless mesh networks. *ACM Mobile Computing and Communications Review*, *8*(2), 50–65. doi:10.1145/997122.997130

Rao, C. R. (1962). Efficient estimates and optimum inference procedures in large samples. *Journal of the Royal Statistical Society. Series B. Methodological*, *24*, 46–72.

Rappaport, T. S. (2006). *Wireless communications* (2nd ed.). New Delhi, India: PHI.

Rashwan, A. H., ElBadawy, H. M., & Ali, H. H. (2009). Comparative ASSESSMENTS FOR Different

Ratha, N. K., Connell, J., & Bolle, R. M. (1999). A biometrics-based secure authentication system. In *Proceedings of the Workshop on Automatic Identification Advances Technologies*, 1999.

Ratha, N., Connell, J. H., & Bolle, R. M. (2001a). An analysis of minutiae matching strength. In *Proceedings of the International Conference on Audio and Video-based Biometric Person Authentication*, Halmstad, Sweden, June 2001, (pp. 223–228).

Ratha, N. K., Connell, J. H., & Bolle, R. M. (2003). Biometrics break-ins and band-aids. *Pattern Recognition Letters*, *24*(13), 2105–2113. doi:doi:10.1016/S0167-8655(03)00080-1

Ratha, N. K., Connell, J., & Bolle, R. (2001b). Enhancing security and privacy in biometrics-based authentication systems. *IBM Systems Journal*, *40*(3), 614–634. doi:doi:10.1147/sj.403.0614

Ratib, O., Swiernik, M., & McCoy, J. M. (2003). From PACS to integrated EMR. *Computerized Medical Imaging and 1020 Graphics*, 2003, (pp. 207–215).

Ratnasamy, S., Francis, P., Handley, M., Karp, R., & Shenker, S. (2001). A scalable content-addressable network. In *Proceedings of ACM SIGCOMM*.

Raymond, K. (1989). *A tree-based algorithm for distributed mutual exclusion*. TOCS.

Raynal, M. (1991). A simple taxonomy for distributed mutual exclusion algorithms. *ACM SIGOPS Operating Systems Review*, *25*(2).

Reid, P. (2003). *Biometrics for network security*. Prentice Hall PTR.

Remagnino, P., & Forest, G. L. (2005). Ambient intelligence: A new multidisciplinary paradigm. *IEEE Transactions on Systems. Man & Cybernetics: Part A*, *35*, 1–6. doi:doi:10.1109/TSMCA.2004.838456

Revet, B. (1997). *DICOM cookbook*. Retrieved from ftp:// ftp-wjq.philips.com/ medical/ interoperability/ out/ DICOM_Information/

Ricart, G., & Agrawala, A. K. (1981). An optimal algorithm for mutual exclusion in computer networks. *Communications of the ACM*, *24*(1). doi:10.1145/358527.358537

Ricci, F. (2002). *Travel recommender systems*. IEEE Intelligent Systems.

Ricker, J. (2006). *Human services - Integrating user interfaces into a service oriented architecture*. Retrieved November 30, 2010, from http://www.jeffreyricker.com/ papers/ Human-Services.pdf

Riva, O. (2003). *Analysis of Internet transport service performance with active queue management in a QoS enabled network*. University of Helsinki, Department of Computer Science.

Roberts, C. (2007). Biometric attack vectors and defenses. *Computers & Security*, *26*(1), 14–25. doi:doi:10.1016/j.cose.2006.12.008

Ross, A. A., Nandakumar, K., & Jain, A. K. (2006). *Handbook of multibiometrics*. New York, NY: Springer.

Rowstron, A., & Druschel, P. (2001). *Pastry: Scalable, distributed object location and routing for large-scale peer-to-peer systems, middleware*.

Royer, E., & Perkins, C. E. (2000). An implementation study of the AODV routing protocol. *Proceedings Wireless Communication and Networking Conference,* (pp. 1003–1008). IEEE Press.

Saint-Andre, P. (2005). Streaming XML with Jabber/XMPP. *IEEE Internet Computing, 9*(5), 82–89. doi:10.1109/MIC.2005.110

Sandhu, S. K., Nguyen, N. D., Center, J. R., Pocock, N. A., Eisman, J. A., & Nguyen, T. V. (2010). Prognosis of fracture: Evaluation of predictive accuracy of the FRAX™ algorithm and Garvan nomogram. *Osteoporosis International, 21*, 863–871. PubMed doi:10.1007/s00198-009-1026-7

Santi, P. (2005). *Topology control in wireless ad hoc and sensor networks.* John Wiley & Sons Ltd. doi:10.1002/0470094559

Satyanarayanan, M. (2002). A catalyst for mobile and ubiquitous computing. [IEEE.]. *Pervasive Computing, 1*, 2–5. doi:doi:10.1109/MPRV.2002.993138

Saunders, S. R., & Zavala, A. A. (2007). *Antenna and propagation for wireless communication systems* (2nd ed.). UK: Wiley.

Schachter, A. D., & Ramoni, M. F. (2007). Clinical forecasting in drug development. [PubMed]. *Nature Reviews. Drug Discovery, 6*, 107–108. doi:doi:10.1038/nrd2246

Schall, D., Truong, H., & Dustdar, S. (2008). Unifying human and software services in Web-scale collaborations. [IEEE.]. *IEEE Internet Computing, 12*(3), 62–68. doi:10.1109/MIC.2008.66

Schmidt-Belz, B., Laamanen, H., Poslad, S., & Zipf, A. (2003). Location-based mobile tourist services - First user experiences. *Information and communication technologies in tourism International Conference* (p. 10). Helsinki, Finland: Springer-Verlag Wein.

Schneier, B. (1999). Attack trees. *Dr. Dobb's Journal, 24*(12), 21–29.

Seong, S., et al. (2010). *PrPl: A decentralized social networking infrastructure.* In Workshop on Mobile Cloud Computing & Services: Social Networks and Beyond. ACM Press.

Seychell, D., & Dingli, A. (2010). *Virtual mobile city guide.* University of Malta.

Shabsigh, A., & Bochner, B. H. (2006). Use of nomograms as predictive tools in bladder cancer. *World Journal of Urology, 24*, 489–498. PubMed doi:10.1007/s00345-006-0122-y

Shahsavar, N., Ludwigs, U., Blomqvist, H., Gill, H., Wigertz, O., & Matell, G. (1995). Evaluation of a knowledge-based decision-support system for ventilator therapy management. *Artificial Intelligence in Medicine, 7*(1), 37–52. PubMed doi:10.1016/0933-3657(94)00025-N

Sharma, A., & Paliwal, K. K. (2008). Cancer classification by gradient LDA technique using microarray gene expression data. *Data & Knowledge Engineering, 66*(2), 338–347. doi:doi:10.1016/j.datak.2008.04.004

Shoniregun, C. A. (2002). The future of Internet security: Should common Internet security technologies be blended with biometrics for accuracy and reliability. *ACM: Ubiquity, 3*(37).

Sierra, B., Inza, I., & Larrañaga, P. (2001). Lecture Notes in Computer Science: *Vol. 2199. On applying supervised classification techniques in medicine* (pp. 14–19).

Singhal, M. (1989). A heuristically-aided algorithm for mutual exclusion in distributed systems. *IEEE Transactions on Computers, 38*(5), 61–77. doi:10.1109/12.24268

Skeels, M., & Grudin, J. (2009). When social networks cross boundaries: A case study of workplace use of Facebook and LinkedIn. In *International Conference on Supporting Group Work* (pp. 95-104). ACM Press.

Sloot, P. M. A., Coveney, P. V., Ertaylan, G., Müller, V., Boucher, C. A. B., & Bubak, M. T. (2009). *HIV decision support: From molecule to man. Philosophical Transactions of the Royal Society of London. Series A: Mathematical and Physical Sciences, 367*, 2691–2703. PubMed.

Smith, D. R. (2004). *Digital transmission systems* (3rd ed.). Kluwer Academic Publishers. doi:10.1007/978-1-4419-8933-8

Sobrinho, J. L. (2002). Algebra and algorithms for QoS path computation and hop-by-hop routing in the internet. [TON]. *IEEE/ACM Transactions on Networking, 10*(4), 541–550. doi:10.1109/TNET.2002.801397

Sombrutzki, R., et al. (2006). Self-organization in community mesh networks: The Berlin roofnet. *Proceedings of the 1st Workshop on Operator-Assisted (Wireless Mesh) Community Networks,* (pp. 1–11). IEEE Press.

Soret, B., Torres, M. C. A., & Entrambasaguas, J. T. (2010). Analysis of the tradeoff between delay and source rate in multiuser wireless systems. *EURASIP Journal on Wireless Communications and Networking,* 2010.

Soutar, C. (n.d.). *Biometric system security White Paper.* Bioscrypt (Online). Retrieved from http://www.bioscrypt. com

Stern, T. E., & Bala, K. (2008). *Multiwavelength optical networks: A layered approach.* Addison Wesley.

Stoica, I. (2001). A scalable peer-to-peer lookup service for Internet applications. In *Proceedings of ACM SIG-COMM,* San Deigo, CA.

Sun, S., Krzymien, W. A., & Jalai, A. (1998). Optimal forward link power allocation for data transmission in CDMA systems. In *Proceedings of Ninth IEEE International Symposium on Personal, Indoor and Mobile Radio Communications,* (pp. 848-852). Boston, MA.

Suzuki, I., & Kasami, T. (1985). A distributed mutual exclusion algorithm. *ACM Transactions on Computer Systems, 3,* 344–349. doi:10.1145/6110.214406

Systems, B. E. A. IBM, Microsoft, SAP AG and Siebel Systems. (2003). *Business process execution language for Web services,* version 1.1. Retrieved from http://www-106.ibm.com/ developerworks/ library/ ws-bpel/

Takayama, Y., Ghiglione, E., Wilson, S., & Dalziel, J. (2009). Human activities in distributed BPM. In Abramowicz, W., Maciaszek, L., Kowalczyk, P., & Speck, A. (Eds.), *Business Process, Services Computing and Intelligent Service Management, Lecture Notes in Informatics 147* (pp. 139–151). Germany: Gesellschaft für Informatik.

Tanenbaum, A. S. (2004). *Computer networks.* New Delhi, India: Pearson Education.

Tang, T., & McCalla, G. (2004). *Utilizing artificial learners to help overcome the cold-start problem in a pedagogically-oriented paper recommendation system. AH 2004* (pp. 245–254). Berlin, Germany: Springer-Verlag.

Tannenbaum, A. S. (1996). *Computer networks* (3rd ed.). Prentice Hall.

Tasic, T. (2009). *Circuits and systems for future generations of wireless communications.* New York, NY: Springer.

Tétard, F., & Patokorpi, E. (2004). Cutural heritage tourism and mobile ICT. *IADIS International Conference e-Society 2004,* (pp. 868-871). Avila, Spain.

Thomas, R. H. (1979). A majority consensus approach to concurrency control for multiple copy databases. *Transactions on Database Systems, 4*(2), 180–209. doi:10.1145/320071.320076

Tistarelli, M., Li, S. Z., & Chellappa, R. (2009). *Handbook of remote biometrics.* New York, NY: Springer.

Tootoonchian, A., Saroiu, S., Ganjali, Y., & Wolman, A. (2009). Lockr: Better privacy for social networks. In *International Conference on Emerging Networking Experiments and Technologies* (pp. 169-180). ACM.

Toral, H., Torres, D., & Estrada, L. (2009). Simulation and modeling of packet loss on VoIP traffic: A power-law model. *WSEAS Transactions on Communications, 8*(10).

Trapani, G., & Pash, A. (2010). *The complete guide to Google Wave.* 3ones, Inc., USA.

Tripathi, A. K., Vidyarthi, D. P., & Mantri, A. N. (1996). A genetic task allocation algorithm for distributed computing system incorporating problem specific knowledge. *International Journal of High Speed Computing, 8*(4), 363–370. doi:10.1142/S0129053396000203

Uludag, U., & Jain, A. K. (2004). Attacks on biometric systems: A case study in fingerprints. In *Proceedings of SPIE-EI Security, Steganography and Watermarking of Multimedia Contents VI,* San Jose, CA, January, (pp. 622–633).

Van Grove, J. (2010). Facebook announces new messaging system: "It's Not E-mail". *Mashable.* Retrieved November 30, 2010, from http:// mashable.com/ 2010/11/15/ facebook-messaging- event/

Vaughan-Nichols, S. (2010). Will HTML 5 restandardize the Web? *IEEE Computer, 43*(4), 13–15. doi:10.1109/ MC.2010.119

Velazquez, M. G. (1993). *A survey of distributed mutual exclusion algorithms*. Technical Report CS-93-116, Colorado State University.

Vidyarthi, D. P., Tripathi, A. K., & Mantri, A. N. (1997). Task partitioning using genetic algorithm. In *Proceedings of International Conference in Cognitive Systems*. New Delhi, India.

Vidyarthi, D. P., & Tripathi, A. K. (2001). Maximizing reliability of distributed computing system with task allocation using simple genetic algorithm. *Journal of Systems Architecture, 47*(6), 549–554. doi:10.1016/S1383-7621(01)00013-3

Von Berg, J., Schmidt, J., & Wendler, T. (2001). *Business process integration for distributed applications in radiology*. Philips Research. In Third International Symposium on Distributed Objects and Applications (DOA_01), Rome, Italy, 2001.

W3C. (2001). Web services description language (WSDL) 1.1. Retrieved from http:// www.w3.org/ TR/ wsdl.html

Wake, G. M. G. H., Boland, N., & Jennings, L. S. (2009). Mixed integer programming approaches to exact minimization of total treatment time in cancer radiotherapy using multileaf collimators. *Computers & Operations Research, 36*(3), 795–810. doi:doi:10.1016/j.cor.2007.10.027

Walker, B., Seastrom, J., Lee, G., & Lin, K. (2010). Addressing scalability in a laboratory-based multihop wireless testbed. *Journal Mobile Networks and Applications, 15*(3).

Wang, X., & Poor, H. V. (2004). *Wireless communication systems: Advanced techniques for signal reception*. New Delhi, India: PE.

Wang, H., Huang, J. Z., Qu, Y., & Xie, J. (2004). Web services: Problems and future directions. *Web Semantics: Science. Services and Agents on the World Wide Web, 1*(3), 309–320. doi:doi:10.1016/j.websem.2004.02.001

Watanabe, S., Hiroyasu, T., & Miki, M. (2002). Neighborhood cultivation genetic algorithm for multi-objective optimization problems. In *Proceedings of the 14th Asia-Pacific Conference on Simulated Evolution and Learning*, (pp. 198-202). Singapore.

Weiser, M. (1995). The computer for the 21st century. *Scientific American, Special Issue: The Computer in the 21st Century.*

Wells, B. J., Jain, A., Arrigain, S., Yu, C., Rosenkrans, W. A., Jr., & Kattan, M. W. (2009). Predicting 6-year mortality risk in patients with type 2 Diabetes. *Diabetes Care, 32*(5), e60. PubMed doi:10.2337/dc09-0327

WiMAX scheduling algorithms. In *World Congress on Engineering and Computer Science 2009 (WCECS 2009)* vol. I. San Francisco.

Wood, M. C. (2010). *An analysis of the design and implementation of QoS over IEEE 802.16.* Retrieved October 18, 2010, from http:// www.cs.wustl.edu/ ~jain/cse574-06/ ftp/ wimax_qos/ index.html

Wu, D., Parsia, B., Sirin, E., Hendler, J. A., & Nau, D. S. (2003). *Automating DAML-S Web services composition using SHOP2* (pp. 195–210). ISWC.

Xue, J. L., Ma, J. Z., Louis, T. A., & Collins, A. J. (2001). Forecast of the number of patients with end-stage renal disease in the United States to the year 2010. [PubMed]. *Journal of the American Society of Nephrology, 12*, 2753–2758.

Xu, G., & Papageorgiou, L. G. (2009). A mixed integer optimisation model for data classification. *Computers & Industrial Engineering, 56*(4), 1205–1215. doi:doi:10.1016/j.cie.2008.07.012

Yang, S., & Chen, I. (2008). A social network-based system for supporting interactive collaboration in knowledge sharing over peer-to-peer network. *International Journal of Human-Computer Studies, 66*(1), 36–50. doi:10.1016/j.ijhcs.2007.08.005

Yu, C.-C., & Chang, H.-P. (2009). *Personalized location-based recommendation services for tour planning in mobile tourism. EC-Web 2009* (pp. 38–49). Berlin, Germany: Springer-Verlag.

Zhang, D., Ray, S., Kannan, R., & Iyengar, S. S. (2003). A recovery algorithm for reliable multicasting in reliable networks. In *Proceedings of IEEE 32nd International Conference on Parallel Processing*, (pp. 493-500). Kaohsiung, China.

Zhang, L. (2003). *Synchronisation techniques for high efficiency coded wireless systems*. PhD Thesis, Department of Electronics University of York July 2003.

Zhang, Z. (2004). *The power of DHT as a logical space*. To appear in FTDCS'04.

Zhang, D. D. (2000). *Automated biometrics technology and systems*. Kluwer Academic.

Zhang, H., & Singer, B. (1999). *Recursive partitioning in the health sciences*. New York, NY: Springer-Verlag.

Zhang, R., Arpinar, I. B., & Aleman-Meza, B. (2003). *Automatic composition of Semantic Web services* (pp. 38–41). ICWS.

Zhan, J. (2001). Unified spatial diversity combining and power allocation for CDMA systems in multiple timescale fading channels. *IEEE Journal on Selected Areas in Communications, 19*(7).

Zhao, D., Shen, X., & Mark, J. W. (2006). Soft handoff and connection reliability in cellular CDMA downlinks. *IEEE Transactions on Wireless Communications, 5*(2), 354–365. doi:10.1109/TWC.2006.1611059

Zhou, L., & Haas, Z. J. (1999). Securing ad hoc networks. *IEEE Network, 13*(6), 24. doi:10.1109/65.806983

Zhu, H., & Rohwer, R. (1995). *Bayesian invariant measurements of generalization for continuous distributions*. Technical Report NCRG/4352, Aston University.

Zhu, H. (2004). A survey of quality of service in IEEE 802.11 networks. *IEEE Wireless Communications, 11*(4), 4–14.

About the Contributors

Deo Prakash Vidyarthi received his Master's Degree in Computer Application from MMM Engineering College Gorakhpur and PhD in Computer Science from Jabalpur University (work done in Banaras Hindu University, Varanasi). He taught UG and PG students in the Department of Computer Science of Banaras Hindu University, Varanasi for more than 12 years. He joined JNU in 2004 and is currently working as Associate Professor in the School of Computer & System Sciences, Jawaharlal Nehru University, New Delhi. Dr. Vidyarthi has published around 50 research papers in various international journals and transactions (including IEEE, Elsevier, Springer, World Scientific, etc.) and around 30 papers in proceedings of various peer-reviewed conferences in India and abroad. He has contributed chapters in many edited books. He is on the editorial board of two international journals and on the reviewer's panel of many international journals. Also, he has co-authored a book (research monograph) entitled "Scheduling in Distributed Computing Systems: Design, Analysis and Models" published by Springer, USA released in December, 2008. Dr. Vidyarthi is the member of the IEEE, International Society of Research in Science and Technology (ISRST), USA, and senior member of the International Association of Computer Science and Information Technology (IACSIT), Singapore. Research interests includes parallel and distributed system, Grid computing, and mobile computing.

* * *

Mohammad Anbar received his B.Tech. in Electronics Engineering from Tishreen University, Lattakia, Syria, in the year 2003, M.Tech. in Computer Science from Jawaharlal Nehru University, New Delhi, India in the year 2007, and Ph.D. in the School of Computer & Systems Sciences, Jawaharlal Nehru University, New Delhi in the year 2010. Currently Dr. Anbar is with the Department of Computer Engineering &Automatic Control, Tishreen Universit, Lattakia, Syria. His research interest includes wireless communication, mobile computing, soft computing techniques, et cetera.

Md. Mejbahul Azam obtained his Bachelor of Science in Engineering degree from Department of Computer Science and Engineering (CSE), Dhaka University of Engineering & Technology (DUET), Gazipur, Bangladesh in 2010. His main research areas includ TCP/IP and Protocol analysis.

Kashinath Basu received his BS and PhD in Computer Science from Oxford Brookes University, UK. Currently, he is a working as a Senior Lecturer in Computer Science at Oxford Brookes University. He has over sixteen years of experience in research and development in various fields of computer networking. His current research interest is focused primarily around next generation of wireline and wireless networking. Dr. Basu has published several papers in journals and conferences and has contributed chapters in a number of books. He has co-chaired and has been in the technical programme committee of several journal and conferences. He is frequently invited as a guest speaker in various academic and business events.

Nabanita Das received the B.Tech. in Radio Physics and Electronics in 1979 from Calcutta University, the M.E. degree in Electronics and Telecommunication Engineering in 1981, and PhD in Computer Science in 1992, from Jadavpur University, Kolkata. Since 1986, she has been on the faculty of the Advanced Computing and Microelectronics Unit, Indian Statistical Institute, Calcutta. She visited the department of Mathematik and Informatik, University of Paderborn, and the Technical Univ., Munich, Germany, under INSA scientists' exchange programme. She has co-authored many papers published in international journals of repute. She has acted as the co-guest Editor of the special issue on "Resource Management in Mobile, Ad Hoc and Sensor Networks" of *Microprocessors and Microsystems*, by Elsevier. She has served in the program committees of several international conferences. She has acted as program chair of the International Workshop on Distributed Computing, IWDC 2004, and also as co-editor of the proceedings published as *LNCS* by Springer. Her research interests include wireless networks, mobile computing, and parallel and distributed algorithms. She is a senior member of IEEE.

Julian Descottes was a MSc. student of the Faculty of Computer Science, University of New Brunswick, Fredericton, NB, Canada during 2006-2008.

José C. Delgado is an Associate Professor at the Computer Science and Engineering Department of the Instituto Superior Tecnico (Lisbon Technical University), in Lisbon, Portugal, where he earned the Ph.D. degree in 1988. He lectures courses in the areas of Computer Architecture, Information Technology, and Service Engineering. He has performed several management roles in his faculty, namely Director of the Taguspark campus, near Lisbon, and Coordinator of the B.Sc. and M.Sc. in Computer Science and Engineering at that campus. He has been the coordinator of and researcher in several research projects, both national and European. As an author, his publications include one book and more than 40 papers in international refereed conferences and journals.

Alexiei Dingli, B.Sc.IT Hons (Malta), Ph.D (Sheffield), MBA (Grenoble) obtained a First Class Bachelor of Science degree in Information Technology from the University of Malta. Immediately after, he continued his studies at the University of Sheffield (UK) where he pursued in a record time, a Doctorate (Ph.D) in Computer Science. Upon his return to Malta, he worked as a Senior Manager with the Employment and Training Corporation and is today a Lecturer at the Department of Artificial Intelligence within the University of Malta where he also represents the Faculty on Gaming-related initiatives. In these past years, he also managed to obtain a Master's in Business Administration with specialisation in Technology Management from the Grenoble Business School (France) where he graduated with distinction. His work was praised by international professors, and it was awarded a World Class status where it was also published in a book, seven book chapters, and in around 40 prominent conferences on the subject. He is also the Mayor of Valletta, the Capital City of Malta.

Lucio Grandinetti, Since 1986, Lucio Grandinetti is a full Professor at the Faculty of Engineering, University of Calabria (UNICAL), Italy. At the same University, he currently holds the position of Vice Rector (since 1999). At the above mentioned University, he was Director of the Department of Electronics, Informatics, and Systems for ten years, as well as member of the University Administration Council. His scientific background is in Electronic Engineering and Systems Science. He is a graduate of the University of Pisa, Italy and the University of California at Berkeley. He has also been a postdoc fellow at University of Southern California, Los Angeles and Research Fellow at the University of Dundee, Scotland. He has been a member of the IEEE Committee on Parallel Processing, and European Editor of a book series of MIT Press on Advanced Computational Methods and Engineering. Currently he is member of the Editorial Board of four international journals. He is author of many research papers in well-established international journals and Editor or co-Editor of several books on algorithms, software, applications of parallel computing, HPC, and Grids. Since 1994, he has been part of several evaluation panels of European Projects within various ICT and Info society programs; he has also been reviewer of many EU Projects in the above programs. He has been recipient and scientific leader of many European-Commission-Funded projects since 1993 (e.g. Molecular Dynamics Simulations by MPP Systems, EUROMED, HPC Finance, WADI). He has been recipient and scientific leader of several national projects (CNR "Progetti Finalizzati," Grid.it, PRIN, FIRB, et al.). Currently, he is: Director of the Centre of Excellence on HPC established at the University of Calabria by the Italian government; Co-managing director of a Supercomputing Centre jointly established by the University of Calabria and NEC Corporation; Recipient and scientific leader of some European-Commission-Funded projects (among others, BEINGRID); and Project leader of a node of the most important European Grid Infrastructure for e-science named EGEE.

Md. Shohidul Islam completed B.Sc Engineering degree in Computer Science & Engineering under the faculty of Electrical & Computer Engineering from Rajshahi University of Engineering & Technology, Rajshahi-6204, Bangladesh in March, 2007. He is a member of IEEE-USA, ACM-USA, IAENG-Hong Kong, IACSIT-Singapore, IEB-Bangladesh, and serving as Lecturer of Computer Science & Engineering in Dhaka University of Engineering & Technology, Gazipur-1700, Bangladesh. His major research interest includes wireless networking, protocol analysis, and algorithm design.

Sk. Shariful Islam obtained his Bachelor of Science in Engineering degree from Department of Computer Science and Engineering (CSE), Dhaka University of Engineering & Technology (DUET), Gazipur, Bangladesh in 2010. His main research areas include wireless and mobile computing.

Rune Hylsberg Jacobsen holds an M.Sc. (1995) degree in Physics and Chemistry and a Ph.D. degree (1997) in Laser Physics and Optoelectronics from Aarhus University, Denmark. In 2010 he was appointed Associate Professor in Communication Technology at Aarhus School of Engineering, Aarhus University. His main research interests include Future Internet, Internet of Things, wireless IP networking, and embedded systems development. His professional career embraces more than 14 years in the telecommunication and IT industry where he has assumed responsibilities in R&D systems engineering and international leadership and management from companies as Tieto, L.M. Ericsson, and the Danish telecommunication operator, TDC. In addition, he works as an expert consultant for the European Commission's Research and Technology Development (RTD) programs.

Jens Kristian Kjaergaard is M.Sc. of Science in Computer Science from Aarhus University (1981). He is an expert in IP-based network architectures with a strong involvement in IPv6 development and deployment and is today the Chief Technology Officer (CTO) of Tieto R&D in Denmark. His broad career includes several aspects of research and development from network equipment vendors as Regnecentralen, Telebit Communications, and L.M. Ericsson. Moreover, from 1989 to 1992 he served as Associate Professor at Aarhus University. In addition, he has been project coordinator of several European Research and Technology Development (RTD) projects under IST and WEU programs.

Rama Krishna Kosaraju was a MSc. student of the Faculty of Computer Science, University of New Brunswick, Fredericton, NB. Canada during 2006-2008.

Niaz Morshed obtained his Bachelor of Science in Engineering degree from Department of Computer Science and Engineering (CSE), Dhaka University of Engineering & Technology (DUET), Gazipur, Bangladesh in 2010. He is pursuing his Master's degree in the same department and university now. His main research areas include wireless and mobile computing and computer networks.

Pattabhirama Pandit is a Technical Manager for Global Test Automation Group in Magnetic Resonance Imaging Group in Philips Healthcare. He has 11 years of experience in the field of software testing and test automation. He has experience in building test frameworks (both White Box & Black Box) and has experience of working in various technological domains. He has published several papers in international journals and conferences.

Ornella Pisacane was born in Catanzaro (Italy) on August 11th 1981. In 2004 she obtained the Laurea degree in Computer Engineering at the University of Calabria (UNICAL) defending a thesis on "Parallel Algorithms of Simulated Annealing for Simulation Optimization," obtaining the maximum score of 110/110 with honours. In 2005 she was Assistant Professor for the Optimization Laboratory course and in 2006 and 2007 for the Logistics course, at UNICAL. From 2005–2006 she was research fellow at DIRO – Universitè De Montrèal – (Canada), collaborating with Prof. L'Ecuyer on Simulation Optimization problems. Her software skills are related to C, C++, Java, JSP, and MPI. In 2008, she completed her Ph.D. in Operation Research at UNICAL. In 2009, she collaborated at the CIRRELT – Universitè De Montrèal – with Prof. Cordeau for managing supply chains by simulation optimization. Her research also includes Grid computing. She is author of scientific publications and co-author of a book.

Neetesh Purohit is working as Assistant Professor at Indian Institute of Information Technology, Allahabad, India since 2006. Previously he was associated with Devi Ahilya University, Indore, India. He has received the Graduation, Master's, as well as Ph.D. degrees in the Electronics and Communication Engineering in 1998, 2001, and 2008, respectively. There exist more than 20 research publications to his credit. He has more than 10 years of teaching experience in undergraduate and post graduate engineering courses. His research and teaching interests includes wireless mobile communication, wireless sensor networks, advanced computer networks, digital communication systems, digital signal processing, and antenna engineering streams.

S. K. Raghuwanshi is working as an Assistant Professor in the Department of Electronics Engineering at Indian School of Mines, Dhanbad. He received the Bachelor's degree in Electronic and Instrumentation Engineering from S.G.S. I.T.S. Indore, Madhya Pradesh, India and the Master's degree in Solid State Technology from Indian Institute of Technology, Kharagpur, in August 1999 and January 2002, respectively. Since July 2009, he has obtained PhD degree in the field of Optics from the Department of Electrical Communication Engineering of Indian Institute of Science, Bangalore India. He is author of one book entitled "Analytical and Numerical Study of Propagation in Optical Waveguide and Devices in Linear and Non-linear Domain" published by VDM Verlag, Germany in 2009. His current research area of interest is inhomogeneous optical waveguide and nonlinear optics.

Manjunath Ramachandra is currently working at Philips, Bangalore. He has about 17 years of work experience in the overlapping fields of signal processing, image processing, Wireless/mobile, and networking. Research in the same field led to PhD, about 110 international publications, patent disclosures, and a book. He represented Philips in international standardization bodies such as Digital Living Network Alliance (DLNA) and serves as the industrial liaison for CE-Linux Forum. He has chaired about 14 international conferences. His areas of interests include networking, signal processing, multimedia, database architecture, et cetera.

Biplab K. Sarker is a Technical Architect at Atwood Technology, New Brunswick, Canada. Biplab has more than 10 years research and development experience designing, architecting, and modeling of user centric innovative systems with end to end solutions. He worked as an Architect and developer in companies like IBM Canada, Innovatia and Primal Fusion to provide them with the solutions based on semantic technology for their innovative products. He has expertise in parallel/distributed/cloud computing systems, Semantic Web technology, and data/text mining. He also worked as a visiting researcher in Kobe University, Japan and postdoctoral fellow in University of New Brunswick, Canada. He has more than 40 publications in refereed journals and conference proceedings. He has been serving as a program committee member for numerous conferences and journals. He obtained his PhD from the Department of Computer Engineering, Banaras Hindu University, India. He is an active member of IEEE Computer Society, USA for last 12 years.

Dylan Seychell graduated in Information and Communication Technology and is currently reading a Master of Science degree in the same field at the University of Malta. During his Bachelor's degree, Mr. Seychell specialised in the areas of Computer Science and Intelligent Systems. Mr. Seychell has both academic and professional experience in the field of mobile technology. Besides having worked with various telecommunications companies in the past years, he is also specialised in this field of intelligent systems on mobile devices. His studies also included all aspects of mobile technology from infrastructure to mobile applications. In October 2010, Mr. Seychell placed first in the GNSS Living Lab Prize of the European Satellite Navigation competition when submitting the idea of DINOS for smart cities.

Farhan Siddiqui received the M.S and Ph.D. degrees in Computer Science from Wayne State University, USA in 2003 and 2007, respectively. During 2008, she was a visiting faculty at Bradley University, IL, USA. Since March 2009, she has been a faculty member in the Information Systems Program at Walden University, Minneapolis, USA. Her research interests are primarily in areas of computer networking, with a focus on wireless networking, mobile and ubiquitous computing, home networking, Voice over IP, and security.

Aruni Singh Assistant Professor in the Department of Computer Engineering, KNIT, Sultanpur, India. His research interests include computational intelligence, biometrics, machine learning, data structures, and parallel algorithms.

Mayank Singh is working as a consultant with IGate Bangalore. He has done M.Tech (IT) and B.Tech (IT) Intergrated Five Year Programme from ABV IIITM Gwalior in 2008. He completed his MBA from IIM Bangalore in 2011. His primary research areas of interest are computer networks, mobile networks, wireless networks, ad hoc networks, et cetera.

Sanjay K. Singh is Associate Professor in Department of Computer Engineering at Institute of Technology, Banaras Hindu University, India. His research interests include computational intelligence, biometrics, video authentication, and machine learning.

Ravi Shankar Singh is Assistant Professor in the Department of Computer Engineering, Institute of Technology, Banaras Hindu University, and Varanasi, India since 2004. His research interests include tasks scheduling techniques in distributed computing, data structures, and parallel algorithms.

Mohsin Sohail was a MSc. student of the Faculty of Computer Science, University of New Brunswick, Fredericton, NB. Canada during 2006-2008.

Shashikala Tapaswi is a Professor at ABV-IIITM Gwalior. She has obtained her Ph.D. (Computer Engineering) from Indian Institute of Technology, Roorkee, India in 2002, M.Tech (Computer Science) from University of Delhi, India in 1993, and B.E. from MITS, Gwalior, India in 1986. Her primary research areas of interest are AI, ANNs, fuzzy logic, digital image processing, computer networks, mobile networks, ad hoc networks, network security, et cetera.

Shrikant Tiwari received his M.Tech. degree in Computer Science and Technology from University of Mysore, India, in 2009. He is currently working toward the PhD degree at the Institute of Technology, Banaras Hindu University, and Varanasi, India. His research interests include biometrics, image processing, and pattern recognition.

Thomas Skjødeberg Toftegaard (formerly Thomas Toftegaard Nielsen) has M.Sc.E.E. (1995) and Ph.D. (1999) in Wireless Communications from Aalborg University, Denmark. In 2009 he was appointed Professor (MSO) in Communication Technology at Aarhus School of Engineering, Aarhus University. He serves as Director of the Electrical Engineering and Information and Communication Technology at Engineering College of Aarhus. Professor Toftegaard is leading a research group on wireless communications. His main research interests is on future intelligent wireless connectivity, mobile communications, sensor networks, dense network architectures, wireless IP, software defined radio, cognitive radio, and ubiquitous wireless networks. In addition, his career includes a 14+ year tenure in the high-tech industry with responsibilities exclusively in the R&D, project management, and product development domains. He has built more than 10 years of experience in R&D leadership and management while working for the mobile operator Telenor, Nokia Telecommunications, L.M. Ericsson, and Tieto.

Sherali Zeadally received the B.A. degree in Computer Science from University of Cambridge, England, and the Doctoral degree in Computer Science from University of Buckingham, England, in1996. He is currently an Associate Professor in the Department of Computer Science and Information Technology at the University of the District of Columbia, Washington DC. He is the Founder of the Network Systems Laboratory (NEST) at the University of the District of Columbia. Sherali Zeadally is the Co-Editor-in-Chief of the *International Journal of Internet Protocol Technology* (IJIPT), and he currently serves on the editorial boards of over 15 peer-reviewed scholarly journals. He has also co-guest edited over 15 special issues of various refereed international journals. He currently serves as Vice/Co-Chair, Program Chair, and General Chair of several international communication workshops and conferences. He is a Fellow of the British Computer Society (FBCS) and a Fellow of the Institution of Engineering and Technology (FIET), England.

Index

A

Access Service Network (ASN) 144, 152
Adaptive Fuzzy Partition (AFP) algorithm 79
add/drop multiplexer 4, 35
adhoc network 173
adversary attacks 132
ambient intelligent network 289, 293, 296
America Online 2
Arpanet 2
ASN Gateways (ASN-GW) 145
augmented reality 258-259, 263-264, 266-273
Authentication Authorization Accounting (AAA) 145

B

beamforming 150
Berners-Lee, Tim 1-2
biometrics 119
biometric traits 122
BrowserConnector 48-49
browser management 47
browserver 38
brutal attack 118
business social networks (BSNs) 41

C

Carrier to Interference and Noise Ratio (CINR) 150
cellular IP network 187, 247-251, 256
Center for Information Technology Leadership (CITL) 64
ciphering - See encoding.
Clinical Classification Tree (CCT) 77
closed-circuit television (CCTV) 130
Concept Learning System (CLS) algorithm 78
congestion 231
congestion detection interval 171
Connectivity Service Network (CSN) 144

ContainerUnits 47-49
cryptographic systems 115
cryptography 117

D

DataHandler 48
deciphering - See decoding.
decoding 118
differentially fed artificial neural network (DANN) 165
distributed hash table (DHT) 214, 228
Domain Name Service (DNS) 145
domain name system (DNS) 2
Doppler Effect 97-99, 113
Dynamic Host Control Protocol (DHCP) 145

E

encoding 118
enterprise social networks (ESNs) 41
erbium-doped fiber amplifier (EDFA) 5
escrow 118
evolutionary algorithm 249
exponential moving average (EWMA) 234
eXtensible Markup Language (XML) 65

F

failure rate 181
feedback control 166
fiber to the cabinet (FTT Cab) 32
fiber to the curb (FTTC) 32
fiber to the home (FTTH) 32
fiber to the node (FTTN) 32
fiber to the premises (FTTP) 32
fourth generation (4G) 96

G

Genetic Algorithm (GA) 181-182, 247
geo-tag 270

H

healthcare administrators 60
health care organizations (HCOs) 60
Health Level 7 Clinical Document Architecture
 (HL7 CDA) 68
HTML (Hyper Text Markup Language) 2
HTTP (Hyper Text Transfer Protocol) 2
hyper text markup language - See HTML.
hypertext technology 2
hyper text transfer protocol - See HTTP.

I

inference engine 76, 291, 296-297
Internet and Mobile Association of India (IAMAI)
 279
Internet Corporation for Assigned Names and Num-
 bers (ICANN) 2
Internet Engineering Task Force (IETF) 3, 192, 212,
 230
Internet of Things 191-193, 210-211, 213
Internet Protocol based Television (IPTV) 180
Internet Protocol (IP) 17, 180, 191, 278
internet protocol version 6 (IPv6) 196
Internet Research Task Force (IRTF) 3
internet security 114-119, 121, 128-129, 137-142
Inverse Fast Fourier Transform (IFFT) 148
IP multimedia services (IMS) 145

L

link quality source routing (LQSR) 278
Link Reliability 205
low power wireless personal area network (LoW-
 PAN) 213

M

MapForce 291, 294-297
media access control (MAC) 281
medical assistants 60-61
Medical Information Systems (MIS) 66
Medical Knowledge Based Decision Support Systems (MKBDSS) 76
medical specialties 60
Medical Web Service (MWS) 66

mesh connectivity layer (MCL) 278
mesh-under architecture 196
microcontroller 200
multiple input, multiple output (MIMO) 150
mutual exclusion (ME) 215

N

Network Access Provider (NAP) 145
network congestion 164
network management 47
Network Service Provider (NSP) 145
network topology 204-205, 208, 217, 246
Network Working Group (NWG) 144
neural network 164
Newham Borough 130

O

ontology 293
operation research (OR) 62
optical line terminal 4, 35
optical network terminal 35
OXCs (Optical Cross-Connects) 28

P

packet arrival rate 252
packet flow 250
packet processing rate 252
particle swarm optimization (PSO) 247
passive optical network 4, 24, 33, 35
Peer-to-Peer (P2P) 214
peer to peer system 216
pervasive computing 1, 158, 303
pervasive internet - See pervasive computing
physical layer (PHY) 144
physical therapists 61
Picture Archiving and Communication System
 (PACS) 66
Point-to-Point Tunneling Protocol (PPTP) 128
power management 202
private key management (PKM) 146
provider-based web 42
provider-centric web 41
Public Switched Telephone Network (PSTN) 145

Q

quality of service (QOS) 143, 167, 180, 279
quorum set 215

R

Radiology Information System (RIS) 66
radio transmission technology (RTT) 96
Random Early Detection (RED) 164, 230, 232-233
Real-Time Protocol (RTP) 180
recommendation system 268
relational database management systems (RDBMS) 294
Reliability 181
reliable mobile multicast protocol (RMMP) 249
remote access service 128
rich internet applications 44
route-over architecture 196
routing 204
routing over low power and lossy networks (ROLL) 206, 212
routing protocol for low power and lossy networks (RPL) 206

S

scalable ODFMA 147-148
second generation (2G) 96
secure electronic transaction (SET) 119
semantic web 1-2, 43, 58, 90, 94, 270, 272-273, 289-290, 301, 303
Service Data Unit (SDU) 146
Service Flow Identifier (SFID) 146
Service Provider Working Group (SPWG) 144
services management 47
Simple Mail Transfer Protocol (SMTP) 115
social networks (SNs) 41
Spatial Augmented Reality 264, 271
synchronization 175

T

TCP protocol 2
third generation (3G) 96
throughput 5, 110, 122, 125, 149, 151, 164, 170, 173-176, 192-193, 197, 231, 238, 244-246, 280-282, 286

tokens 120
Tomlinson, Ray 2
traffic shaping 166
transmission control protocol (TCP) 229-230

U

ubiquitous computing 1, 143, 272, 288, 291, 303
UnitBuilder 47, 49
Universal Description, Discovery and Integration (UDDI) 65
user-based web 43
user-centric web 41
User Datagram Protocol (UDP) 180, 230
user interface management 47

V

Virtual Mobile City Guide (VMCG) 269
virtual private network (VPN) 129
virtual signage 269

W

wavelength-division multiplexing (WDM) 6, 24, 35
Web Service Flow Language (WSFL) 65
Web Services Description Language (WSDL) 66, 88
WiMAX architecture 144
wireless communication systems 95-97, 102, 104, 108, 113
wireless mesh network (WMN) 276
wireless sensor network 203
WISARD 268
Worldwide Interoperability for Microwave Access (WiMAX) 144

X

XML - See eXtensible Markup Language.

Z

zero-effort attacks 132